IMAGES OF BLACKS
IN AMERICAN
CULTURE

IMAGES OF BLACKS IN AMERICAN CULTURE

A Reference Guide to Information Sources

EDITED BY JESSIE CARNEY SMITH

FOREWORD BY Nikki Giovanni

Greenwood Press

NEW YORK · WESTPORT, CONNECTICUT · LONDON

Library of Congress Cataloging-in-Publication Data

Images of Blacks in American culture : a reference guide to
   information sources / edited by Jessie Carney Smith ; foreword by
   Nikki Giovanni.
      p.   cm.
   Bibliography: p.
   Includes index.
   ISBN 0–313–24844–3 (lib. bdg. : alk. paper)
   1. Afro-Americans in art.   2. Arts, American.   I. Smith, Jessie
Carney.
NX652.A37I43   1988   87–24964
700—dc19

British Library Cataloguing in Publication Data is available.

Library of Congress Catalog Card Number: 87–24964
ISBN: 0–313–24844–3

First published in 1988

Greenwood Press, Inc.
88 Post Road West, Westport, Connecticut 06881

Printed in the United States of America

The paper used in this book complies with the
Permanent Paper Standard issued by the National
Information Standards Organization (Z39.48–1984).

10 9 8 7 6 5 4 3 2 1

Copyright Acknowledgments

The author and publisher gratefully acknowledge the following sources for granting permission to
use copyrighted materials:

Lines from ''The Black Mammy'' from *St. Peter Relates an Incident* by James Weldon Johnson.
Copyright © 1935 by James Weldon Johnson, renewed copyright © 1963 by Grace Nail
Johnson. Reprinted by permission of Viking Penguin, Inc.

Selections from Sam Dennison, *Scandalize My Name*. Copyright © 1982 by Garland Publishing
Inc. Used with permission.

John Singleton Copley, *Watson and the Shark*, painting. Used by permission of the Museum of
Fine Arts, Boston.

Henry Ossawa Tanner, *The Banjo Lesson*, painting. Used by permission of Hampton University
Museum. Photograph by Reuben Burrell.

Photograph of Marion Davies in *Operator 13* with Sam McDaniel from the book *Black
Hollywood: The Negro in Motion Pictures*, copyright © 1975 by Gary Null, published by
arrangement with Lyle Stuart, Inc. Used with permission.

Every reasonable effort has been made to trace the owners of copyright materials in this book,
but in some instances this has proven impossible. The publisher will be glad to receive
information leading to more complete acknowledgments in subsequent printings of the book and
in the meantime extend their apologies for any omissions.

To
Helena, Jodie, and Ray

Contents

Illustrations

Foreword

Waring Cuney's poem "No Images" describes the lack of beauty in the life of a Black woman; presumably it would be or could be any woman. The last line rather regretfully recalls that "dishwater gives back no images" (*American Negro Poetry*, ed. Arna Bontemps, rev. ed., New York: Hill and Wang, 1974: 98–99). That is not exactly accurate. A woman standing, whether tall and proud, or heavily leaning, over dirty dishes, *is* an image. The dishwater is not required to reflect it; we are required to acknowledge it. The novelist Toni Morrison shared in an interview that she washes her dishes by hand because it allows her freedom to dream. For the brilliance of her light we may all toss out our automatic anachronism and bloom.

Somehow—in some fascinating way—the Black American community is obsessed with image. The complaint about *The Color Purple* was never about the book or the movie. It was about the image of Black men as if, had the novel never been written, there would be no sexual abuse of children, no wives who were beaten, no women who fell in love with each other. Images are not responsible for reality; quite the opposite is true. The question would be lies.

There are lies about people; personally and ethnically. There are interesting lies, i.e., all Jews are rich. There are helpful lies, i.e., all Asians are smart. There are silly lies, i.e., all Poles are dumb. There are mean lies, i.e., all Hispanics are dope pushers. There are venal lies, i.e., all Blacks are stupid, childlike, irresponsible, welfare-loving people who don't want to work. Some lies can, and perhaps ought to be refuted; some lies we all learn to ignore; but some lies are so terribly bad that they can be neither refuted nor ignored. They have to be fought. Proctor and Gamble, recently the target of a big lie, had to bring out in the open the fungus that was devouring their company to say "We are not a company run by the devil." That must have been embarrassing to even have to say. Some lies are so venal one's own sense of propriety is offended by the simple act of denial. Yet truth, though never as strong as a lie, must fight for its share of light. It is said that in order for evil to triumph all that is required is for good men to say nothing.

Jessie Carney Smith has said something. *Images of Blacks in American Culture* allows us to look at the use and abuse to which Black Americans have been subjected. It is not, as no look at the carnage of war is, a pretty picture. A people have been hurt. And more, those who have needed the lies are exposing their disease. Not since the Middle Ages have we humans considered dark, dank quarters the proper housing for the ill, the infirmed, the insane. As we do not lock Aunt Emma upstairs because she is forgetful, as we do not put John in a dungeon because he has pleurisy, as we would not dream to strap Junior to his bed because he suffers from polio, we cannot keep hidden the products of our emotional disorders. We bring forth *Images* to proclaim that though we have erred in the past we still do believe "all men are created equal."

Nikki Giovanni
Poet
San Francisco, 1987

Preface

Mammy, Sambo, Rastus, and pickaninny are cultural icons in American history. These traditional figures permeate the art, literature, music, theater, film, and other forms of expression in which some non-Black artists, writers, and others have portrayed their own images of Blacks. The pattern set early in American history could well be explored under the theme "two centuries of negative and stereotyped images of Blacks." Coupled with these cultural icons are the positive views, the other side of the coin: Other artists and commentators, themselves usually Black, have celebrated images of strength, beauty, and achievement.

The two views are often intertwined, however, as James Weldon Johnson's "The Black Mammy" illustrates:

> O whitened head entwined in turban gay,
> O kind black face, O crude, but tender hand,
> O foster-mother in whose arms there lay
> The race whose sons are masters of the land!
> It was thine arms that sheltered in their fold,
> It was thine eyes that followed through the length
> Of infant days these sons. In times of old
> It was thy breast that nourished them to strength.
>
> So often hast thou to thy bosom pressed
> Thy golden head, the face and brow of snow;
> So often has it 'gainst thy broad, dark breast
> Lain, set off like a quickened cameo.
> Thou simple soul, as cuddling down that babe
> With thy sweet croon, so plaintive and so wild,
> Came ne'er the thought to thee, swift like a stab,

That it some day might crush thy own black child (*Saint Peter Relates an Incident*, New York: Viking Press, 1935: 40).

Johnson's poem is written in obvious awareness of the mammy, celebrated by non-Blacks for her nurturing and nonthreatening stamina. However, Johnson highlights the irony and possible tragedy of a mother required to give care and love to those who may destroy her own children. The images emphasize contrast, first physically in the mammy herself ("whitened head . . . gay turban," "crude but tender hands") and then her dark skin against the white of her foster child. Observing from a distance in this meditative ode, the narrator sees these contrasts even if the mammy figure herself does not. The overall effect is to capture the burden and the complexity of the situation.

This reference volume explores images of Blacks as they have been presented in the study and development of American culture. Ten chapters introduce and analyze key issues on a variety of themes. What are the images? What led to their development? How have they emerged? What impact have they had on the shaping of Black and American culture? What has been Black America's response? What current developments are taking place to help today's audiences understand and eradicate negative images and to promote more positive ones? These are some of the questions addressed throughout the ten chapters. What has remained foremost in each author's mind, however, has been an effort to build bridges to understanding American culture and the various images within it.

Although some subjects do not receive explicit attention, for example, history and the press, clearly those that are discussed cover key and comprehensive topics. In fact, cultural history is inescapably a part of most chapters' analyses. Furthermore, what seems to be subject matter duplication is actually additional evidence of the interrelationships between topics. Readers are thus able to trace a recurring theme, such as images of women, within a wide backdrop which does not ignore dimensions unique to specific fields. For example, David C. Driskell's exploration of "Aspects of Black Imagery in American Art, 1700–1900," analyzes the negative and positive elements of the imagery and includes a section on Black women. A similar pattern is followed in other chapters, such as Nagueyalti Warren's analysis "From Uncle Tom to Cliff Huxtable, Aunt Jemima to Aunt Nell: Images of Blacks in Film and the Television Industry," Arlene Clift-Pellow's discussion of "Literary Criticism and Black Imagery," Thomas Riis' chapter "Blacks on the Musical Stage," as well as Janet Sims-Wood's chapter on "The Black Female: Mammy, Jemima, Sapphire, and Other Images," which is, as the title suggests, the primary chapter for the exploration of images of women. Joseph Boskin's chapter on "Sambo and Other Male Images In Popular Culture" balances Sims-Wood's chapter by concentrating on the popular male image.

Sims-Wood shows that the film image of the Black woman has been defined by others rather than by Black women. This statement bears directly on images of Blacks in general as discussed throughout this work. As noted at the outset, the images portrayed by Mammy, Sambo, and pickaninny were set by non-Blacks who defined the Black position in American society in terms many non-Blacks found unacceptable but reworked more positively. In this connection, T. J. and Lois Anderson examine "Images of Blacks in Instrumental Music and Song" and note an early practice of selecting "symbols of Black culture which are constant in their recycling." As a result, the "negative transformation of a people has taken place." In examining Black images in the early theater, Thomas Riis calls slaves and free Blacks what they were—a despised minority who had little or no influence over the literature or drama addressed to the general public. Since Blacks remained a despised minority for so many years—and indeed in some circles still are considered unequal to the white American majority—the struggle to take control over that part of the art, literature, music, theater, films and television, and published works that discuss Blacks has been tireless and difficult. Thus, as Driskell also notes, early Black artists Joshua Johnston, Henry O. Tanner, Edward M. Bannister, and William Simpson were pathmakers for other Black artists, and they defined Black art in terms of reality. Other pioneers in a move to present black talent in a positive vein on the musical stage and in music and song include the Theater Owners' Booking Association, a racially integrated organization, and Black writers, actors, and musicians such as Eubie Blake, Noble Sissle, William Grant Still, and the noted minstrel team Williams and Walker. The Andersons examine the true Black American music—spirituals, ragtime, blues, gospel and jazz—and note their importance in Black-American image building.

That the negative and stereotyped views of Blacks have been so deeply ingrained in American culture is easily understood, considering the point at which these images have been introduced—in childhood. Jessie M. Birtha's chapter, "Images of Blacks in Children's Books," looks at the images in such works and concludes that children's literature historically has deliberately presented negative stereotypes of Blacks in both factual and imaginative material for young minds during their formative stages. Since many white writers were insensitive to Black character portrayal, it was not until the publication of more books by Black writers that positive images displaced distasteful ones. Even the titles of some of the books themselves, for example, *Ten Little Niggers*, helped to perpetuate a negative stereotype. In recent years, the work of groups such as the Council on Interracial Books for Children and the American Library Association has led to the publication of books that present realistic and positive views of Blacks. Children's toys were equally instrumental in perpetuating the unacceptable images by presenting comparable caricatures and distortions of Black children and adults. Doris Wilkinson's research on "The Toy Menagerie: Early Images of Blacks in Toys, Games, and Dolls" reveals that play objects are important cultural products and can lead to a biographical and psychological sketch of the society that produced them. The Sambo-like figures and the mammy and Aunt Jemina dolls have finally given way to lifelike figures and to images of noted Blacks, such as Paul Laurence Dunbar and Diahann Carroll.

The chapter "Black Americana Resources and Collections: Evidences of Black Imagery" addresses the timely topic which increasingly appeals to Black and white collectors alike—that of collecting Black Americana. The chapter identifies the recurring motifs discussed in the other nine essays and documents the presence of these motifs in various collections, most of which are in private hands.

The reader will find additional leads in the suggested readings and bibliographies that conclude each chapter. Of varying lengths, the bibliographies serve as guides to fuller discussions on the thematic emphases of the chapters. Some chapters include special compilations of information and resources relating to their subjects, such as award-winning books, Black museums, and filmography.

The publication of this volume represents nearly seven years of work to address the need for educators, researchers, students, and Black memorabilia collectors to have a current, historically based overview of the images presented in a variety of works by and about Black Americans. At first, the interest blossomed into a lecture/exhibit series, "Images in Black Artifacts: Negative and Positive," funded at Fisk University by the Tennessee Committee for the Humanities (now the Tennessee Humanities Council). During the public series, however, the need to publish the work became clear. Those who attended the lectures and/or exhibits were overwhelmed. Such curiosity over the subject matter and the items on exhibit warranted more attention as well as answers to the continuing questions. The increasing popularity of the subject matter, the growing number of collectors, and the publication of several books on the theme, particularly P. J. Gibbs's *Black Collectibles Sold in America* (Paducah, Ky.: Collector Books, 1987) and Dawn Reno's *Collecting Black Americana* (New York: Crown Publishers, 1986), document this point. What was clearly needed, then, was a reference guide with bibiliographical leads to subject matter to help the reader interpret more accurately and comprehensively what has been identified and presented either in scattered studies or limited to particular fields heretofore. This book aims to fill that need.

Rarely do writers complete their work without assistance in many forms and from many people. I have been no exception. Those who contributed to this volume at some point from inception to publication and whose assistance I gratefully acknowledge include the former Tennessee Committee for the Humanities for funding initial research and the collecting of memorabilia for study; collectors and Black Americana scholars Ron Carr, Don Kader, Edgar Orchard, and Ronald Rooks for invaluable insights into subject matter, leads to other collections, advice on compiling the "Black Americana" chapter, and genuine words of encouragement; the authors of chapters for the book, some of whom wrote under very pressing deadlines; respondents to the questionnaires used for my chapter on collections; Ann Scott of the Fisk University Library staff for research assistance; Queen E. B. Couts, my secretary, who worked diligently on the information collected, handled the many necessary details, and who always called my attention to the receipt of a questionnaire completed for my essay or the arrival of a chapter from one of the authors; Sue Varga-Ward, director of Fisk's Microcomputer Laboratory, for making my use of the computer less frustrating; Gary Ridner, director of the University Computer Center, for sharing his expertise in emergencies; Greenwood Press for accepting the manuscript, and Marilyn Brownstein for understanding and accepting my unavoidable tardiness; and Henry Ponder, president of Fisk University, for granting me a sabbatical leave to complete my book. Considering the financial obligations of one on sabbatical who is researching and preparing a manuscript for publication, I am especially grateful to the United Negro College Fund for presenting to me a Distinguished Scholar's Award—a distinct honor and a source of financial support as well.

Aspects of Black Imagery in American Art, 1700–1900

Until the latter half of the nineteenth century, the portrayal of the Black image in American painting and in the larger context of art remained somewhat elusive and descriptively narrow. The problem of interpretation is seldom a simple one. Thus, with a subject as controversial as the depiction of race and how it should be rendered in the name of honest imagery, artists often were at the mercy of clients who were not objective in their description of race. The actual observations of subjects from within the Black race had little impact on the making of Black images in painting. Much of what emerged from white artists as a sympathetic statement about the Black race in the eighteenth and nineteenth centuries came largely from the imagination of the artists. Often, they willfully stereotyped Black subjects by carrying out the wishes of clients who wanted a portrait of their favorite Black servant recorded along with themselves. The results of such a practice were Black images in the art of painting that covered a gamut of visual responses, from the more positive sophisticated imagery of John Singleton Copley's *Watson and the Shark*, in which a Black man is shown as an equal, awestruck spectator in the boat, to the tattered-torn destitute Black people in the paintings of William Aiken Walker in which field hands are seen picking cotton on southern plantations.

By contrast, from 1700 to 1900, very few images of Blacks appeared in sculpture other than in folk items. Those which have survived were often made to show subjects with exaggerated features highlighting what most would describe as unfavorable stereotypic characterizations of the Black race. Some of these grotesque characterizations of Blacks have survived into the twentieth century. Many of these images have been transferred into artifacts and found in related subject areas discussed throughout this book. In order to outline specifically one area in which this descriptive characterization appears, I have chosen to concentrate on Black images that are to be found in American painting from 1700 to 1900. This chapter briefly examines a number of Black images in painting and broadens our inquiry to include select examples in portraiture that depart from the stereotypes associated with the artistry of the period.

Since there is no particular period delineation that characterizes the works that I have selected, for reasons of clarity, I have divided the work discussed into six distinct categories: (1)pre-Revolutionary images, 1700–1775; (2) immediate post-Revolutionary Images, 1776–1800; (3) pre–Civil War images, 1800–1860; (4) late nineteenth-century images, 1861–1900; (5) Black American artists of the nineteenth century, and (6) images of Black women.

One could all but characterize the subjects which occur in the first four time periods listed by citing the recurring themes which white American artists chose to depict in which Blacks were the principal subjects. The first paintings to be discussed in which Blacks are depicted show them as servants and slaves, noble savages, or servant/war heroes; a few are seen as "gentlemen of color." As early as 1838, Blacks were seen as entertainers of whites, serving as musicians and comic capers. Among the visual documentation found are slave sales and slave market scenes, field scenes depicting work experiences as well as those sharing the "laziness of the race," and Blacks who serve to promote the sale of food. These are among the constant images that recur in the work of American artists from 1840 until the end of the Civil War.[1]

A cursory study of Blacks in American painting reveals that they were virtually ignored as primary figures. When depicted, they were presented more often as servants in the employ of wealthy householders or in scenic settings in which they provide music as entertainment and on occasion singing and dancing for self-entertainment (Epstein 1). As time passed, such images have come to be looked upon as stereotypic and only partially accurate in showing the full range of the lifestyle and activities of Blacks in colonial and post-Revolutionary America.

Dimension is not a term which can readily describe the treatment that Blacks received from the hands of artists of the majority culture prior to the latter half of the nineteenth century. In all ways of visual description, Blacks were depicted with contempt. What is seen today as an appreciable change among mainstream artists in their portrayal of the Black subject is a trend which began to change with the imagery of William Sidney Mount (1807–1868) and Winslow Homer (1836–1910), both of whom depicted Black subjects with reasonable likeness in their time in history. Of the two, Mount showed limited sensibilities to the plight of the race.

Homer directed his artistry toward articulating personal characteristics of the race, painting distinct individuals who lived separate lives devoid of the stereotypic cast placed on previous Black sitters. Homer avoided placing Black figures into a cramped space devoid of compositional clarity. Examples are to be found in the numerous compositions painted between 1895 and 1899 that emphasized the individual masculinity of Black fishermen braving the rough seas of Nassau (Beam 168–69). While one tends to look favorably on those images created by William Sidney Mount and on those still-unknown artists of the period that show Blacks as musicians, farmers, and members of their own households, in the main, those images were most often rendered in a manner that singled out Black Americans as being happy with their fate and destitute state in life. More often, they appeared untutored in the cultural ways of white society and visually represented a helpless people without civilized roots and a distinct ethnic history.

American literature in the eighteenth and nineteenth centuries did little to correct the imposed image of savagery and aloofness from the ideals of society that Blacks were said to have had. Few models in the printed word emerged to counteract the widespread misconceptions that abounded throughout this young nation regarding the subject of Blacks being inferior to whites. Since many prominent painters were influenced by the literature and the illustrations that appeared in print during their lifetimes and since there were few intellectual models from which to draw, much of what is seen in painting echoes the same inaccurate depictions of Black life. Most white artists had infrequent contact with Black people. Often, those whom they saw were slaves or household servants who lived a life dictated by a dual standard of living.[2]

One asks, could a more realistic image of Blacks have been painted by the artists of the period, and to what extent would white artists have been singled out as liberal-minded illustrators seeking to disrupt the peace and harmony of white society when portraying a more realistic picture of Blacks? While a comprehensive answer to these questions may yet be forthcoming, there is little doubt that in the eighteenth and nineteenth centuries the politics of race was a volatile matter for many artists. Few felt compelled to risk the chance of peer ridicule by being labelled a "colored sympathizer." One example seems to illustrate clearly this issue. When William Sidney Mount was praised for his depiction of bravery and conviction in portraying a Black woman at the helm of a rowboat steering it to safety on Long Island Sound, he later confessed that the painting about which the comments had been made, *Eel Spearing at Setauket*, to be discussed in this chapter under "Images of Black Women," had been painted somewhat out of context in relation to the real subject. Mount told of having seen a Black man, rather than a Black woman, perform the task of rowing the boat. No doubt Mount felt that he would alienate white clients who had begun to question the depiction of a positive image of Black males in the art of painting (Frankenstein 164).

PRE-REVOLUTIONARY IMAGES, 1700–1775

It is both significant and interestingly curious for historians of the Southeastern region to note that the earliest recorded image of a person of African ancestry to be seen in a painting done in this nation comes from the state of Maryland and from the hand of an artist born in Germany. Adopting the young town of

Annapolis as his new home, Justus Engelhardt Kühn (d. 1717) is said to have settled there just prior to the end of the year 1708. He set up a studio in Annapolis and made known his desire to paint likenesses of the local townspeople. One of his first assignments at the easel was that of painting a portrait of Eleanor Darnell and her brother, Henry. *The Portrait of Henry Darnell III* (Maryland Historical Society) was executed in 1710. The principal subject in the painting is the young Henry at eight years of age (Sadik entry 1). The well-dressed youngster stands straight and tall against a background of palaces and gardens that would rival Versailles. The sitter's environment was intended by the artist not only as an important indication of class but also as a selling tool for the have-nots who dreamed of such luxury and splendor. Here our interest turns from the young Henry, who later became the Collector of Customs for the Potomac and Receiver of Revenues for Lord Baltimore, to the portrait of his faithful, though nameless Black servant. The servant appears to be an adolescent somewhat older than Henry. He is also well dressed and wears garments that are normally associated with those who attended to the affairs of the house. Kühn does not reveal the servant's exact height. He places him behind the figure of the young white master clutching with one hand the partridge no doubt felled by the arrow of the well-dressed youngster. The artist did not intend for the figure of the Black servant to be a subject of importance equal to that of Henry Darnell. In spite of this observation, the work becomes a celebrated image for two reasons: it is an early portrayal of the role of the Black slave in this society, and it strongly romanticizes a preconceived notion as to what pre-Revolutionary life in colonial America was like (Driskell, "Black Images in American Painting" 5).

The early portrayal of the role of the Black laborer in America is best depicted in the many illustrations that graphic artists executed as important visual documents for books and administrative memorabilia. From such works we are able to glean the historical picture of the Black worker/slave and, at the same time, view the mercantile system in which the slave fitted and spent much of his daily existence. A scene depicting a wharf on the Chesapeake Bay, a cartouche from a map in the Maryland Historical Society dated 1751, shows a number of partially clothed slaves serving their master, helping to load and unload a cargo of tobacco while ships wait at the wharf in the background where the work occurs. Similar scenes often appeared in the broadsides and general advertisements that were printed for commercial distribution.[3]

IMMEDIATE POST-REVOLUTIONARY IMAGES, 1776–1800

The post-Revolutionary image in general in American art is one of sophistication and stylistic development which speaks of the coming of age of art and the artist in America. Charles Willson Peale (1741–1827), John Trumbull (1756–1843), Gilbert Stuart (1775–1828), and Benjamin West (1738–1820), all of whom went to Europe to study art, had developed in their work important stylistic characterizations winning them praise by European critics as gifted artists.

Images of Blacks in the paintings of this period portray the servant's role discussed earlier. Valentine Green (1739–1813), an English artist, created a mezzotint after the work of John Trumbull entitled *General Washington*. The original portrait by Trumbull, *George Washington*, painted in 1780, is in the Metropolitan Museum of Art in New York. General Washington was a popular subject. A French artist, Noel le Mire (1724–1800), did an engraving of him called *Le General Washington*, ca. 1796 (Library of Congress). Whether or not le Mire actually saw a portrait of General Washington or a copy by Jean Baptiste le Paon is unclear. Le Mire's engraving was taken from one of the first authentic likenesses of Washington known in Europe at that time (Kaplan 33–36). It came from a miniature portrait of the general by Charles Willson Peale, a work done for the Marquis de Lafayette in 1779. Peale painted at least fourteen portraits of Washington between 1772 and 1795, some of which served as models for European artists who had ventured to America or who had not seen the general in real life (Kinnaird 156). In both prints, by the Englishman Green and the Frenchman le Mire, General Washington stands in the foreground of a vast landscape and is accompanied by a turban-wearing Black servant or attendant who holds the reins of the general's horse.

A third print, *[G]eneral Washi[ngton]*, ca. 1796 (location unknown) by an anonymous American engraver, illustrates what may be described as an early expressionistic treatment of the Le Mire theme and is altogether removed from the appearance of the original Peale miniature painted for Lafayette. Though one rarely finds any reference in the literature to slaves or servants wearing Eastern and Middle Eastern style turbans fitting for the personages of a maharajah or the like, this romantically perceived notion of Black attire was often placed upon the heads of unsuspecting servants in early American paintings as seen in Trumbull's *George Washington*. Washington referred to the handsomely tur-baned slave, William (Lee), simply as William. William added the name Lee himself, knowing that he had been purchased by Washington from Mary Lee in 1768. He was the general's faithful servant, always by his side. William was with Washington in Massachusetts in 1775 and remained with him until the end of the Revolutionary War. He is the servant seen standing in Edward Savage's famous painting of the Washington family executed in 1796 and referred to as Billy Lee (Kinnaird 44).

Washington referred to William as a mulatto and decreed in his will that, upon his death, "my Mulatto man William (calling himself William Lee) I give immediate freedom. . . . I allow him an annuity of thirty dollars during his natural life . . . and this I give him as a testimony of my sense of his attachment to me, and for his faithful services during the Revolutionary War."[4] Washington granted William the extraordinary favor of permitting him to take a wife, a free woman of color from Philadelphia, in the year 1784. Lee brought his bride to Mount Vernon to reside thereafter. Because of the close bond between Lee and Washington, we are able to identify an early Black subject in several artists' works, many of whom give diverse treatment to the subject.

Other subjects in which Blacks were depicted prior to the nineteenth century dealt with historic events in which acts of courage and heroic deeds were seen. Such is the case in the masterworks by John Singleton Copley (1738–1815) entitled *Watson and the Shark*, 1778. The painting in the Museum of Fine Arts in Boston is one of several by the artist with the same title. It was completed in time to be entered into the Royal Academy Exhibition in London in 1779. A second version of the work, painted in 1782, is in the collection of the Detroit Institute of Arts. In each work, a Black man is seen standing with outstretched arms gesturing in a manner so as to help rescue young Brook Watson who lost a leg to a shark in the waters of Havana harbor. The incident is said to have taken place there when Watson was a young man of fourteen years (Driskell, "Black Images in American Painting" 9). The Black man, shown at the top of the picture, is an equal passenger not only in the sense of his humanity and concern but also in the compositional soundness of Copley's understanding of the construction of a painting which honors the pyramidal grouping employed by a composition of this nature (Barker 214–15). Copley used a Black sitter, with whom he was acquainted, as his model in London.

Again, it is in an early portrayal of the Black slave and his role as war servant and hero that we come upon the action portrait: Peter Salem from Framingham, Massachusetts. Salem, an enlistee or a private in the American Army in Captain Simeon Edgel's company, became a celebrated hero for his act of bravery at Bunker Hill. *Lt. Grosvenor and Negro Servant Peter Salem at the Battle of Bunker Hill*, 1786 (Yale University Art Gallery), by John Trumbull, shows Salem grasping the musket of the lieutenant after which he fires at the encroaching British militia men, killing the gallant Major Pitcairne by a shot aimed straight at the head. The king's soldiers are shown retreating following Salem's act of bravery. Salem's heroism brought about a limited victory for the American soldiers (Kaplan 14).

Trumbull is said to have been on hand to talk to Salem a few days after the incident and commented on witnessing the fireworks from the Battle of Bunker Hill in Roxbury across the harbor. Trumbull painted this major work in 1786 after he had returned to London. It has been suggested that he worked from a Black model in his London Studio believed to be the same person who posed for the Black subject in *Watson and the Shark*. Salem is said to have died in 1816 in a Framingham poorhouse, having spent his post war years without pension or a position of security.

In 1795, Ralph Earl (1751–1801), a native of Massachusetts, painted an oil now in the New Britain (Connecticut) Museum of American Art called *Gentleman with Negro Attendant*. The Black attendant who remains unidentified looks admiringly at his master as he hands him a message to read. Earl's painting takes on the stylistic attributes of a work by Gilbert Stuart and other masters of the period and pointedly describes the master-servant role observed in earlier works by Trumbull and Kühn.

1. *Watson and the Shark*, 1778, John Singleton Copley, American, 1738–1815. Oil on canvas. Gift of Mrs. George von Lengerke Meyer. Courtesy of the Museum of Fine Arts, Boston.

PRE–CIVIL WAR IMAGES, 1800–1860

Several painters of this period attempted to break with the tradition of pre-senting stereotypic images of Blacks in their works. One such artist was Jeremiah Person Hardy (1800–1888). His work, in some ways, parallels the attempts of Black artist Joshua Johnston (discussed later in this chapter under "Black American Artists of the Nineteenth Century") to render the Black image with dignity in defiance of the stereotypes of the period. Born in New Hampshire in 1800, in 1811 Hardy settled in Northern Massachusetts, a region later to become the State of Maine. There he worked from 1824 until his death in 1888. His portrait of the well-known Black Bangor, Maine, barber-abolitionist and humorist, en-titled *Abraham Hanson*, 1828 (Addison Gallery of American Art), is among the first images by a white artist of a Black to celebrate a Black individual as a professional man. Executed in basic subtleties of grays, browns, and blacks, the painting, completed in 1828, shows that the artist understood the basic formula for naturalistic painting. Abraham, as he was affectionately known in the city of Bangor's lively circles, is said to have taken the development of the abolitionist cause very seriously. He offered his talent as a respected barber to an exclusive white community and used some of his profits to politic in favor of antislavery causes and for freedom movements as far away as Greece. He was equally well-known for the sale of sumptuous dinners, the proceeds from which he turned over to abolitionists and freedom-fighting causes (Cummings 3).

Another painting, entitled *Portrait of a Gentleman* in the collection of the Bowdoin College Museum of Art, executed two years after Hardy's portrait of Abraham, shows a handsome Black gentleman of mixed ancestry graciously attired in the fashionable style of his day. Painted around 1830, the work is unsigned and, at the present time, is not attributed to any known artist (Sadik entry 12).

Here it seems important to share with the reader what some writers have singled out as the Black portrait which, while attempting to show dignity of character, instead reveals how white American artists rendered the prime depic-tion of the "noble savage." The work to which I refer is the famous painting *Portrait of Cinqué* (New Haven Colony Historical Society) by Nathaniel Jocelyn (1796–1811), executed in 1840. Doubtless, Jocelyn considered that he was giving an actual portrait of bravery and heroism through his depiction of Cinqué, the Mendi prince from Sierre Leone enslaved aboard the *Amistad*, a Spanish slave ship on which a revolt by Black slaves took place in the waters off Havana harbor.[5] The historical symbols one would expect to see in a portrait of this type are neither present nor alluded to in Cinqué's character. Though the slaves aboard the *Amistad* took the guns and swords of the Spanish captors to carry out the mutiny, Jocelyn shows Cinqué with a spear in his hand, not posing with the firearms that contributed to the slaves' revolt. Yet Jocelyn attempted to create an image fitting the description of this historical event, one said to have singularly prevailed in helping to change the course of history in matters pertaining to justice for slaves in America and promoting missionary zeal crying for the end of slavery in America.

James G. Clonney (1812–1867) was born in England. When he arrived in America, he still devoted much of his time to painting miniatures. He turned from miniature painting to create scenes such as *The Militia Training*, 1841 (private collection, New York City), in which whites provide music for Black dancers. These genre scenes provided a mixture of entertainment, patriotism, and frolicking. Subjects which emphasized state of character among Blacks, the ability to be good workers and provide laughter for leisure class whites while indulgingly patronizing the status quo, were popular themes at this time and all but dominated the painting scenes in which Blacks were seen.

William Sidney Mount (1807–1868), a prolific painter of people, genre scenes, landscape, fauna, and themes of the common order, was born in the small village of Setauket on Long Island, New York. At the age of eighteen he was apprenticed to his oldest brother as a signmaker. This exposure provided him the ease with which he was able to move into painting, and he took advantage of every possible chance to see original paintings in New York City where he later worked. He became interested in portrait painting at the beginning of his career and concentrated on depicting likenesses of others while working in the city.

By the time Mount was twenty-three, he had created a relatively small painting showing a large crowd of people, all with individualized faces in a canvas format of approximately 22 inches by 27 inches. On this small canvas, entitled *Rustic Dance after a Sleigh Ride*, 1830 (Museum of Fine Arts, Boston), thirty-one faces are seen, three of which are Black. It would appear that this work represents the earliest known painting by Mount in which Blacks appear. Here, the music for the ensuing frolic is provided by a Black musician while two Black boys look on approvingly. Hereafter, Mount was to seek out Blacks as subjects for his paintings partly because of his interest in music but also because of his acquaintance with a number of Blacks who were musicians at Stony Brook, on Long Island, where he lived. Thereafter, he would undertake the depiction of many Black subjects as individuals instead of grouping them together in one scene. His treatment of the Black subject in *Farmers Nooning*, 1836 (The Museum at Stony Brook), was meant to show equality of sharing the noon lunch period on a Long Island farm. *Negro Asleep—Hay Making* is the name William Sachus, an agent for Goupil and Company of New York City, gave the picture when writing to Mount about rights to reproduce it by engraving on September 1, 1852. Sachus was also interested in obtaining *Banjo Player*, 1856 (The Museum at Stony Brook) and *The Bone Player*, 1856 (Museum of Fine Arts, Boston). He anxiously asked in the same letter, "How soon can I have one or both of these pictures?" Mount responded to Sachus' letter eight days later and indicated that he "liked the tone of it. . . . I am ready to negotiate with you," he stated. It is here that we see the true convictions of Mount as he is being challenged about painting so many themes of Blacks. He continues his response to Sachus by saying, "I will undertake those large heads (heads of Negroes) for you, although I have been urged not to paint anymore such subjects'' (Frankenstein 164). It is by now obvious that Mount was under pressure to return to the depiction of white subjects, without which there would be the threat of economic reprisal. Mount decided to stick by his decision to continue painting Black subjects. He further stated to Sachus: "I had as leave paint the character of some negroes as to paint the characters of some whites, as far as the morality is concerned." Then it appears that Mount thought very seriously about the question of morality and the economic reality of patronage, and he ended his letter to Sachus by saying, "A Negro, is as good as a White man—as long as he behaves himself" (Frankenstein 164). Mount's explanation of his portrayal of the Black theme seems to suggest that he was on the verge of breaking with the stereotyped image of how Blacks should be represented, yet he did not take the giant step of affirming his commitment to the Black subject.

Prior to the time of this exchange of ideas on the subject of the morality of depicting Black themes between the artist and his new dealer, William Sachus, Mount had painted numerous works in which Blacks were no longer subordinate props in the composition but were the main subject. But of utmost importance here is the fact that the Black figure emerged as something other than a prop in the work of William Sidney Mount. Though not completely emancipated as the supreme subject of celebration, the Black personage became an isolated individual just as whites were in earlier works. Thus, with the advent of the art of William Sidney Mount, Blacks became major subjects in works of art by American painters.

To the viewer, *Farmers Nooning*, a painting done for Jonathan Sturges, projected the stereotype image of a Black male sunning himself in a carefree manner seemingly uncaring about the world around him. A young white boy teases the Black male who is the principal subject. Was Mount astute enough to paint a subtle allegory which was not understood by his contemporaries? Is not the Black man at the center of the composition? The white subjects who are a lesser part of the composition are grouped around the Black man; some exhibit a pose of anonymity which suggests that they are less important to the scene than the Black. The scythe, the jug, and the act of sharpening the saw suggest something other than leisure. The teaser is the reverse of the amuser role Blacks previously assumed in paintings by white Americans where the entertainment was always done by Blacks. The small boy serves as a comic device. He performs the playful or foolish prank associated with Black adults in other paintings. The Black figure, relaxed and sensuous in pose, anticipates the Ariadne posture of love and pleasure. Yet, the stereotype of Black lust was built into the work to appease the common audience. Blacks were not thought of in the larger context of mid-nineteenth-century American society as being capable of sustaining intellectual thought. But more profoundly put in this context of how Blacks were viewed in American society are the comments of President Abraham Lincoln on the naiveté of Blacks published in the *Final Report of the American Freedman's Inquiry Commission*:

The Anglo-Saxon race, with it great force of character, much mental activity, an un-
flagging spirit of enterprise, has a certain hardness, a stubborn will, only moderate
genialty, a lack of habitual cheerfulness. Its intellectual powers are stronger than its social
instincts. The head predominates over the heart. There is little that is emotional in its
religion. . . . It is a race more calculated to call forth respect than love, better fitted to do
than to enjoy. The African race is in many respects the reverse of this. Genial, lively,
docile, emotional, the affections rule; the social instincts maintain the ascendent except
under cruel repression, its cheerfulness and love of mirth overflow with the exuberance
of childhood. It is devotional by feeling. It is a knowing rather than a thinking race. . . .
As regards the virtues of humility, lovingkindness, resignation under adversity, reliance
on Divine Providence, this race exhibits these, as a general rule, in a more marked manner
than does the Anglo-Saxon. . . . With time, if we but treat these people in a Christian
fashion, we shall have our reward. The softening influence of their genial spirit, diffused
throughout the community, will make itself felt as an element of improvement in the
national character (n.p.).

The fact that Blacks were not seen as people with a record of accomplishments
as forgers of ideas and conquerors of space did not take into account the salient
history of the Black race. Instead, theories were advanced which sought to justify
slavery and the lowly life Blacks lived under human bondage. What was even
more frightening, as we see these ideas and events more than one hundred years
later, is that the belief in the inferiority of the Black race was advanced and
clothed in acceptable Christian doctrine. Mount and other American artists had
little moral pressure to provide a more enlightened point of view in the visual
interpretation of the race.

In other pictures by Mount, in which one may attempt to rearrange hindsight
to accommodate nineteenth-century thought, Blacks seem to be mysterious
strangers intruding in a white man's world. *The Lucky Throw*, 1851 (The Museum
at Stony Brook), a lithograph by LaFarge & Company, was done in 1851 after
a painting of the same title by Mount. It illustrates the quality of the kind of
reproduction that William Sachus was referring to in his earlier correspondence
with Mount. This image is believed to be the prototype on which stereotypic
images of Blacks were copied later on business, trade, and postcards that advertised such products as hams, stoves, turkeys, pills, stove polish, sewing
machines, threads, soaps, and other items in this country, providing important
media images of Blacks beyond the first quarter of this century.

The Bone Player was painted by Mount in 1856 and so was the *Banjo Player*.
Other works such as *Dawn of Day*, 1867 (The Museum at Stony Brook), which
was painted eleven years later, suggest that Mount became interested in the use
of the Black image as a political statement, but only perhaps to show the lack
of political astuteness on the part of the Black race. One could also imply a
longing for the nostalgic master-servant relationship as suggested in the long
sleep. To Mount, the painting showed the Republican rooster after the Democratic
victories trying to awaken the Negro race. Mount felt the crowing to be of no
avail. He was painting not a sleeping Black man but one who was dead. Mount

painted the *Dawn of Day* one year before his own death, which occurred on November 18, 1868 (Frankenstein 201).

While Mount's treatment of the Black theme may seem compromising and indeed tame to some today, we must consider the prevalence of the myths and racial notions about the inferiority of Blacks, which were rampant though acceptable to all but a few liberal-minded antislavery crusaders and abolitionists at that time.

LATE NINETEENTH-CENTURY IMAGES, 1861–1900

A positive approach to seeing Black people as subjects deserving human compassion and a more realistic portrayal of racial themes can be observed in the work of numerous artists of the last part of the nineteenth century. Indeed, it may be rightly said that the art of Winslow Homer, Eastman Johnson (1824–1906), and Thomas Eakins (1844–1916) advanced a more dignified and realistic portrayal of the image of persons of African ancestry in art than the combined artistry of all who painted before them.

Eastman Johnson, a contemporary of Mount, was a man of little less than two decades Mount's junior. Mount is sometimes associated with Johnson as though the two artists were close friends. This is by no means the case, although Johnson chose to paint some subjects very much in the genre of those painted by Mount. Johnson's study of *Negro Boy*, 1860 (National Academy of Design), shows a sensitively painted Black lad sitting in the door of a log cabin playing a reed flute. In 1862, two years after *Negro Boy* was completed, Johnson executed a painting in which a small Black child and a man are seen listening in the background to music. *A Ride for Freedom—the Fugitive Slaves* (The Brooklyn Museum), completed in 1862, was said by the artist to be a scene he witnessed at Centerville, Virginia, on the morning of March 2, 1862, when McClellan's troops advanced on Manassas, Virginia (Sadik entry 35). Johnson was interested in Black life, and he is well known for his celebrated work. *Old Kentucky Home*, 1859 (New York State Historical Society), depicts Black life in mid-nineteenth-century Washington, D.C., in which the social concept of the extended family is readily observed. Johnson's *Portrait of a Negress*, 1866 (Hirschl and Adler Galleries), shows an old woman leaning forward to rest on her walking stick.

In addition to the artistry of Johnson, Homer, and Eakins, the talents of European artists Emanuel Gottlieb Leutze (1816–1868), born in Germany; Frank Buscher (1828–1890), of Switzerland; and Thomas Hovenden (1840–1895), a native of Ireland, all of whom settled in America, were joined by a host of artists of the pre–Civil War era and late nineteenth century to produce images that mirrored the various ways in which Blacks were viewed by whites in American life. Much of what they observed and painted reflected positive images of the race. Leutze, a painter of murals in the U.S. Capitol, was caught up in recounting historical themes such as *Mrs. Schuyler Burning Her Wheat Fields on the Approach of the British*, 1852 (Los Angeles County Museum of Art). Mrs. Schuyler is accompanied by a Black servant who carries the lantern which supplies the fire. John Quidor (1801–1881) was a painter of solid imagination who often filled his compositions with suspense and drama, a quality one observes in the minstrel-like characterizations given the fightened Black subject in *The Money Diggers*, 1832 (private collection).

In contrast to the drama seen in *The Money Diggers, Guitar Player*, 1867 (Kennedy Galleries), by Buscher, shows the confidence of the Black musicians who relaxes in a well-appointed home. Buscher seems to be closer to Mount in theme and concept in his representation of the Black figure than to his contemporaries.

Among the most acceptable as well as the most stereotypic images of Blacks produced during the post–Civil War period were those from the hand of William Aiken Walker (1838–1921), a native of Charleston, South Carolina. Walker's first recorded painting was done in 1850 when he was twelve years of age. The work depicted a Black man on the docks in Charleston. By far one of the lesser craftsmen among the nineteenth-century artists whom I have cited, Walker was, however, the most prolific; he produced more images with Black subjects than any other white American artist of the period. Trained as a photographer, he often painted directly from his snapshots of Black life, resulting in the stiff, scarecrow-type figures that stand motionless against the southern landscape.

Views of Blacks in cotton fields, *Cotton Plantation in Mississippi*, 1881 (Los Angeles County Museum of Art), are descriptive of these themes; hoeing cotton, wharf scenes, Blacks travelling and good timing along the way, market scenes (*Girl Eating Melon*, 1885, private collection), harvest scenes, and cabin scenes are among the many images Walker created in which the subjects were often anatomically ill-proportioned and were used in the same manner that one would use dolls or other lifeless props in a still life. What appears to be an accurate account of how white southerners felt about Blacks is best described in an account by an observer of Walker's work.

Walker's drawings of the Negro in his native cotton and cane fields is immutably given with all of the half pathetic raggedness of costume and love of gay colors that renders the darky such good artistic material for one who has the skill (New Orleans *Daily Picayune*, November 30, 1884:2).

Walker's portrayal of Blacks in the South is vastly different from Winslow Homer's portrayal. Walker revived the stereotypic image while Homer drew on sources directly from black life. Homer found the Black subject one to his liking and he used it for historical documentation, first for magazines, then for general interpretation of the power of the Black image in the making of formal composition. Most interesting is the contrast to be noted in the way in which Homer paints Blacks in a cotton field, *Cotton Pickers*, 1876 (Los Angeles County Museum of Art) and *Upland Cotton*, ca. 1879 (Hirschl and Adler Gallery), and Walker's version of the same subject. Homer gave a living quality to the working figures that does not occur in Walker's studies. But beyond this observation, Homer used Black images as principal subjects that included aspects of life other than the field experience. Although Homer also produced sketches with the pickaninny image in which Blacks dance wildly while white soldiers looked on amusedly, he redeemed himself amicably during his sojourns to the Caribbean where he showed Black subjects in control of the waters there just as he had done in his paintings of white seamen in the North Atlantic. Such an account is observed in *Shark Fishing*, 1885 (Cooper Union Museum). The furies of the storm and the unpredictable currents of the sea give title to the watercolor *After the Tornado*, 1888–89 (Art Institute of Chicago), in which the still body of a Black fisherman lies sprawled against the debris of a wrecked boat on a Bahamian Island.

Homer's documentation of Black life is reminiscent of the depiction Walker gave in theme only. Homer's sophistication as an artist is most telling in *Sunday Morning in Virginia*, 1877 (Cincinnati Art Museum) and *The Visit of the Mistress*, 1876 (National Museum of American Art). These works raise our interest level to see sensitively the pity and deprivation associated with the newly freed slaves, a quality not seen in Walker's work.

Thomas Eakins employed Blacks as models for portraits, some of whom he painted as individual characters as seen in the portrait of his pupil entitled *Henry O. Tanner*, ca. 1900 (The Hyde Collection); the portrait of a mulatto woman, *The Red Shawl*, 1890 (Philadelphia Museum of Art); and a work entitled *Negress*, 1867 (private collection) (Sadik entries 51, 52). *Whistling for Plover*, 1874 (The Brooklyn Museum), shows a Black man waiting in the marshes offshore readying himself to aim a gun at the ducks that are about to answer his call. *Negro Boy Dancing*, 1878 (Metropolitan Museum of Art), a composition with a subject similar to that later to appear in Tanner's work, is one of the few genre scenes in which Eakins uses a Black subject. A study for *Negro Boy Dancing*, 1878 (private collection), shows how observant the artist was to capture even the emotion of the mouth of the young dancer who bucks it out to the theme of the banjo. Eakins brought a breath of fresh air and a fine sense of interpretation to the black theme, a quality in painting he seemed highly capable of doing. He was a keen observer of nature and was equally able to discern with certainty the spiritual qualities of his sitter (Barker 654). He restored the dignity to the portrait that was lost in American painting after the widespread move to landscape painting.

BLACK AMERICAN ARTISTS OF THE NINETEENTH CENTURY

The nineteenth century saw the emergence of a number of Black artists whose principal interest in art moved away from portraiture to landscape painting. Principal among those who came after Joshua Johnston (ca. 1765–ca. 1832), a Baltimore artist who specialized in portraits, were Robert S. Duncanson (1821–

1872), Edward M. Bannister (1828–1901), and Henry O. Tanner (1859–1937). William Simpson (1818–1872), to be discussed later in this chapter under "Images of Black Women," worked in Boston from 1860 to 1866 as a portrait painter as did Robert Douglas, Jr. (1809–1887) of Philadelphia. David Bustill Bowser (1820–1900), also of Philadelphia, a relative of Douglas, was trained as an artist by him. These artists are among the few persons of African ancestry whose works have survived and are regularly seen in twentieth-century exhibits of works by Black artists.

Johnston, the former slave limner whose portraits were highly sought after by wealthy sea merchants and farmers along the Chesapeake Bay region and in the city of Baltimore, is thought to have practiced his craft between the years 1795 and 1832 in the vicinity of Baltimore (Driskell, *Two Centuries of Black American Art* 35). While more than ninety portraits have been attributed to Johnston to date, less than five works have surfaced in which the sitter is Black. *Portrait of a Cleric*, 1810 (Bowdoin College Museum of Art), is one such Black subject painted by Johnston. The sitter is a Black minister. The question has arisen as to whether the painting is taken from a likeness of the Reverend Daniel Coker, a founder of the African Episcopal Methodist Church in Baltimore (Bearden and Henderson 13). To date, no documents exist that would affirm what many have speculated: that the painting may indeed be a portrait of Reverend Coker. Johnston may have known several community ministers and likely requested a sitting of the Black cleric who posed without props for his painting, which was done between 1805 and 1810.

Johnston sought to emancipate himself completely as an artist and as a human being. He was a limner equal to most who lived during his time. Since his style is closely associated with those painters who studied with or who were influenced by Charles Willson Peale, one can assume that he, too, was under the tutelage of the acknowledged American master.

The sitter is attired in the simple garb worn by eighteenth-century preachers. He wears a full clerical collar covering his neck and a black jacket characteristic of the clothing worn by religious figures of the Protestant faith at the turn of the nineteenth century. The work shows the dignity of the sitter in a manner not commonly done with Black subjects. One would assume that a Black artist would be sympathetic to the portrayal of people of his own race. Johnston is not deceptive in the exercise of judgement; he renders facial features that are convincingly Negroid yet without exaggeration, a characterization not often seen among the white artists who painted Black subjects.

Little is known about the circumstances of Johnston's life after 1830. In previous years his name had appeared in the Baltimore city directory from time to time, and he is said to have been in the ownership of more than five families during his tenure as a slave (James Porter, *Modern Negro Art* 27). What is known about him proves that wealthy white merchants and seamen sought him to paint portraits of their families, creating compositions which captured the likeness of his sitter with a measure of satisfaction. Johnston's sitters were usually white, well attired, and posed to show a three-quarter view of the face. His work registered a sense of confidence and order about which he modestly spoke when, on December 19, 1798, he placed the following advertisement in the *Baltimore Intelligence*:

Portrait painting . . . as a self-taught genius, deriving from nature and industry his knowledge of Art . . . experienced many unsuperable obstacles in the pursuit of his studies, it is highly gratifying to him to make assurances of his ability to execute all commands, with an effect, and in a style, which must give satisfaction. Apply at House, in the alley leading from Charles to Hanover Street, back of Sear's Tavern (Driskell, *Two Centuries* 35).

Johnston's formula for painting people in a setting which emphasized their dignity and pride was by no means a phenomenon which he, as a Black artist, alone possessed. He chose not to use the caricature as a model for depicting any subject. The ideal for him was a close likeness of the sitter. Even through the barriers of a stiffly given limner formula, there emerged in Johnston's *Portrait of a Cleric* a quiet dignity apart from the ordinary expression, a quality which helped to validate, in a positive way, the art of America's first Black portrait painter.

Robert S. Duncanson was a follower of the Hudson River School tradition and a second generation away from those landscape artists who heeded the call of Thomas Cole and followers to escape to the American wilderness and show nature in its unfolding beauty and strength. Thus, few works of a figurative mode by Duncanson exist. Yet one prominent painting shows Black and white subjects occupying the foreground of an otherwise well-composed landscape. The title of the work, *Uncle Tom and Little Eva*, 1853 (Detroit Institute of Arts), was a popular one in the time and is said to have been inspired by the writings of Harriet Beecher Stowe. *Uncle Tom and Little Eva* provide no relief from the stereotypic image often associated with Black lifestyle and unsympathetic literature of the period (Driskell, *Two Centuries* 42). Duncanson lived a quiet and dignified life painting first in the city of Cincinnati, then travelling to Rome and later to Scotland, the place where so many of his landscapes derive their themes.

While Duncanson chose to work in the tradition of the Hudson River School painters, his contemporary, Edward M. Bannister of Providence, Rhode Island, was far more taken with the expressive mood of the Barbizon painters. Unlike Duncanson, Bannister never travelled abroad; in fact, he is not known to have ventured south of New York City in his lifetime. He too, felt the call to the wilds—often painting pastoral scenes in which man and his herd of cattle are shown at peace living in harmony with nature. Among the few works by Bannister in which Black or mulatto images are seen are *The Hay Gatherers*, ca. 1870 (private collection) and *Newspaper Boy*, 1869 (National Museum of American Art).

Bannister's death in 1901 occurred seven years after Henry O. Tanner turned

2. *Banjo Lesson*, 1893, Henry O. Tanner. Oil on canvas. Courtesy of Hampton
University Museum. Photo by Reuben Burrell.

from Black genre painting, a subject he convincingly mastered as early as the year 1893, to pursue religious painting until his death in 1937. His celebrated *Banjo Lesson*, 1893 (Hampton University), provides us with an important definition of the Black experience as seen by a Black artist. His *Thankful Poor*, 1894 (private collection), and the *Banjo Lesson* are two of the major Black genre paintings in which the artist uses the same two models as the subject. When he turned to painting religious themes, they were void of Black subjects. Tanner's work was greatly informed by the art of the Impressionists, but he chose not to become an exponent of their style. He variously took from the Impressionists the tonal feeling for color, a characteristic in his work which was much admired, the plein-air veil of mystery so often associated with atmospheric light in late nineteenth-century French painting and a lyrical and poetic way of seeing people and the land. Tanner is often hailed as America's most important Black painter and increasingly receives widespread attention as the preeminent twentieth-century American artist of religious themes.

IMAGES OF BLACK WOMEN

Images of Black women are rare in American painting in the pre-Revolutionary and post-Revolutionary periods. When women were shown, they were domestics in the role of servant or slave nurse guiding the directions of young children. Among the earliest of such scenes is a painting by an unknown artist entitled *Alexander Spotwood Payne and His Brother John Robert Dandridge Payne with Their Nurse*, dated 1790, in the Virginia Museum of Fine Arts in Richmond. Many artists in the South often depicted Black women nursing and protecting young white children left in their care, while others showed, in portrait form, a favorite octoroon or mulatto mistress. The Bavarian artist François Fleischbein (ca. 1804–1868) is credited with painting the charming portrait of *Marie LeVeau's Daughter* after 1860 (New Orleans Museum of Art). LeVeau is regarded as the voodoo queen of New Orleans, but so is her daughter (Bundy, *Painting in the South: 1564–1980*, 242).

William Matthew Prior did a portrait of a Black woman entitled *Mrs. Lawson*, 1843 (Shelburne [Vt.] Museum), in which he includes the name of the sitter, Nancy Lawson, in print near his own signature. Mrs. Lawson is graciously attired in well-appointed fashions including a white lace bonnet and matching collar. She holds a book in her right hand and wears a double ring on the fourth finger of the same hand. A distant landscape painting is seen with two figures, perhaps those of Reverend and Mrs. Lawson.

In genre scenes by artists such as John Adams Elder (1833–1895) and Winslow Homer, Black women became principal subjects. In *A Plantation Burial*, 1860 (Historic New Orleans Collection) by John Antrobus (1837–1907), Black women are shown in prominent positions throughout the composition sharing their grief at the passing of a close friend and relative. The *Portrait of Charity Banks*, 1870 (Maryland Commission of Afro-American History and Culture) by William

Simpson, a Black American artist from Boston, reveals how middle-class free people of color lived in Baltimore in the 1860s. Charity and her husband were painted by Simpson at a time when they were prosperous business partners in Maryland's port city. Mrs. Banks is elegantly dressed in black and is bedecked with fine jewelry, a symbol of her uncommon wealth.

When fledging Fisk University's newly organized Jubilee Singers toured Europe in the 1870s, they posed for Queen Victoria's court painter, Edmund Havel (ca. 1820–1895), and the result was a handsome portrait of America's first Black professional choral group, one whose fame would soon spread throughout the Western world. Of the eleven singers in the portrait, seven are women. The portrait, *The Fisk Jubilee Singers*, painted in 1873, now hangs in historic Jubilee Hall, built in 1875 on the famous Black college campus from funds raised by the Jubilee Singers on their European tour. Jubilee Hall stands today refurbished in memory of these courageous singers; it is the first permanent edifice for the instruction of students on a Black campus.

The works of many anonymous artists also inform us about how Black women were seen by outside observers. Such is the case of a painting by an unknown artist who painted *The Slave Market*, ca. 1850 (Museum of Art, Carnegie Institute). The work shows a Black mother clinging to an older child while all but forsaking an infant lying nearby on the ground. She is under the lash of the whip of condemnation and receives little or no sympathy from the audience. The painting also shows a mulatto woman on the steps of a hotel porch dressed in clothing reminiscent of garments worn by octoroons in New Orleans. She is being examined gently by a prospective buyer. Gavel in hand, the auctioneer awaits the highest bid to close the sale and release the beautiful young woman of color to the purchaser.

Mount's *Eel Spearing at Setauket*, 1845 (New York State Historical Society), mentioned earlier, shows a Black woman aiming her spear to capture an eel while the boat is oared into position by a young white boy. This is perhaps the very first time in American art that a Black woman is seen as the principal subject, other than in a portrait, in a composition so importantly rendered and not cast in a position of servitude.

In 1888, Thomas Pollock Anshutz (1851–1912) revived the stereotype of laziness, work evasion, and the tired mammy in a composition entitled *Aunt Hannah*, 1888 (Detroit Institute of Arts). It is the headwrap, the broom, and the nodding woman that provide us with the particular frame of reference for the stereotypic image.

Christian Mayr (1805–1850) created a composition in 1838 in which he depicts a *Kitchen Ball at White Sulphur Springs* (North Carolina Museum of Art). Many of those who celebrate out front by participating in the party as dancers are women. In an outburst of merrymaking and relaxing in the warmth of each other's company, women graciously dressed in pleasant styles of the day win the approval of their male counterparts, many of whom sit and admire them from a distance. Black women dominate a composition in which Eyre Crowe

(1824–1910) describes a sale of slaves in Richmond, Virginia. *Slave Market, Richmond, Virginia*, 1853 (private collection), shows a more humane version of the treatment of slaves at auction and sales than that which is normally recorded in the literature and visual compendia.

Mention has been made earlier of the positive image that Homer rendered in connection with the Black subject. In his composition *Captured Liberators*, 1865–1866 (Edward Eberstadt & Sons), Homer shows a Black woman occupying the central area of a painting in which soldiers of the Confederacy carry their flag past a Virginia residence. Domestic props such as gourds, often used in the South to make dippers for drinking from buckets, can be seen at the left side of the woman. Homer's *The Visit of the Mistress* and *Sunday Morning in Virginia*, previously discussed, highlight the skill by which the artist was able to render concise likenesses of women in various styles of dress in one composition while commenting equally on the social status of a number of subjects, most of which were Black women.

Black women were seldom depicted by white artists for their physical beauty before Thomas Eakins broke with prevailing traditions and painted, with an endowed sensibility to reason, the charm and energy he saw in them. Thus, he created a standard of excellence in painting which acknowledged the moral obligation of the artist to be in tune with the spirit of the sitter capturing more than the physical shell or outside appearance of form.

The advance in the positive depiction of images of Black women did not end with the art of Eakins. His influence on artists of the twentieth century helped establish a positive atmosphere in painting which continues into our own time.

VIEWING THE BLACK IMAGE: A RETROSPECT

Prior to the summer of 1964, the image of Blacks in American art had not been undertaken as a subject around which a major exhibition was worthy of presentation. Marvin Sadik, former director of the National Portrait Gallery, assembled the first such exhibition at Bowdoin College Museum of Art. It was called "The Portrayal of the Negro in American Painting." For the first time, students of American art, other than Blacks themselves, took special note of the Black theme as it appeared from colonial times to the mid-twentieth century. And, perhaps for the first time, art historians realized the deliberate biases of some of America's visual artists and recognized the contributions they made to the development and perpetuation of racial myths so commonly associated with the electronic media of our own times.

In the mid-nineteenth century there developed a sentimental attitude toward genre painters who saw poverty and the deprived conditions under which most Blacks lived as a picturesque theme and not one which spoke of the illness of the societal order. One notes in recent years, however, a change among visual artists in their portrayal of a more positive treatment of the Black image in American art, much of which came from the hands of Black artists who looked at themselves during the great Black cultural revolution of the 1920s known as the Harlem Renaissance. Thus came the beginning of positive images of Blacks in American art—but from the hands of Black American artists.

This brief overview is by no means a comprehensive study of the subject of race in American art, nor is it meant to be a sociological study. It was intended to bring to our attention a view of how American artists saw Blacks, first as exotica, in the manner that some European artists saw them, but seldom as personalities. Further, the chapter is meant to show how Blacks were seen and interpreted by white artists as picturesque creatures who loved music, fun, and dance and who regarded their own deprived state of life as being a part of God's will. These artists were reinforced in their beliefs by notions they learned through the teachings of Christian principles. But along with the various views depicted by white artists of Blacks in their works, there has been a significant parallel development of the Black artist whose works present another view of Black images in American art, and who are master builders both in the presentation of these images and in those of other genres as well.

NOTES

1. Popular images of Blacks appeared in stereotypic form which showed a stylized treatment of the runaway slave, happy slaves dancing for their masters, and those who served a household faithfully over several generations.

2. When under the direct supervision of their master, slaves were often docile and willingly engaged in exercises of humor and comedy that amused an easily deceived owner. In their own family circles, however, they often exhibited patterns of behavior which showed them to be heroically brave and even militant by the standards of the time.

3. Among newspapers that descriptively advertised such scenes were the *Baltimore Intelligencer* and the *Maryland Gazette*, both of which accepted paid advertisements and solicitations of payments owed artists. Private printers such as William Hunter of Williamsburg also engaged in the making of descriptive broadsides and decorative cartouches.

4. Excerpted from the will of George Washington and illustrated in Sidney Kaplan, *The Black Presence in the Era of the American Revolution* (Washington, D.C.: Smithsonian Institution Press, 1973):32.

5. For a complete historical description of the revolt known as The Amistad Incident, see David C. Driskell, *Amistad II: Afro American Art* (New York: United Church Board for Homeland Ministries, 1975):15–34.

LOCATION OF ART WORKS DISCUSSED IN TEXT

Works of art that include Blacks either as primary or secondary subjects are cited below. For an extensive list of Black museums and others that house works by Black painters and artists, see chapter 10 of this book.

Anonymous. *Alexander Spotwood Payne and His Brother John Robert Dandridge Payne with Their Nurse*. 1790. Virginia Museum of Fine Arts, Richmond, Va.
Anonymous. *[G]eneral Washi[ngton]*. Engraving. ca. 1796. Location unknown.

Anonymous. *Portrait of a Gentleman*. ca. 1830. Bowdoin College Museum of Art, Brunswick, Maine.

Anonymous. *The Slave Market*. ca. 1850. Museum of Art, Carnegie Institute, Pittsburgh, Pa.

Anshutz, Thomas Pollock (1851–1912). *Aunt Hannah*. 1888. Detroit Institute of Arts, Detroit, Mich.

Antrobus, John (1837–1907). *A Plantation Burial*. 1860. Historic New Orleans Collection, New Orleans, La.

Bannister, Edward M. (1828–1901). *The Hay Gatherers*. ca. 1870. Private collection.

————. *Newspaper Boy*. Also recorded as *Mulatto Boy*. 1869. National Museum of American Art, Smithsonian Institution, Washington, D.C.

Buscher, Frank (1828–1890). *Guitar Player*. 1867. Kennedy Galleries, New York, N.Y.

Clonney, James G. (1812–1867). *The Militia Training*, 1841. Private collection, New York, N.Y.

Copley, John Singleton (1738–1815). *Watson and the Shark*. 1778. Museum of Fine Arts, Boston, Mass.

————. *Watson and the Shark*. 1782 version. Detroit Institute of Arts, Detroit, Mich.

Crowe, Eyre (1824–1910). *Slave Market, Richmond, Virginia*. 1853. Private collection.

Duncanson, Robert S. (1821–1872). *Uncle Tom and Little Eva*. 1853. Detroit Institute of Arts, Detroit, Mich.

Eakins, Thomas (1844–1916). *Henry O. Tanner*. ca. 1900. The Hyde Collection, Glens Falls, N.Y.

————. *Negress*. 1867. Private collection.

————. *Negro Boy Dancing*. 1878. Metropolitan Museum of Art, New York, N.Y.

————. *The Red Shawl*. 1890. Philadelphia Museum of Art, Philadelphia, Pa.

————. *Whistling for Plover*. 1874. Brooklyn Museum, Brooklyn, N.Y.

Earl, Ralph (1751–1801). *Gentleman with Negro Attendant*. 1795. Museum of American Art, New Britain, Conn.

Fleischbein, François (ca. 1804–1868). *Marie LeVeau's Daughter*. ca. 1860. New Orleans Museum of Art, New Orleans, La.

Green, Valentine (1739–1813). *General Washington*. Mezzotint, ca. 1775. Location unknown.

Hardy, Jeremiah Person (1800–1888). *Abraham Hanson*. 1828. Addison Gallery of American Art, Phillips Academy, Andover, Mass.

Havel, Edmund (ca. 1820–1895). *The Fisk Jubilee Singers*. 1873. Fisk University, Jubilee Hall, Nashville, Tenn.

Homer, Winslow (1836–1910). *After the Tornado*. 1888–89. Art Institute of Chicago, Chicago, Ill.

————. *Captured Liberators*. 1865–66. Edward Eberstadt & Sons, New York, N.Y.

————. *Cotton Pickers*. 1876. Los Angeles County Museum of Art, Los Angeles, Calif.

————. *Shark Fishing*. 1885. Cooper Union Museum, New York, N.Y.

————. *Sunday Morning in Virginia*, 1877. Cincinnati Art Museum, Cincinnati, Ohio.

————. *Upland Cotton*. 1879–95. Hirschl and Adler Gallery, New York, N.Y.

————. *The Visit of the Mistress*. 1876. National Museum of American Art, Smithsonian Institution, Washington, D.C.

Jocelyn, Nathaniel (1796–1881). *Portrait of Cinqué*. 1840. New Haven Colony Historical Society, New Haven, Conn.

Johnson, Eastman (1824–1906). *Negro Boy*. 1860. National Academy of Design, New York, N.Y.

————. *Old Kentucky Home*. 1859. New York State Historical Society, Cooperstown, N.Y.

————. *Portrait of a Negress*. 1866. Hirschl and Adler Galleries, New York, N.Y.

————. *A Ride for Freedom—The Fugitive Slaves*. 1862. The Brooklyn Museum, Brooklyn, N.Y.

Johnston, Joshua (ca. 1765-ca. 1832). *Portrait of A Cleric*. 1810. Bowdoin College Museum of Art, Brunswick, Maine.

Kühn, Justus Engelhardt (d. 1717). *The Portrait of Henry Darnell III*. 1710. Maryland Historical Society, Baltimore, Md.

LaFarge & Company. *The Lucky Throw*. 1851. Lithograph. The Museum at Stony Brook, Stony Brook, Long Island, N.Y.

le Mire, Noel (1724–1800). *Le General Washington*. ca. 1796. Engraving. Library of Congress, Washington, D.C.

Leutze, Emanuel Gottlieb (1816–1868). *Mrs. Schuyler Burning Her Wheat Fields on the Approach of the British*. 1852. Los Angeles County Museum of Art, Los Angeles, Calif.

Mayr, Christian (1805–1850). *Kitchen Ball at White Sulphur Springs*. 1838. North Carolina Museum of Art, Raleigh, N.C.

Mount, William Sidney (1807–1868). *Banjo Player*. 1856. Museum of Fine Arts, Boston, Mass.

————. *The Bone Player*. 1856. Museum of Fine Arts, Boston, Mass.

————. *Dance of the Haymaker*. 1845. The Museum at Stony Brook, Stony Brook, Long Island, N.Y.

————. *Dawn of Day*. 1867. The Museum at Stony Brook, Stony Brook, Long Island, N.Y.

————. *Eel Spearing at Setauket*. 1845. New York State Historical Society, Cooperstown, N.Y.

————. *Farmers Nooning*. Also referred to as *Negro Asleep—Hay Making*. 1836. The Museum at Stony Brook, Stony Brook, Long Island, N.Y.

————. *The Power of Music*. Also referred to as *Music Hath Charms*. 1847. The Century Association, New York, N.Y.

————. *Rustic Dance after a Sleigh Ride*. 1830. Museum of Fine Arts, Boston, Mass.

Prior, William Matthew (1806–1873). *Mrs. Lawson*. 1843. Shelburne Museum, Shelburne, Vt.

Quidor, John (1801–1881). *The Money Diggers*. 1832. Private collection.

Savage, Edward (1761–1817). *Painting of the Washington Family*. 1796. National Gallery of Art, Washington, D.C.

Simpson, William (1818–1872). *Portrait of Charity Banks*. 1870. Maryland Commission of Afro-American History and Culture, Annapolis, Md.

Tanner, Henry O. (1859–1937). *Banjo Lesson*. 1893. Hampton University Museum, Hampton, Va.

————. *Thankful Poor*. 1894. Private collection.

Trumbull, John (1756–1843). *Lt. Grosvenor and Negro Servant Peter Salem at the Battle of Bunker Hill*. 1786. Yale University Art Gallery, New Haven, Conn.

————. *George Washington*. 1780. Metropolitan Museum of Art, N.Y.

Walker, William Aiken (1838–1921). *Cotton Plantation in Mississippi*. 1881. Los Angeles County Museum of Art, Los Angeles, Calif.

————. *Girl Eating Melon*. 1885. Private collection.

BIBLIOGRAPHY

Adams, Russell. *Great Negroes Past and Present*. Chicago: Afro-American Publishing Co., 1969.

Aptheker, Herbert, ed. *Documentary History of the Negro People in the United States*. 2 vols. 2d ed. New York: Citadel Press, 1964.

Atkinson, J. Edward, and David C. Driskell, comps. and eds. *Black Dimensions in Contemporary American Art*. New York: New American Library, 1971.

Bardolph, Richard. *The Negro Vanguard*. Reprinted. Westport, Conn.: Negro Universities Press, 1959.

Barker, Virgil. *American Painting*. New York: Macmillan, 1950.

Barnes, Albert C. "Negro Art and America." *Survey* (March 1, 1925): 668–69.

Barr, Alfred, ed. *Painting and Sculpture in the Museum of Modern Art*. New York: Museum of Modern Art, 1942.

Baur, John I. H., ed. *New Art in America: 50 Painters of the 20th Century*. Greenwich, Conn.: Graphic Society, 1957.

Beam, Phillip C. *Winslow Homer at Prouts Neck*. Boston: Little, Brown & Co., 1966.

Bearden, Romare, and Harry Henderson. *Six Black Masters of American Art*. New York: Zenith Books, 1972.

Bergman, Peter M. *The Chronological History of the Negro in America*. New York: Harper and Row, 1969.

Black American Artists of Yesterday and Today. Black Heritage Series. Dayton, Ohio: George A. Pflaum, Publisher, 1909.

The Black Photographers Annual 1973. Brooklyn, N.Y.: Black Photographers Annual, 1973.

Boning, Richard A. *Profiles of Black Americans*. Rockville Centre, N.Y.: Dexter and Westbrook, 1969.

Boswell, Peyton, Jr. *Modern American Painting*. New York: Dodd, Mead, 1939.

Brawley, Benjamin. *Negro Builders and Heroes*. Chapel Hill: University of North Carolina Press, 1937.

———. *The Negro in Literature and Art in the United States*. Rev. ed. New York: Dodd, Mead, 1934.

———. *The Negro Genius, a New Appraisal of the Achievement of the American Negro in Literature and the Fine Arts*. New York: Biblo and Tannen, 1965.

Brown, Sterling. *The Negro Caravan*. New York: Dryden Press, 1942.

Bryan, Michael. *Bryan's Dictionary of Painters and Engravers*. 5 vols. New York: Macmillan Co., 1903–1905.

Bundy, David S. *Painting in the South: 1564–1980*. Richmond, Va.: Virginia Museum of Fine Arts, 1983.

Burnett, W. C., Jr. "Black Art Evolves." *Atlanta Journal and Constitution*, January 9, 1977: F1–2.

Burroughs, Margaret, et. al. *National Conference of Negro Artists*. Atlanta: Atlanta University, 1959.

Butcher, Margaret Just. *The Negro in American Culture*. New York: Alfred A. Knopf, 1967.

Cahill, Holger, and Alfred Barr, Jr., eds. *Art in America in Modern Times*. New York: Reynal and Hitchcock, 1934.

———. *New Horizons in American Art*. New York: Museum of Modern Art, 1936.

Callaway, Thomas J. "The American Negro Exhibits at the Paris Exposition." *Hampton Negro Conference*. Hampton, Va.: Hampton Institute Press, 1901. 74–80.

Celebrating Negro History and Brotherhood: A Folio of Prints by Chicago Artists. Chicago: Seven Arts Workshop, 1956.

Chase, George Henry, and Chandler R. Post. *A History of Sculpture*. New York: Harper and Brothers, 1925.

Chase, Judith W. *Afro-American Art and Craft*. New York: Van Nostrand Reinhold Co., 1971.

Clapp, Jane. *Art Reproductions*. New York: Scarecrow Press, 1961.

———. *Sculpture Index*. Vol. 2. Metuchen, N.J.: Scarecrow Press, 1970.

Clement, Clara E., and Laurence Hutton. *Artists of the Nineteenth Century: Their Works*. Boston: Osgood, 1885.

Coen, Rena N. *The Black Man in Art*. Minneapolis, Minn.: Lerner Publications Co., 1970.

Coleman, Floyd. "African Influences on Black American Art." *Black Art* (Fall 1976): 4–15.

Craven, Thomas, ed. *A Treasury of American Prints*. New York: Simon and Schuster, 1939.

Cummings, Paul. *A Dictionary of Contemporary American Artists*. New York: St. Martin's Press, 1966.

Dabney, Wendell P. *Cincinnati's Colored Citizens*. Cincinnati, Ohio: Dabney Publishing Co., 1926.

Dannett, Sylvia G. L. *Profiles of Negro Womanhood*. 2 vols. Negro Heritage Library. Yonkers, N.Y.: Educational Heritage, 1964, 1966.

Davis, John P., ed. *The American Negro Reference Book*. Negro Heritage Library. Yonkers, N.Y.: Educational Heritage, 1966.

Davison, Ruth M., and April Legler, comps. *Government Publications on the American Negro, 1948–1968*. Focus: Black America Bibliography Series. Bloomington: Indiana University, 1969.

Diamond Jubilee Exposition Authority. *Cavalcade of the American Negro*. Chicago: Illinois Writers' Project, 1940.

Dover, Cedric. *American Negro Art*. Greenwich, Conn.: New York Graphic Society, 1960.

Driskell, David C. "Afro-American Art." *American Quarterly* 30, No. 3 (1978): 390–94.

———. *Amistad II: Afro American Art*. New York: United Church Press, 1975.

———. "Art by Blacks: Its Vital Role in U.S. Culture." *Smithsonian* (October 1976): 86–93.

———. "Black Images in American Painting." Unpublished manuscript delivered at Fisk University, October 12, 1981.

———. *Hidden Heritage: Afro-American Art, 1800–1950*. San Francisco, Calif.: Art Museum Association of America, 1985.

———. *Two Centuries of Black American Art*. New York: Alfred Knopf, 1976.

DuBois, W. E. B. *Encyclopedia of the Negro*. 2d ed. New York: Phelps-Stokes Fund, 1946.

———. *The Negro Artisan*. Atlanta: Atlanta University Press, 1902. Reprinted. New York: Arno Press and *The New York Times*, 1969.

Editors of *Ebony*. *The Negro Handbook*. Chicago: Johnson Publications Co., 1966.

Fax, Elton C. *Seventeen Black Artists*. New York: Dodd, Mead, 1971.

Final Report of the American Freedman's Inquiry Commission. n.p., 1864.

Frankenstein, Alfred. *William Sidney Mount*. New York: Harry N. Abrams, Publishers, 1975.

Franklin, John Hope. *From Slavery to Freedom*. 5th ed. New York: Alfred A. Knopf, 1980.

French, H. W. *Art and Artists of Connecticut*. Boston: Lee and Shepard, 1879.

Fuller, Edmund B. *The Sculpture of William Edmondson*. Pittsburgh, Pa.: University of Pittsburgh Press, 1973.

Fuller, Thomas O. *Pictorial History of the American Negro*. Memphis, Tenn.: Pictorial History, 1933.

Gayle, Addison. *The Black Aesthetic*. Garden City, N.Y.: Doubleday, 1971.

Geldzaher, Henry. *American Painting in the Twentieth Century*. New York: The Metropolitan Museum of Art, 1965.

George Cleveland Hall Branch Library. *The Special Negro Collection at the George Cleveland Hall Branch Library*. Chicago: n.p., 1968.

Greene, Lorenzo Johnson. *The Negro in Colonial New England, 1620–1776*. New York: Columbia University Press, 1942.

Hale, R. B., ed. *One Hundred American Painters of the Twentieth Century*. New York: The Metropolitan Museum of Art, 1950.

The Harlem Renaissance Art of Black America. Introduction by Mary S. Campbell. Essays by David Driskell, David L. Lewis, and Deborah W. Ryan. New York: The Studio Museum in Harlem, Harry Abrams, Publishers, 1987.

Harvard University Library. *Resources of the Harvard University Library for Afro-American and African Studies*. Cambridge, Mass.: Harvard University Press, 1969.

Hatch, John Davis. *Up Til Now: The Negro Artist Comes of Age*. Albany, N.Y.: Albany Institute of History and Art, 1946.

Huggins, Nathan. *The Harlem Renaissance*. New York: Oxford University Press, 1971.

Hughes, Langston, and Milton Meltzer. *A Pictorial History of the Negro in America*. New York: Crown, 1956.

Hunter, Sam. *American Art of the Twentieth Century*. New York: Harry N. Abrams, 1972.

Jackson, Giles B., and D. Webster Davis. *The Industrial History of the Negro Race in the United States*. Richmond, Va.: n.p., 1980.

Johnson, James Weldon. *Black Manhattan*. New York: Alfred A. Knopf, 1930.

Kaplan, Sidney. *The Black Presence in the Era of the American Revolution*. Washington, D.C.: Smithsonian Institution Press, 1973.

Kinnaird, Clark. *George Washington, the Pictorial Biography*. New York: Hastings House, 1967.

Larkin, Oliver. *Art and Life in America*. New York: Holt, Rinehart and Winston, 1960.

Lewis, David Levering. *When Harlem Was in Vogue*. New York: Alfred A. Knopf, 1981.

Locke, Alain. "Negro Art." *Encyclopaedia Britannica*. 14th ed. Chicago: Encyclopaedia Britannica, Inc.

———. "Negro Art." *Encyclopaedia Britannica*. 15th ed. Chicago: Encyclopaedia Britannica, Inc., 1979.

————. *Negro Art: Past and Present*. Washington, D.C.: Associates in Negro Folk Education, 1936.

————. *The Negro in Art*. Washington, D.C.: Associates in Negro Folk Education, 1940.

————. *The New Negro*. New York: Albert & Charles Boni, 1925. Reprinted. Boston: Atheneum Press, 1968.

Louisiana: A Guide to State W.P.A. in the State of Louisiana. New York: Hastings House, 1941.

McCausland, Elizabeth. "Jacob Laurence." *Magazine of Art* 38 (November 1945): 250–54.

Mallett, Daniel Trowbridge. *Mallett's Index of Artists: International-Biographical: Including Painters, Sculptors, Illustrators, Engravers, and Etchers of the Past and Present. Orig. and Supplement*. New York: Peter Smith, 1948.

Mendelowitz, Daniel M. *A History of American Art*. New York: Holt, Rinehart and Winston, 1960.

National Conference of Artists. *A Print Portfolio by Negro Artists: A Souvenir in Observation of the Emancipation Proclamation Centennial, 1863–1963*. Chicago: n.p., 1963.

New Orleans *Daily Picayune*, November 30, 1884: 2.

Patterson, Lindsay, comp. and ed. *The Negro in Music and Art*. International Library of Negro Life and History. Under the auspices of the Association for the Study of Negro Life and History. New York: Publishers Co., 1968.

Pincus-Witten, Robert. "Black Artists of the 1930's." *Artforum* 7 (February 1969): 65.

Pleasants, J. Hall. "Joshua Johnston. The First Negro Portrait Painter." *Maryland Historical Magazine* 37 (June 1942): 121–49.

Ploski, Harry A., Ernest Kaiser, and Otto J. Lindenmeyer, eds. "The Black Artists." *Reference Library of Black America*. New York: Bellwether Publishing Co., 1971.

Porter, Dorothy B. *The Negro in the United States: A Working Bibliography*. Ann Arbor, Mich.: University Microfilms, 1969.

Porter, James A. *Modern Negro Art*. New York: Dryden Press, 1943. Reprinted. New York: Arno Press, 1969.

————. "The Negro Artist." Master's thesis, New York University, 1937.

————. "Robert S. Duncanson, Romantic Realist." *Art in America* 39, 3 (October 1951): 99–154.

————. "The Transcultural Affinities of American Negro Art." *Africa Seen by American Negroes*. Dijon, France: Présence Africaine, 1958.

Roberts, Lucille. "The Negro in American Arts: A Gallery of Light." *Topic* (1966): 21–25.

Robinson, Wilhelmina S. *Historical Negro Biographies*. International Library of Negro Life and History. Under the auspices of the Association for the Study of Negro Life and History. New York: Publishers Co., 1967.

Roelof-Lanner, T. V., ed. *Prints by American Negro Artists*. Los Angeles, Calif.: Los Angeles Cultural Exchange Center, 1965.

Rose, Barbara. *American Art Since 1900: A Critical History*. New York: Frederick A. Praeger, 1967.

————. "Black Artists in America." A symposium. *Bulletin of the Metropolitan Museum of Art* (January 1969): 245–61.

————. "Blacks in American Art." *Art in America* 58 (September-October 1970): 65.

Roucek, Joseph S., and Thomas Kiernan, eds. *The Negro Impact on Western Civilization*. New York: Philosophical Library, 1970.

Sadik, Marvin. *The Portrayal of the Negro in American Painting*. Catalog notes. Brunswick, Maine: Bowdoin College Museum of Art, 1964.

Schoener, Allon, comp. *Harlem on My Mind: Cultural Capital of Black America, 1900–1968*. New York: Random House, 1968.

Siegel, Jeanne. "Four American Negro Painters, 1940–1965, Their Choice and Treatment of Themes." Master's thesis, Columbia University, 1966.

Simmons, William J. *Men of Mark, Eminent, Progressive and Rising*. Cleveland, Ohio: Revel, 1887.

Simon, Leonard. "The American Presence of the Black Artist." *American Art Review* (November–December 1976): 105–19.

West, Earl H., comp. *A Bibliography of Doctoral Research on the Negro: 1933–1966*. Ann Arbor, Mich.: University Microfilms, 1969.

Wheadon, Augusta Austin. *The Negro from 1863 to 1963*. New York: Vantage Press, 1964.

Wilson, Joseph. *Sketches of the Higher Classes of Colored Society in Philadelphia, by a Southerner*. Philadelphia: Marrihew and Thompson, 1841.

Woodruff, Hale. "My Meeting with Henry O. Tanner." *Crisis* 77 (January 1970): 7–12.

Blacks on the Musical Stage

In his preface to *Blacks in the American Theatre*, Leonard C. Archer has pointed out that before the ferment of the 1950s favorable black images were "almost invisible" (Archer 6). While polemic and confusion over terms have clouded the discussion of Black contributions to American musical theater, Archer's basic point is indisputable. Distinctive characterizations of Blacks unrelated to stereotypes are a comparatively recent development on the American stage.

But what images were created and how have the images of Blacks been made and fixed in the public mind? What was the history of this image making before the turmoil of the nineteenth century and the rigid minstrel show stereotypes that grew up and calcified at that time? Perhaps the greatest deprivation for us as cultural historians is the lack of information about the orally transmitted performance traditions before the nineteenth century. Many shades of subtlety with respect to musical performing practices, comedic gestures, and dance steps have been lost in the passage of time. Occasionally iconography can help to fill the gap, but more often than not picture evidence only reminds us of the incompleteness of our knowledge. Written accounts are often heavily biased; nevertheless, at least a general impression of "the Black image" can be gained from carefully scrutinizing the available material.

IMAGES IN THE EARLY THEATER

Since slaves and free Blacks both constituted despised minority populations with little or no influence over the literature or drama of the general public, it is hardly surprising that even before the nineteenth century grotesque caricatures arose in connection with white-run musical theater—the ballad opera. This was a form of entertainment with strength in its identification with popular senti-ments—sentiments that held Blacks to be pathetic, laughable, or stupid.

Theater in America before the 1820s, consisting of importations from Europe in many instances, included Black characters played by whites and, for the most part, conveying images derived from older traditions. Blacks were comic serv-ants: Mungo in *The Padlock* (1769); Sambo in *The Triumph of Love* (1795). Occasionally contrasting images appeared; John Leacock's more historically derived work, *The Fall of British Tyranny* (1776) portrayed Black troops eager to serve the British and kill their former slave masters.[1]

The opening of the African Grove Theater in New York in 1821 signaled the formal appearance of Black acting in a musical entertainment "agreeable to Ladies and Gentlemen of Colour" (quoted in Southern 119). Shows were an-nounced for September and October, one to be a benefit for James Hewlett (d. 1849?), the company's principal actor and singer. Characteristic of the time, several songs were offered as an opening section; a play (Shakespeare's *Richard III*) followed; and a pantomime entitled *Asama* concluded the evening. The theater was plagued by hecklers and hoodlums who sought to disrupt the per-formances, and it was finally closed by the police in 1829 (Southern 116–21). Hewlett toured abroad calling himself "The New York and London Coloured Comedian." A young Ira Aldridge, who later gained fame as a tragedian playing Othello opposite Edmund Kean's Iago, sang songs at the Grove. Charles Mathews (1776–1835), the English actor, mimicked the Black actors of the African Grove and recorded James Hewlett's song "Possum Up a Gum Tree." He also created the stage character of Agamemnon, a fat fiddle-playing runaway slave. Despite the obvious family resemblance of Agamemnon to other comic Black servants, the image of Mathews' creation was not entirely without merit. Mathews was highly critical of America in general and penned what may well be the first abolitionist play, *Jonathan in England*, in about 1824, in which Agamemnon is informed about the chance of being free in England (Hodge 67–68). In the so-called Yankee plays of the early nineteenth century, such as *The Green Mountain Boy* (1832), by Joseph Jones, or *The Vermont Wool Dealer, or The Yankee* (1840), by C. A. Logan, Black servants remained characters to be mocked and abused, although on rare occasions they protested their lot (Hodge 58, 70, 172, 233).

THE LITERATURE OF THE COLONIAL PERIOD

The bibliography for the colonial period and the early nineteenth century is not exhaustive. Eileen Southern's summary of events in *The Music of Black Americans* represents original research not yet matched in more extended sources (Southern 116–21). Her bibliography contains several sources which incidentally mention Black attendance at predominantly white theaters and demonstrate en-thusiasm among Blacks—even slaves—for the theater. Evidence for a truly independent Black musical theater of any permanence in the antebellum United

States is rare, although a few tantalizing bits of information hint that more activity than has yet come to light existed. In his study of the highly musical and racially diverse population of pre–Civil War New Orleans, *Music in New Orleans* (1966), Henry Kmen has unearthed announcements of the opening of a theater for the "free colored population" of that city—the Theatre de la Renaissance. One of the announcements suggests that, in all likelihood, the music director and the orchestra members were Black. The theater is reported to have opened on January 19, 1840, featuring among its offerings dramas, opera-comiques, and vaudevilles (Kmen 235–36). Southern has also noted a few passing references to thespian groups in Philadelphia (Southern 121). Presumably, these groups offered a variety of images to their audiences.

THE BLACKFACE MINSTREL

In the 1840s the birth of blackface minstrelsy took place. Whites blackened their faces with burnt cork and sang and danced in a program imitating the supposed habits of southern blacks. Performers such as Thomas "Daddy" Rice, George Washington Dixon, George Nichols, and Bob Farrell had made blackface characters popular in the 1820s and 1830s, but not until Dan Emmett and his Virginia Minstrels took the stage in 1843 did blackface characters become a virtually indispensable part of extended variety shows, called minstrel shows.[2]

The minstrel show was a theatrical entertainment in which "images of Negroes [were] shaped by white expectations and desires and not by Black realities," says Robert Toll in the most thoroughly documented of recent books on the subject. Minstrelsy by all accounts was the most widely viewed form of theater in America from the 1850s to the 1880s. These two facts help to explain why the images of minstrelsy have so overwhelmed the discussion of Black stage entertainment in general. As "the first American popular entertainment form to become a national institution," minstrelsy has shaped all subsequent forms—vaudeville, burlesque, musical comedy, legitimate theater, radio, and television (Toll vi).

At least ten major minstrel show companies were playing in New York City by the mid–1850s, and groups soon sprang up in other cities. Although Black actors themselves were active by the 1860s as minstrel show performers—sometimes they appeared in "genuine" blackface, without makeup—the preponderance of minstrel images were created by whites, sometimes contradicted, sometimes confirmed by Black actors. Although the original spoof of the 1840s involved mostly exaggerated mimickry of dancing and playing and may actually have been rooted in the Black folk experience, by the 1870s even this link all but disappeared in performances by white blackface minstrels.

Minstrel men (the profession was always predominately male) were experts in caricature. Along with cork-darkened faces, lips were painted extra large and white; players wore rags or ludicrously fancy clothes and told jokes loudly in a dialect not necessarily resembling Black speech. Although minstrelsy began to turn away from overt Black caricature in the 1870s and 1880s, the link between inferiority, foolishness, and a black face was retained. Most audible and visible elements of the minstrel actor dictated that Blacks be viewed as farcical, laughable types. By the 1890s even the songs they sang (the so-called coon songs) supported this utterly demeaning characterization (Toll 160–63; Dennison). "Coon" songs are further discussed in chapter 4.

The most galling aspects of minstrelsy (to modern viewers) were mitigated somewhat by the all-Black minstrel troupes of the late nineteenth century. In these shows, the Old South was romanticized; memories were sweetened. References to freedom, Emancipation, and the comforts of religion were more common in Black than in white minstrel acts. Black minstrels were tremendously popular with the mass of Black common folk, supporting Toll's suggestion that Black minstrels were "freed" by the theatrical conventions and so enabled to comment wryly and truthfully on the attitudes and mores of the time (Toll 195–233). We can almost certainly assume that the language and poses of genuinely Black minstrels were developed and shown in ways that may have been lost completely on white audiences. Upper- and middle-class Blacks disdained the minstrels, but even the erudite James Monroe Trotter found their music worthy of praise in his collective biography *Music and Some Highly Musical People* (Trotter 274–82). The most active Black troupes included those headed by Lew Johnson; Charles Callender; Sprague and Blodgett; J. H. Haverly; Richard and Pringle; Billy Kersands; McCabe, Young, and the Hun Brothers; and W. S. Cleveland. Sometimes white and Black minstrel troupes were run by the same manager, but the shows were not integrated.

Among the earliest Blacks to cross the color line on the antebellum stage was the legendary dancer William Henry Lane, who did not work in blackface but toured in 1845 and later with three white showmen calling themselves the Ethiopian Minstrels. His dancing skills were widely hailed. (Charles Dickens reported on the dazzling skills and unique act of a dancer who may have been Lane in his *American Notes* [1842].) Lane was called Master Juba, possibly after a type of African dance step called a *giuba* (Stearns and Stearns 27–29).

THE IMPACT OF *UNCLE TOM'S CABIN*

Harriet Beecher Stowe's highly influential novel *Uncle Tom's Cabin* has long been recognized as a landmark in American literature and politics. It was most widely disseminated in dramatic form, with musical interludes, almost immediately after the publication of the book in 1852. The importance and the centrality of music to *Uncle Tom's Cabin* productions is easily verified from available prompt books and programs.[3] Because the drama addressed the slavery issue squarely and vehemently, the images of Blacks within the play obviously had a wide impact. The term "Uncle Tom" is still with us, indicating the current negative value placed on the title character, but, in fact, the variety of Black characters in the novel and in some play versions, as well as the unequivocal abolitionist stance of the author, meant that it was considered essentially a pro-Black play in the nineteenth century.

Although it is pervaded by a melodramatic tone typical of the time, *Uncle Tom's Cabin* recognized that Blacks were human beings and embodied human emotions, a fact that worked powerfully on its audiences. As late as 1904, leading Black composer/comedian Bob Cole could write: "More good has been wrought to the American people by the advent of [*Uncle Tom's Cabin*] on the literary and dramatic horizon than volumes could record" (Cole 301–307). A more recent critique by James Baldwin, which appeared in *Partisan Review* (1949, 578–85), "Uncle Tom's Cabin: Everyone's Protest Novel," marked the beginning of a process which has consigned Uncle Tom to the list of outcast images in American life. From a musical standpoint, however, *Uncle Tom's Cabin* was important in a way similar to minstrelsy in becoming a vehicle for the presentation of Black singing, dancing, and acting talent. Individual Black peformers, such as virtuoso banjoist Horace Weston, became the foci around which whole productions were planned. Professional singers, imitating the approach of the Fisk University student group known as the Jubilee Singers, began to be included in increasingly larger numbers in *Uncle Tom's Cabin* productions. Some ambitious producers of the 1890s featured multiple groups of instrumentalists, singers, and dancers together with military drill demonstrations, animal acts, show wagons, and floats, in Barnum-like extravaganzas. Rather than constituting a countervailing force to the imagery of minstrelsy, ironically, *Uncle Tom's Cabin* shows and minstrel shows moved to occupy common territory and expressed similar ideas and images. The original antislavery message of Stowe had been overwhelmed by circus trappings by the twentieth century (Birdoff; Riis, "Music in Nineteenth-century Productions of *Uncle Tom's Cabin*," 268–86). The strongest and most consistent images that arose from *Uncle Tom's Cabin* were those associated with emotions or emotion-filled activity—music, dance, and religion. Blacks were "natural" creatures of God; however, by implication, higher, rational activities and abilities were still denied them.

Blacks themselves began to act the roles in the play in the 1870s. A "genuine" black Topsy was advertised in San Francisco in 1877, and Sam Lucas (1840–1916), a minstrel star, is generally credited as the first Black man to take the title role in 1878. After these pioneering efforts, several companies moved to include Black actors or even to stage all-black productions (Riis, "Music in Nineteenth-century Productions of *Uncle Tom's Cabin*," 274–77.)

THE LITERATURE OF MINSTRELSY

The bibliography of minstrelsy is large (see Southern 88–96, 228–40, especially as they relate to music). Tom Fletcher's *100 Years of the Negro in Show Business* (1954) provides one of the rare first-person accounts of a Black showman who lived through the latter part of the minstrel age of the late nineteenth century, and so forms a link to the modern era. Fletcher's concern is to record the large amount of activity by Black entertainers in his day. He makes no effort to evaluate images. His interests are those of a professional showman trying to make a living, not of a sociologist trying to prove a point about Black oppression. But much social history related to the opportunities that were open or closed to Blacks can be read between the lines. *Old Slack's Reminiscence and Pocket History of the Colored Profession from 1865 to 1891*, by Ike Simond (1974), "banjo comique," is less well known and less comprehensive than Fletcher's *100 Years*. The attraction of Simond's account is his listing of dozens of names not even mentioned by Fletcher, a circumstance that hints at an even greater amount of Black theatrical activity in the nineteenth century than has been imagined by historians and which is hitherto unexplored.

BLACK TOURING COMPANIES AND PERFORMERS

Nineteenth-century entertainments that contradicted the dominant images of minstrelsy did exist, but their reticence and propriety was such that they remain a largely unknown chapter of Black theater history. On April 1, 1876, the *New York Clipper* announced that

The Hyers' Sisters Troupe, colored vocalists, have taken a new departure, having appeared on March 20 . . . in a new musical drama, written expressly for them by Joseph Bradford, called 'Out of the Wilderness.' . . . The new drama is said to have achieved success (7).

Here was an entertainment mounted by acclaimed singers, related to the Black experience yet apparently not based on minstrelsy, at least not containing the surface features of it. By July of that year, the Hyers were offering a three-act drama filled with "jubilee songs, duets and quartets," called "Out of Bondage," also by Bradford. Their week at the Boston Theater in August 1877 was deemed a "complete success" by the *Folio*, which noted that "the Hyers Sisters have excellent and well-cultivated voices, which were never heard to better advantage than during this week" (Vol. 19, Dec. 1880, p. 452). Sam Lucas and the concert singers John Lucas (1832–1910) and Wallace King (1840–1903) also appeared with the touring company.

Black concert companies, which combined concert singers, instrumentalists, and comedians, were also actively touring in the late 1800s. The Redpath Lyceum Bureau sponsored both the Hyers Sisters and a group calling itself the Ideal Colored Musical Combination in the 1880s. Other short-lived shows are reported in the pages of *Billboard*, the *New York Dramatic Mirror*, and the Indianapolis *Freeman* in the 1890s.[4]

Sam T. Jack's Creole Burlesque Show set out on the road in the autumn of 1890. Its chief attraction was beautiful Black show girls presented in a tropical scene, wearing "fine and costly" costumes, swinging in hammocks, and then dancing and singing along in routines with other individual male and female stars. The Creole's burlesque play was entitled "The Beauty of the Nile, or

Doomed by Fire.'' It was liberally praised by the *Freeman* and lauded as ''novel and excellent'' by the *Clipper*.[5] The Creoles toured all over the country in their own railroad car from 1891 to 1896, presenting a variety of acts and many newly written songs by Black composers.

Among other touring companies of the nineties were Whalen and Martell's *South Before the War*; *Suwanee River*, under the management of Davis and Keogh; *Darkest America*, under Al G. Fields; and *Black America*, sponsored by Nate Salsbury, whose previous ventures had included Buffalo Bill Cody's Wild West Show. The touring shows showcased increasingly larger aggregations of Black talent, often in stereotyped plots which idealized life in the Old South but which vividly confirmed the strength of Black ensemble performance capabilities—in singing, playing instruments, and dancing.[6]

A sizable influx of Black performers into the New York City area in the late 1890s helped to spark the creation of the first full-fledged Black musical comedies. Beginning with *A Trip to Coontown* (1898), created by Bob Cole, Black performers eventually wrote and staged some thirty shows in the period from 1898 to 1915, mostly with all-Black casts. The individuals who were most instrumental in bringing about this remarkable flowering included the composing team of Bob Cole and J. Rosamond Johnson (although Cole worked on *A Trip to Coontown* with an earlier partner also named Johnson), the multitalented Ernest Hogan, the comedy team of Bert Williams and George Walker, Walker's wife (the dancer Aida Overton), and composer/conductor Will Marion Cook. Spinning off the minstrel tradition in many instances, these shapers of the new shows included modern songs and adopted the revue format (a succession of topical songs and skits using the same actors in different roles). The early shows of Williams and Walker, *The Policy Players* (1899) and *The Sons of Ham* (1900), were extended versions of the team's comedy and cakewalk routines of the middle 1890s. The standout show of 1903, and one of the first American shows to become a big European success, was Williams and Walker's *In Dahomey*. It succeeded in building its songs, dances, and jokes around a plot which involved a scheme by American Blacks to colonize Africa. Even this remarkable show (which enjoyed a royal command performance in London) revealed its minstrel ancestry in the inclusion of characters, labeled ''Tambo'' and ''Bones,'' who according to the surviving libretto carry on a dialogue in the minstrel manner. But the significance of these shows should not be slighted. The mere presence of an all-Black cast acting in an autonomous and original production was a tonic to Black show business and a portent of things to come. For two decades the Williams and Walker shows were held up as critical models. Their singer/comedians dealt with current issues in songs about education (''Vassar Girl''), roots and self-image (''Miss Hannah from Savannah,'' ''Where My Forefathers Died''), and Black social caste (''Leader of the Colored Aristocracy''). Other contemporary productions included the vehicles created by Ernest Hogan, ''the unbleached American,'' *Rufus Rastus* (1906) and *The Oyster Man* (1907). Though not as lavish as the Williams and Walker shows, Hogan's efforts were filled with catchy, topical songs and subtle humor. Meanwhile, Bob Cole and J. Rosamond Johnson were developing Black operettas, *The Shoo-Fly Regiment* (1907) and *The Red Moon* (1909). The classification "operetta" was suggested by critics at the time who felt that such entertainments were perhaps too sophisticated, too musically high-brow, in a word, too white, to be attempted by an all-Black company.[7] With white critics having decided that the Black arena was to be minstrelsy and its spinoffs, it is no wonder that Black entertainers looking to broaden their scope were frustrated and thwarted at every turn.

An attempt to buck the trend to operetta without returning to minstrel conventions first occurred prominently in the shows of the Darktown Follies of 1915. J. Leubrie Hill organized a show that celebrated singing—Black choral singing had often been cited as striking and original—and especially dancing, not sets, costumes, or tableaux. By this time, Black shows were finding it impossible to get booking on Broadway as Williams and Walker and Cole and Johnson had, and so Hill and his company generally played in Harlem's Lafayette Theater when it came to New York. It attracted huge crowds, white as well as Black.

Despite the vitality that the Follies exuded and the flashy kinds of vernacular dance that it displayed, even this company was chided by white writers for adopting stage conventions from downtown, as if Black shows should always be free of the eclecticism that pervaded the rest of the musical comedy world. The "incontestably mulatto" flavor of Afro-American culture which Albert Murray discusses in *The Omni-Americans* (Murray 22) was still being contested when Carl Van Vechten objected to "the actors on the stage singing conventional hymns to the moon, with accompanying action which Ned Wayburn [a well-known Broadway choreographer] might have devised. . . . '' (Kellner 24).

Although the Darktown Follies shows drew packed houses in Harlem in successive seasons, the effervescent dancing style of the shows was not successfully imitated by whites, or, for that matter, by other Black companies. Black dancers made a better living on vaudeville circuits. Not until May 1921 at the opening of *Shuffle Along* did New York see a show to rival the spirit of Hill's Follies.[8]

What was it about the shows in the period from 1898 to 1915 that was so special? After all, dozens of musicals dating back to the middle of the nineteenth century had included elements derived from the minstrel show, the farce comedy, the extravaganza, and the pantomime. Almost always it seems that the determining factor in critical reviews was the originality of the music, and that combined with a chorus which both sang and danced. Beyond the encouragement the shows gave to Black audiences through the presentation of plots which commented humorously on Black life, the turn-of-the-century musicals demonstrated a competency in musical *composition* (not only improvisation) and revealed to whites a facet of Black life which might best be termed spontaneity of style—epitomized in the gritty, determined, and unrelentingly exuberant activity in ensembles and finales.

THE LITERATURE OF EARLY BLACK MUSICALS

Among the best sources on the Black musicals of the turn-of-the-century stage are James Weldon Johnson's books *Black Manhattan* (1930) and *Along This Way* (1933). The first is a cultural history of Harlem in emergence; the second is an autobiography which provides a detailed account of his career as a songwriter in collaboration with his brother J. Rosamond and Bob Cole. This work also makes mention of several contemporaries, such as Will Marion Cook and Bert Williams. A more recent history of the turn of the century in Harlem, including some discussion of music, is found in Jervis Anderson's *This Was Harlem: A Cultural Portrait, 1900–1950* (1981). *Jazz Dance* (1968), by Marshall and Jean Stearns, is a remarkable narrative summary of observations and interviews with hundreds of Black performers with careers dating from the turn of the century through the 1960s. Its value far exceeds that of a mere dance history, owing to its inclusion of extensive details about all aspects of the musical theater of concern to Black show people. Henry Sampson's *Blacks in Blackface* (1980) is essentially a collection of lists, titles, plot summaries, and excerpts from reviews. It illustrates the remarkably large amount of musical theater activity by Blacks in the 1910s, 1920s, and 1930s, although its usefulness is weakened by careless dating and inadequate references. The only books devoted to an individual performer in the shows of the period are two on the life of Bert Williams, Mabel Rowland's collection of anecdotes and song lyrics interspersed with short biographical chapters, entitled *Bert Williams: Son of Laughter* (1923), and Ann Charters' *Nobody: The Story of Bert Williams* (1970). The former is an informal but touching tribute; Rowland was Williams' publicity agent. The latter attempts to place Williams in the stage environment of the era in conjunction with his partner, George Walker. Neither book contains detailed citations, but both are useful in assessing the impact that Williams had on Black musical theater.

THE BLACK MUSICAL STAGE, 1920–1940

Black notoriety on the musical theater stage came before a comparable recognition in the legitimate dramatic arena (the first drama by a Black playwright to appear on Broadway was Willis Richardson's *The Chip Woman's Fortune* in 1923). In musicals, most Blacks, whether in blackface makeup or not, were singers, dancers, and comedians. These roles were open to them thanks to the dominant images of minstrelsy and the long involvement of Black actors with that old genre. While the loose structure of the turn-of-the-century musical comedy did not preclude the treatment of serious subjects, it did require that the action conclude happily and that everyone have a smile on his or her face. Few scenes with serious emotional expressions were tolerated. That the ugliest horrors of Jim Crow legislation coupled with Klan-inspired violence should have grown up simultaneously with the gradual replacement of minstrelsy by all-Black musical comedies might superficially suggest contradictory historical tendencies at work. In reality, the move away from minstrelsy, a somewhat old-fashioned entertainment in the large United States urban centers by the 1890s in any case, in the direction of musical comedy did not alter the fixed roles expected of Black actors.

The early 1920s saw a new emphasis on straight plays in Harlem, although touring musical comedies and dance revues remained popular around the country. What might be called a second wave of all-Black-cast shows followed the rollicking and tuneful hit of 1921, *Shuffle Along*.[9] Although in many ways *Shuffle Along*, created by the combined efforts of Eubie Blake, Noble Sissle, Flournoy Miller, and Aubrey Lyles, was merely a well-produced and outstandingly executed example of a type of show familiar to Black theatergoers of the previous twenty years, it possessed a special attractiveness. Featuring an extraordinary array of young faces who later became stars (including Josephine Baker, Caterina Yarboro, Hall Johnson, and William Grant Still), it bubbled to success with good songs ("I'm Just Wild About Harry," "Love Will Find a Way," "In Honeysuckle Time," "Dixie Moon"), innocuous comedy, and infectious dancing. It chalked up a record of over 500 performances on Broadway and toured nationwide for over two years. The vivacity and charm of the show's star Florence Mills, not to mention the potential box-office receipts, spurred a host of imitators: *Put and Take* (1921), *Strut Miss Lizzie* (1922), *Go-Go* (1923), *Runnin' Wild* (1923), *Dinah* (1924), *Dixie to Broadway* (1924), *Lucky Sambo* (1925), *My Magnolia* (1926), and *Rang Tang* (1927). Although all were not carbon copies of *Shuffle Along* and many were invigorated with the spirit of "syncopated music," as rag and jazz songs were then politely called, the links to the past were also clear. African and jungle motifs were omnipresent, the Old South nostalgia was rampant, and blackface makeup was still surprisingly common. The prologue for *Dixie to Broadway*, for example, is nobly entitled "The Evolution of the Colored Race," an uplift theme typical of the twenties, but this is immediately followed by scenes which suggest old formulas, "Put Your Old Bandanna On" and "Dixie Dreams." Characters named Mammy and Mandy are revived in *Liza* (1922), and the Plantation Revue called its grand finale "Minstrels on Parade" (Sampson 278).

New images of women begin to crop up in the musicals of the 1920s, and scenes appear which place Blacks in the new urban environments of the North. The Harlem street scene became a cliché as did the plot about the migration of a poor southern girl to an evil northern city. The participation of women in minstrelsy had been limited, but now roles were expanded and modernized. The Hyers Sisters had tearfully sung songs of the Old South, like "Good-Bye Old Cabin Home." Modern songstresses Ma Rainey and Bessie Smith sang about their troubles and feelings in the blues, unvarnished comments about love, pain, loss, and joy. The women of the twenties embodied glamour and sexuality in shocking new ways. Comparatively discreet chorus girls, like those of the 1890s Creole Shows, were supplanted by dynamic stars like Josephine Baker, the American sensation in the French Revue Negre. Baker's star rose abroad, but it created ripples at home. The image of the primitive, sensual but tough jungle woman—the exotic—was paraded in the floor shows of the Cotton Club and on the dance floor of the Savoy Ballroom, where whites came to ogle the latest Black dance steps.

Although the large shows did not always reflect the new, looser attitudes of the clubs and vaudeville, as the twenties ended, more variety could be found among the plots than had earlier been the case. *Great Day* (1929) contained a lovers' triangle set in the 1913 New Orleans Mardi Gras; *Brown Buddies* (1930) paired soldiers and YMCA entertainers and featured a romance between Adelaide Hall and Bill Robinson. *Sugar Hill* (1931) claimed to be a "sketch of life in Harlem's aristocratic section." *Fast and Furious* (1931) seemed to approach the eclectic heights of the 1890s by including a Georgia street scene, a Shakespearian spoof (on *Macbeth*), a football game, several dance numbers including "Rhumbatism," a parody of another show called "The Band Wagon," and a drag show called "Pansies." It lasted a week in New York (Sampson 74, 200).

These shows often took the road and joined dozens of other more modest musical comedies known as tab shows, short for tabloid musical comedy.[10] The tabs carried fewer than two dozen people and presented shows that worked from a written script, although they also featured many specialty acts—stand-up comedians, piano players, and always a chorus line of leggy young women. The tab show was a mainstay of the Black theater circuits in the 1920s and 1930s, particularly the Theater Owners' Booking Association (T.O.B.A.)

THE THEATER OWNERS' BOOKING ASSOCIATION

The T.O.B.A. was founded as a joint Black-white effort in 1920 by S. H. Dudley, a star from the Black shows of the 1910 decade, and white theater owner Milton Starr of Chattanooga, who were responding to the growing number of theaters catering to Blacks and the consequent booking problems that resulted. By 1921 approximately 300 theaters were serving Blacks nationwide; Ninety-four of these were Black owned and managed.[11] Although plagued with complaints from disgruntled theater owners, underpaid entertainers, and competing circuits in several regions of the country, by the autumn of 1921, the T.O.B.A. could claim in the pages of *Billboard* that it "controls the attractions playing 80 of 107 theaters devoted to colored road shows and vaudevilles. More than 50 companies travel over the circuit and 179 vaudeville acts find almost continuous work with the association."[12] By 1925 the Colored Actors' Union included over 500 names as dues payers.

The ties between touring vaudeville acts, tab shows, and larger, less mobile musical comedies were strong. Without the apprenticeship opportunities provided by vaudeville there would have been no Black musical theater in the 1920s and 1930s. On the circuit, one learned the art of improvising in the dance and comedy traditions of earlier Black shows, as well as the art of survival. Days were long, travel difficult, audiences demanding, and pay low. The hoped-for reward was a spot on a "big time" bill, a job on the Keith-Albee or Orpheum circuit, which would bring with it more recognition, higher salaries, and better working conditions.

The variety of acts offered on the T.O.B.A. and other Black circuits was extensive. Among vocalists not only blues singers, such as Ma Rainey, Bessie Smith, Mamie Smith, or Edmonia Henderson, appeared regularly, but yodeler Charles Anderson and the "Oklahoma Prima Donna," Bernice Ellis, were popular. "Jubilee," i.e., spirituals singers, remained as attractive as they had been in the 1880s. Bronco Billy Verne did a weight-lifting, balancing, and lariat-throwing demonstration. Harrison Blackburn described himself as "the one-man circus."[13] Dancing acts abounded and were often original, consisting of innumerable combinations of tap, acrobatic, and comic routines.

Probably most of the performers on the T.O.B.A. circuit were southerners. Northern-born dancer Dewey Weinglass told Marshall and Jean Stearns that when he started his own act in the 1920s "going on T.O.B.A. never entered my head" (Stearns and Stearns 83). Doing travelling shows in the South was something to be feared by a non-southerner who associated the region with Jim Crow and lynching. When Ethel Waters announced a southern tour in 1922, it was considered a bold and courageous act. She was forced to replace some band members who refused to go.[14]

The full impact of the T.O.B.A. on the musical comedy stage has yet to be calculated, but even a brief glance at the long list of participants suggests that there was much more going on than minstrel shows and plantation medlies. It is hardly credible that Black musical comedies would not have felt the impact of this newly trained generation of performers. Granted that the image of the vaudeville entertainer was less than exalted, but then neither the image nor the low social standing of actors could have served as a strong deterrent to talented individuals prejudged to be inferior within the dominant culture. With all of its drawbacks, the musical stage continued to provide opportunities for employment and an outlet for creative imaginations as it had in the nineteenth century. The "Black image" was becoming more diversified.

The Depression and the advent of sound films weakened the institution of vaudeville and eventually saw the demise of the T.O.B.A. Films also reintroduced stereotypical portrayals of Blacks which Black theater critics of twenty years before had worked to abolish in musicals.[15] The Black cast musicals of the late 1930s and after were written mostly by whites, an indication that the new Black images developed in the 1920s, while not as blatantly repulsive or unsavory as the minstrel stereotypes, still consisted of an array of types relatively easy to reproduce and market if one knew the formulas (Sampson 22, Southern 540). In addition to the continuation of the familiar revue in shows such as Lew Leslie's *Blackbirds*, a pair of more distinctive and controversial items appeared in the 1930s: Hall Johnson's *Run Little Chillun* (1933), a play filled with rousing renditions of spirituals as well as Bahamian folk songs, and George Gershwin's opera *Porgy and Bess* (1935). Neither offered new images, but both succeeded as ambitious efforts to showcase Black talent and were recognized as artistic achievements. Optimists predicted better times ahead for the Black entertainer.

THE FEDERAL THEATRE

The good times were slow in coming. In order to counteract the sustained hardship of the Depression, in 1935, the Federal Theatre was created as part of the Works Progress Administration (WPA), and some of the theatre's regional units included musicals. In Chicago *Did Adam Sin?* (1936), created from elements of Black folklore, and *Swing Mikado* (1939), a jazz version of the Gilbert and Sullivan classic, provided some work for struggling Black singer-actors. Broadway exploited the public's interest in Black versions of familiar pieces by staging the *Hot Mikado* (1939), but this D'Oyly-Carte-twice-removed show was counted only moderately successful, despite the sparkling gold-suited presence of Bill Robinson as star. Cecil Mack and Eubie Blake's *Swing It* (1937) had also appeared under WPA auspices as had the Seattle unit's tribute to the folk hero John Henry, *The Natural Man* (1937) and the Philadelphia production *Prelude to Swing* (1937), a panoramic potpourri of Black music history (Southern 436, Flanagan 305).

BLACK WRITERS, ACTORS, AND MUSICIANS OF LATER YEARS

Shows of the 1940s were relatively few in number and received mixed critical reviews. *Cabin in the Sky* (1940) was an exceptional vehicle for Ethel Waters. *Carmen Jones* (1943), a production of Bizet's *Carmen* in an American setting with an all-Black cast, enjoyed a Broadway run of 503 performances. *Carib Song* (1945), featuring Katherine Dunham's dancers and a villainous Avon Long in a West Indian plot, lasted barely a month. *St. Louis Woman* (1946), although it combined the talents of writers Arna Bontemps and Countee Cullen with the musical skills of Harold Arlen and Johnny Mercer (whose songs includued "Come Rain, Come Shine," "Ridin' on the Moon," and "Any Place I Hang My Hat") with the young singer Pearl Bailey, also had a short run.

The production of the stage version (no music included) of Richard Wright's *Native Son* in 1941, with its direct presentation of interracial sexual themes and tensions, showed how far audiences had come in their willingness to accept more racially charged material and more modern images. (In the eyes of some, the depiction of Bigger Thomas as primitive, violent, and dangerous was only a new version of an old idea with racist roots.) The long-running fight of the National Association for the Advancement of Colored People on behalf of actors began to show results when an agreement was reached with movie studio producers in 1942 on the abolition of old stereotyped roles and the inclusion of more realistic Black characters in movie scripts (Cripps 3–7, Archer 25–67). The presence of a larger number of Black performers in mainly white musical shows of the late 1940s was less significant musically than it was a signal development that social change was in the wind. It hinted that Black entertainers might not need to conform much longer to a short list of types in order to succeed in show business; Juanita Hall's appearance in *South Pacific* (1949) and Todd Duncan's in *Lost in the Stars* (1949) were especially noticeable, in the former instance because of the prominence of the show and in the latter because of the fame of the star.

Biracial musical entertainments had existed since the "double mammoth" minstrel shows had offered one white and one Black cast (though the different groups seldom worked on the stage at the same time). Will Marion Cook's *The Southerners* (1904), which featured an integrated chorus, was considered quite controversial during its short New York run.[16] But none of the forerunners of the integrated Broadway show tampered with the basic Black character types: mammies, servants, simpletons, and children who sang, danced, and uttered few lines. However, several shows of the 1950s, *Mr. Wonderful* (1956) led by Sammy Davis, Jr., *Shinbone Alley* (1957) with Eartha Kitt, and *Jamaica* (1957) featuring Lena Horne, helped to make integrated shows with individualized Black stars not merely acceptable but fashionable.

THE REVOLUTIONARY THEMES

By the 1960s more revolutionary themes began to appear regularly in straight plays.[17] While opportunities were increasing for actors and actresses, serious themes related to the Black struggle, such as alienation and anger, Black nationalism, and the real substance of Black life, seemed less comfortable to a musical theater setting, especially a musical comedy format. Also in the 1960s television displaced live theater (and radio) as the principal American mass entertainment, weakening still further the interest of investors in new Broadway shows. The recession of the early 1970s heightened this conservatism. Under these conditions, it is hardly surprising that the most successful musical theater efforts of the 1960s and 1970s were revivals and revues, not new book shows or experimental productions. In the wake of the civil rights movement, Black folk and religious music was rediscovered and brought to the stage in productions such as *Tambourines to Glory* (1963), adapted from Langston Hughes' novel. *Your Arm's Too Short to Box with God* (1976), the outstanding example in this group of shows, used both spirituals and gospel music. The gospel song-play *Black Nativity* (1962) achieved its greatest success on tour in Europe and the Far East, and it was provided a sequel in *Trumpets of the Lord* (1963) (Patterson 81–84, Archer 275).

The devoutly (and nonviolently) triumphant man of God as a stage character had its most famous antecedent in Uncle Tom. But because the Black consciousness movement grew directly out of the inspirational leadership provided by the men of the Black church—first and foremost Martin Luther King, Jr.—a new vigor was imparted to Black religious sentiment suggesting the possibility of its modern use on stage. The Black images that arose from the Black church and that were resuscitated by Black actors and singers through the use of genuine Black musical styles rang truer than any *Uncle Tom's Cabin* ever could have done in the twentieth century.

CONTEMPORARY BLACK THEATER GROUPS

An attempt to make a stronger Black nationalist statement came in the formation of the National Black Theatre (N.B.T.) in Harlem in 1968. The N.B.T. stressed the need for community involvement and—to avoid an elitist star system—the importance of developing players who participated in all aspects of the theater, the designing and building as well as the acting, singing, and dancing. Its musical productions featured African and West Indian rituals and dances in the spirit reminiscent of the historical musicals of the 1910 decade, all but forgotten pieces such as *Children of the Sun* (1919) and *African Prince* (1920). The N.B.T. staked its future on community support and refused to compromise its ideology by accepting outside funds. It folded in 1972. The less ideologically bound Negro Ensemble Theatre (NET) was founded in 1967, an outgrowth of experiments in the Group Theatre Workshop. The NET has become a major positive force in Black theater with productions such as Douglas Turner Ward's *Day of Absence* (1966) and Joseph Walker's *The River Niger* (1972), but its emphasis has not been placed on musical theater (Southern 541–42).

BLACKS ON THE MUSICAL STAGE—THE SEVENTIES AND EIGHTIES

The early 1970s saw more Black productions on Broadway than at any time since the 1920s and with a far wider variety of fantastic and realistic images than had previously appeared. *Don't Bother Me, I Can't Cope* (1972), *Ain't Supposed to Die a Natural Death* (1971), *The Wiz* (1975), *Me and Bessie* (1975), and *Bubbling Brown Sugar* (1976) spanned the range from the novel to the nostalgic in their musical contents (although stressing the latter), and *Ain't Misbehavin'* won the Tony Award of 1978 for best musical of the year. Many of the Black shows from the seventies and eighties proved successful at the box office as well, including *Purlie* (1970), *Raisin* (1973), *Timbuktu* (1978), and *Dream Girls* (1982).

THE MUSIC, HISTORY AND LITERATURE

The escape from the necessity of creating absolutely stereotyped and artificial characterizations has been accompanied ironically by the use of much music from earlier periods—mostly songs that were certified hits. This reliance on old music is only partially attributable to caution on the part of producers. Like the vaudeville stars of the 1920s who found better pay in working off Broadway, the potential Black composers for new musicals find more financial incentive in Hollywood. Many Black composers who once might have written for live touring shows now have turned to the movies. Curtis Mayfield, Isaac Hayes, Donny Hathaway, and Quincy Jones have all gained recognition in providing music for commercials, motion pictures, and music videos.

No definitive history of Black musical theater has yet appeared. Much of a preliminary nature still needs to be done. Studies could be made of Black musicals in the 1920s and 1930s and the impact of the T.O.B.A., and a thorough sorting of theatrically related material from the dozens of entertainer biographies and autobiographies included in Russell Brignano's 1984 listing (*Black Americans in Autobiography*) might yield new insights. An assessment of the recorded music from twentieth-century Black musicals is also in order. (Ann Charters' biography of Bert Williams, for example, contains a list of the comedian's recorded songs, some of which might be usefully transcribed and compared with the sheet music of those songs.)

Langston Hughes and Milton Meltzer's *Black Magic: A Pictorial History of the Negro in American Entertainment* (1969), with over 300 pages of illustrations, conveys the exuberant history of Blacks on stage, ranging from opera to jazz to straight theater to films. Though filled with rare material, it is badly in need of updating, expansion, and revision. *Anthology of the American Negro in the Theatre: A Critical Approach* (1968), edited by Lindsay Patterson, is a compilation of essays, many of which pertain to musical theater, including Will Marion Cook's first-person account of the creation of his show *Clorindy* in 1898 and Hall Johnson's insightful comments on *Porgy and Bess* in "Porgy and Bess— A Folk Opera?" Alain Locke's *The Negro and His Music* (1936) places the Black show composer within the broad spectrum of Black musicians of all types, and his *The New Negro* (1925) is a fascinating anthology of writings by and about poets, musicians, and other Black artists of the Harlem Renaissance. But, obviously, neither of Locke's books presents an up-to-date account. Gerald Bordman, in his *American Musical Theatre: A Chronicle* (1978), has written a 749-page study of remarkable thoroughness and trenchant insight, containing much valuable information about the Black contribution to the American musical. His is the first comprehensive history of the American stage to do so without condescension or significant omissions. His new *Oxford Companion to American Theatre* (1984) is similarly conscientious in its inclusion of major Black stage figures. Among the most thoughtful assessments to appear recently is a brief essay by Martin Williams in *Jazz Heritage* (1985) entitled "Cautions and Congratulations: An Outsider's Comments on the Black Contribution to American Musical Theater." Williams' provocative comparisons and piquant queries constitute fresh perspectives on the Black contribution to American musicals.

THE EVOLVING IMAGE

Black images are still evolving in American musical theater. As one-dimensional Black characters and white blackfaced actors become odd and isolated

3. Minstrel sketches. Courtesy of Special Collections, the Ernest R. Alexander Collection, Fisk University Library.

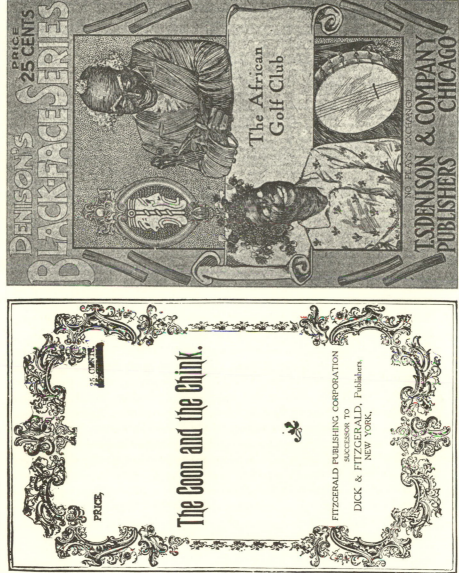

historical objects for us, minstrelsy's usefulness as a vehicle of parody and fresh topical comment, rather than a means of perpetuating a stereotype, may be revived. The "comic fool" tradition is an ancient one and need not be made a partner with ethnic slurs. All sorts of singing, dancing, and "shuffling along" have been interpreted by someone as cooperating in a racist system; the charge of playing the Uncle Tom is still hurled with regularity at Black entertainers. America's consciousness of the Black images on its musical stage will change as our appreciation of the stage itself changes and as we inevitably put time between ourselves and the great obsessions of minstrelsy. All the while, individual Black artists will continue to shatter the stereotypes and transcend the clichés that inevitably arise in a field where imitation must of necessity be both embraced and shunned, where images both reflect and change reality.

Actors speak the past and the present—and even at times suggest the future. Magically, paradoxically these things are done all at the same moment. Images on the stage, like photographic images, may be fixed for a long period or fade when exposed to strong light. But even those that are seemingly permanent will be reinterpreted in each successive generation.

NOTES

1. Succinct descriptions of early American Black theater can be found in Eileen Southern, *The Music of Black Americans*, 2d ed. (New York: Norton, 1983) and Gerald Bordman, *American Musical Theatre: A Chronicle* (New York: Oxford University Press, 1978). The early volumes of George Odell's *Annals of the New York Stage*, 15 vols. (New York: Columbia University Press, 1927–1949) contain several references to the African Grove. Secret traditions of musical play and satire dating to the early eighteenth century known to slaves yet hidden from white masters, as tantalizingly reported by Hennig Cohen (183–84), remain as fragments of an unrecorded history.

2. The bibliography of minstrelsy is huge. Three of the more useful studies are Hans Nathan, *Dan Emmett and the Rise of Early Negro Minstrelsy* (Norman: University of Oklahoma Press, 1962), although it deals mostly with blackface, not genuine Black minstrels; Gary D. Engle, ed., *This Grotesque Essence: Plays from the American Minstrel Stage* (Baton Rouge: Louisiana State University Press, 1978), whose commentary is helpful in understanding the consistent themes of the minstrel repertory; and Robert Toll, *Blacking Up: The Minstrel Show in Nineteenth-century America* (New York: Oxford University Press, 1974).

3. Many of the prompt books and programs for the dramatic form of this work, with musical interludes, can be found in the Harvard Theatre Collection, Houghton Library, Harvard University.

4. *Folio* 19 (December, 1880): 453. Some other especially helpful periodicals are the Baltimore *Afro-American*, 1892– (from 1901 to 1916 titled the *Afro-American Ledger*); *Crisis*, 1910–1940; and Chicago *Defender*, 1905–. Among all of these the *Freeman*, 1884–1924 is the most consistently rich and least dispensable.

5. *Freeman*, September 5, 1891: 5; September 20, 1890: 6; *Clipper*, August 16, 1890: 358.

6. On these touring shows and the musicals that followed them see Thomas Riis,

"Black Musical Theatre in New York, 1890–1915," Ph.D. diss., University of Michigan, 1981.

7. A large clipping file is preserved in scrapbooks in the Billy Rose Theatre Collection, New York Public Library, Lincoln Center.

8. Marshall Stearns and Jean Stearns, *Jazz Dance*, pp. 125–39, give an extensive discussion of the Darktown Follies and *Shuffle Along*.

9. Robert Kimball and William Bolcom's book *Reminiscing with Sissle and Blake* (New York: Viking Press, 1973) colorfully documents in words and pictures the genesis and growth of *Shuffle Along*.

10. *Billboard*, December 10, 1921: 15.

11. Statistical calculations can be made from reports in *Billboard*, which regularly reported Black vaudeville news in the 1920s. See *Billboard*, August 6, 1921: 63–64 for one of the several lists that appeared.

12. *Billboard*, August 6, 1921: 61. Bart Kennett, *Colored Actors' Union Theatrical Guide* (Washington, D.C.: n.p., c. 1925).

13. *Billboard*, July 21, 1923: 51; May 31, 1924: 46.

14. *Billboard*, February 18, 1922: 43.

15. For a full discussion of the impact of films, see Thomas Cripps, *Slow Fade to Black: The Negro in American Film, 1900–1942* (New York: Oxford University Press, 1977).

16. A folder of undated reviews of *The Southerners* can be found in the Harvard Theatre Collection.

17. Lindsay Patterson, ed., *Anthology of the American Negro in the Theatre*, 2d ed. (New York: Publishers Company, 1968) devotes several articles to these developments. See also Loften Mitchell, *Black Drama* (New York: Hawthorne Publishers, 1967).

BIBLIOGRAPHY

Books

Aiken, George. *Uncle Tom's Cabin, or, Life Among the Lowly.* New York: Samuel French, [1853].

Anderson, Jervis. *This Was Harlem: A Cultural Portrait, 1910–1950.* New York: Farrar, Straus, Giroux, 1981.

Archer, Leonard C. *Black Images in the American Theatre.* Brooklyn, N.Y.: Pageant-Poseidon, Ltd., 1973.

Baldwin, James. "Uncle Tom's Cabin: Everyone's Protest Novel." *Partisan Review* 16 (1949): 578–85.

Birdoff, Harry. *The World's Greatest Hit: Uncle Tom's Cabin.* New York: Vanni, 1947.

Bordman, Gerald. *American Musical Theatre: A Chronicle.* New York: Oxford University Press, 1978.

————. *The Oxford Companion to American Theatre.* New York: Oxford University Press, 1984.

Brignano, Russell C. *Black Americans in Autobiography.* Rev. ed. Durham, N.C.: Duke University Press, 1984.

Brown, Sterling. *Negro Poetry and Drama.* 1937. Reprint. New York: Atheneum, 1969.

Bubna, Augusta da. "The Negro on the Stage." *The Theatre* 3 (1903): 96–98.

Butcher, Margaret Just. *The Negro in American Culture*. 2d ed. New York: Alfred A. Knopf, 1972.

Charters, Ann. *Nobody: The Story of Bert Williams*. London: Macmillan, 1970.

Cohen, Hennig. "A Negro 'Folk Game' in Colonial South Carolina." *Southern Folklore Quarterly* 16 (1952): 183–84.

Cole, Robert. "The Negro and the Stage." *Colored American Magazine* 4 (1904): 301–307.

Cripps, Thomas. *Slow Fade to Black: The Negro in American Film, 1900–1942*. New York: Oxford University Press, 1977.

Daughtry, Willia. "Sissieretta Jones: A Study of the Negro's Contribution to Nineteenth-century American Concert and Theatrical Life." Ph.D. diss., Syracuse University, 1968.

Dennison, Sam. *Scandalize My Name: Black Imagery in American Popular Music*. New York: Garland Publishing, 1982.

Dickens, Charles. *American Notes*. London: Chapman and Hall, 1842.

Dormon, James H., Jr. *Theater in the Ante Bellum South, 1815–1861*. Chapel Hill: University of North Carolina Press, 1967.

Engle, Gary D., ed. *This Grotesque Essence: Plays from the American Minstrel Stage*. Baton Rouge: Louisiana State University Press, 1978.

Flanagan, Hallie. *Arena*. New York: Duell, Sloan and Pearce, 1940.

Fletcher, Tom. *The Tom Fletcher Story: 100 Years of the Negro in Show Business*. 1954. Reprint. New York: Da Capo Press, 1984.

Foster, William. *1928 Edition . . . the Official Theatrical World of Colored Artists*. New York: n.p., 1928.

Gayle, Addison, Jr. *The Black Aesthetic*. Garden City, N.Y.: Doubleday, 1971.

Gilbert, Douglas. *American Vaudeville: Its Life and Times*. New York: Whittlesey House, 1940.

Gottfried, Martin. *Broadway Musicals*. New York: Abrams, 1979.

Grimsted, David. *Melodrama Unveiled: American Theatre and Culture, 1800–1850*. Chicago, Ill.: University of Chicago Press, 1968.

Hamm, Charles. *Yesterdays: Popular Song in America*. New York: Norton, 1979.

Handy, W. C. *Father of the Blues*. New York: Macmillan, 1941.

Hartnoll, Phyllis. *The Oxford Companion to the Theater*. 4th ed. Oxford: Oxford University Press, 1983.

Hatch, James V. *Black Image on the American Stage: A Bibliography of Plays and Musicals, 1770–1970*. New York: DBS Publications, 1970.

Hatch, James V., and OMANii Abdullah. *Black Playwrights, 1823–1977: An Annotated Bibliography of Plays*. New York: R. R. Bowker and Co., 1977.

Hodge, Francis. *Yankee Theatre: The Image of America on the Stage, 1825–1850*. Austin: University of Texas Press, 1964.

Hughes, Langston. "Black Influences in the American Theater: Part I." *The Black American Reference Book*. Ed. Mabel M. Smythe. Englewood Cliffs, N.J.: Prentice-Hall, 1976.

Hughes, Langston, and Milton Meltzer. *Black Magic: A Pictorial History of the Negro in American Entertainment*. Englewood Cliffs, N.J.: Prentice-Hall, 1967.

Isaacs, Edith. *The Negro in the American Theatre*. 1947. Reprint. College Park, Md.: McGrath Publishing Co., 1968.

Jefferson, Miles M. "The Negro on Broadway, 1947–48." *Phylon* 9.2 (1948): 99–107.

Johnson, Helen Armstead. "Black Influences in the American Theater: Part II." *The Black American Reference Book*. Ed. Mabel M. Smythe. Englewood Cliffs, N.J.: Prentice-Hall, 1976.

————. "Blacks in Vaudeville: Broadway and Beyond." American Popular Entertainment Papers and Proceedings of the Conference on the History of American Popular Entertainment. Ed. Myron Matlaw. Westport, Conn.: Greenwood Press, 1977.

Johnson, James Weldon. *Along This Way*. New York: Viking, 1922.

————. *Black Manhattan*. New York: Alfred A. Knopf, 1930.

Kahn, E. J., Jr. *The Merry Partners: The Age and Stage of Harrigan and Hart*. New York: Random House, 1955.

Kellner, B., ed. *"Keep A-Inchin' Along": Selected Writings of Carl Van Vechten about Black Arts and Letters*. Westport, Conn.: Greenwood Press, 1979.

Kennett, Bart. *Colored Actors' Union Theatrical Guide*. [Washington, D.C.]: n.p., [c. 1925].

Kimball, Robert, and William Bolcom. *Reminiscing with Sissle and Blake*. New York: Viking Press, 1973.

Kmen, Henry A. *Music in New Orleans*. Baton Rouge: Louisiana State University Press, 1966.

Levine, Lawrence. *Black Culture and Black Consciousness: Afro-American Folk Thought from Slavery to Freedom*. New York: Oxford University Press, 1977.

Lichtenwanger, William. "Matilda Sissieretta Joyner Jones." In *Notable American Women 1607–1950*. Cambridge, Mass.: Belknap Press of the Harvard University Press, 1971.

Locke, Alain. *The Negro and His Music*. 1936. Reprint. New York: Arno Press and the New York Times. 1969.

————. *The New Negro*. New York: A. and C. Boni, 1925.

McLean, Albert. *American Vaudeville As Ritual*. Louisville: University of Kentucky Press, 1965.

Marks, E. B. *They All Sang from Tony Pastor to Rudy Vallee*. 1934. Reprint. New York: Viking, 1959.

Mathews, Charles. *The London Mathews: Containing an Account of This Celebrated Comedian's Trip to America*. Philadelphia, Pa.: Morgan and Yager, 1824.

Mitchell, Loften. *Black Drama*. New York: Hawthorne Publishers, 1967.

Morath, Max. "The Vocal and Theatrical Music of Bert Williams and His Associates." American Popular Entertainment Papers and Proceedings of the Conference on the History of American Popular Entertainment. Ed. Myron Matlaw. Westport, Conn.: Greenwood Press, 1977.

Murray, Albert. *The Omni-Americans: New Perspectives on Black Experience and Black American Culture*. New York: Outerbridge and Dienstfrey, 1970.

Nathan, Hans. *Dan Emmett and the Rise of Early Negro Minstrelsy*. Norman: University of Oklahoma Press, 1962.

Odell, George. *Annals of the New York Stage*. 15 vols. New York: Columbia University Press, 1927–1949.

Ottley, Roi, and William J. Weatherby, eds. *The Negro in New York: An Informal Social History*. New York: New York Public Library, 1967.

Patterson, Cecil L. "A Different Drum: The Image of the Negro in the Nineteenth-century Popular Song Book." Ph.D. diss., University of Pennsylvania, 1961.

Patterson, Lindsay, ed. *Anthology of the American Negro in the Theatre: A Critical Approach*. 2d ed. New York: Publishers Company, 1968.

Riis, Thomas L. "Black Musical Theatre in New York, 1890–1915." Ph.D. diss., University of Michigan, 1981.

————. "Music in Nineteenth-century Productions of *Uncle Tom's Cabin*." *American Music* 4 (1986): 268–86.

Root, Deane. *American Popular Stage Music, 1860–1880*. Ann Arbor, Mich.: UMI Research Press, 1981.

Ross, Roland. "The Role of Blacks in the Federal Theatre, 1935–1939." *Journal of Negro History* 59 (1974): 38–50.

Rowland, Mabel. *Bert Williams: Son of Laughter*. 1923. Reprint. New York: Negro Universities Press, 1969.

Sampson, Henry. *Blacks in Blackface: A Sourcebook on Early Black Musical Shows*. New York: Negro Universities Press, 1980.

Schatz, Walter, ed. *Directory of Afro-American Resources*. New York: R. R. Bowker Co., 1970.

Simond, Ike. *Old Slack's Reminiscence and Pocket History of the Colored Profession from 1865 to 1891*. 1891. Reprint. Bowling Green, Ohio.: Popular Press, 1974.

Smith, Cecil. *Musical Comedy in America*. New York: Theatre Arts Books, 1950.

Sobel, Bernard. *Burleycue: An Underground History of Burlesque Days*. New York: Farrar and Rinehart, 1931.

Southern, Eileen. *The Music of Black Americans: A History*. 2d ed. New York: Norton, 1983.

Stearns, Marshall, and Jean Stearns. *Jazz Dance*. New York: Schirmer Books, 1968.

Toll, Robert. *Blacking Up: The Minstrel Show in Nineteenth-century America*. New York: Oxford University Press, 1974.

Trotter, James Monroe. *Music and Some Highly Musical People*. 1880. Reprint. Chicago: Afro-Am Press, 1969.

Williams, Martin. "Cautions and Congratulations: An Outsider's Comments on the Black Contribution to American Musical Theater." In *Jazz Heritage*. New York: Oxford University Press, 1985. 229–37.

Winter, Marian H. "Juba and American Minstrelsy." *Dance Index* 6 (1947): 28–47.

Periodicals

Afro-American. Baltimore (1892–) From 1901 to 1916 titled the *Afro-American Ledger*.

Billboard (1893–).

Clipper (1853–1924).

Crisis (1910–1940).

Folio (1869–1895).

Freeman (1884–1924).

From Uncle Tom to Cliff Huxtable, Aunt Jemima to Aunt Nell: Images of Blacks in Film and the Television Industry

In the beginning was "Tom." Tom was the image and the image was tom. Later came the "coons," the "mammies," the "bucks," and the "mulattoes." Donald Bogle's classic work, *Toms, Coons, Mulattoes, Mammies, and Bucks* (1973) is an exposé of the various images of Black people in American films. Bogle's thesis identifies five basic images. The stereotypes, enumerated in the book's title, change guises over the years, but the types remain basically unaltered. In *Famous Black Entertainers of Today* (1973), Raoul Abdul focuses on Black people who have ostensibly destroyed the old stereotypes. Interestingly, Abdul's thesis, which contradicts Bogle's, appeared at almost the same time.

A review of the literature on Black people in film and television generally reveals the perceptiveness of Bogle's analysis and exposes an uncanny similarity and consistency between the images created in literature and those brought to life on the silver screen and in countless living rooms through television sets. Sterling Brown's "A Century of Negro Portraiture in American Literature" (1966; discussed in chapter 5) identifies the following stereotypes: (1) the contented slave/wretched freedman, (2) the comic minstrel, (3) the persecuted victim, (4) the noble savage, (5) the submissive Christian, (6) the tragic mulatto, and (7) the brute Negro (*Massachusetts Review* 7, Winter 1966: 73–96). One can readily see the parallels in film. Lawrence Reddick expands the identification of stereotypes in his article "Of Motion Pictures" (1944) to include those which appear in all media. These types supplement each other, although they are sometimes contradictory. Reddick lists the following images:

Savage African

Happy slave

Devoted servant

Corrupt politician

Irresponsible citizen

Petty thief

Social delinquent

Vicious criminal

Sexual superman

Superior athlete

Unhappy non-white (Brown's tragic mulatto)

Natural-born cook

Perfect entertainer

Superstitious churchgoer

Chicken and watermelon eater

Razor and knife "toter"

Uninhibited expressionist

Mental inferior

Natural-born musician (Lindsay Patterson, ed., *Black Films and Film–makers* 23)

While this list is exhaustive, one must also add lazy and shiftless as adjectives for depicting Black males in particular. All of the stereotypes found in literature, on the stage, and on radio are captured and reinforced by the camera's eye.

Gordon Allport notes in *The Nature of Prejudice* (1954) that stereotypes are "socially supported, continually revived and hammered in, by our media . . . by novels, short stories, newspaper items, movies, stage, radio, and television" (200). Negative images have always been portrayed in one form or another, but with the expansion of visual images, stereotypes are vividly reinforced generation after generation. Richard Maynard's work, *The Black Man on Film: Racial Stereotyping* (1974) questions the impact of negative images on race relations. What kinds of attitudes do they shape in the minds of white children? What kinds of self-images do they project to young Blacks? Several studies seek to answer these questions. Early, enlightening works include Herbert Blumer's *Movies and Conduct* (1933), Henry Forman's *Our Movie Made Children* (1933), and W. W. Charters' *Motion Pictures and Youth: A Summary* (1933). While the questions raised by Maynard are still being discussed (see Roy Madsen's *The Impact of Film: How Ideas are Communicated through Cinema and Television*, 1973), they are not satisfactorily resolved in the literature. One thing, however, is clear: In the United States, education and the transmission of culture take place not so much in the schools as at the movies and before television sets. The part Hollywood has played in the formation of black images in movies and on television has been examined by a number of film critics and historians. Thomas Cripps, in the essay "The Death of Rastus: The Negro in American Films Since 1945," says that "Hollywood and any national film industry is both a leader and a follower of public opinion'' (Maynard 18). Hollywood, and all that it personifies, turns attitudes into concrete images, and concrete images, in turn, influence attitudes.

SILENT FILMS

Edward Mapp discusses stereotypes in *Blacks in American Films: Today and Yesterday* (1972) from silent movies to the films of the 1960s. He scrutinizes numerous films and the portrayals of Black people in them. Mapp's book documents the involvement of Black Americans in film since the beginning of the industry around 1888 when Thomas Edison invented the motion picture camera. Jim Pines, in *Blacks in Films* (1975), calls the Black image a permanent feature in the history and evolution of the American film (Pines 72). He discusses the earliest images of Blacks in short silent films such as *Pickaninnies* (1894), *Three Man Dance* (1894), *Negro Dancers* (1895), and *Dancing Darkey Boy* (1897), all produced by the Edison Company. These negative images contributed to the first film versions of black stereotypes.

The Uncle Tom Image

The film version (the negative stereotype already existed in literature) of Uncle Tom was born in 1903 on Edward S. Porter's 12-minute film *Uncle Tom's Cabin*. Uncle Tom, America's first black movie character, paradoxically was played by a white man in blackface (Bogle, *Toms, Coons* 3). The image that Tom projects is submissive, stoic, and faithful to whites—very much like the literary version of the contented slave. Books that discuss the birth and development of Uncle Tom include Bogle's, Thomas Cripp's *Slow Fade to Black: The Negro in American Film 1900–1942* (1977), Edward Mapp's *Blacks in American Films: Today and Yesterday* (1972), and James P. Murray's *To Find an Image: Black Films from Uncle Tom to Super Fly* (1974). Numerous articles about the image of Uncle Tom exist in both scholarly and popular journals.

Noteworthy works of history and criticism on the period in which Tom developed include James R. Nesteby's *Black Images in American Films, 1896–1954* (1982), Peter Noble's *The Negro in Films* (1970), Gary Null's *Black Hollywood: The Negro in Motion Pictures* (1975), Lindsay Patterson's *Black Films and Filmmakers: A Comprehensive Anthology from Stereotype to Superhero* (1975), and William Schechter's *The History of Negro Humor in America* (1970). These books provide a good historical background, though by no means an exhaustive one, for studying the formation of early Black images. Null's book is especially useful for the number and selection of photographs it provides. Together, these books reveal a format for racist depictions of Black people, from about 1894 to 1910, heavily influenced by the vaudeville stage traditions as well as by the blackface minstrel shows.

Uncle Tom is a pathetic rather than a comic figure. The influence of vaudeville and minstrel shows brought to life the comic image. Unfortunately, the distorted image of Black people is not limited to American filmmakers. As early as 1902, *Off to Bloomingdale*, a French film produced by George Melies, depicted four Black men as buffoons who erected the stereotype of the bug-eyed, eye-rolling, grinning, head-scratching, Black fool. In America, this image was born in the minstrel tradition and developed in the coon pictures described by Bogle and others. The coon is a Black, adult, male idiot or a Black child (pickaninny) cast as a clown or buffoon. The coon stereotype premiered in the 1905 film short *Wooing and Wedding of a Coon*. This film was a denigration of Black people and their ability to function as normal human beings.

The Birth of Coon and Rastus

The birth of the coon allowed for the exploitation of so-called ethnic events. Pines (1975) discusses ragamuffin plantation entertainments, buck dancing, cakewalking, watermelon-eating contests, fish fries, and Black culture in general, and he illustrates how these events are used in the most extreme and distorted comic terms. Coon soon took on the name Rastus or Sambo and expanded into what Bogle describes as "the most blatantly degrading of all black stereotypes. The pure coons emerge as no-account niggers, those unreliable, crazy, lazy, subhuman creatures, good for nothing more than eating watermelons, stealing chickens, shooting crap, or butchering the English language" (Bogle, *Toms, Coons* 8). In 1910 a barrage of Rastus films appeared. The first in this series of slapstick comedy was *How Rastus Got His Turkey*. Rastus tries to steal a turkey for Thanksgiving (petty thief image). Next, *Rastus in Zululand*, set in deepest, darkest, savage Africa, portrayed the "no-account nigger" who prefers death to matrimony. *Rastus and Chicken, Pickaninnies and Watermelon*, and *Chicken Thief* appeared between 1910 and 1911, but the films did not end there. *How Rastus Got His Pork Chop* appeared in 1914 and *Sambo's Wedding Day* in 1919.

These images are further discussed by Daniel Leab in *From Sambo to Superspade: The Black Experience in Motion Pictures* (1975). Leab traces black images in film through 1974 and concludes that, with a few exceptions, movies about Blacks were as negative as ever. The images of Black people are useful not just in terms of entertainment value, although entertainment is an important part; the real significance of the Southern plantation myth with its toms, coons, and mammies embodies the seminal ideas of American racism and cultural bigotry. These first images from movies and silent films form "the content of all plasticised black images" (Pines 7).

The Mulatto Image

The mulatto image emerged from the problematic theme of miscegenation. In the films *For Massa's Sake* (1911), *The Debt* (1912), and *In Slavery Days* (1913), the mulatto was depicted basically as an evil and degrading type. The concept

4. Marion Davies as mulatto in *Operator 13* with Sam McDaniel, 1934.

of the "tragic" mulatto emerged somewhat later in the 1915 film *The Nigger*.
The tragedy, apparently, is having one drop of Black blood. Sympathetic treatment of the character is reserved for the mulatto/octoroon only; thus black
characters are continually and consistently maligned. The significance of this
image is profound; its effect has yet to be completely analyzed. With this one
image, the standards of beauty, especially for females, seems set for all time.
If one could not be white (a tragedy), the closer one could approximate white
features, the more physically beautiful one was believed to be. Thin lips, sharp
pointed features, fair skin, and straight hair were the order of the day. But even
when Blacks met the standard, the parts were often played by whites.

Images of Black Women

The Masher (1907) is a blatant example of the maligning of the image of
Black womanhood in American films. The film shows a white man hotly pursuing
women, but the only one he can catch (who allowed herself to be caught) is
veiled mysteriously. When the man discovers the woman is Black, he runs the
other way. Thus was the image of the Black woman as undesirable established.

Much research needs to be conducted on the topic of the image of Black
women in film and on television. Several efforts have been made. In 1974
Adelaide Gulliver edited *Black Images in Films: Stereotyping and Self-Perception
As Viewed by Black Actresses*, which presents an interesting approach to the
issue of images. Donald Bogle's *Brown Sugar: Eighty Years of America's Black
Female Superstars* (1980) presents another effort to examine the often ignored
topic. "Ain't Beulah Dead Yet?" by Liz Gant (1973) is a less than satisfactory
analysis of the topic of Black female images, albeit a start. Maryann Oshana's
new study, *Women of Color: A Filmography of Minority and Third World Women*
(1987), represents an effort on an international scale. The images of Black women
have been restricted, on the one hand, to undesirable, sexless mammies or
exaggerated, on the other hand, to promiscuous, amoral, exotic sirens.

According to Bogle in *Toms, Coons*, the mammy image is closely related to
the coon; the stereotype is usually big, fat, black, ugly, and cantankerous.
Mammy first appeared in the 1914 film *Lysistrata*, which presents a blackface
version of this figure. In that year also the comedy *Coon Town Suffragettes*
further promoted the image of mammies. This film shows a collection of mammies trying to keep their "no-account nigger men" out of saloons. Aunt Jemima,
sometimes known as "handkerchief head," is the offshoot of the mammy and
the counterpart of Uncle Tom. Whereas the mammy is often irascible, Aunt
Jemima is characterized as sweet, jolly, and even-tempered. Jemima is polite,
never headstrong like mammy.

The Remaining Stereotypes

The appearance in 1915 of one single film introduced the remaining stereotypes
and reinforced those already delineated. This film, like *Uncle Tom's Cabin* before

it, and other box-office hits that followed, was based upon and adapted from a 1905 novel, *The Clansman* by Thomas Dixon. The film version, D. W. Griffith's *The Birth of a Nation*, presents the most pyschotic racist fears embedded in the American psyche. Every work that deals with Black images in films credits *The Birth of a Nation* for creating and displaying the most virulent racial stereotypes. Bogle credits the film for introducing the final mythic type: the buck (Sterling Brown's brute).

The most controversial Civil War film ever released in the United States, *The Birth of a Nation* narrates the physical and ideological birth of the Ku Klux Klan. It distorts the Civil War and Reconstruction periods in order to establish the need for the Klan to save the South and white womanhood. Black images in this monumental and impressive piece of film propaganda include the now classic mammy and Uncle Tom, the faithful souls who remain with the white family and defend them from other Blacks, and the pickaninny slaves who sing, dance, and clown in their quarters. These types represent Brown's contented slaves. The film also presents black bucks/brutes. The brute is a physically violent, subhuman, feral, and nameless character on a rampage and full of rage (Bogle, *Toms, Coons* 13). In *The Birth of a Nation*, a buck character attacks and beats white men; he also beats faithful Black servants. According to Bogle, the "pure black bucks" are Griffith's great archetypal figures. "Bucks are always big, baadddd niggers, over-sexed and savage, violent and frenzied as they lust for white flesh" (Bogle, *Toms, Coons* 13). This stereotype exposes the link between sex and racism in America.

Pines presents an interesting summation of this moviemaking era when he observes that "White American progressivism along with its nineteenth-century moralism and racism . . . went hand-in-hand to define this period. It was precisely this milieu which made possible the poisonous excrements of Griffith's film" (Pines 10).

Should one doubt the powerful influence of films, one need only note the ironic improvement of minority images during wartime. By 1918 propaganda films had come to the fore, the result of government efforts to improve their image and relationship with Blacks as a result of World War I. One surprising example of these propaganda films is D. W. Griffith's *The Greatest Thing in Life* which depicts a Black soldier in a heroic role, albeit as a Tom. Other films followed; examples are *Our Colored Fighters* (1918) and *Our Hill Fighters* about the 367th all-Black regiment.

Black Filmmakers

In light of all the negative images of Black people in the movies, one wonders what Blacks were doing to alter them. The action/reaction to negative images proceeded along the same lines it followed in literature and politics: accommodation and protest. Those Blacks who took over the blackface roles formerly played by whites helped extend the stereotype, thus accommodating themselves to the negative images. Others, individuals and organizations, chose to protest. The NAACP through *The Crisis* magazine still wages a very active campaign against negative images in films as elsewhere. Some Black filmmakers sought to counter the Hollywood image with positive films of their own. Emmett J. Scott's attempt to produce *Lincoln's Dream* (*The Birth of a Race*) in 1916 was an effort to counteract *The Birth of a Nation*. Oscar Micheaux, considered the first and most oustanding Black producer in American film, founded his New York (Harlem) based company in 1918. Micheaux is said to have written, directed, produced, and personally promoted over twenty-one feature films and shorts (Pines 35). Finally, in January 1987, Micheaux was honored with a star on Hollywood's famed walk.

More research needs to be directed toward Black filmmakers. Lindsay Patterson's *Black Films and Filmmakers* (1975) deals more with the Black film than the filmmaker. Henry T. Sampson's *Blacks in Black and White* (1977), a good sourcebook on Black films, contains an extensive film synopsis and discusses several Black-owned corporations. Sampson's book claims to list all Black films produced between 1904 and 1950. Additionally, the book contains chapters on the Lincoln Motion Picture Company, an early Black enterprise in Los Angeles; the Micheaux Film Corporation; and other Black independents. Pines includes a section in his book on independent Black filmmakers. Thomas Cripps' *Slow Fade to Black* (1977) includes a chapter titled "Two Early Strides Toward Black Cinema," which discusses Oscar Micheaux and the Lincoln Company. In an article "New Black Cinema and Uses of the Past," Cripps calls for a detailed study of Black pioneer filmmakers (*Black Cinema Aesthetics* 19–27).

For the most part, Black filmmakers functioned outside Hollywood conventions, or they tried to do so. They produced low-budget films; by the late 1920s, as many as a dozen independent Black companies were producing films across the United States. They produced full-length features and newsreels and distributed them to ghetto cinemas or for once-a-week matinees in white theaters (Pines 33). Most, though not all of the companies, were Black owned.

The 1920s provided conditions that fostered the development of films. The great Black Northern migration and the resulting urban Black ghettos, the rise in Black business given impetus by the National Negro Business League, as well as all of the cultural activities of the Harlem Renaissance promoted the Black film movement. Black films could depict life from a Black point of view, something which Hollywood failed miserably to do. But Black films contain stereotypes too. Pines states that the stereotypes exist only in the sense that all popular narrative conventions are subject to stocktype situations and characterizations. A more critical assessment is postulated by Haile Gerima who says that, while early Black filmmakers should be recognized, they often provide decadent solutions to various ethnic problems. Oscar Micheaux, for example, glorified the standard of white beauty over Black with his mulatto/octoroon characters. The real issue of Black beauty and sexuality was ineffectively dealt with. Both *Body and Soul* (1924) and *God's Step Children* (1938) suffer from color psychosis (*Black Cinema Aesthetics* 106–12).

The George Johnson Negro Film Collection housed in the Special Collections section of the University of California, Los Angeles Research Library provides a massive melange of information on the Black film company of George and Nobel Johnson (Lincoln Motion Picture Company). The collection contains a listing of Black and white companies that produced films from 1915 through 1962, a moving picture film history, and a large collection of information from newspaper clippings, articles from journals, and other sources on racism in entertainment. There is also a significant number of film reviews of pictures containing Black characters in major and minor roles. Advertising handbills and playbills round out the collection of memorabilia.

Daniel Leab's *From Sambo to Superspade* (1975) includes an interesting chapter, "All-Colored—But Not Very Different," which explores the efforts of Black film producers. Leab discusses the attempts of William Foster to "put his race right with the world" (Leab 59). Foster's Chicago-based company produced several films but was financially unsuccessful. Leab also discusses the Los Angeles–based Lincoln Motion Picture Company which he credits with being the first company to produce serious Black films for a Black audience. In the majority of Black films, "light skins" are the rule, and themes are middle class.

James Nesteby devotes several chapters in *Black Images in American Films, 1896–1954* (1982) to the Afro-American effort. One chapter is devoted to all-Black silent films, one to all-Black sound films, and one to all-Black Hollywood movies. Richard Maynard's work, *The Black Man on Film: Racial Stereotyping* (1974) is a good source for understanding the fight that has been waged against negative images in films.

Black filmmakers faced many problems; they had no economic strength. But despite the problems, the films they were able to produce contradicted the Hollywood plantation milieu. Many films are set in the North, utilizing the urban ghetto context and focusing on Black nightlife, nightclubs, dives, and other settings popular among urban Blacks. The all-Black films avoided the "race problem" altogether. Many of the themes are rural versus urban experiences, and moral versus immoral values. Often, the themes follow a middle-class ethos. They encourage Black youth to aspire to any profession, for example, in *The Flying Ace* (1926). Other films inspire a sense of community for transplanted southerners in the urban North. Research on early Black films and filmmakers awaits interested scholars, film critics, and historians. To aid in this effort, the researcher should explore the collection of thirty films uncovered in 1983 that were made between 1939 and 1953 by Black directors. These films were designed for showing to Black audiences primarily in segregated theaters of the South. Included are feature-length movies, such as *Miracle in Harlem* (released in 1948 and featuring Stepin Fetchit) and *Souls of Sin*, as well as musical shorts and newsreels. Fourteen of the films are available in 16mm for purchase or rent from the Tyler Texas Black Film Collection, Phoenix Films & Video, 468 Park Avenue, South, New York, NY 10016.

SOUND

Sound film marks the beginning of the modern movie industry. Sound augments the image and moves closer toward cinematic realism, thus extending the credibility of the medium, its range and the persuasiveness of the image. Sound also has made the greatest impact on the Black image process in American film. Other advanced technologies such as screen size, perspective, and color have a less immediate impact on racial imagery.

In 1922 the *Our Gang* comedy shorts were released. Running into the talkie period, these comedies (pickaninny stereotypes) became *The Little Rascals*. The 1927 premiere of *The Jazz Singer*, starring Al Jolson in blackface, launched the talking motion picture and ended the era of blackface performances. The *History of the American Film Industry* (1970) by Benjamin Hampton offers interesting insights on the transition from silent films to sound. Following the introduction of sound, parts for Black actors increased. By the end of the decade, Hollywood's first attempt to deal with the Black family appeared in the all-Black musical *Hallelujah*. This film was the precursor of the all-Black musicals that followed. With *Hallelujah*, King Vidor presented idealized Black people who are devoutly religious, gullible, and, in other ways, unrealistic. Whites praised the film; Blacks criticized it for the caricatures that are presented. *Hallelujah* introduced the first Black woman as an exotic sex-object. Nina Mae McKinney played the first Black whore in the character Chick. *Hearts of Dixie* (1929), which was released before *Hallelujah*, is an all-Black movie which introduced Stephin Fetchit, Clarence Muse, and Mildred Washington to the silver screen. According to Bogle in *Toms, Coons*, the movie presented the first all-Black cast ever seen in an American film. The actors accommodated themselves to the slick, but negatively stereotyped, roles created by Hollywood filmmakers. The chronicle of this accommodation is detailed in numerous articles from the 1929 article by C. M. Pierce on "Primitive Emotions Aflame in a Negro Film," to the 1972 James Murray article, "Do We Really Have Time for a Shaft?" Murray also provides a book-length study in *To Find an Image: Black Films from Uncle Tom to Super Fly* (1974).

THE 1930s

The beginnings of television in the United States can be credited to the inventions in 1923 of Vladimir Zworyken and Philo Farnsworth; however, the first public television broadcasts were made in 1927 in England. Television came to America in 1930. Broadcasting began on a regular basis on April 30, 1939, in connection with the New York World's Fair. Scheduled broadcasting was soon interrupted by World War II and resumed after the war's end.

Of the movies, Bogle says "no other period [1930s] could boast of more black faces carrying mops and pails or lifting pots and pans than the Depression years" (Bogle, *Toms, Coons*, 36). Pines describes this era as one distinguished by personalities rather than by films. Edward Mapp devotes a section in *Blacks in American Films* (1972) to the description of motion pictures produced during the 1930s. *Arrowsmith* (1932), *Emperor Jones* (1933), *Imitation of Life* (1934), *So Red the Rose* (1935), *The Green Pastures* (1936), *Show Boat* (1936), and *Gone with the Wind* (1939) are all worth mentioning for their portrayal of Black people. Leonard Archer discusses the majority of these movies in his chapter "Black Images on the Silver Screen" (Archer 183–225). Archer claims the black stereotypes from American literature and stage find their way into motion pictures. He describes the stereotypes in familiar terms: comics, savages, contented slaves, loyal servants, and buffoons. Archer's chapter is particularly interesting because it simultaneously traces the fight waged by the NAACP and the National Urban League against the negative images found in films, and refers to the sermons that were preached from pulpits condemning the showing of negative films. Magazine reviews and criticism are also discussed. The controversy over *Imitation of Life* is documented by the heated argument between Sterling Brown, film critic for *Opportunity Magazine* (while it was published, it was the official journal of the National Urban League), and Fannie Hurst, author of the novel. Brown criticizes the film for portraying the same old Black stereotypes. Hurst asserts that Black people should be "grateful" for the opportunity to appear on screen (Archer 188).

A favorite theme of the 1930s seems to have been the South: The Civil War setting, Mississippi River life, and plantations all appear in the major films of the era. *Gone with the Wind* is the most popular of the 1930s films. Thomas Cripps' "Politics of Art" in *Slow Fade to Black* describes this film as the one most reflective of its time. Nesteby rates *So Red the Rose*, directed by King Vidor, as the worst of the films about the South—a film that portrays Black people as pro-South and against their own freedom.

The Green Pastures is a major all-Black film that was produced during this era. Langston Hughes describes the film as "a quaint funny heaven full of niggers" ("Is Hollywood Fair to Negroes" 21). *The Green Pastures*, based upon Marc Connelly's Pulitizer Prize-winning play of the same title, was highly acclaimed both as a film and a play. Black newspapers found the play "enjoyable," but some Black critics blasted the film. Roi Ottley, film critic for the *Chicago Defender* (13 March 1930), called *The Green Pastures* "the phoniest panorama of hocus pocus that has yet come from Hollywood." Daniel Leab calls the characterization in *The Green Pastures* "niggerisms" that find expression in other media; for example, in the hit radio show of the 1930s, "Amos 'n' Andy," and in the Aunt Jemima Pancake Mix advertisements. The Jemima images showed "a broad-bosomed, fat, handkerchief-headed, gingham-dressed, black mammy who told worried housewives, 'Don' yo' fret none, honey. . . . Jus' follow dese directions for de world's mos' delicious pancakes' " (Leab 98).

5. Plastic plates showing Hattie McDaniel as "mammy" in *Gone with the Wind*, and "Buckwheat" from "Our Gang," and later the "Little Rascals" series. From the editor's collection. Photo by Vando Rogers.

Emperor Jones, the film version of Eugene O'Neill's play, expands the role of Brutus Jones, played by Paul Robeson, from pullman porter to emperor of an all-Black island kingdom. While Robeson portrays a strong character, "'crap-shooting, gin-guzzling, immorality, cutting, killing, fear of ghosts,'" and other stereotypes are present (Leab 111). Robeson also appears in *Show Boat*. Publicity for this film describes him as the "lazy, easy-going husband" of the cook (mammy type) played by Hattie McDaniel (Handbill, Manuscript Collection UCLA, 1936).

The films of the 1930s for the most part reinforced the negative stereotypes introduced in silent films. Sound provided another method through which the entrenchment of stereotypes could occur. Blacks in silent films are portrayed as foolish; with the coming of sound movies, they are seen and heard as buffoons. By the middle of this era, one sensitive writer in a *New York Age* article, "Negro Movie Characters" (23 February 1935), asked when the film industry would have the gut and moral courage "to stop pandering to society's 'prejudice and fanaticism' '' (Leab, *From Sambo* 117).

THE 1940s

The use of film as propaganda can be seen clearly during wartime. The government wanted the movie industry to stress national unity. In response,

Hollywood used Black soldiers in crowd scenes. But, as Leab points out, "even as American propaganda castigated axis racism, the traditional stereotypes of the movie black failed to disappear" (Leab, *From Sambo* 119).

Films of the 1940s include efforts such as *Casablanca* (1942); *In This Our Life* (1942); *Cabin in the Sky* (1943), an all-Black musical; *Stormy Weather* (1943); *Lifeboat* (1944); and *The Negro Soldier* (1944). These war movies portray Blacks somewhat differently from the usual caricatures. Rather than "shuffle along" in *Casablanca*, the character of Sam (played by Dooley Wilson) appears as Humprey Bogart's piano-playing companion. *In This Our Life* is a film that presents a Black man (Ernest Anderson) in the dignified role of a clerk and law student. It is, however, not without its stereotypes; namely, Hattie McDaniel appears in the usual mammy role. *Life Boat* is another film which presents a Black man in a human role. *Cabin in the Sky* has the distiction of being "the most acceptable all-Negro movie musical ever made"; yet it is often called "a stale insult (Leab, *From Sambo* 128)." To be sure, the movie is patronizing and in some ways resembles *The Green Pastures*. *Cabin in the Sky* is important for the cast it presents. Ethel Waters plays Petunia, a leading lady; Eddie Anderson and Rex Ingram have leading roles; and Lena Horne plays Georgia Brown. The screen play is by a Black man, Carlton Moss. Moss also acts in the film (Leab 128). Both World War I and World War II newsreels used Black soldiers for comic relief, if they were used at all. Moss himself offers valuable insight on this era in his article, "The Negro in American Films" (1971).

The 1940s resurrect an older theme often exploited in literature: the tragic mulatto. The most famous of these movies appears in the postwar era. *Lost Boundaries* (1949) is a film which exposes the tenacity of racism in a small American town. The film is based on a true story of a black New England family that for twenty years passed for white. Bogle describes the film as starkly realistic with a documentary flavor. He analyzes this film in detail in the section of his book entitled "The Problem People" (Bogle, *Toms, Coons* 118). *Pinky* (1949) presents the same old tragic mulatto theme but adds the dimension of a strong female character as well as an interracial romance. It is also noteworthy that the film is set in the racially troubled South. Ethel Waters presents the image of the now archetypal strong-Black-woman. These films are reviewed and the characters criticized by Herman Hill ("Stereotype Roles Cause of Dispute in Film Industry" 1946), Siegfried Kracaver ("National Types as Hollywood Presents Them" 1949), Daniel Leab (*From Sambo*), among others.

Finally, MGM brought the image of a "defiantly proud black man" to the silver screen. William Faulkner's *Intruder in the Dust* (1949) introduced the actor Juano Hernandez who played the role with dignity. The film, shot in Oxford, Mississippi, revealed racism in a "typical" American small town. The film has been called a melodrama, a detective story, a murder mystery, but, as Bogle aptly perceives, "it [is] a subtle study of a fearless and proud black man" (*Toms, Coons* 155).

The censorship of the NAACP finally began to pay off near the end of the 1940s. Hollywood became aware of the need to change the depiction of Black people. Leab (*From Sambo*) describes the change as "a limited response"; Patterson (*Black Films and Filmmakers*) observes "patterns of change" turn out to be nothing more than the same old stereotypes forcing him to recognize that the limitations placed on Black actors hindered the development of the movies in general, and prevented films from becoming a true art form in a democratic culture.

In 1946 twelve commercial television stations began operating in the United States. At first, telecasts of sporting events were especially popular. As advertisers entered the field on a large scale, stations grew. By 1948 there were forty-six stations in operation. The rising number of television viewers caused thousands of theaters to close (Mast 326). It appears that old vaudeville and minstrel show entertainment influenced early programming. The most popular shows were the variety type: "Toast of the Town," which used a vaudeville format is an example. Comedy was paramount in early television. In 1949 CBS televised an all-Black variety show, "Uptown Jubilee." The show, hosted by Willie Bryant, starred Jimmie Rogers and Harry Belafonte, but it lasted only one month (George Hill, *Blacks on Television* 1). The show raised the hopes of Black people who expected fairer treatment from television producers than they had received from movie producers. Enthusiasm was so high that *Ebony* magazine (July 1950) went on record saying that television offered better roles for Blacks than did any other medium.

THE 1950s

Television took the 1950s by storm. The beginnings were promising for Black actors. In 1950 Hazel Scott became the first Black woman to host a network series. George and Sylvia Hill presented a brief but informative history of Blacks on television in *Blacks on Television* (1985). "Harlem Detective," a show aired by a local station in 1953 (WOR-TV, New York), was the precursor to "I Spy." In "Harlem Detective," William Marshall (Black) is paired with William Harriston (white). The duo investigate crime in Harlem. These positive images, relatively speaking, however were short lived. Griffin and Hill pointed to one fact that became clear to television executives: "it would be bad business to change the skillfully crafted and accepted black image film and radio had created" (Hill and Hill 2).

The appearance of "Beulah" in October 1950 reestablished the norm. "Amos 'n' Andy" presented the toms, mammies, and coons rolling and bucking their eyes and scratching their heads in the style popularized in films from the 1920s and 1930s. Other early television shows that featured Blacks include "The Hallmark Hall of Fame" with Staats Cosworth in the role of *MacBeth* in 1954; "Kraft Theater" with Ossie Davis in 1955; and "Studio One" in which Juano Hernandez and Frank Silvera were showcased in 1957. "Green Pastures" also made a television debut. But, it was "Beulah," "Amos 'n' Andy," and "Green

Pastures,'' all of which presented negative images, that dominated the television images of the fifties.

Music and variety shows gave Black entertainers an opportunity to expose their talent. In 1956 "The Nat King Cole Show" became the first Black show in a network series. The show appeared first as a 15-minute spot on NBC just before the network news. By the summer of 1957, the show had expanded to 30 minutes and aired on Tuesdays at 10:00 P.M.; however, problems caused cancellation of the show after about one year (Griffin and Hill 2). A great deal of information on early television shows can be found in *Ebony* and *Jet* magazines.

The "Ed Sullivan Show" (1948–1971), "The Steve Allen Show" (1950–1952), and "The Jack Benny Show" (1950–1965) all premiered Black talent. On the other hand, Blacks were conspicuously absent from television Westerns. The Westerns turned out to be extremely popular; yet no Black actor had a main role. Sammy Davis, Jr., made a spot appearance in *Black Saddle* (1959). Scholars note that the decade that began with such promise ended like a "twilight zone full of deja vu. This new, oh-so-promising medium was shaping up to become no better than movies and certainly no better than radio" (Griffin and Hill 3).

Movies of the 1950s show little change in the Black images presented or in the roles that Blacks played. However, the decade produced a number of Black movie stars. Ethel Waters, Dorothy Dandridge, Harry Belafonte, Sidney Poitier, Eartha Kitt, and Nat King Cole were the cynosures. Hollywood made numerous changes in an effort to recapture the moviegoing audience seduced by television. The film industry introduced the giant wide screen cinerama, cinemascope, vista vision, and three-dimensional pictures to woo back the public. Bold themes were adopted to get the viewer's attention. Perhaps more important than any of these changes was the *Zeitgeist* of this historical period. Historians point to the incongruities that characterized this era: the red scare of McCarthyism, the Korean conflict, Ralph Bunche as a Nobel Peace Prize winner, Marian Anderson at the Metropolitan Opera, the Supreme Court decision of 1954 (on civil rights), the lynching of Emmett Till in Mississippi, the courage of Rosa Parks to begin a bus boycott, the leadership of Martin Luther King, Jr., bus boycotts, sit-ins, marches—this clearly was a time of change. The mood of the 1950s precipitated change in the motion picture industry. Bogle (Toms, Coons) recognizes these changes and groups the films that produced more dignified images in a category by themselves, calling them "problem films." Pines also discusses the changes that took place in the films of this era. Cripps (1967) presents an interesting summary of this period in his article, "The Death of Rastus: The Negro in American Films Since 1945."

Ethel Waters was the first actress to benefit from the changing mammy stereotype. A veteran performer, in *Pinky* she introduces the image of the strong black woman. In the 1950s she won mass audience approval and created the "earth mother" image out of the mammy role. *The Member of the Wedding* (1952) provided the vehicle for Waters' rise to stardom. This film has been called "a motion-picture event." *The Member of the Wedding* is the first film to use a Black woman as a lead in a white production (Bogle, *Toms, Coons* 161). Bogle presents a sensitive analysis of Ethel Waters' career.

Dorothy Dandridge is referred to as the second Black star to emerge on the fifties' horizon. Her rise as Hollywood's most successful leading lady obviously owe in part to the sensuous Black women who "paid dues" before her time; namely, Nina Mae McKinney and Lena Horne. *Carmen Jones* (1954) is the film that catapulted Dandridge to stardom. The movie also typecast her as the "definitive tragic mulatto" (Bogle, *Toms, Coons* 168). The character Carmen Jones is, according to Leab, "a direct descendent of Chick, the vamp in Vidor's *Hallelujah*" (Leab, *From Sambo* 203). James Baldwin also analyzes the role of Carmen in "Carmen Jones: The Dark Is Light Enough" (Patterson 1975). Despite the stereotype of the loose, amoral, exotic, Black woman as sex-object, Dandridge was admired for her performance. In fact, her performance earned her an Oscar nomination as the best actress of the year, making her the first Black woman nominated in the category for a leading role. Both Hattie McDaniel and Ethel Waters had been nominated for best supporting role.

Sidney Poitier was the third Black star to rise. Bogle describes him as a "model integrationist hero" ascending to stardom in an integrationist age (*Toms, Coons* 175). Poitier succeeded in breaking the tom, coon, and buck stereotype; yet the image he created suffers from a sexless, almost sterile quality. He clearly is no threat to the white film goer, Leab insists, because he is not sexually aggressive (Leab, *From Sambo to Superspade* 226). The films that contributed to Poitier's success are *Edge of the City* (1957) and *The Defiant Ones* (1958). The Poitier image has come under closer scrutiny since the 1960s when attitudes toward integration began to change. Poitier's acceptability to Black audiences diminished; their elan for Poitier waned; and the image seems incredulous by contemporary standards. Contemporary Black film goers see him as unreal, says Bogle. Poitier's characters are "still the old type that America [has] always cherished. They were mild-mannered toms, throwbacks to the humanized Christian servants of the 1930s"; but, Bogle concedes, Poitier "may have played the old tom dressed up with modern intelligence and reason, but he digified the figure" (Bogle, *Toms, Coons* 176).

Pines describes the fifties as an era of racial liberalism and classifies many of the movies of this period as racial genre films. This is an interesting epoch of varying images covered best by Pines, Bogle, and Leab, as well as by a good number of articles in *Ebony, Sepia*, and *Jet*, and even in the more scholarly journals listed in the bibliography for this chapter.

THE 1960s

The flux that characterized the motion picture images of the previous decade took over the television images of the 1960s. Television was neither left behind nor excluded from the changes that gripped America. John F. Kennedy, who came into office at the beginning of the decade, instituted major changes which impacted on the television industry. He appointed the Federal Communications Commission, which requires television stations to enforce affirmative action policies (Hill and Hill 2). Perhaps the single most significant contribution television made to the Black experience took place during the sixties. A nonfictional image of civil rights activists and freedom fighters was projected by Blacks during this decade. Television captured that image and flashed it into nearly every American home and around the world.

Again, the social environment prompted better roles for Black actors. "Eastside/Westside" (1964) cast Cicely Tyson as an actress who, at the time, was the only Black with a continuing role. "I Spy" (1965–1968), starring Bill Cosby and Robert Culp, was the first adventure series to contain a Black actor since "Harlem Detectives." Blacks also gained roles in daytime television—another first. This decade can accurately be dubbed the era of "firsts", "onlies," and "showcase Negroes." The television stars of this era include Diahann Carroll, Bill Cosby, Ruby Dee, James Earl Jones, Eartha Kitt, Greg Morris, Diana Sands, and Ethel Waters, all of whom won Emmies for their achievements. The riots of the sixties and the Kerner Commission Report brought the decade to a close and aided in the airing of Tony Brown's "Black Journal" (1968), the only national Black affairs show on either public or commercial television (Douglas 1973).

The movies of the sixties managed to capture the image of the "militant" Black that emerged from television news. The industry also hired more Blacks as extras, cast them in minor roles, and featured them as ordinary people—a result of the NAACP's threat to take legal and economic action against them (Leab, *From Sambo to Superspade* 208).

Take a Giant Step (1960), a movie adapted from the off-Broadway play by Louis Peterson, opened the decade. According to several film critics, the movie's significance lay in the fact that Peterson is one of Hollywood's few Black screenwriters. The film adaptation of *A Raisin in the Sun*, which appeared the following year, was more successful than Peterson's effort. Both films present nineteen-fiftyish integrationist images. It was not until the appearance of the "Black Art films" that militant images emerged. Bogle lists a number of Black Art films; that is, films made for other than commercial purposes that honestly depict racism in America. Accordingly, *Shadows* (1961), *The Cool World* (1963), *One Potato, Two Potato* (1964), and *Nothing but a Man* (1964) erected the image of a Black protagonist demanding freedom on his own terms without assimilation or accommodation. The sixties can be characterized as a period in which contradictory images coexisted. Bogle says *Hurry Sundown* (1967) is the first commercial motion picture to capture the militant spirit and Black revolt of the late 1960s. This film, however, is an example of the old images in new guises. The movie, Bogle's witty analysis claims, is "way down in de New Old South with Tom-Tom, Miss Bronze Barbie Doll, and Ms. Militant Mammy" (Bogle, *Toms, Coons* 208–13). Other critics tend to agree.

Pines detects other problems with the militant image. The image—popularized by Jim Brown in *Rio Conchos* (1964) and *100 Rifles* (1968)—of the big, black, angry, rapist perpetuates the buck/brute myth and exploits the American phobias concerning racial sexuality. Still another antiquated image surfaced during the 1960s: blackface. This old image in new guise is dubbed by Pines as "sociological blackface"—the white "passing" for Black for the purpose of study as portrayed in the film *Black Like Me* (1964) or a more recent example, *Soul Man* (1986).

THE 1970s

The movies of the 1970s that vulgarize ethnic material and aim the image at a Black audience have been labeled blaxploitation films. Melvin Van Peebles' *Watermelon Man* (1970) opened the period but reflects virtually no representation of the blaxploitation genre. Rather, Pines says, the movie is viewed best as a transitional one in that it represents Hollywood's last attempt at the message film. The so-called film with a message or lesson turns out to be a 1970s production of the time-worn tragic mulatto image with a few twists for comedy. *Cotton Comes to Harlem* (1970), produced by Ossie Davis and based on the work of novelist Chester Himes, established the blaxploitation genre. Bogle harshly criticizes the film, Pines is kinder, and Leab focuses on its commercial success. In general, these blaxploitation films are characterized by their appeal to Black audiences. There is little doubt that *Cotton Comes to Harlem* abounds with familiar stereotypes. The difference, perhaps, is that the writer and director are Black. Thus, the difference, subtle, but significant, is like a Black person saying "nigger" instead of a white person saying it.

The movies of the seventies are well known. Those that stand out and are most controversial are *Sweet Sweetback's Baadasss Song* (1971) and *Shaft* (1971). The first film is the subject of a great deal of scholarly debate. Bogle (*Toms, Coons*) discusses *Sweet Sweetback* and appears to remain neutral; Pines discusses the film's impulsion within the Black genre; Patterson devotes an entire chapter of his *Black Films and Film-makers* to Van Peebles who claims that the film is a "black odyssey." Lerone Bennett's article in *Ebony* crystallizes the controversy. "There is a certain grim white humor," Bennett writes, "in the fact that the black marches and demonstrations of the '60s reached artistic fulfillment in the '70s with Flip Wilson's Geraldine and Melvin Van Peebles' Sweetback, two provocative and ultimately insidious reincarnations of all the Sapphires and studs of yesteryear" (Bennett 106).

Yearwood and Rose in *Black Cinema Aesthetic* (1982) present a colloquy with Van Peebles, St. Clair Bourne, Haile Gerima and Pearl Bowser. In this forum, the controversy rages. Issues similar to those raised by the Black Arts movement and the Black Aesthetic movement in literature regarding the artist's commitment and responsibility are raised. Gerima questions the filmmaker's responsibility to the Black community, and Yearwood argues for artistic freedom.

The Black images projected by the films of the seventies, the most notorious of which is *Superfly* (1972), consist of glorified pimps, whores, drug addicts and dealers, and sexually violent superstuds. Gary Null in *Black Hollywood: The Negro in Motion Pictures* (1975), which is little more than a picture book, states that "these stereotypes express the images black screenwriters, producers, and directors have of their race" (Null 230). It could also be that these images are marketable.

Black images on television during the 1970s were less blatantly negative than the images that emerged from the blaxploitation movies. The number of Blacks on television increased dramatically during the seventies. Between 1970 and 1979, Black actors either starred in or had supporting roles in at least fifteen shows (Hill and Hill 5); however, the majority of those shows were comedies. With "The Bill Cosby Show" (1970), the comedy casting began. "Sanford and Son" appeared in 1971, followed by "Good Times" (1973), "The Jeffersons" (1974), and "What's Happening" (1976), and the decade ended with "Benson" and "Sanford" (1979). The detective shows were "Shaft," "Paris," "Tenafly," "Get Christy Love," "Mannix," "The Rookies," "Ironside," and "Mod Squad." Even though only some of the images were positive, it was certainly an improvement for television. The seventies represent a period of growth. Black people were offered more multidimensional roles and were cast as doctors, lawyers, nurses, and other professionals as well as ordinary workers.

George and Sylvia Hill's *Blacks on Television* (1985) is a valuable bibliography useful for its annotations. Pamela Douglas' article "Black Television: Avenues of Power" in *The Black Scholar* (September 1973) represents a major analysis of the financial and political functioning of various stations, both public and commercial. In her research, Douglas finds that 96 percent of American homes have at least one television set (Douglas 27). It is thus apparent how far reaching and important the issue of Black image is. In "Women and Blacks on Prime-Time Television," Judith Lemon (1977) reports the results of a scientific study that analyzes the images of Blacks and women. The study reports that the images of Blacks and women fair best in situation comedies. The more serious the drama, the worse these two groups appear (J. Lemon 70–79).

Pamela Trotman Reid's illuminating article on racial stereotyping on television (1979) compares the behavior of both Black and white television characters. She finds that "racial stereotypes and sex role stereotypes are the basis for character portrayals on television" (Reid 465). Reid's study is important for its analysis of the difference in the female image based upon race. She finds that white female characters are shown to be submissive and helpless; they rated low on dominance and high on succorance. On the other hand, Black female characters are rated low on achievement, succorance, and self-recognition, but rated high on dominance and nurturance. Her findings are supportive of the mammy image for Black women.

The 1970s presented new opportunities in television, if not new images.

Unfortunately, many of the gains of the previous ten years have disappeared in the current decade.

THE 1980s AND CONTEMPORARY IMAGES

In television, several of the Black roles of the 1970s have been integrated into groups of white shows; others have disappeared altogether. Examples of this role integration can be seen in NBC's "The A-Team" with its Black star Mr. T, "Trapper John, M.D." with Madge Sinclair and Brian Mitchell, "Hill Street Blues" with Michael Warren and Taurean Blacque, and Roger Mosley on "Magnum P.I.," Greg Morris in "Vegas," Ted Lang in "Love Boat," Debbie Allen in "Fame," and, most recently, Philip Michael Thomas in "Miami Vice." Opportunities for one or two Blacks to appear in both daytime and nighttime soaps have also come about. Diahann Carroll and Billy Dee Williams are popular examples. The effect of this type of integrating is twofold. First, it makes Black actors highly visible (the fly in buttermilk effect). Second, it creates the illusion that Black people have finally "made it"—they have finally arrived and are now well integrated into American society.

While the 1980s have provided the opportunity for Blacks to become hosts and cohosts on several programs, for example Bryant Gumbel on the "Today Show" and Byron Allen on "Real People," and Oprah Winfrey on her own syndicated show, the period still projects worn out mammy images in new guise. In "Gimme' a Break," Nell Carter plays nursemaid/housekeeper/mammy to a modern-day white family. Particularly negative segments have referred to Al Jolson as grandpa's hero showing Nell standing back watching while Little Master Joey Lawrence sings "Swanee."

Perhaps the most virulent images on television thus far in this decade have come by way of documentaries. CBS's "The Vanishing Family: Crisis in Black America," which aired on January 25, 1986, resembled a throwback from a bygone era. It presented the no good nigger male image and the amoral, promiscuous, whorish black female image, as well as a variety of pickanninnies as juvenile delinquents. These images were strengthened by the style of presentation. Reporter Bill Moyer actually interviewed the persons who best fit the stereotypes. The format of the documentary is probably the most convincing method for presenting clichéd images.

Often, when the horizon appears the bleakest, a glimmer of hope appears. Such is the case with the appearance of the top-rated "Bill Cosby Show" and the "Oprah Winfrey Show." The Cosby show projects a positive Black male in the role of husband, father, and breadwinner; a positive, beautiful, and intelligent woman lawyer as the wife and mother; and five lovely, smart, and good Black children. Heathcliff Huxtable and his family represent new and exciting possibilities for writers and producers of Black shows—creators of Black images. This show has earned top ratings without pandering to racist preconceptions. Nevertheless, Cosby and his fictional characters in the Huxtable family have not escaped criticism. Ironically, several white critics have charged that the show is not "Black" enough. Obviously, it fails to conform to their preconceptions of the Black experience. The "Oprah Winfrey Show" projects the image of an intelligent, capable, and articulate Black woman—a significant change made all the more meaningful because she is not acting; she is real.

Little scholarly research exists on the shows of this era. We are too close to develop much perspective. Movies of the 1980s present many of the same problems as the television images. Gone are the blaxploitation films, and black actors are being integrated into white films—one at a time: Lou Gossett in *An Officer and a Gentleman*, Billy Dee Williams in *Star Wars*, and Lou Gossett, again, in the recently released *Fire Walker*. One of the most controversial "Black" films of 1986 was *The Color Purple*, which was adapted from Alice Walker's novel of the same title. Despite the merits of the novel, the movie brings to life images of negative stereotypes: the brute/buck in the character of Mr., the tom in the character of Harpo, the whore in Shug Avery, and the religious, superstitious figure of Shug's father, who interestingly enough does not appear in the novel. This movie, along with others of the era, awaits serious study and analysis.

The study of images alone is a fascinating subject. The images of minorities and of Blacks in particular are especially provocative and offer a fertile area for research. Several scholars—Bogle, Cripps, Patterson, Pines—have made significant contributions by documenting and analyzing the history of Black images in film. Television has fewer scholars who have published book-length studies. George and Sylvia Hill are welcome pioneers in this field. Reference is made to stereotype studies in *Role Portrayal and Stereotyping on Television*, edited by Nancy Signoreielli (1986). This work describes 423 studies on television's depiction of women, racial and ethnic minorities, and other groups. Sources are primarily scholarly journals and books, with some articles from popular journals and government publications. The annotations include a bibliographic citation. Suggestions are given for improving the portrayal of women and minorities on television.

Bogle's ending comments are mots justes for summarizing the topic of black images in films and on television:

What can we say about film history that carries us from the submissive stoicism of Tom in . . . *Uncle Tom's Cabin* to the equally submissive stoicism of the Sidney Poitier characters in *Lillies of the Field* and *In the Heat of the Night*? What are we to think when some morning we see on television the notorious pranks of a slowwitted shuffling Stepin Fetchit and then the same evening we visit the local movie house and view the demeaning shenanigans of a dim-witted, shifty character played by Sammy Davis, Jr.? When we compare the actors of the past with those of the present or when we contrast the movies of yesteryear with those of today, . . . all of us ask ourselves despairingly just how far American movies have progressed in the past half-century in recording the black experience accurately or sensitively (*Toms, Coons* 230).

Other areas of investigation regarding black images remain to be examined, such as the recently developing videotapes. Educational films are another means of projecting Black images that need to be examined. Some excellent historical and educational pieces are appearing on PBS video, such as "Eyes on the Prize," which chronicles the civil rights years. While they are increasing in popularity, video cassette recorders are less accessible than are movies and television. Only an estimated 40 percent of Americans own a VCR (*Consumer Report* 1987).

The information which follows is in no way exhaustive. It presents, instead, an overview of the topic of prominent actors, a filmography, a list of Black-owned television stations, and, finally, the bibliography with listings which provide historical and critical information on the topic of Black images in television and film.

IMAGE MAKERS

The image, that is, the impression, idea, and concept, of Black people in the United States is heavily influenced by the projections we see on film and on television. To what extent people are influenced by images is still being researched, but that images do have an effect is without doubt. Listed here are those men and women responsible for presenting a likeness or imitation of Black people through the confines of the character prescribed to him or her. Countless thousands of Black men and women in both major and minor roles, before the camera and behind the scenes, have contributed to the image that America has of Black people and that Black people have of themselves. Since it was impossible to list all of them, only the most well-known stars are included. Film and television credits are listed along with special studies that have been conducted regarding them.

Bailey, Pearl

Film Credits

Variety Girl, 1947

Isn't It Romantic, 1948

Carmen Jones, 1954

Porgy and Bess, 1959

That Certain Feeling, 1956

St. Louis Blues, 1959

All the Fine Young Cannibals, 1958

The Landlord, 1970

Norman—Is That You?, 1976

Special Studies

Bailey, Pearl. *The Raw Pearl*. New York: Harcourt, 1968.

Belafonte, Harry

Film Credits

Bright Road, 1953

Carmen Jones, 1954

Island in the Sun, 1956

The World, the Flesh and the Devil, 1958

Odds Against Tomorrow, 1959

Tamango, 1959

The Angel Levine, 1969

Buck and the Preacher, 1972

Special Studies

"Belafonte Plays Angel on and off Screen." *Ebony* 22 (October 1969): 76–82.

Brown, Nick. "Would You Believe Belafonte as a Jewish Angel?" *New York Times*, April 27, 1969:D–17.

"Harry Belafonte." *TV Guide* (January 10, 1959):13–15.

"Movie Maker Belafonte." *Ebony* 14 (June 1959):94–96, 98–100.

Shaw, Arnold. *Belafonte*, New York: Chilton, 1960.

Beavers, Louise

Film Credits

Barnum Was Right, 1928

Coquette, 1929

Annabelle's Affair, 1931

Girls about Town, 1931

Ladies of the Big House, 1931

Sundown Trail, 1931

Bombshell, 1932

Girl Missing, 1933

In the Money, 1933

She Done Him Wrong, 1933

Imitation of Life, 1934

Gentlemen of the Navy, 1935

Bullets or Ballots, 1936

Life Goes On, 1938

Reckless Living, 1938

Scandal Street, 1938

Brother Rat, 1939

Reform School, 1939 (all Black)

No Time for Comedy, 1941

Shadow of the Thin Man, 1941

Holiday Inn, 1942

Jack London, 1942

Reap the Wild Wind, 1942

The Big Street, 1943

Dubarry Was a Lady, 1943

Top Man, 1943

The Vanishing Virginian, 1943

Barbary Coast Gents, 1944

Follow the Boys, 1944

Dixie Jamboree, 1945

West of the Pecos, 1945

Delightfully Dangerous, 1948

Mister Blandings Builds His Dream House, 1948

The Jackie Robinson Story, 1950

I Dream of Jeannie, 1952

You Can't Run Away from It, 1956

The Goddess, 1958

All the Fine Young Cannibals, 1960

Facts of Life, 1961

TV Credits

"Beulah," 1952 ABC

"Playhouse 90," 1957 CBS

"World of Disney," 1959 ABC

Special Studies

"My Biggest Break." *Negro Digest* 8 (December 1949):21–22.

Brooks, Clarence

(One of the founders of the Black Lincoln Motion Picture Company)

Film Credits

Realization of a Negro's Ambition, 1916

Law of Nature, 1918

By Right of Birth, 1921

Absent, 1928

George Rose, 1930

Lem Hawkins' Confession, 1935

Bargain with Bullets, 1937

Dark Manhattan, 1937

The Bronze Buckaroo, 1938

Spirit of Youth, 1938

Bad Boy, 1939

Harlem Rides the Range, 1939

Two-Gun Man from Harlem, 1939

Am I Guilty, 1940

Up Jumped the Devil, 1941

The Negro Soldier, 1944

Brown, Jim

Film Credits

Rio Conchos, 1966

The Dirty Dozen, 1967

Dark Side of the Sun, 1968

Ice Station Zebra, 1968

100 Rifles, 1968

The Riot, 1969

El Condor, 1970

Tick Tick Tick, 1970

Black Gunn, 1972

Slaughter, 1972

I Escaped from Devil's Island, 1973

Slaughter's Big Rip-off, 1973

TV Credits

"I Spy," 1967 CBS

Special Studies

Stone, Judy. "Jim Brown, Fighting Southern Sheriff." *New York Times*, July 26, 1969: D–9.

Carroll, Diahann

Film Credits

Carmen Jones, 1954

Porgy and Bess, 1959

Paris Blues, 1961

Hurry Sundown, 1966

The Split, 1968

Claudine, 1974

TV Credits

"Peter Gunn," "Sing a Song of Murder," 1960 NBC

"Naked City," "A Horse Has a Big Head," 1962 ABC

"Eleventh Hour," "And Man Created Vanity," 1963 NBC

"Julia," 1968–1970 NBC

"Hotel Ninety," 1973 CBS

"Death Scream," 1975 ABC

"Dynasty," 1984 ABC

Special Studies

"Chance of a Lifetime: Diahann Carroll Wins Fame, Fortune and a Celebrity's Headaches on TV Talent Show." *Our World* 10 (May 1954):12–17.

"Diahann Caroll." *People* 16 (August 23, 1976):54–59.

"Diahann Carroll and Joan Collins Renew Their Feud in 'Dynasty' Roles." *Jet* (September 29, 1986):58–60.

"Diahann Carroll Stars in Sisters." *Los Angeles Sentinel* February 1, 1979:B–1.

Efron, E. "Diahann Carroll's Struggle between Two Worlds." *TV Guide* (May 27, 1967):12–15.

Gardella, Kay. "TV Casts Diahann as a Pioneer." *Sunday News* September 1, 1968:C–39.

Sanders, Charles. "Diahann and Billy Dee: Dynasty's Newest Stars." *Ebony* 39 (October 1984):155–63.

See, C. "Diahann Carroll's Image." *TV Guide* (March 14, 1970):26–30.

Cosby, Bill

Film Credits

Hickey and Boggs, 1972

Man and Boy, 1972

Uptown Saturday Night, 1975

Let's Do It Again, 1978

Beverly Hills Suite, 1979

TV Credits

"I Spy," 1965–1968 NBC

"Murder at NBC," 1967 NBC

"The Bill Cosby Show," 1969 NBC

"Aesop's Fables," 1971 CBS

"To All My Friends on Shore," 1972 CBS

"Fat Albert and the Cosby Kids," 1973 CBS

"Top Secret," 1978 NBC

"The New Fat Albert Show," 1980–1981 CBS

"The Bill Cosby Show," 1986–Present NBC

Special Studies

"Bill Cosby: TV's Top Dad." *Jet* (June 16, 1986): 23.

Black, Doris. "What's Next for Bill Cosby?" *Sepia* 27 (June 1971): 44–48.

"Close-up of Bill Cosby." *Michigan Chronicle*, December 3, 1977: B–4.

Cosby, William H., Jr. "An Integration of the Visual Media via 'Fat Albert and the Cosby Kids' into Elementary School Curriculum as a Teaching Aid and Vehicle to Achieve Increased Learning." Ph.D. diss., University of Massachusetts, 1976.

"Cosby Forms TV Company, Opens with 14-City Market." *Jet* (March 12, 1981):16.

Davidson, M. "Bill Cosby—Ph.D." *TV Guide* (August 18, 1973): 28–30.

"December Is Bill Cosby's Month." *Soul* (December 8, 1966):18.

"I Spy: Comedian Bill Cosby Is First Negro Co-Star in TV Network Series." *Ebony* 47 (September 1965): 65–66.

Olsen, James. *Bill Cosby: Look Back in Laughter*. Los Angeles: Creative Education, 1970.

Ryan, C. "Bill Cosby: The Man in Studio 41." *TV Guide* (February 3, 1973):28–31.

Dandridge, Dorothy

Film Credits

A Day at the Races, 1939 (debut as child actress)

Four Shall Die, 1940

Moo Cow Boogie, 1943

Pillow to Post, 1945

Flamingo, 1946

Jungle Queen, 1946

Ebony Parade, 1947

The Harlem Globetrotters, 1951

Tarzan's Peril, 1951

Bright Road, 1953

Carmen Jones, 1954

Island in the Sun, 1957

The Decks Ran Red, 1958

Moment of Danger, 1959

Porgy and Bess, 1959

Tamango, 1959

TV Credits

"Light's Diamond Jubilee," "A Chance for Adventure," 1964 CBS

"Cain's Hundred," "Blues for a Junkman," 1962 NBC

Special Studies

Dandridge, Dorothy, and Earl Conrad. *Everything and Nothing*. New York: Abelard-Schuman, 1970. (autobiography)

Dee, Ruby. "The Tattered Queens." *International Library of Negro Life and History*. *Anthology of the American Negro in the Theatre*. Ed. Lindsay Patterson. New York: Association for the Study of Negro Life and History, 1966. 131–34.

Mills, Earl. *Dorothy Dandridge*. Los Angeles: Hawthorne Books, 1967.

"Mystery of Dorothy Dandridge." *Color* 10 (March 1956):7–9.

"Private World of Dorothy Dandridge." *Ebony* 14 (June 1962):116–21.

Young, A. S. "Doc." "Dorothy Dandridge Marries." *Sepia* 40 (September 1959):38–43.

———. "Life and Death of Dorothy Dandridge." *Sepia* 21 (December 1965):8–12.

Davis, Ossie

Film Credits

No Way Out, 1950

Anna Lucasta, 1958

Gone Are the Days, 1963

Shock Treatment, 1963

The Hill, 1965

A Man Called Adam, 1966

Sam Whiskey, 1968

The Scalphunters, 1968

Slaves, 1969

Cotton Comes to Harlem, 1970

Kongi's Harvest, 1970 (produced by Davis)

Black Girl, 1972 (directed by Davis)

Gordon's War, 1973 (directed by Davis)

TV Credits

"Showtime U.S.A.," "Green Pasture," 1951 NN

"Kraft Theatre," "The Emperor Jones," 1955 NBC

"John Brown's Raid," 1960 NBC

"Play of the Week," "Seven Times Monday," 1960 NN

"Defenders," "The Riot," 1961 CBS

"Car 54 Where Are You?" "Bennie the Bookie's Last Chance," 1963 NBC

"Defenders," "Metamorphosis," 1963 CBS

"Defenders," "Star-Spangled Ghetto," 1963 CBS

"Great Adventure," "Go Down, Moses," 1963 CBS

"Defenders," "Mind Over Murder," 1964 CBS

"Defenders," "Turning Point," 1964 CBS

"Doctors/Nurses," "A Family Resemblance," 1964 CBS

"Defenders," "Fires of the Mind," 1965 CBS

"Defenders," "Nobody Asks What Side You're On," 1965 CBS

"Defenders," "The Sworn Twelve," 1965 CBS

"Slattery's People," "What Can You Do with a Wounded Tiger," 1965 CBS

"Look Up and Live," "Continuity of Despair," 1966 CBS

"Fugitive," "Death Is the Door Prize," 1966 ABC

"Run for Your Life," "A Game of Violence," 1966 NBC

"Outsider," 1967 NBC

"N.Y.P.D.," "Nothing Is Real but the Dead," 1968 ABC

"Bonanza," "The Wish," 1969 NBC

"Hallmark Hall of Fame," "Teacher, Teacher," 1969 NBC

"Name of the Game," "The Third Choice," 1969 NBC

"Night Gallery," 1969 NBC

"The Sheriff," 1971 ABC

"Today Is Ours," 1974 CBS

"Hawaii Five-O," 1974 CBS

"The 10th Level," 1976 CBS

"Billy: Portrait of a Street Kid," 1977 NBC

"King," miniseries, February 12, 14, 1978 NBC

"Roots: The Next Generation," miniseries, 1979 ABC

"Freedom Road," 1979 NBC

"All God's Children," 1980 ABC

"Don't Look Back," 1981 ABC

Special Studies

Davis, Ossie. "Purlie Told Me!" *International Library of Negro Life and History. Anthology of the American Negro in the Theatre.* New York: Association for the Study of Negro Life and History, 1963. 165–69.

Davis, Sammy Jr.

Film Credits

Rufus Jones for President, 1931

Season's Greetings, 1932

The Benny Goodman Story, 1957

Anna Lucasta, 1958

Porgy and Bess, 1959

Ocean's Eleven, 1960

Sergeants Three, 1961

Reprieve, 1962

Johnny Cool, 1964

Robin and the Seven Hoods, 1964

A Man Called Adam, 1966

Salt and Pepper, 1968

Man without Mercy, 1969

Sweet Charity, 1969

One More Time, 1970 (sequel to *Salt and Pepper*)

TV Credits

"G.E. Theatre," "Auf Widerschen," 1958 CBS

"Zane Grey Theatre," "Mission, 1959 CBS

"G.E. Theatre," "The Patsy," 1960 CBS

"Lawmen," "Blue Boss and Willie Shay," 1961 ABC

"Dick Powell Theatre," "The Legend," 1962 NBC

"Frontier Circus," "Coal of Fire," 1962 CBS

"Hennessey," 1962 CBS

"Rifleman," "The Most Amazing Man," 1962 ABC

"Ben Casey," "Allie," 1963 ABC

"Burke's Law," "Who Killed Alex Debbs?" 1963 ABC

"Patty Duke Show," "Will the Real Sammy Davis Stand Up," 1965 ABC

"Wild, Wild West," "The Night of the Returning Dead," 1966 CBS

"Danny Thomas Show," "The Enemy," 1967 NBC

"I Dream of Jeannie," 1967 NBC

"Beverly Hillbillies," 1969 CBS

"Mod Squad," "Keep the Faith, Baby," 1969 ABC

"The Pigeon," 1969 ABC

"Here's Luck," 1970 CBS

"Make Room for Granddaddy" [sic], 1970 ABC

"Mod Squad," "The Song of Willie," 1970 ABC

"Name of the Game," "I Love You Billy Baker," 1970 NBC

"The Trackers," 1971 ABC

"All in the Family," 1972 CBS

"Old Faithful," 1973 ABC

"Poor Devil," 1973 NBC

"Chico and the Man," 1975 NBC

"Charlie's Angels," "The Sammy Davis, Jr. Kidnap Caper," 1977 ABC

"One Life to Live," 1979 (several episodes) ABC

Special Studies

"*Anna Lucasta*: Eartha Kitt, Sammy Davis Star in Film." *Ebony* 14 (December 1958): 72–76.

Davis, Sammy, Jr., Jane Boyer, and Bert Boyer. *Yes I Can: The Story of Sammy Davis, Jr.* New York: Farrar, Straus and Giroux, 1965.

Lucas, Bob. "The Many Lives of Sammy Davis." *Sepia* 20 (August 1971):18–22.

"Robin and the Seven Hoods: Sammy Davis, Jr. Co-Stars in Spoof of Mob." *Ebony* 19 (June 1964): 90–100.

Young, A. S. Doc. "Sammy Davis, Jr. Speaks Out." *Negro Digest* 12 (June 1963):19–25.

Dee, Ruby

Film Credits

Love in Syncopation, 1946

The Fight That Never Ends, 1947

That Man of Mine, 1947

What a Guy, 1947

The Jackie Robinson Story, 1950

No Way Out, 1950

St. Louis Blues, 1950

The Tall Target, 1951

Go, Man Go!, 1954

Edge of the City, 1957

Take a Giant Step, 1960

Virgin Islands, 1960

A Raisin in the Sun, 1961

The Balcony, 1963

Black Girl, 1963

Gone Are the Days, 1963

The Incident, 1967

Uptight, 1968 (script by Ruby Dee)

Buck and the Preacher, 1972

Countdown at Kusini, 1975

TV Credits

"Play of the Week," "Seven Times Monday," 1960 NN

"Play of the Week," "Black Monday," 1961 NN

"Alcoa Premiere," "Impact of an Execution," 1962 ABC

"East Side/West Side," "No Hiding Place," 1963 CBS

"Fugitive," "Decision in the Ring," 1963 ABC

"Great Adventure," "Go Down, Moses," 1963 CBS

"Nurses," "Express Stop from Lenox Avenue," 1963 CBS

"Defenders," "The Sworn Twelve," 1965 CBS

"Look Up and Live," "Continuity of Despair," 1966 CBS

"Peyton Place," 1968 ABC

"Deadlock," 1969 NBC

"The Sheriff," 1971 ABC

"N.E.T. Playhouse," "To Be Young, Gifted and Black," 1972 NN

"D.H.O.," 1973 ABC

"Tenafly," "The Window That Wasn't," 1973 NBC

"It's Good to Be Alive," 1974 CBS

"Today Is Ours," 1974 CBS

"Wedding Band," 1974 ABC

"Police Woman," 1975 NBC

"I Know Why the Caged Bird Sings," 1979 CBS

"Roots: The Next Generation," 1979 ABC

Special Studies

"Critic Keeps Her Cool on *Up Tight.*" *New York Times*, December 29, 1968: D–1, 29.

Dee, Ruby. *My One Good Nerve: Rhymes, Reasons*. Chicago: Third World Press, 1986. (a collection of poems and short stories)

Fetchit, Stepin

Film Credits

In Old Kentucky, 1927

Big Time, 1929

Fox Movietone Follies of 1929, 1929

The Ghost Talks, 1929

Hearts in Dixie, 1929

Salute, 1929

David Harum, 1934

The House of Connelly, 1934

Helldorado, 1935

Judge Priest, 1935

The Littlest Rebel, 1935

Steamboat Round the Bend, 1935

Virginia Judge, 1935

Showboat, 1936

Elephants Never Forget, 1939

His Exciting Night, 1939

Bend of the River, 1952

The Sun Shines Bright, 1953

Special Studies

"Stepin Fetchit Comes Back." *Ebony* 7 (February 1952): 58–62.

Hernandez, Juano

Film Credits

Girl From Chicago, 1932

Lying Lips, 1940

Intruder in the Dust, 1949

Kiss Me Deadly, 1955

Something of Value, 1956

The Pawnbroker, 1964

The Extraordinary Seaman, 1968

TV Credits

"Studio 57," "The Goodwill Ambassadors," 1957 CBS

"Studio One," "Escape Route," 1957 CBS

"Alfred Hitchcock Presents," "An Occurrence at Owl Creek Bridge," 1959 CBS

"Adventure in Paradise," "Isle of Eden," 1960 ABC

"Adventure in Paradise," "The Good Killing," 1961 ABC

"Play of the Week," "Black Monday," 1961 NN

"Route 66," "Good Night, Sweet Blues," 1961 CBS

"Defenders," "The Savage Infant," 1962 CBS

"Dick Powell Theatre," "Safari," 1962 NBC

"Naked City," "Howard Running Bear Is a Turtle," 1963 ABC

Special Studies

"From Actor to College Professor." *Ebony* 8 (November 1952):122–26. (Hernandez' return to Puerto Rico and his new career as English professor)

"Hollywood's 'Hottest' Negro Actor." *Ebony* 5 (August 1950):22–26.

"Trial: Cast as a Judge, Actor Juano Hernandez Is Given Best Role of His Hollywood Career." *Ebony* 11 (November 1955):29–32.

Horne, Lena

Film Credits

The Duke Is Tops, 1938

Bronze Venus, 1940 (available on videocassette)

Harlem Hot Shot, 1940

Bip Bam Boogie, 1941

Cabin in the Sky, 1943 (available on videocassette)

Panama Hattie, 1943

Stormy Weather, 1943 (available on videocassette)

Swing Fever, 1943

Thousands Cheer, 1943

Boogie Woogie Dream, 1944

Broadway Rhythm, 1944

Two Girls and a Sailor, 1944

Mantan Messes Up, 1946

Till the Clouds Roll By, 1946

Ziegfield Follies, 1946

Harlem on Parade, 1948

Words and Music, 1948

Duchess of Idaho, 1950

Meet Me in Las Vegas, 1957

Death of a Gunfighter, 1969

That's Entertainment, 1974

The Wiz, 1978

Special Studies

Buckley, Gayle. *The Hornes: An American Family*. New York: Alfred A. Knopf, 1986.

Horne, Lena. *In Person: Lena Horne*. New York: Greenberg, 1950.

Horne, Lena, and Richard Schickel. *Lena*. New York: Doubleday, 1965.

Lane, Bill. "Lena Horne Changes Course." *Sepia* 10 (June 1980):34–38.

"Lena Horne." *Ebony* 13 (May 1980):39–45.

"Lena Horne: Our World's First Cover Girl." *Our World* 7 (April 1950):11–13.

"Million Dollar Beauty, Lena Horne." *Sepia* 2 (January 1958):7–13.

Norman, Shirley. "Lena Horne at 60." *Sepia* 9 (June 1977):26–33.

Ingram, Rex

Film Credits

Huckleberry Finn, 1932

Harlem after Midnight, 1934

Captain Blood, 1936

Green Pastures, 1937

Thief of Bagdad, 1941

Cabin in the Sky, 1943

Sahara, 1944

Anna Lucasta, 1958

TV Credits

"Kraft Theatre," "The Emperor Jones," 1955 NBC

"Your Play Time," "The Intolerable Portrait," 1955 NBC

"Black Saddle," 1959 NBC

"Law and Mr. Jones," "The Storyville Gang," 1960 ABC

"Dick Powell Theatre," "Sea Witch," 1962 NBC

"Lloyd Bridges Theatre," "Gentlemen in Blue," 1962 CBS

"Sam Benedict," "A Split Week in San Quentin," 1963 NBC

"Breaking Point," 1964 ABC

"I Spy," "Weight of the World," 1965 NBC

"Daktari," 1967–1968 CBS

"Cowboy in Africa," 1968 ABC

"The Bill Cosby Show," December 21, 1969 NBC

"Gunsmoke," "The Good Samaritans," 1969 CBS

Lee, Canada

Film Credits
Keep Punching, 1939

Henry Brown Farmer, 1942 (narrated by Lee)

Lifeboat, 1944

Lost Boundaries, 1949

Cry, The Beloved Country, 1951

TV Credits
"Tele Theatre," "The Final Bell," 1950 NBC

McDaniel, Hattie

Film Credits
Story of Temple Drake, 1933

Judge Priest, 1935

The Prisoner of Shark Island, 1936

Showboat, 1936

Nothing Sacred, 1938

Gone With the Wind, 1939

In This Our Life, 1942

The Little Colonel, 1945

Song of the South, 1947

McKinney, Nina Mae

Film Credits

Hallelujah!, 1929

Pie, Pie, Blackbirds, 1932

Gang Smashers, 1938

St. Louis Gal, 1938

The Devil's Daughter, 1939 (available on videocassette)

Straight to Heaven, 1939

Swanee Show Boat, 1940

McNeil, Claudia

Film Credits

The Last Angry Man, 1959

A Raisin in the Sun, 1961

There Was a Crooked Man, 1970

Black Girl, 1973

TV Credits

"Du Pont Show of the Month," "The Member of the Wedding," 1958 CBS

"Look Up and Live," "Death," 1959 CBS

"Play of the Week," "Simply Heavenly," 1959 NN

"The Dick Powell Theatre," "Thunder in a Forgotten Town," 1963 NBC

"Nurses," "Express Stop from Lenox Avenue," 1963 CBS

"Look Up and Live," 1964 (three episodes) CBS

"Profiles in Courage," 1965 NBC

"CBS Playhouse," "Do Not Go Gentle into That Good Night," 1967 CBS

"Incident in San Francisco," 1971 ABC

"Mod Squad," "The Connection," 1972 ABC

"Moon of the Wolf," 1972 ABC

"N.E.T. Playhouse," "To Be Young, Gifted and Black," 1972 NN

McQueen, Butterfly (Thelma)

Film Credits

Gone With the Wind, 1939

Affectionately Yours, 1941

The Great Life, 1941

They Died with Their Boots On, 1942

Cabin in the Sky, 1943

Duel in the Sun, 1947

Killer Diller, 1947

Song of the South, 1947

TV Credits

"Beulah," 1950 ABC

"Studio One," "Give Us Our Dream," 1950 CBS

"Hallmark Hall of Fame," "The Green Pastures," 1959 NBC

"The ABC Afterschool Special," "The Seven Wishes of a Rich Kid," 1979

Muse, Clarence

Film Credits

Hearts in Dixie, 1929

Hill's Highway, 1933

Huckleberry Finn, 1933

Laughter in Hell, 1933

O'Shaughnessy's Boy, 1935

Showboat, 1936

So Red the Rose, 1936

Spirit of Youth, 1938

Way Down South, 1939 (screenplay by Muse and Langston Hughes)

Broken Earth, 1940

Broken String, 1940

Maryland, 1940

Gentlemen from Dixie, 1942

Tales of Manhattan, 1942

Shadow of Doubt, 1943

In the Meantime Darling, 1944

Night and Day, 1946

TV Credits

"Four Star Playhouse," "Bourbon Street," 1954 CBS

"Casablanca," 1955 ABC

Parks, Gordon

Film Credits

The Learning Tree, 1969 (directed and written by Parks)

Shaft, 1971 (directed by Parks)

Special Studies

Parks, Gordon. *A Choice of Weapons*. New York: Harper, Row, 1965. (autobiography)

————. *The Learning Tree*. Greenwich, Conn.: Fawcett, 1963. (novel)

Poitier, Sidney

Film Credits

From Whom Cometh Help, 1949 (Army documentary)

No Way Out, 1950

Cry, The Beloved Country, 1951

Red Ball Express, 1952

Go Man, Go!, 1953

The Blackboard Jungle, 1955

Edge of the City, 1956

Goodbye My Lady, 1956

Something of Value, 1956

Bands of Angels, 1957

The Defiant Ones, 1958

The Mark of the Hawk, 1958

Virgin Islands, 1958

Porgy and Bess, 1959

All the Young Men, 1960

Paris Blues, 1961

A Raisin in the Sun, 1961

Pressure Point, 1962

Lilies of the Field, 1963

The Long Ships, 1964

The Bedford Incident, 1965

The Greatest Story Ever Told, 1965

A Patch of Blue, 1965

The Slender Thread, 1965

Duel at Diablo, 1966

In the Heat of the Night, 1967

To Sir, With Love, 1967

For Love of Ivy, 1968 (also written by Poitier)

Guess Who's Coming to Dinner, 1968

The Lost Man, 1969

Brother John, 1970

They Call Me Mister Tibbs, 1971

The Organization, 1971

Buck and the Preacher, 1972 (also directed by Poitier)

A Warm December, 1973

Up Town Saturday Night, 1974

TV Credits

"Philco Playhouse," "Parole Chief," 1952 NBC

"Philco Playhouse," "The Man Is Ten Feet Tall," 1955 NBC

"Pond's Theatre," "Fascinating Stranger," 1955 ABC

"The Strollin' 20s," 1966 CBS

"ABC Stage 67," "A Time for Laughter," 1967

Special Studies

"*All the Young Men*: Anti-bias Korean War Movie Casts Sidney Poitier, Alan Ladd in Lead Roles." *Ebony* 15 (August 1960):83–88.

Baldwin, James. "Sidney Poitier." *Look* 23 (July 1968):4, 50–58.

Barrow, William. "A Gallery of Leading Men." *Negro Digest* 12 (October 1963):45–48.

Bennett, Lerone Jr. "Hollywood's First Negro Movie Star: Sidney Poitier Breaks Film Barrier to Become Screen Idol." *Ebony* 14 (May 1959):100–108.

————. "How Sidney Poitier Won an Oscar." *Sepia* 8 (June 1964):14–17.

Black, Doris. "A Quarter Century in Movies for Sidney Poitier." *Sepia* 23 (August 1974):36–42.

"*Blackboard Jungle*: Sidney Poitier Has Key Role in Brutal Film about Teacher, Juvenile Delinquents." *Ebony* 10 (May 1955):87–93.

Canby, Vincent. "Milestones Can Be Millstones." *New York Times*, July 19, 1970:D–2. (Marks the beginning of Poitier's negative criticism: says his Blackness is invisible)

Champlin, Charles. "Sidney Poitier: The Burden of Power." *New York Post*, February 3, 1969:48.

Cripps, Thomas. "Movies in the Ghetto, B. P. (Before Poitier)." *Negro Digest* 7 (February 1969):17–22.

Crowther, Bosley. "The Negro in Films: Poitier Points a Dilemma Which *The Cool World* Helps Rebuff." *New York Times*, August 26, 1964:E–4.

Ellston, Maxine Hall. "Two Sidney Poitier Films." *Film Comment* 36 (Winter 1969):85.

Ewers, Carolyn. *Sidney Poitier: The Long Journey*. New York: New America Library, 1969.

Flatley, Guy. Sidney Poitier as Black-Militant. *New York Times*, November 10, 1968: C–10.

"For Love of Ivy." *Ebony* 23 (October 1968):52–59.

Geale, Gloria. "ME by Sidney Poitier." *Sepia* 17 (October 1968):56.

Goodman, George. "Durango: Poitier Meets Belafonte." *Look* 35 (August 25, 1971): 56–60.

Greeley, Andrew. "Guess Who's Coming to Dinner." *The Reporter* (March 21, 1968):39.

Hernton, Calvin C. "And You, Too, Sidney Poitier!" *White Papers for White Americans*. Ed. C. Hernton. New York: Doubleday, 1966. 53–70.

Keyser, Lester. *The Cinema of Sidney Poitier*. San Diego, Calif.: A. S. Barnes, 1980.

Landry, Robert J. "Films, Poitier and Race Riots." *Variety* 3 (January 1968):7–12.

Marell, Alvin. *The Films of Sidney Poitier*. New York: Citadel, 1978.

Mason, Clifford. "Why Does White America Love Sidney Poitier So?" *New York Times*, September 10, 1967: 17.

Poitier, Sidney. *This Life*. New York: Ballantine Books, 1981. (autobiography)

———. "Walking the Hollywood Color Line." *American Film* 5 (April 1980):24–29.

———. "Why I Became an Actor." *Negro Digest* 11 (March 1962):80–97.

"Poitier Credits Robeson with Much of His Success." *Jet* 36 (September 14, 1978):58.

"Poitier Heads Production Company." *Chicago Daily Defender*, December 16, 1978:I–13.

"Poitier's New Film Makes Black Beautiful." *Jet* 64 (May 3, 1973):56–60.

Prelutsky, Burt. "Hollywood's Negro Mired in Stereotypes." *Los Angeles Times*, February 19, 1967:D–2. (compares Poitier to Fetchit)

Robinson, Louie. "The Expanding World of Sidney Poitier: Superstar, Director, Producer Eyes Future." *Ebony* 27 (November 1971):100–113.

———. "Sidney Poitier Tells How to Stay On Top in Hollywood." *Ebony* 33 (November 1977):53–62.

Sanders, Charles L. "Sidney Poitier: The Man Behind the Superstar." *Ebony* 23 (April 1968):172–82.

"The Secret Private Life of Sidney Poitier." *Sepia* 221 (June 1972):47–56.

"Sidney Poitier." *Ebony* 23 (May 1968):172–74, 176, 178, 180, 182.

Thompson, M. Cornell. "Sidney Poitier Makes Relevant Film for Blacks. *Jet* (May 13, 1971):58–61. (a positive review of *Brother John*)

"To Sir, With Love." *Sepia* 16 (April 1967):76–79.

"To Sir, With Love: Sidney Poitier Stars Brightly in British Film." *Ebony* 22 (April 1967):68–74.

Wilkins, Roy. "Poitier's Ivy." *New York Post*, July 27, 1968: 27.

Pryor, Richard

Film Credits

Lady Sings the Blues, 1972

Hit, 1973

Wattstax, 1973

Car Wash, 1975

Which Way Is Up, 1978

Family Dreams, 1979

Stir Crazy, 1980

Jo, Jo Dancer Your Life Is Calling You, 1986 (available on videocassette)

In Critical Condition, 1987

Robeson, Paul

Film Credits

Voodoo, 1922

Body and Soul, 1925

Borderline, 1930

The Emperor Jones, 1933 (available on videocassette)

Sanders of the River, 1934

Show Boat, 1935

Song of Freedom, 1936

Big Fella, 1937

Jericho, 1937

King Solomon's Mines, 1937 (available on videocassette)

Proud Valley, 1939

Tales of Manhattan, 1942

Special Studies

"Chronology of Paul Robeson's Life." *Michigan Chronicle*, April 29, 1978: A–3.

Cripps, Thomas R. "Paul Robeson and Black Identity in American Movies." *The Massachusetts Review* 11 (Summer 1970):468–85.

Davis, Lenwood. *A Paul Robeson Research Guide: A Selected Annotated Bibliography*. Westport, Conn.: Greenwood Press, 1982.

"Detroit Relives Life and Times of Paul Robeson." *Michigan Chronicle*, April 15, 1978: A–1.

"Detroit's Celebration of Robeson's Life." (*Adams Column*) *Michigan Chronicle*, April 29, 1978:A–8.

"Paul Robeson Honored at United Nations." *New York Amsterdam News*, October 21, 1978:A–3.

Robeson, Eslanda Goode. *Paul Robeson: Negro*. London: Victor Gollanez, 1930.

Robeson, Paul. *Here I Stand*. New York: Othello, 1958.

Robeson, Susan. *The Whole World in His Hands*. Secaucus, N.J.: Citadel Press, 1981.

Schlosser, Antol. "Paul Robeson." Ph.D. diss., New York University, 1970.

Weaver, Harold D. "A Bibliographic, Discographic and Filmographic Note." (On Robeson). *The Black Scholar* 5 (December 1973): 32.

―――. "Paul Robeson and Film: Racism and Anti-Racism in Communications." *Negro History Bulletin* 37 (January 1974):204–6.

White, Walter. "The Strange Case of Paul Robeson." *Ebony* 6 (February 1951):78–84.

Ross, Diana

Film Credits

Lady Sings the Blues, 1972

Mahogany, 1975

The Wiz, 1979

TV Credits

"Tarzan," "The Convert," 1968 NBC

"Make Room for Granddaddy" [sic], February 4, 1971 ABC

Special Studies

Wilson, Mary. *Dreamgirl: My Life As a Supreme*. New York: St. Martin's Press, 1986.

Tucker, Lorenzo

Film Credits

Veiled Aristocrat, 1927

Wages of Sin, 1928

When Men Betray, 1929

A Daughter of the Congo, 1930

Easy Street, 1930

The Black King, 1932

Harlem after Midnight, 1934

Temptation, 1936

Underworld, 1937

Straight to Heaven, 1939

Boy, What a Girl, 1946

One Round Jones, 1946

Reat, Petite and Gone, 1947

Sepia Cinderella, 1947

Tyson, Cicely

Film Credits

The Last Angry Man, 1959

A Man Called Adam, 1966

The Comedians, 1967

The Heart Is a Lonely Hunter, 1968

Sounder, 1972

Autobiography of Miss Jane Pittman, 1974 (TV film)

The River Niger, 1976

A Hero Ain't Nothin But a Sandwich, 1977

Roots, 1977 (TV film)

Family Dream, 1979

TV Credits

"Eastside/Westside," 1963 CBS

"I Spy," "So Long," 1965 NBC

"Slattery's People," "Who You Taking to the Main Event, Eddie?" 1965 CBS

"I Spy," "Trial by Treehouse," 1966 NBC

"Cowboy in Africa," 1967 ABC

"The Guiding Light," 1967 CBS

"Judd for the Defense," 1967 ABC

"FBI," "The Enemies, 1968 ABC

"Courtship of Eddie's Father," 1969 ABC

"FBI," October 12, 1969 ABC

"FBI," "Silent Partner," 1969 ABC

"Here Come the Brides," 1969–1970 ABC

"Medical Center," "The Last Ten Yards, 1969 CBS

"On Being Black," "Johnny Ghost," 1969 NN

"The Bill Cosby Show," 1970 NBC

"Gunsmoke," "The Scavengers," 1970 CBS

"Mission Impossible," March 15, 1970 CBS

"Hollywood Television Theatre," "Neighbors, 1971 NN

"Marriage: Year One," 1971 NBC

"Emergency," April 15, 1972 NBC

"Wednesday Night Bout," 1972 NBC

"The Autobiography of Miss Jane Pittman," 1974 CBS

"Just an Old Sweet Song," 1976 CBS

"Roots," 1977 ABC

"Wilma," 1977 NBC

"King," 1978 NBC

"A Woman Called Moses," 1978 NBC

"The Body Human: Becoming a Woman," 1981 CBS

"The Marva Collins Story," 1981 CBS

Special Studies

"Cicely Tyson." *Afro-American*, Baltimore, August 18, 1979:2–11.

"Cicely Tyson." *Bilalian News*, February 16, 1979:14.

"Cicely Tyson." *Chicago Daily Defender*, January 23, 1979: 17.

"Cicely Tyson." *Michigan Chronicle*, December 23, 1978:A–1.

"Cicely Tyson." *Pittsburgh Courier*, December 30, 1978: F–10.

"Cicely Tyson Criticizes Media Images of Black Women." *Afro-American*, Baltimore, June 23, 1979:6.

"Cicely Tyson Speaks in Indianapolis on Roles for Blacks." *Bilalian News*, August 17, 1979:12.

"Cicely Tyson Speaks to Black Women's Forum in L.A." *Los Angeles Sentinel*, July 26, 1979:A–1.

"Cicely Tyson's Performance in Atlanta." *Atlanta Daily World*, April 29, 1979:5.

"Cicely Tyson's Transformation in the Autobiography . . . " *Jet* 65 (January 3, 1974): 56–57.

Klemesrud, Judy. "Cicely, the Looker from Sounder." *The New York Times*, March 18, 1973:D–7.

Norment, Lynn. "Interview with Cicely Tyson." *Ebony* 36 (February 1981):124–38.

Robinson, Louie. "Cicely Tyson: A Very Unlikely Movie Star." *Ebony* 29 (May 1974): 33–38.

Van Peebles, Melvin

Film Credits

The Story of a Three Day Pass, 1967 (director, French film)

Watermelon Man, 1970

Sweet Sweetback's Badasss Song, 1971 (director and actor)

Special Studies

Bennett, Lerone. "Sweetback in Wonderland." *Ebony* 26 (September 1971):106.

Lee, Don L. "The Bittersweet of Sweetback or, Shake Yo Money Maker."*Black World* 20 (November 1971):1–8.

"Pathological Symbolism in Sweetback." *Muhammad Speaks*, July 30, 1971:C–11.

Waters, Ethel

Film Credits

On With the Show, 1929

Rufus Jones for President, 1931

Bubbling Over, 1942

Cairo, 1942

Cabin in the Sky, 1943

Stage Door Canteen, 1943

Tales of Manhattan, 1943

Pinky, 1949

Member of the Wedding, 1953

The Sound and the Fury, 1959

TV Credits

"Beulah," 1950 ABC

"Climax," "The Dance," 1955 CBS

"G.E. Theatre," "Winning by Decision," 1955 CBS

"Favorite Playhouse," "Speaking to Hannah," 1955 CBS

"Playwrights '56," "The Sound and the Fury," 1955 NBC

"Matinee Theatre," "Sing for Me," 1957 NBC

"Whirlybirds," "The Big Lie," 1959 NN

"Route 66," "Good Night, Sweet Blues," 1961 CBS

"Great Adventures," "Go Down, Moses," 1963 CBS

"Professor Hubert Abernathy," 1967 CBS

"Daniel Boone," 1970 NBC

"Owen Marshall," "Run, Carol, Run," 1972 ABC

Special Studies

Morrison, A. "Ethel Waters Comes Back." *Negro Digest* 17 (April 1950):6–10.

Waters, Ethel. *His Eye Is on the Sparrow*. New York: Doubleday, 1950.

———. "Men in My Life; Famous Actress Looks Back to Recall Intimate Off-Stage

Story of Tumultuous Loves in Her Stormy Life on Stage.'' *Ebony* 7 (January 1952):24–32.

Williams, Billy Dee

Film Credits

Brian's Song, 1971

The Final Comedown, 1972

Lady Sings the Blues, 1972

Hit!, 1973

The Take, 1974

Mahogany, 1975

Bingo Long and the Travelling All-Stars, 1976

Star Wars, 1978

Return of the Jedi, 1979

Fear City, 1985

Special Studies

Sanders, Charles. "Diahann and Billy Dee: Dynasty's Newest Stars." *Ebony* 41 (October 1984):155–63.

SELECTED FILMOGRAPHY

The following list includes all-Black films and films containing Black characters. Although omissions have certainly been made, the purpose of this brief listing is to illustrate that almost without exception Black films and Blacks in films have been projecting and reinforcing various images from the very beginning of filmmaking in America. In the years in which many films were made, the effort here has been to list the lesser known films along with those more widely recognized. In some instances, more than one film is listed during a single year. This has been done in the case of films that have produced a profound impression in terms of images, production, and/or direction and that have in some other significant way affected film genre.

1897   *Dancing Darkey Boy*, Thomas A. Edison

1903   *Cotton Spinning*, AM & B Productions
       Uncle Tom's Cabin, Siegmund Lubin

1904   *A Nigger in the Woodpile*, AM & B Productions

1905   *The Wooing and Wedding of a Coon*, American Mutoscope

1907   *Jamaica Negroes Doing a Two-Step*, Thomas A. Edison

1908   *How Rastus Got His Pork Chop*, Siegmund Lubin

1909 *Coon Town Parade*, Lubin Manufacturing Company

1910 *Confederate Spy*, AM & B Productions

1911 *For Massa's Sake*, Edison Company

1912 *The Debt*, Rex

1913 *In Slavery Days*, Otis Turner
      The Octoroon, Kalem

1914 *Coon Town Suffragettes*, Siegmund Lubin

1915 *The Birth of a Nation*, D. W. Griffith
      The Nigger, Fox

1916 *Natural Born Gambler*, Biograph
      Realization of a Negro's Ambition, Lincoln Motion Pictures (all Black)
      The Wooing of Aunt Jemima, Horace Davey

1917 *The Law of Nature*, Lincoln Motion Pictures (all Black)

1918 *A Man's Duty*, Lincoln Motion Pictures (all Black)

1919 *Circumstantial Evidence*, Micheaux Film Corporation (all Black)

1920 *Within Our Gates*, Micheaux Film Corporation (Black production with mixed cast; controversial film on lynching in the South)

1921 *By Right of Birth*, Lincoln Motion Pictures (Black production with whites in cast)

1922 *The Dungeon*, Micheaux Film Corporation (all Black)

1923 *The Heart of a Negro*, Lincoln Motion Pictures (all Black)

1924 *Birthright*, Micheaux Film Corporation (all Black)

1925 *Body and Soul*, Micheaux Film Corporation (all Black), stars Paul Robeson
      Free and Equal, Thomas Ince (this film was said to be a response to *Birth of a Nation*)

1926 *Broken Violin*, Micheaux Film Corporation (all Black)

1927 *The Millionaire*, Micheaux Film Corporation (all Black)

1928 *Tenderfeet*, Midnight Productions (all Black)

1929 *Black and Tan*, RCA Photone Studios
      Melancholy Dame, Cohen (all Black; first Black talking film)

1930 *Georgia Rose*, Aristo Films (all Black)

1931 *Darktown Revue*, Micheaux Film Corporation (all Black)

1932 *The Black King*, Southland Pictures (white production billed as satire on the life of Marcus Garvey) (available on videocassette)

1933 *Dixie Love*, Paragon Pictures

1934 *Voodoo Drums*, International Stage Play Pictures

1935 *Lem Hawkins' Confession*, Micheaux Film Corporation (all Black)

1936 *Showboat*, Universal

1937 *Dark Manhattan*, Renaldo Films (all Black)

1938 *The Duke Is Tops*, Million Dollar Productions (all Black; Lena Horne's first picture)
      Harlem on the Prairie, Buell (first Black Western)

1939 *Double Deal*, Argus Pictures, Inc.

1940 *George Washington Carver*, Bryant Productions Biograph

1941 *Murder on Lenox Avenue*, Colonade Pictures Corporation (all Black)

1942 *Second News Reel*, All American News (footage of Meharry Medical College and the Fisk University Choir)

1943 *We've Come a Long Way*, The Negro Marches On Company (Black documentary)

1944 *Go Down Death*, Harlemwood Studios (available on videocassette)
Negro Soldier, U.S. War Department (semidocumentary)

1945 *It Happened in Harlem*, All American News
The Negro Sailor, U.S. Navy Department (documentary/propaganda film focusing on the need for racial harmony in order to win the war)

1946 *The Highest Tradition*, Alexander Productions (documentary based on Black involvement in the U.S. Army)

1947 *Ebony Parade*, Astor Pictures (all-Black star cast including Cab Calloway, Count Basie, and Dorothy Dandridge)

1948 *Miracle in Harlem*, Herald Pictures (all Black)

1949 *Mr. Atom's Bomb*, Sepia Film Co.

1950 *Harlem Follies*, Herald Pictures (all Black)

1951 *The Harlem Globetrotters*, Columbia Pictures

1952 *Member of the Wedding*, Columbia Pictures

1953 *Bright Road*, MGM

1954 *Carmen Jones*, Twentieth Century Fox Productions

1955 *Mambo*, Paramount Productions

1956 *The Ten Commandments*, Paramount Pictures

1957 *Meet Me in Vegas*, MGM

1958 *The Defiant Ones*, United Artists Studio

1959 *The Last Angry Man*, Columbia Pictures

1960 *Take a Giant Step*, United Artists

1961 *A Raisin in the Sun*, Columbia Pictures (all Black)

1962 *The Man Who Shot Liberty Valence*, Paramount Pictures

1963 *Gone Are the Days*, Trans Flux

1964 *Nothing But a Man*, Duart Film Laboratories

1965 *A Patch of Blue*, MGM

1966 *The Slender Thread*, Paramount Pictures

1967 *In the Heat of the Night*, United Artists
The Incident, Twentieth Century Fox

1968 *Uptight*, Paramount Pictures (script written by Ruby Dee)

1969 *Death of a Gunfighter*, Universal Studios

1970 *They Call Me Mister Tibbs*, United Artists Studios

1971   *Shaft*, MGM (blaxploitation)
       Sweet Sweetback's Baadasss Song, Yeah Inc. (blaxploitation)

1972   *Lady Sings the Blues*, Paramount Pictures (all Black; available on videocassette)
       Superfly, Warner Brothers (blaxploitation; available on videocassette)

1973   *Black Girl*, Cinerama Releasing (blaxploitation; available on videocassette)

1974   *Uptown Saturday Night*, Warner Brothers (all Black; available on videocassette)

1975   *Mahogany*, Paramount Pictures

1976   *The River Niger*, Columbia Pictures (all Black)

1977   *A Hero Ain't Nothin But a Sandwich*, Radnitz Mattel Productions

1978   *Which Way Is Up*, Universal Studios (blaxploitation; available on videocassette)

1979   *Family Dream*, Universal Studios

1980   *Penitentiary*, Amaa Fanaka Films (Black production, mixed cast; available on videocassette)

1981   *Body and Soul*, Amaa Fanaka Films (available on videocassette)

1982   *Quest for Fire*, Lorimar

1983   *An Officer and a Gentleman*, Paramount Pictures (available on videocassette)

1984   *A Soldier's Story*, Columbia Pictures (all Black; available on videocassette)

1985   *The Color Purple*, Warner Brothers (all Black) (available on videocassette)

1986   *Soul Man*, Orion (available on videocassette)

1987   *In Critical Condition*, Paramount Pictures
       Native Son, Cinecom International (available on videocassette)

A SELECTED VIDEOGRAPHY

Unlike the filmography, the videography is brief and decidedly different in the images it projects. The use of videotapes did not commence until 1956. Playback units perfected in 1959 have only recently become affordable for popular use. Naturally, a large portion of entertainment video reflects what already exists in film and on television, for many of these videos are simply tapes of original shows (see notations in filmography and in film credits). However, a large number of recordings have been prepared for educational services and public television stations. In educational tapings, there seems to have been a concerted effort to avoid old stereotypes. These tapes, listed in the videography, offer a corrective to the negative images in films and on television.

1961   *Othello*, CAROUF

1963   *Malcolm*, CAROUF

1968   *Color Us Black*, IU

1969   *Carpetbag Regimes and 'Negro Rule,'* GPITVL

1970   *Junkie Junior—Life in the South Bronx*, TVC

1971   *Harlem in the Twenties*, EBEC

1972   *Bill Cosby on Prejudice*, PUBTEZ
       Purlie Victorious, MSSTV

1973   *A Slave's Story: Running a Thousand Miles to Freedom*, LCOA

1974   *Dead Ends and New Dreams*, MGHT

1975   *No Vietnamese Ever Called Me Nigger*, CNEMAG

1976   *Black Shadows on Silver Screen*, LVF (studies the Black motion picture industry
       from 1915 to 1950)

1977   *Autobiography of Miss Jane Dubois*, HERTZ
       The Old African Blasphemer, TIMLIF

1978   *El-Hajj Malik El-Shabazz*, MGHT

1979   *Dance to the Music*, GPITVL

1980   *The Black Athelete*, PFP
       Black Girl, UCEM

1981   *Martin Luther King, Jr.*, JOU

1982   *The Cotton Club*, BCNFL
       Oscar Micheaux Film Pioneer, BCNFL

1983   *New Image for Black Women*, PBS

1984   *Electric Boogie*, FLMLIB

1985   *Marcus Garvey—Toward Black Nationhood*, FOTH

1986   *Eyes on the Prize*, PBS
       Toni Morrison, PERSPF

BLACK-OWNED TELEVISION STATIONS

KONG-TV, 660 Sacramento Avenue, Suite 330, San Francisco, CA 94111.
KSTS-TV, 2349 Bering Drive, San Jose, CA 95131.
WFTY-TV, 6507 Chillum Place, NW, Washington, DC 20012.
WHCT-TV, 555 Asylum Street, Hartford, CT 96105.
WHMM-TV (PBS), Howard University, 2600 4th Street, Washington, DC 20059.
WWLG-TV, P.O. Box 340, Macon, GA 31297.
WVII-TV, 41 Farm Road, Bangor, ME 04401.
WGPR-TV, 3140 East Jefferson Street, Detroit, MI 48207.
KXLI-TV, P.O. Box 1776, St. Cloud, MN 56302.
WAOE-TV, P.O. Box 858, South Oneida Avenue, Rhinelander, WI 54501.

BIBLIOGRAPHY

The bulk of published material on the images of Blacks in films and television falls
into two categories, each of which can be subdivided. These are history/criticism and
bibliography/filmography. Information on television is located mainly in periodicals. Film
and motion picture data are contained in both books and journals. Scholarly journals,
popular magazines, and newspapers are listed first; these represent useful sources on
Black images in films and on television. General references, listed next, include books

that provide pertinent background information on stereotyping and prejudice on television and in motion pictures in general. Dissertations and theses are listed following the general references. Black images on television follow; entries on Black images in motion pictures are listed last.

Journals and Newspapers

The following items are Black publications which frequently contain articles on Blacks in film and on television. Other valuable information can be found in journals such as *Film and Filming, Television Weekly*, and *TV Guide*, as well as in major newspapers such as the *New York Times* and *Washington Post*.

Journals (scholarly and popular)

Black Collegian, 1970–.
Black Enterprise, 1970–.
Black Filmmakers Hall of Fame, 1974–. First issue contains programs of the Oscar Micheaux Awards Ceremony.
Black Images, 1972–.
Black Scholar, 1969–.
Black Star Review, 1977–.
Black World, 1962–1976. See also *Negro Digest*.
The Crisis, the official journal of the NAACP, 1910–.
Ebony, 1945–.
Ebony Man, 1986–.
Encore, 1969–.
Essence, 1970–.
Freedomways, 1966–.
Jet, 1951–.
Negro Actors Guild Newsletter, 1940–.
Negro Digest, 1942–. Name changed to *Black World* in May 1970.
Opportunity, journal of the National Urban League, 1923–1949.
Our World, 1946–.
Phylon, 1940–.
Right On, 1971–.
Sepia, 1954–.
Soul, 1950–.

Newspapers

Afro-American, Baltimore, 1892–.
Bilalian News, 1977–.
Chicago Defender, 1905–.
Los Angeles Sentinel, 1934–.
Muhammad Speaks, 1961–.
New Pittsburgh Courier, 1910–.
New York Amsterdam News, 1909–.

General References

Allport, Gordon. *The Nature of Prejudice*. Reading, Mass.: Addison-Wesley, 1954.

Archer, Leonard C. *Black Images in the American Theatre*. New York: Pageant-Poseidon, 1973. Includes NAACP protest campaigns against stage, screen, and television industries.

Batty, Linda. *Retrospective Index to Film Periodicals, 1930–1971*. New York: Bowker, 1975.

Blumer, Herbert. *Movies and Conduct*. New York: Macmillan Co., 1933.

Brown, Sterling. "A Century of Negro Portraiture in American Literature." *The Massachusetts Review* 7 (Winter 1966):73–96.

Charters, W. W. *Motion Pictures and Youth: A Summary*. New York: Macmillan Co., 1933.

Consumer Report. Mt. Vernon, N.Y.: Consumers Union, Inc., 1987.

Doane, Mary Ann. *The Desire to Desire*. Bloomington: Indiana University Press, 1987. The woman's film of the 1940s.

Ellis, Ethel. *The American Negro: Selected Checklist of Books*. Washington, D.C.: Howard University Press, 1968.

Film-TV Daily Yearbook of Motion Pictures. v. 1-, 1915–1970. Basic tool on film history; contains reviews.

Foreman, Henry. *Our Movie Made Children*. New York: Macmillan, 1933.

Friedman, Norman L. "Theory Number Two: Studying Film Impact on American Conduct and Cultures." *Journal of Popular Film* 3 (1974): 173–81.

Gilman, Sander L. *Difference and Pathology*. Ithaca, N.Y.: Cornell University Press, 1986. Examines stereotypes of sexuality, race, and madness in literature, fine arts, popular culture, film, and science.

Gottesman, Ronald, and Harry Geduld. *Guidebook to Film*. New York: Holt, Rinehart & Winston, 1972.

Heath, Stephen. *Questions of Cinema*. Bloomington: Indiana University Press, 1981.

Hillier, Jim, ed. *The 1950s: Neo-Realism, Hollywood, New Wave*. Cambridge, Mass.: Harvard University Press, 1985.

————. *The 1960s: New Wave, New Cinema, Reevaluating Hollywood*. Cambridge, Mass.: Harvard University Press, 1986. An anthology of film criticism.

Hull, Gloria T., Patricia Bell Scott, and Barbara Smith, eds. *All the Women Are White, All the Blacks Are Men, but Some of Us Are Brave*. Old Westbury, N.Y.: The Feminist Press, 1982.

Jacobs, Lewis. *The Rise of the American Film*. New York: Teachers College Press, 1967.

Kawin, Bruce F., ed. *Faulkner's MGM Screenplays*. Knoxville: University of Tennessee Press, 1986.

Lauretis, Teresa. *Alice Doesn't*. Bloomington: Indiana University Press, 1984. Deals with feminism, semiotics, and cinema.

The Library of Congress Catalog—Motion Pictures and Filmstrips. Published as part of the *National Union Catalog*. New York: Rowman & Littlefield, 1972.

Lindenmeyer, Otto. *Black History: Lost, Stolen, or Strayed*. New York: Avon, 1970.

Lippmann, Walter, "Stereotypes." *Thought and Statement*. Eds. William Leary and James Smith. New York: Harcourt, Brace, and World, 1960. 228–36.

Madsen, Roy Paul. *The Impact of Film: How Ideas Are Communicated through Cinema and Television*. New York: Macmillan, 1973.

Manchel, Frank. *Film Study: A Resource Guide*. Crainbury, N.J.: Fairleigh Dickinson University Press, 1973.

Mast, Gerald. *A Short History of the Movies*. New York: Bobbs-Merrill, 1976.

Media Review Digest. Ed. Elinor Schwartz. Ann Arbor, Mich.: Pierian Press, 1979. A complete guide to reviews of nonbook media.

Metz, Christian. *The Imaginary Signifier*. Bloomington: Indiana University Press, 1982. Psychoanalysis and the cinema.

Oshana, Maryann. *Women of Color: A Filmography of Minority and Third World Women*. New York: Garland Publishers, 1987.

Peterson, Ruth, and L. I. Thurstone. *Motion Pictures and Social Attitudes of Children*. New York: Macmillan, 1933.

Readers' Guide to Periodical Literature. New York: H. W. Wilson Co., 1900–. Films listed in 1905–1909 volume under "Moving Pictures."

Rehraver, George. *Cinema Booklist*. Metuchen, N.J.: Scarecrow Press, 1972.

Sadoul, Georges. *Dictionary of Films*. Berkeley, Calif.: University of California Press, 1972. Discussion of 1,200 films, gives a list of credits and plot summaries.

Samples, Gordon. *How to Locate Reviews of Plays and Films*. A bibliography of criticism from the beginnings to 1975. Metuchen, N.J.: Scarecrow Press, 1976.

Sarris, Andrew. *The American Cinema: Directors and Directions, 1929–1968*. New York: Dutton, 1968.

Schechter, William. *The History of Negro Humor in America*. New York: Free Press, 1970.

Scheyer, Steven H. *Movies on TV*. New York: Bantam Books, 1958.

Shuttleworth, Frank, and Mary May. *The Social Conduct and Attitude of Movie Fans*. New York: Macmillan, 1933. New York: Arno Press, 1970.

U.S. Copyright Office. *Motion Pictures, 1894–*. Washington, D.C.: U.S. Government Printing Office, 1951–1960.

U.S. National Advisory Commission on Civil Disorders. *Kerner Report*. New York: Dutton, 1968.

Woll, Allen L., and Randall M. Miller. *Ethnic and Racial Images in American Film and Television*. New York: Garland Publishers, 1987. A collection of historical essays and bibliography.

Theses and Dissertations

Bloom, Samuel W. "A Psychological Study of Motion Picture Audience Behavior: A Case Study of the Negro Image in Mass Communication." Ph.D. diss., University of Wisconsin, 1956.

Bowmani, Kwame N. "Black Television and Domestic Colonialism." Ph.D. diss., Stanford University, 1977.

Brenner, William M. "Comparative Analysis of Black and White Student Attitudes toward Television." Master's thesis, Ohio State University, 1971.

Buchanan, Singer. "A Study of the Attitudes of the Writers of the Negro Press toward the Depiction of the Negro in Plays and Films 1930–1965." Ph.D diss., University of Michigan, 1968.

Burke, William Lee. "The Presentation of the American Negro in Hollywood Films, 1945–1961." Ph.D. diss., Northwestern University, 1965.

Chaudhuri, Arun K. "A Study of the Negro Problem in Motion Pictures." Master's thesis, University of Southern California, 1951.

Clift, Charles E. "The WLBT-TV Case, 1964–1969: An Historical Analysis." Ph.D. diss., Indiana University, 1976.

Colle, Royal D. "The Negro Image and the Mass Media." Ph.D. diss., Cornell University, 1967.

Cosby, William H., Jr. "An Integration of the Visual Media Via 'Fat Albert and the Cosby Kids' into the Elementary School Curriculum as a Teaching Aid and Vehicle to Achieve Increased Learning." Ph.D. diss., University of Massachusetts, 1976.

Deneroff, Harvey. "A Historical Study of Early American Film Criticism, 1907–1915." Master's thesis, University of Southern California, 1968.

Dimas, Chris. "The Effect of Motion Pictures Portraying Black Models on the Self-Concept of Black Elementary School Children." Ph.D. diss., Syracuse University, 1970.

Ferguson, Gloria. "From 'Amos 'n' Andy' to 'Sanford & Son': An Historical Survey and Criticial Analysis of the Chacteristics and Images of Blacks on American Network Television and Drama." Master's thesis, University of Southern California, 1975.

Ferrow, Donald L. "The Treatment of Social Problems in the Entertainment Film." Master's thesis, University of Southern California, 1952.

Goldberg, Albert L. "The Effects of Two Types of Sound Motion Pictures on Attitudes of Adults toward Minority Groups." Ph.D. diss., Indiana University, 1956.

Hutchins, Charles. "A Critical Evaluation of the Controversies Engendered by D. W. Griffith's *The Birth of a Nation*." Master's thesis, University of Iowa, 1961.

Jackson, Harold. "From 'Amos 'n' Andy' to 'I Spy': A Chronology of Blacks in Prime Time Television Programming, 1950–1964." Ph.D. diss., University of Michigan, 1982.

Jewell, Karen Sue Warren. "An Analysis of the Visual Development of a Stereotype: The Media's Portrayal of Mammy and Aunt Jemima as Symbols of Black Womanhood." Ph.D. diss., Ohio State University, 1976.

Kurimi, Amir Massoud. "Toward a Definition of the American Film Noir: 1941–1949." Ph.D. diss., University of Southern California, 1970.

Mapp, Edward C. "The Portrayal of the Negro in American Motion Pictures 1962–1968." Ph.D. diss., New York University, 1970.

Merritt, Russell. "The Impact of D. W. Griffith's Motion Pictures from 1908 to 1914 on Contemporary American Culture." Ph.D. diss., Harvard University, 1970.

Moore, Douglas Cameron. "A Study in the Influence of the Film, *The Birth of a Nation* on the Attitudes of Selected High School White Students toward Negroes." Ph.D. diss., University of Colorado, 1971.

Nesteby, James R. "The Tarzan Series of Edgar Rice Borrough's Lost Races and Racism in American Popular Culture." Ph.D. diss., Bowling Green State University, 1978.

Poe, Lillian A. "Elder Lightfoot Solomon Micheaux: His Social and Political Interests and Influence." Ph.D. diss., College of William and Mary, 1975.

Schlosser, Arnold. "Paul Robeson: His Career in the Theatre, in Motion Pictures, and on the Concert Stage." Ph.D. diss., New York University, 1970.

Solomon, Paul J. "A Laboratory Experiment to Assess the Aspect of Black Models in Television Advertising." Ph.D. diss., Arizona State University, 1974.

Stillwell, Robert R. "A Study of the Effects of Motion Pictures on the Attitudes of Seventh Grade Students." Master's thesis, Ohio State University, 1939.

Television

Alexander, H. B. "Negro Opinion Regarding 'Amos 'n' Andy.' " *Sociological and Social Research* (March 1932): 345–54.
Allen, Steve. "Talent is Color-Blind." *Ebony* 10 (September 1955): 49.
"B.A.D.C. Organization Combats Negative Images of Blacks in TV and Movies." *Los Angeles Sentinel* December 16, 1982: A–1.
Barbara, R. "James Earl Jones Comes to TV." *TV Guide* (October 12, 1974): 12–17.
"Benny and Rochester; TV's Hottest Team." *Our World* (August 1955):51–55.
Benny, Jack. "My 24 Years with Rochester." *Sepia* (March 1962):34–37.
" 'Beulah Land' Happy Slave TV Movie Attacked in Hollywood." *Jet* 58 (April 3, 1980):56.
" 'Beulah Land' Postponed." *Washington Post*, April 12, 1980: B4.
" 'Beulah Land' Review." (Robertson Column) *Los Angeles Sentinel*, August 29, 1980: A3.
"Black Comedians on TV." (Editorial) *Afro-American*, Baltimore, October 8, 1977: I4.
"Black Television, Its Problems & Promises; Programming for and by Blacks Faces Uphill Struggle." *Ebony* 24 (May 1969):88.
"Black TV Directors." *Sepia* (May 1971): 28–32.
Bond, Jean Carey. " 'Flip Wilson,' 'The Mod Squad,' 'Mission Impossible': Is This What It's Really Like to Be Black?" *Redbook* (February 1972):82–83, 127–32.
Brown, Les. "ABC Took a Gamble with 'Roots' and Is Hitting Pay Out." *New York Times*, January 28, 1977: 2–1.
———. " 'Good Times' Will Drop Male Parent; Black Media Coalition Protest Move."*New York Times*, June 7, 1978:18.
——— " 'Roots' Success in South Seen as Sign of Change." *New York Times*, February 10, 1955:15.
Brown, M. D. "Cable TV and the Black Community." *Black Politician* (April 1971):4.
Buck, Jerry. "Making TV History: Viewers Pulled in by 'Roots.' " *Los Angeles Times*, January 29, 1977:2–4.
Bush, R. F, and others. "There Are More Blacks in TV Commercials." (Bibliography). *Journal of Advertising Research* (February 1977):21–25.
Chisolm, Earle. "Minorities & TV Viewers' Surveys." *Bilalian News*, July 6, 1979: 24.
Clark, Cedric. "Television and Social Controls: Some Observations on the Portrayals of Ethnic Minorities." *Television Quarterly* (Spring 1969): 18–22.
Colle, Royal D. "Negro Image in the Mass Media Market: A Case Study in Social Change." *Journalism Quarterly* (Spring 1968):55–60.
Comstock, G. "Television and the Children of Ethnic Minorities." *Journal of Communication* 29 (Winter 1979): 104–15.
Cripps, Thomas. "Noble Black Savage: A Problem in the Politics of Television Art." *Journal of Popular Culture* (Spring 1975):687–95.
Dalron, Fik. "Why Television Is a Wasteland for Negroes." *Negro Digest* (June 1963): 27–30.
Darden, B. J., and J. A. Bayton. "Self-Concept and Blacks' Assessment of Black Leading

Roles in Motion Pictures and Television." *Journal of Applied Psychology* 62 (October 1977):620–23.

Douglas, Pamela. "Black Television: Avenues of Power." *Black Scholar* 5 (September 1973): 23–31.

Douglas, Robert L. "Black Males and Television: New Images versus Old Stereotypes."*The Western Journal of Black Studies* 11 (Summer 1987): 69–73.

Dowling, E. "Color Us Black; Failure of Commercial TV to Report Adequately on Race Relations and Ghetto Problems." *New Republic* 8 (June 1968): 41–43.

Epstein, B. R. "Stereotypes." *Community* (September 1961): 9–10.

"Esther Rolle Discusses 'Good Times' Role." *Afro-American*, Baltimore, May 27, 1978, I–8.

"Federal Communication Commision Orders More Blacks." *Soul* (May 10, 1971): 14.

Fee, Debi. "Brian Mitchell of 'Trapper John.' " *Right On* (May 1982):52; (January 1983): 24–25.

———. "Mr. T.: The Gentle Giant." *Right On* (August 1982): 58–59.

———. "Nell Carter: She Deserves a Break Today." *Right On* (October 1982): 24–25.

Ferdinand, Val. "Taking the Weight: TV Broadcasting of News." (Max Robinson) *Black Collegian* (November-December 1978): 56–57ff.

Fife, Marilyn D. "Black Image in American TV: The First Two Decades." *Black Scholar* (November 1974): 7–15.

Fine, Marilyn G. "Dialectual Features of Black Characters in Situation Comedies on Television." *Phylon* (December 1980): 396–409.

Forbes, C. "From These Roots; the Real Significance of Haley's Phenomenon." *Christianity Today* (May 6, 1977): 19–21.

Fraser, Gerald C. "Blacks and Whites Found to Have Misapprehensions on Impact of 'Roots.' " *New York Times* June 7, 1977: 71.

Gates, Henry Lewis. "Portraits in Black: From 'Amos 'n' Andy' to 'Coonskin.' " *Harper's* 252 (June 1976): 16–19ff.

Gehman, R. "The Negro in Television." *TV Guide* (June 20, 1964): 15–23; (June 27, 1964): 15–22.

Gelman, Steve. "Robert Guillaume." *TV Guide* (September 15, 1979): 26.

Gray, Oliver. "Black Politics and Cable TV: Problems & Possibilities." *Black World* 23 (December 1973): 43–48, 68–74.

Greenberg, P. "Georg Stanford Brown of 'The Rookies.' " *TV Guide* (May 4, 1974):21–26.

Greenfield, M. "Uncle Tom's Roots." *Newsweek* (February 14,1977): 100.

Gupta, Udayan. "Black Television Station Owners; How They Did It." *Black Enterprise* (February 1980): 106–11.

Haggerty, Sandra. "TV and Black Womanhood." *Los Angeles Times*, November 6, 1974: 4–1.

Hay, Samuel A. "Roots—A Corrected Image." *Media & Methods* (April 1977): 16–18.

Hays, Scott. "Look What Happened to the Stars of Roots." *TV Guide* 34 (November 29, 1986):10–14.

Hill, George. *Black Media in America: A Resource Guide & Bibliography*. Los Angeles, Calif. R & E Associates, 1983.

———. *Ebony Images: Black Americans and Television*. Carson, Calif.: Daystar Publications, 1985.

Hill, George H., and Sylvia Hill. *Blacks on Television*. Metuchen, N.J.: Scarecrow Press, 1985.

Hinton, J. L. "Tokenism and Improving Imagery of Blacks in TV Drama and Comedy, 1973."*Journal of Broadcasting* (Fall 1974): 423–32.

Hobson, Sheila Smith. "The Rise and Fall of Blacks in Serious Television." *Freedomways* (Third Quarter 1974): 185–99.

Holly, Ellen. "Role of Media in the Programming of an Underclass." *Black Scholar* 10 (January 1979): 31–37.

Holsendolph, E. "Coloring the Image of Public Television." *Black Enterprise* (March 1979): 13.

Jacob, John. "TV Accused of Perpetuating Stereotypes." *Washington Post*, August 16, 1977: 27.

"James Earl Jones: Race Is Still the Important Thing."*Sepia* (January 1971): 16–20.

Jones, Marquita. "Racism in Television." *Black World* 20 (March 1971): 72–78.

"Julian Dixon, California Congressman, Blasts Images of Blacks on TV."*Jet* (December 20, 1979): 59.

"Julian Dixon Column on TV Programming and Blacks." *Los Angeles Sentinel*, November 8, 1979: A–8.

Kirk, Cynthia. "Black TV Shows Are Still Programmed for Whites." *Soul* (May 26, 1975): 6–10.

———. "The Screen Goes to Black as TV Opens Its Eyes."*Soul* (April 29, 1974): 22–24.

Kisner, Ronald. "Blacks Get Bigger Roles This TV Season."*Jet* (September 22, 1977):58–61.

Koiner, Richard. "Black Image on TV: Good or Bad?" *Los Angeles Herald Dispatch*, Part I, November 14, 1980:4; Part II, November 21, 1980:4.

Lane, Bill. " 'Roots I' vs. 'Roots II.' " *Sepia* (May 1979):18–30.

———. "TV and Publishing Industries and Blacks." *Afro-American*, Baltimore, May 10, 1980:11.

Lemon, Judith. "Women and Blacks on Prime Time Television." *Journal of Communication* 27 (Autumn 1977):70–79.

Lemon, Richard. "Black Is the Color of TV's Newest Stars." *Saturday Evening Post* (November 30, 1968):44.

Levin, Eric. "Television Takes to the Street." *TV Guide* (December 28, 1974):12–13.

———. "Under New Management (TV Station WLBT in Mississippi Emphasizes Black Programs, Management)." *TV Guide* (April 5, 1975):3ff.

Levine, Richard M. "Why Unconscious Racism Persists." *TV Guide* (July 18, 1981):2–6; July 25, 1981:26–32.

Lewis, R. W. "The Importance of Being Julia." *TV Guide* (December 14, 1968):24–28.

"Linda Avery Discusses Blacks and Minorities in TV Industry." *Michigan Chronicle*, July 11, 1981:A–3.

Lloyd, R. G. " 'Roots,' The Book; The TV Version; The Message."*Negro Education Review* (April 1977):58–62.

Lucas, Bob. "Blacks on TV." *Jet* (March 6, 1980):54–56.

———. "New Faces, New Shows and Old Racism Mark New Television Season." *Jet* (October 23, 1975): 55–57.

———. "Pam: Why Are Black Women Fading from Films?" *Jet* (November 6, 1980): 58–61.

MacDonald, J. Fred. "Black Perimeters—Paul Robeson, Nat King Cole and the Role of Blacks in American TV." *Journal of Popular Film and Television* 3 (1979): 246–64.

———. *Blacks in White TV*. Chicago: Nelson-Hall, 1983.

McGhee-Jordan, Kathleen. "View from Within: Television as a Profession." *Encore* (May 17, 1978): 48.

Maloney, M. "Black Is the Color of Our New TV." In *Television: A Selection of Readings from TV Guide*. Ed. Barry Cole. New York: Free Press, 1970:255–58.

Mason, Clifford. "Can Negroes Jingle TV's Jangles?" *New York Times* Arts and Leisure Section, December 10, 1967:25.

Merritt, Carole. "Looking at Afro-American 'Roots.' " *Phylon* (June 1977): 211–12.

"Minority Employment in TV Field Survey." *New York Amsterdam News*, February 12, 1977: D–5.

Morris, Allen. "One Hundred Years of Negro Entertainment." *Ebony* (September 1963): 122–24.

Morton, C. A. "Public Service for Black Viewers, Some Other Choices Besides Off/On." *Black Enterprise* (August 1979):49.

Moses, K. "Black Image on Television: Who Controls It?" *Black Enterprise* (September 1979):33–36ff.

"Negroes and Television." *Sepia* (April 1976):5.

"Newest Black Women Who Have Won TV and Movie Roles." (Ronalda Douglas, Darcel Wynne, Lydia Nicole, Claudette Wells, Diane Day, Rose Dursy) *Ebony* 38 (April 1983): 63–66.

Nolan, Tom. "Says Nell Carter . . . 'There Was a Time I Didn't Like Nell.' " *TV Guide* (August 21, 1982):17–20.

Obatala, J. K. "Blacks on TV: A Replay of 'Amos 'n' Andy?' " *Los Angeles Times*, November 26, 1974:5–5.

"Passing of 'Beulah.' " *Our World* (February 1953):12–15.

"Pastore Bill Restricts Black TV Ownership." *Soul* (November 17, 1979):18.

Peters, Art. "What the Negro Wants from TV." In *Television: A Selection of Readings from TV Guide*. Ed. Barry Cole. New York: Free Press, 1970: 259–64.

Phillips, J. "Distortions of 'Roots' on Television Are Inflammatory." *TV Guide* (February 19, 1977: A–6.

Pierce, C. M. "Experiments in Racism: TV Commercials." *Education and Urban Society* 10 (November 1977):61–87.

Pitts, Leonard. "Norman Lear and the Black TV Image." *Soul* (June 5, 1978): 20–22.

———. "Stalking the Elusive Perfect Black Image." *Soul* (July 3, 1978):19.

Pollard, Gayle. "From Amos 'n' Andy to Bill Cosby." *Boston Globe*, October 29, 1981: C–4.

"The Portrayal of Minorities and Women on Television Hasn't Improved in Recent Years and Neither Has Their Employment in the Industry the U.S. Civil Rights Commission Reported." *Wall Street Journal*, January 16, 1979: 34.

Reed, Claude. "Film and TV: Blacks Still in the Background." *National Scene Supplement* January 1983:14–17.

Reid, Pamela Trotman. "Racial Stereotypes on Television: A Comparison of Both Black and White Television Characters." *Journal of Applied Psychology* 64 (October 1979):465–71.

Roberts, C. "The Presentations of Blacks in Television Network Newscasts." *Journalism Quarterly* (Spring 1955):50–55.

Roberts, Churchill. "The Portrayal of Blacks on Network Television on Programs and in Commercial Advertisements over American Television." *Journal of Broadcasting* (Winter 1970–71):45–53.

Robinson, Eugene. "Happy Negroes Make a Comeback: Critique of the Treatment of Blacks in TV Programs." *New West* 16 (July 1979):72.

Rowe, Billy. "Eyeing 'Amos 'n' Andy.' " *The Pittsburgh Courier*, July 7, 1951:21.

———. "TV Bias against Blacks." *New York Amsterdam News*, March 29, 1980:20.

Sampson, C. A. "Black Image; the More It Changes, the More It Remains the Same." *Encore* (May 1980):40–42.

Scotch, Norman A. "The Vanishing Villains of TV." *Phylon* (Spring 1960):58–62.

See, C. "Diahann Carroll's Image." *TV Guide* (March 14, 1970):26–30.

Seggar, J. F. "Television's Portrayal of Minorities and Women, 1971–1975." *Journal of Broadcasting* 2 (Fall 1977):435–46.

Shankman, Arnold. "Black Pride and Protest; the Amos 'n' Andy Crusade." *Journal of Popular Culture* 12 (Fall 1978):236–52.

Shaynon, Robert L. " 'Julia' Breakthrough or Letdown." *Saturday Review* (April 20, 1968):49.

———. "Living Color on TV—Part 2." *Saturday Review* 46 (February 9, 1963):57.

Signoreielli, Nancy, ed. *Role Portrayal and Stereotyping on Television*. Westport, Conn.: Greenwood Press, 1986.

Slater, Jack. "Does TV Have a Secret Formula for Blacks?" *Ebony* 35 (January 1980): 104.

Small, William J. *To Kill a Messenger: Television News and the Real World*. New York: Hastings House, 1970.

Spiegelman, Judy. "More Black Shows, More Blacks Working." *Soul* (October 5, 1970):4–6.

"Stereotyped Black TV Roles Discussed." *Chicago Defender*, December 17, 1977:A–10.

Stevens, John D. "Reflections in a Dark Mirror." *Journal of Popular Culture* 10 (Summer 1976):239–44.

Stewart, Gail. "Black Comedy TV Shows Replacing Shoe Shine Boy." *Soul* (February 16, 1976: 6–7.

Stewart, Ted. "Blacks and Television." *Sepia* (February 1979):82.

———. "Negroes and Television." *Sepia* (November 1975):82.

———. "What's Happening to Black TV Stars." *Sepia* (October 1974):36ff.

Stoehr, Chris. "Where Have All the Black Series Gone." *Detroit Free Press*, August 20, 1978:1.

"Study Shows Portrayal of Women on TV." *Bilalian News*, September 23, 1977:31.

Sullivan, E. "Can TV Crack America's Color Line?" *Ebony* (May 1951):58–62ff.

Sutton, C. "Blacks Fight TV Censoring." *Black Enterprise* 13 (March 1983):25–26.

Tait, E. V. "Women Behind the Television." *Essence* (June 1979):37–38.

Tan, A. S. "Television Use and Self-Esteem of Blacks." *Journal of Communication* 29 (Winter 1979):129–35.

"TV Discovers the Black Man; Afro-Americans Make Mass Debut on Network Shows."
    Ebony 24 (February 1969):27.
"TV: It's Not a Negro Medium." *Sponsor* 5 (July 1967):52–55.
"TV Medium and Black Family Conference." *Michigan Chronicle*, June 14, 1980:B–
    4.
"TV News 'Blacks and Women Cyclops.' " *Life* June 30, 1972:20.
"TV Portrayal of Blacks." *New York Amsterdam News*, April 21, 1979:37.
"TV Rated First in Care about Blacks; The Harris Survey." *Washington Post*, August
    30, 1971:A–3.
"TV Versus Black Survival." *Black World* 23 (December 1973):30–42.
Webster, Ivan. "Three Black TV Pilots Stay a Ground." *Encore* (July 1979):4–41.
" 'What's Happening!' ABC's Popular Teen-Age Sitcom Succeeds in Spite of Itself."
    Ebony (June 1978):74–82.
White, A. "From Tom-Toms to Television." *Our World* (February 1951):30–38.
"Will New TV Series about a Negro Open Eyes of Some Whites?" *Wall Street Journal*,
    April 18, 1968:1.
Wolcott, James. "Black Perspectives on the News." *Village Voice* October 24,1977:51.
Wood, B. "Black Women in Television News." *Essence* (July 1972):3, 31.
Yette, Samuel. "Image of Blacks on TV." *Baltimore Afro-American*, August 27, 1977:I–
    5.
Young, A. S. "Blacks and Cable TV." *Los Angeles Sentinel*, May 8, 1980:A–7.

Film

Abdul, Raoul. *Famous Black Entertainers of Today*. New York: Dodd, 1973.
    Discusses Black stars who have ostensibly destroyed the old stereotypes of Black
    people.
Adler, Renata. "The Negro That Movies Overlook." *New York Times*, March 22,
    1968:D–1.
Archer, Leonard C. "Black Images on the Silver Screen." In *Black Images in the
    American Theatre*. New York: Pageant Poseidon, 1973. 183–225.
Asendio, James. "History of Negro Motion Pictures." *International Photographer* (Jan-
    uary 1940):16–17.
Baldwin, James. "Carmen Jones: The Dark Is Light Enough." In *Notes of a Native Son*.
    New York: Dial, 1964:107–12.
———. "Life Straight in de Eye." *Commentary* 16 (January 1955):456–63.
Barrett, C. A. "Role of the Press, Radio, and Motion Picture and Negro Morale."
    Journal of Negro Education 22 (July 1943):474–89.
Bart, Peter. "The Still Invisible Man." *New York Times* July 19, 1966: D–21.
    NAACP issue of the accurate portrayal of Black life in the movies and on television
    is discussed.
Bennett, Lerone. "Sweetback in Wonderland." *Ebony* 26 (September 1971):106–18.
Bixler, P. "Uncle Tom Walks Again." *Antioch Review* 1 (September 1941):368–75.
"The Black Man as Movie Hero: New Film Offers a Different Male Image." *Ebony* 27
    (August 1977):144–48.
"The Black Screen Image: Where Is It Going in the Seventies?" *Soul Illustrated* 2 (3
    November 1970):18–20.
"The Black Woman as a Sex Image in Films." *Black Stars* 2 (December 1971):32–39.

"Black Women Image Makers." *Black World* 23 (August 1974):24–33.

"Blacks in Selected Films." *The Ebony Handbook*. Chicago: Johnson Publishing Co., 1974. 449–57.

Bloomfield, Maxwell. "Dixon's the Leopard's Spots: A Study in Popular Racism." *American Quarterly* 16 (Fall 1964):387–401.

Blumen, Herbert. *Movies and Conduct*. New York: Macmillan, 1933.

Bogle, Donald. *Brown Sugar: Eighty Years of America's Black Female Superstars*. New York: Harmony Books, 1980.

——. *Toms, Coons, Mulattoes, Mammies, and Bucks: An Interpretive History of Blacks in American Films*. New York: Viking Press, 1973.

——. "Transcending Racist Trash: A Legacy of the First Black Movie Stars." *Saturday Review of the Arts* 1, 2 (February 3, 1973):25–29.

Bourne, St. Clair. "The Development of the Contemporary Black Film Movement." In *Black Cinema Aesthetics*. Eds. V. Rose and Y. Gladstone. Athens: Ohio University Center for Afro-American Studies, 1982. 53–67.

Bowser, Pearl. "Sexual Imagery and the Black Woman in Cinema." In *Black Cinema Aesthetics*. Eds. V. Rose and Y. Gladstone. Athens: Ohio University Press, 1982. 42–53.

Brown, Roscoe C. "Film as a Tool for Liberation." *Black Creation* (Winter 1973):36–37.

Brown, Sterling. "Imitation of Life: Once a Pancake." *Opportunity* 13 (March 1935):87–88.

Burke, Virginia. "Mammy Didn't Mean No Harm; Little Black Sambo." *Language Arts* 53 (March 1976):272–75.

Canby, Vincent. "The Movies That Still Haunt Hollywood." *The New York Times*, January 26, 1969:D–22.

Carter, Elmer Anderson. "Of Negro Motion Pictures." *Close Up* (August 1929):119.

Carter, Everett. "Cultural History Written with Lightening: The Significance of *The Birth of a Nation*." *American Quarterly* 12 (Fall 1960):347–57.

Cartwright, Wesley. "Motion Pictures of Negroes." Microfilm. Carnegie Study. New York: Schomburg Collection, New York Public Library, 1940.

Chaudhuri, Arunk. *Black Projections: The History of the Black American Film*. Englewood Cliffs, N.J.: Prentice-Hall, 1973.

Covington, Floyd C. "The Negro Invades Hollywood." *Opportunity* 11 (April 1929):113–14.

Cripps, Thomas. "The Death of Rastus: The Negro in American Films Since 1945." *Phylon* 28 (Fall 1967):267–75.

——. "The Myth of the Southern Box Office: A Factor in Racial Stereotyping in American Movies, 1920–1940." *The Black Experience in America; Selected Essays*. Ed. James Curtis and Lewis Gould. Austin: University of Texas Press, 1970. 116–44.

——. "New Black Cinema and Uses of the Past." In *Black Cinema Aesthetics*. Eds. V. Rose and Y. Gladstone. Athens: Ohio University Press, 1982. 19–27.

——. *Slow Fade to Black: The Negro in American Films, 1900–1942*. New York: Oxford University Press, 1977.

——. *Black Film as Genre*. Bloomington: Indiana University Press, 1979.

——. "Negroes in Movies: Some Reconsiderations." *American Literature Forum*, 2, 1 (Spring 1968):6–7.

Darden, Betty, and James Bayton. "Self-Concept and Blacks' Assessment of Black Leading Roles in Motion Pictures and Television." *Journal of Applied Psychology* 62 (October 1977):620–23.

Davis, George. "Black Motion Pictures: The Past." *New York Amsterdam News*, Black Academy of Arts and Letters Supplement, September 18, 1971:D–13, D–14.

"The Death of Rastus: Negroes in American Films Since 1945." *Phylon* 28 (Fall 1967):267–75.

Dent, Tom. "The Negro in Recent Films: Reality or Illusion?" *Rights and Reviews* 2, 1 (Winter 1965):19–21.

Dismond, Geraldyn. "The Negro Actor and the American Movies." *Close Up* 5, 2 (August 1929):91.

Dister, P. A. "Exit the Racial Comics." *Educational Theater Journal* 18 (October 1966):247–54.

Draper, Arthur. "Uncle Tom Will You Never Die?" *New Theatre* (January 1936):10–17.

Ellison, Ralph. "The Shadow and the Act." In *Shadow and Act*. New York: Random House, 1949.

———. "Stormy Weather." *New Masses* 37 (September 24, 1940):20–21.

"Encore Document: Black Stereotypes." *Encore* (July 1973):37–46.

"The Expanding World of Black Film"; "A Studio Count of Black Films, 1967–72"; "Ten Most Important Black Films between 1962 and 1972"; and "Film as a Tool for Liberation?" *Black Creation* 4 (Winter 1973):25–43.

Fleming, T. "Real Uncle Tom." *Reader's Digest* 106 (March 1975):124–28.

Franklin, John Hope. "Birth of a Nation—Propaganda as History." *Massachusetts Review* 20 (Autumn 1979):217–34.

Gant, Liz. "Ain't Beulah Dead Yet? Or Images of the Black Woman in Film." *Essence* 4,1 (May 1973):60–61, 72–75.

Gebhart, Myrtle. "The Chocolate Comedy." *Extension Magazine* (November 1929):17–18, 42, 44.

Gent, George. "Exit Darkies, Enter Blacks." *The New York Times*, July 3, 1968:71.

Gerima, Haile. "On Independent Black Cinema." In *Black Cinema Aesthetics*. Eds. V. Rose and Y. Gladstone. Athens: Ohio University Press, 1982. 106–15.

"G.I.'s Resent Uncle Tomism on Screen and Radio." *The Pittsburgh Courier*, September 1, 1945:15.

Gittens, Tony. "Cultural Restitution and Independent Black Cinema." In *Black Cinema Aesthetics*. Eds. V. Rose and Y. Gladstone. Athens: Ohio University Press, 1982. 115–19.

Golden, Herb. "The Negro and Yiddish Film Boom." *Variety*, January 3, 1940:10–14.

Gulliver, Adelaide C., ed. *Black Images in Films: Stereotyping and Self-Perception as Viewed by Black Actresses*. Boston, Mass.: Boston Universiity Afro-American Studies Program, 1974.

Gunther, Lenworth. "Can Blacks Escape . . . American Stereotypes?" *Encore* 2 (July 1973):39–46.

Hall, Susan. "African Women on Film." *Africa Report* 22, 1 (January-February 1977):15–17.

Hampton, Benjamin. *History of the American Film Industry*. New York: Dover, 1970.

Harmon, Sidney. "How Hollywood Is Smashing the Color Bar." *Films & Filming* 5 (March 1959):7ff.

Harrison, William. "The Negro and the Cinema." *Sight & Sound* (London) (Spring 1939):16–22.

Hill, Herman. "Stereotype Roles Cause of Dispute in Film Industry." *The Pittsburgh Courier*, March 9, 1946:19.

Holly, Ellen. "Where Are the Films about Real Black Men and Women?" *Freedomways* (First Quarter 1974):270–73.

Howard, V. "How to Skin a Coon." *Twentieth Century* 160 (July 1956):26–34.

Hudson, Benjamin. "Another View of Uncle Tom." *Phylon* 24 (Spring 1963):51–61.

Hughes, Langston. "Is Hollywood Fair to Negroes?" *Negro Digest* 1 (April 1943):19–21.

Hughes, Langston, and Milton Meltzer. *Black Magic: A Pictorial History of the Negro in American Entertainment*. Englewood Cliffs, N.J.: Methusen, 1967.

Hyatt, Marshall. *The Afro-American Cinematic Experience, an Annotated Bibliography and Filmography*. Wilmington, Del.: Scholarly Resources, 1983.

Jerome, V. J. *The Negro in Hollywood Films*. New York: Masses & Mainstream, 1950.

Johnson, Albert. "Beige, Brown, or Black." *Film Quarterly* 13 (Fall 1959):38–43.

———. "The Negro in American Films: Some Recent Work." *Film Quarterly* 18 (Summer 1965):14–30.

Jordan, Vernon. "How Hollywood Degrades Blacks." *New York Amsterdam News*, October 14, 1972:D–1.

Kael, Pauline. "Notes on Black Movies." *New Yorker* 47 (December 2, 1972):43–54.

Kagan, Norman. "Black American Cinema." *Cinema* 6 (Fall 1970):2–3.

———. "A Primer Black American Cinema." *Cinema* 6 (Fall 1970):2–7.

Kaiser, Ernest. "Black Images in the Mass Media: A Bibliography." *Freedomways* (Third Quarter 1974):274–87.

Killens, John O. "Hollywood in Black and White." *The Nation*, September 20, 1965:157–60.

Kisner, Ronald E. "What Films Are Doing to the Image of Black Women." *Jet* (June 29, 1972):56–61.

Klotman, Phyllis R. *Frame by Frame: A Black Filmography*. Bloomington: Indiana University Press, 1979.

Kracaver, Siegfried. "National Types as Hollywood Presents Them." *Public Opinion Quarterly* 23 (Spring 1949): 53–72.

Kristal, I. "Few Kind Words for Uncle Tom." *Harper's* 230 (February 1965):95–99.

Lacy, Dan. *The White Use of Blacks in America*. New York: Atheneum, 1972.

Landay, Eileen. *Black Film Stars*. New York: Drake, 1973.

Leab, Daniel J. *From Sambo to Superspade: The Black Experience in Motion Pictures*. Boston: Houghton Mifflin, 1975.

———. "The Gamut from A to B: The Image of the Black in Pre–1915 Movies." *Political Science Quarterly*. 88 (March 1973):53–70.

———. "A Pale Black Imitation: All Colored Films 1930–1950." *Journal of Popular Film* 4 (June 1975):57.

Lee, Don L. "The Bittersweet of Sweetback, or Shake Yo Money Maker." *Black World* 20 (November 1971):1.

Lemons, Stanley J. "Black Stereotypes as Reflected in Popular Culture, 1880–1920." *American Quarterly* 29 (Spring 1977):102–16.

Manchel, Frank. "The Afro-American in Hollywood Films." In *Film Study: A Resource Guide*. Crainbury, N.J.: Fairleigh Dickinson University Press, 1973. 102–22.

Mapp, Edward. "Black Women in Films." *The Black Scholar* 4; 6, 7 (March-April, 1973): 42–46.

———. *Blacks in American Films: Today and Yesterday*. Metuchen, N.J.: Scarecrow Press, 1972.

———. "Images Makers." *Negro History Bulletin* 26 (October 1962):127–28.

Mattox, Michael. "The Day Black Movie Stars Got Militant." *Black Creation* (Winter 1973):40–43.

Maynard, Richard A. *The Black Celluloid Curriculum*. New York: Hayden, 1971.

———, ed. *The Black Man on Film: Racial Stereotyping*. Rochelle Park, N.Y.: Hayden, 1974.

"Metro's 'Cabin in the Sky' May Pave the Way for More Negro Films." *Variety* 166 (April 8, 1942):3.

Michener, Charles. "Black Movies: Renaissance or Ripoff?" *Newsweek* 23 (October 1972):74–82.

Miller, Loren. "Uncle Tom in Hollywood." *The Crisis* 61 (November 1934):329.

Morrison, Allan. "Do Negroes Have a Future in Hollywood?" *Ebony* 11 (December 1955):24, 27–30.

Moss, Carlton. "The Negro in American Films." In *Harlem U.S.A*. Ed. John Henrik Clarke. New York: Macmillan, 1971.

Murray, James P."Do We Really Have Time for a Shaft?" *Black Creation* (Winter 1972):26–31.

———. *To Find an Image: Black Films from Uncle Tom to Super Fly*. Indianapolis, Ind.: Bobbs-Merrill, 1974.

"NAACP, CORE and Other Civil Rights Groups Attack Black Films (*Shaft, Super Fly, Sweet Sweetback, Cotton Comes to Harlem, Come Back Charleston Blue, Blacula*) as Representing Black Men as Pimps, Dope Pushers, Gangsters, Robbers and Supersexed Males." *Jet* September 14, 1972: 50–51.

Neal, Larry. "Beware of Tar Baby." *New York Times*, August 3, 1969:G–6.

"Negroes Ask for Better Shade in Pictures." *Variety* 167 (June 17, 1942):5.

Nelsen, Anne K., and Hart Nelsen. "The Prejudicial Film: Progress and Stalemate, 1915–1967." *Phylon* 31 (Summer 1970):142–47.

Nesteby, James R. *Black Images in American Film, 1896–1954*. Washington, D. C.: University Press of America, 1982.

Noble, Peter. "The Coming of Sound Film." In *International Library of Negro Life and History*. Ed. Lindsay Patterson. New York: Publishers Co., 1967. 247–69.

———. *The Negro in Films*. 1948. Reprinted. New York: Arno Press, 1970.

Null, Gary. *Black Hollywood: The Negro in Motion Pictures*. Secaucus, N.J.: Citadel Press, 1975.

Okoge, Felix N. *The American Image of Africa: Myth and Reality*. Buffalo, N.Y.: Black Academy Press, 1971.

Opubur, Alfrede E., and Adebayo Ogunbi. "Ooga Booga: The African Image in American Films." In *Other Voices, Other Views*. Ed. Robin Winks. Westport, Conn.: Greenwood Press, 1978. 343–75.

Patterson, Lindsay. "Hollywood's Boy and Girl Next Door—Color Them White." *New York Times*, June 16, 1968:A–2.

———. "Not by Protest Alone!" *Negro History Bulletin* 31 (April 1968):12–14.

———. "To Make the Negro a Living Human Being." *New York Times*, February 18, 1968:F–18.

————, ed. *Black Films and Film-Makers: A Comprehensive Anthology from Stereotype to Superhero*. New York: Dodd, Mead, 1975.

————, ed. "Radio and Television. In *International Library of Negro Life and History*. New York: Publishers Co., 1967. 269–81.

Peterson, Bernard L. "Black Imagery on the Silver Screen." *Essence* 3 (December 1972):34.

————. "The Films of Oscar Micheaux: America's First Fabulous Black Filmmaker." *The Crisis* 86 (April 1979):34.

————. "A Flood of Black Films." *Essence* 3 (September 1972):28.

Pfaff, Françoise. "Negro Images in American Films from 1900 to 1960." *Negro History Bulletin* 43 (October/November/December 1980):92–94.

Pierce, C. M. "Primitive Emotions Aflame in a Negro Film." *Literary Digest* (October 5, 1929):42–56.

Pines, Jim. *Blacks in Films*. London: Studio Vista, 1975.

Popkin, Henry. "Hollywood Tackles the Race Issue." *Commentary* 24 (October 1957):354–57.

Potamkin, Harry Alan. "The Aframerican Cinema." *Close Up* (August 1929):107–17.

Pouissant, Alvin. "Cheap Thrills That Degrade Blacks." *Psychology Today* 7 (February 1974):22, 26–27, 30, 38, 98.

Powdermaker, Hortense. *Hollywood: The Dream Factory: An Anthropologist Looks at the Movie-Makers*. Boston, Mass.: Little, Brown, 1950.

Powers, Ann. *Blacks in American Movies: A Selected Bibliography*. Metuchen, N.J.: Scarecrow Press, 1974.

Ramsaye, Terry. "Progressive Protest against Anti-Negro Film." *The Survey* 34 (June 5, 1915):209–10.

Reddick, Lawrence. "Educational Program for the Improvement of Race Relations in Films, Radio, Press and Libraries." *Journal of Negro Education* 13 (Summer 1944):9.

————. "Of Motion Pictures." In *Black Films and Film-Makers: A Comprehensive Anthology from Stereotype to Superhero*. Ed. Lindsay Patterson. New York: Dodd, Mead, 1975. 3–24.

Riggio, Thomas. "Uncle Tom Reconstructed a Neglected Chapter in the History of a Book." *American Quarterly* 28 (Spring 1976):56–70.

Riley, Clayton. "The Blue Collar Critic—Theatre and Film." *New York Amsterdam News*, Black Academy of Arts and Letter Supplement (18 September 1971):D–18.

Rose, Vattel. "Afro-American Literature as a Cultural Resource for a Black Cinema Aesthetic." In *Black Cinema Aesthetics*. Eds. V. Rose and G. Yearwood. Athens: Ohio University Center for Afro-American Studies, 1982. 27–42.

Rose, Vattel, and Gladstone Yearwood. *Black Cinema Aesthetics: Issues in Independent Black Filmmaking*. Athens: Ohio University Center for Afro-American Studies, 1982.

Sampson, Henry T. *Blacks in Black and White*. Metuchen, N.J.: Scarecrow Press, 1977.

Sanders, Charles. "New Bad Guy of the Movies." *Ebony* 22 (June 1967):27–30.

"Screen Actors Guild to Fight Bias Against Negro in Movies." *Pittsburgh Courier*, September 28, 1946:19.

Shapiro, Marc. "Black Actresses: Are They Getting the Short End of the Stick?" *Soul* (March 19, 1979):14–15.

Showboat Handbill, UCLA, 1936.

Sloan, William J. "The Documentary Film and the Negro: The Evolution of the Integration Film." *Journal of the Society of Cinematologists* 4, 5 (1964–65):66–69.

Smith, Barbara. "Black Women in Film Symposium." *Freedomways* (Third Quarter 1974):266–69.

Sprecher, David. *Guide to Films (16mm) about Negroes*. Alexandria, Va.: Serina Press, 1970.

Stebbins, Robert. "Hollywood's Imitation of Life." *New Theatre* (July 1935):10–12.

Stewart, Gail. "Black Actress: Just Sleeping on Cold Sheets." *Soul* (May 24, 1976):15.

Still, William G. "The Negro and His Music in Film." *Proceedings of the Writers Congress*. Berkeley: University of California Press, 1944.

Thompson, Era Bell. "Why Negroes Don't Like Porgy & Bess." *Ebony* 10 (October 1959):50–60.

Trumbo, Dalton. "Minorities and the Screen." *Proceedings of the Writers Congress*. Berkeley: University of California Press, 1959.

Ward, Francis. "Super Fly: The Black Film Rip Off." In *The Black Position*. Ed. Gwendolyn Brooks. Detroit, Mich.: Broadside Press, 1972. 37–42.

Ward, Rene. "Lights! Camera! Action! Black Movies Make It Big." *Soul* (May 26, 1975):12–14.

Warner, Virginia. "The Negro Soldier: A Challenge to Hollywood." In *The Documentary Tradition*. Ed. Lewis Jacobs. New York: Hopkinson & Blake, 1971.

Weales, Gerald. "Pro-Negro Films in Atlanta."*Phylon* 13 (December 1952):298–304.

Weaver, Harold. "The Politics of African Cinema." In *Black Cinema Aesthetics*. Eds. V. Rose and G. Yearwood. Athens: Ohio University Center for Afro-American Studies, 1982. 83–92.

Wesley, Richard. "Toward a Viable Black Film Industry." *Black World* 11 (July 1973):23–28.

———. "Which Way the Black Film." *Encore* 2 (January 1973):52–54.

Wiggins, Curtis. "Media Power and the Black American." *The Crisis* 82 (June/July 1975):205–10.

Winter, Ella. "Hollywood Wakes Up." *New Republic* (January 12, 1928):276–78.

Yearwood, Gladstone. "Issues in Independent Black Filmmaking." In *Black Cinema Aesthetics*. Eds. V. Rose and G. Yearwood. Athens: Ohio University Center for Afro-American Studies, 1982. 1–18.

Yearwood, Gladstone. "Towards a Theory of a Black Cinema Aesthetic." In *Black Cinema Aesthetics*. Eds. V. Rose and G. Yearwood. Athens: Ohio University Center for Afro-American Studies, 1982. 67–83.

Images of Blacks in Instrumental Music and Song

Historiography has generally viewed the images of Blacks in instrumental music and song with a jaundiced eye. Through the neglected and often omitted features of culture, Black contributions and worth have been reduced to an available cliché. This stereotype, which is restrictive in understanding and lacking in sensitivity, has developed its own system of gestures, patterns of identification, stylistic expressions, and semantic features within a popular music style. Through selected symbols of Black culture, which are constant in their recycling, the negative transformation of a people has taken place.

This chapter surveys the Black image as seen in music and song. The review is based on two forms of identity by society—that by the Blacks themselves and that projected by the external culture's estimate of what Blacks are as a people. Titles of songs and texts, musical examples from recordings, and published music will serve as illustrative material.

Fortunately, in recent years a number of writers have attempted to document accurately the literature on aspects of this theme. This chapter identifies and analyzes from various perspectives selected literature on Black music. In no way are these references meant to be exhaustive. Dominique-René deLerma has filled this need with his monumental *Bibliography of Black Music* (1981–1984). Four volumes of a projected ten-volume set have been completed to date. *Afro-American Idioms*, volume 2 of this set, is rather broad in its coverage of materials relating to all forms of Black music. References to specific titles, both instrumental and vocal, are included. In addition, the section on "Politics and Sociology—U.S." in volume 4 cites references involving projected images in the music. Another comprehensive bibliographical source is Samuel A. Floyd, Jr.'s *Black Music in the United States* (1983), an annotated bibliography of books, periodicals, recordings, and collections of printed music. A list of repositories and archives, arranged by state, is also included.

The history of Black music has gone from the slave narratives to James Monroe Trotter's *Music and Some Highly Musical People* (1878), to Maud Cuney Hare's *Negro Musicians and Their Music* (1936, 1974), to Eileen Southern's definitive book *The Music of Black Americans: A History* (1983) and its supplement *Readings in Black American Music* (1983). Continued explorations can be seen in the two-volume publication *Black American Music: Past and Present* (1973 and 1985) by Hildred Roach and in *America's Black Musical Heritage* (1984) by Tilford Brooks. In the two publications, great emphasis is placed on the literature generated by composers. Current periodicals can be accessed through *The Music Index*, and American popular songs are indexed in *Popular Music*. Notable among periodicals are *Black Perspective in Music*, edited by Eileen Southern, and the *BMR* Journal, published by the Center for Black Music and Research, Columbia College (Chicago).

From field cries and laments, calls, hollers, and shouts to work songs, Black music has always been aware of its cognitive potential. Through its insistence on African-derived rhythms, which placed accented syllabic transmissions on the newly acquired English language, the roots of a new culture were beginning to take place. The text of these songs shows a high degree of emotional involvement and verbal imagery. Examples of these texts can be found in John W. Work's *American Negro Songs* (1940), Samuel Coleridge-Taylor's *Twenty-Four Negro Melodies, Op. 59* (1905), and Harry T. Burleigh's *Plantation Melodies, Old and New* (1901). Many other writers virtually ignored the contributions of Black Americans in their anthologies. This practice is exemplified in *Music in America: An Anthology from the Landing of the Pilgrims to the Close of the Civil War, 1620–1865* (1964).

It is interesting to note that the tempo or speed of play songs, work songs, and other vocal expressions of Black Americans was generally faster than their counterparts found in white society. Syncopation of beats is also characteristic. In these lines, "Shake it to the east and shake it to the west" from the popular chorus of "Little Sally Walker," one can clearly see the emphasis on the fourth beat and not the characteristic first and third beats of the measure:

To understand this important trait in Black American music, we can review the differences in the spoken language of Africa and England. In the English words, Am-ster-dam or Li-ver-pool or Wash-ing-ton,

we notice that the accentuated beat is on the first syllable. However, in pron-
ouncing the African words Da-ho-mey or Zim-bab-we or Mo-zam-bique, the
accent is placed on the syncopated beat.

This rythmic interpolation was to become a major contribution of Africa to the
Americas. Music goers generally associate this characteristic with jazz. However,
the parameters go far beyond that particularly important style and can be seen
in most of our nationalistic musical expressions.

A review of melodic invention would show that, historically, musical practices
have moved from simplicity to complexity: The older the music in general, the
fewer the notes that are systematically used. Most early field cries, hollers,
shouts, work, and play songs contain about three or four notes. With an extension
of this development, we can observe a five-note formation based on the pentatonic
scale in Negro spirituals.

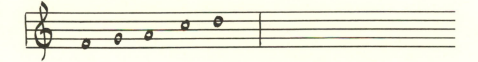

This influence from European music, with its adaptability into three kinds of
religious songs, provided a significant vehicle for Afro-American expression.
John W. Work identified these types as classical; slow, long phrase melodies;
and segmented syncopated melodies (Work, ''The Negro Spiritual'' 23). The
classical examples contain linear lines and were traditionally performed without
the aid of keyboard instruments. They were also heavily influenced by the African
''call and response'' format. ''Swing Low, Sweet Chariot'' is an example of

this type. "Deep River" represents the slow, long phrase melody. The final type, with its repetition of small patterns, is illustrated in the spiritual "Little David Play on Your Harp." Throughout these religious songs, allusions or hidden meanings functioned as a form of metaphor. The singers expressed in these songs a sense of community and a commitment to freedom. Crossing the "River Jordan" meant moving from the slave side of the Ohio River to a free state. "Steal Away to Jesus" was used as a signal for the coming of the underground railroad or of a religious retreat which took place within the spiritual bonds of captivity. The code also included names like "Moses" for a militant slave or "Pharaoh" for a slave owner. The artistic stability of the Negro spiritual lasted through Reconstruction to the present day. For a discussion of masks and symbols in Negro spirituals, the researcher should consult John Lovell, Jr.'s *Black Song: The Forge and the Flame* (1972). This major work on the history of the Negro spiritual also analyzes the texts of these songs.

Many of our nation's most popular Black singers have built their careers on this great musical literature. The names of Harry T. Burleigh, Roland Hayes, Marian Anderson, Paul Robeson, Robert McFerrin, Leontyne Price, and college groups such as the Fisk Jubilee Singers, conducted by Matthew W. Kennedy, the Morehouse College Glee Club, conducted by Wendell Whalum, and the Morgan State University Choir, conducted by Nathan Carter, are well known. The Fisk Jubilee Singers, who toured America and Europe between 1871 and 1878, were chiefly responsible for spreading these Black songs throughout the world. Contemporary Black composers who continue to draw on this wellspring are Hale Smith, Olly Wilson, George Walker, Ulysses Kay, Undine Smith Moore, Frederick Tillis, Billy Taylor, Alvin Singleton, David Baker, and Noel Da Costa. An excellent guide to biographical information on composers and musicians is found in *Black Music Biography: An Annotated Bibliography* (1987) by Samuel A. Floyd, Jr.

According to author Lester Levy in his *Grace Notes on American History: Popular Sheet Music from 1820 to 1900* (1967), the development of the United States can be traced through its popular music—songs serious or humorous, laudatory or derogatory. "The singer has been the reporter, and the interpreter of history, free to describe and criticize, to praise and to scoff, and to retell events in his own particular way" (Levy 15). Along with a historical perspective and a few biases, Levy has produced a representative collection of popular sheet music, illustrated with covers and title pages.

THE MINSTREL SHOW

In the middle of the nineteenth century, Black language was besieged by the vulgarities of white composers. This structure and style were called minstrel shows. These shows relied heavily on the use of text for substance. Attitudes of the time were reflected in the songs and dances of these performances. In fact, most of the images that continue to haunt society today were created during the period of minstrelsy and coon songs. The grotesque, exaggerated caricatures of Blacks as stupid, loose-jointed, good-hearted simpletons with thick lips, flat noses, big ears and feet, wooly hair, and names like Solomon Crow, Had-A-Plenty, Sambo, and Wan-na-mo marched across the stage and across the covers of sheet music. In addition, derogatory terms such as nigger, darkey, coon, pickaninny, buck, and yaller hussey were common. Blacks were seen as gossipy, emotional, prone to stealing chickens, lying, ignorant, lazy, childlike, dishonest, and drunken. Giles Oakley, in the introduction to *The Devil's Music: A History of the Blues* (1977), delineates these images and says that Negroes were seen not as human beings but as caricatures (Oakley 21–22). One can also observe that the economy of the South was built by the hard-working Black slave.

Traditionally, the format of the shows contained a white interlocutor and a Black glee club which sat in a semicircle. In the center, Mr. Interlocutor presided while the comic figures of Mr. Bones and Mr. Tambo entertained on the ends of the semicircle. Originally, minstrel shows were performed entirely by white casts; the Black parts were done in blackface. Later, these shows were performed by a single white and a Black cast using black makeup. In the composition *Thomas Jefferson's Minstrels*, one can find a contemporary usage of the old format in which the roles of Blacks and whites have become inverted. The work is scored for a Black interlocutor, a white glee club, and a jazz band. The following quotation was taken from that show:

> Interlocutor: Gentlemen be seated.
> Bones: Hey fellers, Minstrels comin'!
> Tambo: How many in the show?
> Bones: One gentleman and fifteen white crows! (Anderson, *Thomas Jefferson's Minstrels* 2)

The fad of minstrel songs was introduced in about 1828 by Thomas Dartmouth "Daddy" Rice in blackface and ragged clothes with a song in dialect called "Jim Crow" (Dennison 53).

Sam Dennison analyzes six versions of this song in his exceptional book on imagery in Black popular music, *Scandalize My Name: Black Imagery in American Popular Music* (1982). An example of a verse of this song is as follows:

> I met a Philadelphia niggar
> Dress'd up quite nice and clean,
> But de way he 'bused de Yorkers
> I thought was berry mean
> So I knocked down dis Sambo,
> And shut up his light,
> For I'm jist about as sassy
> As if I was half white (Dennison, 53–54).

Numerous examples of these pejorative images in song are recorded by Dennison.

The development of coon songs was also taking place; Black composers

6. Paper toy depicting the "Zip Coon" image and showing the Black male as entertainer. From the editor's collection. Photo by Vando Rogers.

Ooooh, my darling!

became participants. "All Coons Look Alike to Me," by black composer Ernest Hogan, represents one of the crowning, or clowning, achievements of this era.

> Talk about a coon having trouble
> I think I have enough of my own
> It's all about my Lucy Janey Stubbles,
> And she has caused my heart to mourn,
> There's another coon barber from Virginia,
> In Soci'ty he's the leader of the day,

And now my honey gal is gwine to quit me,
Yes she's gone and drove this coon away.

She'd no excuse
To turn me loose,
I've been abused,
I'm all confused,
Cause these words she did say:

All coons look alike to me,
I've got another beau, you see,
And he's just as good to me as you,
nig' ever tried to be,
He spends his money free,
I know we can't agree,
So I don't like you no how,
All coons look alike to me (Dennison 371–72).

This song is illustrative of the fickle female stereotype of the Black woman as well. Coon songs also placed emphasis on syncopated rhythm and racist humor.

Other subjects which appeared in song around the same time were the image of craps-playing and the creation on stage of the characters of Uncle Tom and Topsy in the musical play based on the book by Harriet Beecher Stowe, *Uncle Tom's Cabin*, by George C. Howard. Topsy sings "Oh! I'se so wicked." By contrast, Little Eva and Uncle Tom are pictured in song thus:

I am going there, I am going there,
She said in a voice so gentle sweet,
That Uncle Tom smooth'd her golden hair,
And mused like a child at Eva's feet (Levy 136).

Stephen Foster, a white composer writing in a Black style, was creating sentimental images of Blacks leading happy, carefree lives on the plantation through songs like "Old Black Joe" and "The Old Folks at Home." One of the major contributors to the music of the period was James A. Bland, a Black composer well known for "Oh, Dem Golden Slippers" and "Carry Me Back to Old Virginny."

An example of the long-range influence of minstrel and coon songs can be seen in the attitudes expressed in the 1920s song, "Bring Back Those Minstrel Days":

Oh! won't you bring back, bring back those minstrel days
Out of the long ago–
Bring back those old faces in black–
Features we all loved so–.

Efforts to eradicate these undesirable references continued to be a concern for Black composers. James Weldon Johnson writes:

I now began to grope toward a realization of the importance of the American Negro's cultural background and his creative folk-art, and to speculate on the superstructure of conscious art that might be reared upon them. My first step in this general direction was taken in a song that Bob Cole, my brother, and I wrote in conjunction during the last days in New York. It was an attempt to bring a higher degree of artistry to Negro songs especially with regard to the text. The Negro songs then the rage were known as "coon songs" and were concerned with jamborees of various sorts and the play of razors, with the gastronomical delights of chicken, pork chops, and watermelon, and with the ex-periences of red-hot "mammas" and their never too faithful "papas." These songs were for the most part crude, raucous, bawdy, often obscene. Such elements frequently are excellencies in folk-songs but rarely so in conscious imitation. The song we did was a little love song called *Louisiana Lize* and was forerunner of a style that displaced the old "coon songs" (Johnson, *Along This Way* 152–53).

As late as 1967, author Lester Levy stated

It is a great pity that today the defensive attitude of minority groups has robbed us of much of our uncomplicated fun of days gone by. The early stage comics, the German, the Irishman, the Jew, the Italian, can no longer be represented in primitive comedy form for fear of treading on sensitive toes. Most of all, we mourn the decline of the blackface minstrel, a development of America's entertainment media which brought delight to our ancestors (Levy 103–5).

The obvious delight has reference to the "good old days" when Blacks were forcibly kept "in their place" and the projected image was always singular. Today, we have moved slightly away from this concept, yet the total range of the Black experience is not made available to the general public. Until we witness the concept of the totality of the Black style, it is safe to assume that these objections will remain. Additional discussion on the minstrel and coon songs is given in chapter 2.

Former slaves created ballads that sang about heroes good and bad. "John Henry" was a "super" Black folk hero, and "Stackolee" and "Frankie and Johnny" represented another viewpoint. These positions should be expanded in our understanding of Black-related music.

THE EMERGENCE OF RAGTIME

The derogatory depiction of the well-established stereotype was detrimental to Black aspirations, yet without these songs, ragtime would not have become an important part of America's musical history. At the turn of the century, this music became internationally popular. The piano style, with its African–derived syncopated rhythm in the melodic right hand and the German march accompanied by the left, generated literature which influenced world music. These pieces also showed an increased use of augmented and diminished chords. Significant Black composers who pioneered this style were Scott Joplin, Arthur Marshall, James Scott, and Eubie Blake. On the covers of printed music, one could find pictures of a stereotypical Black image. As the sheet music gained popularity, these images were replaced by white faces in parlor scenes or ballrooms. The new norm was established; popular culture created by Blacks would be represented by white visuals. The researcher will want to refer to Edward A. Berlin's *Ragtime: A Musical and Cultural History* (1980) for a scholarly study of this American form and to Terry Waldo's *This Is Ragtime* (1976) for a more popular look at its beginnings and form.

A comparison of the texts of coon songs to the words in ragtime songs makes an interesting study. Coon songs placed great emphasis on color with frequent use of words like "black," "high tone," or "colored." Ragtime, on the other hand, was more interested in sentimental love. Occasionally, one could find a novelty song of the period which sang of popular dances of the time: the cakewalk, prance, slow drag, or ragtime dance. The composition of "Pine Apple Rag," with music by Scott Joplin and words by Joe Snyder, demonstrates these ideas.

> Come, honey love, my money love, Slide me;
> Come syncopate, don't hesitate, Glide me
> Say, you're a daisy
> I'm going crazy,
> Oh, that Pine Apple Rag (*Classic Rags and Ragtime Songs*).

Black people were viewed as loving, carefree, irresponsible, and—the continued vestige of slavery—childlike. The imitation of a false life was an acceptable form for white society. However, there was one major difference; now there was significant participation by the Black performer. Blacks had arrived on stage. Robert Cole's "A Trip to Coontown," Will Marion Cook and Paul Laurence Dunbar's "Clorindy, the Original of the Cakewalk," James Weldon Johnson and John Rosamond Johnson's "The Shoo Fly Regiment," and Noble Sissle and Eubie Blake's "Shuffle Along" clearly established a shift in characteristics. There occurred a gradual shift away from insensitive use of texts. Names were substituted for the word "coon," and the word "nigger" was eventually eliminated from these songs. Increased attention was given to the universally experienced love songs. Emphasis was also placed on dance. The use of syncopated rhythms, breaks, and faster speeds all led to this exceptional contribution.

Shortly after the start of the twentieth century, Black musicals made a major instrumental statement. This statement has been called New Orleans jazz or Dixieland. Most of the music was performed by small instrumental groups consisting of about six players. The key factor of this style was improvisation.

Earlier musical styles gave way to stomps and blues. This polyphonic or con-trapuntal music also had a vocal component. These songs focused on personal experiences and represented dramatic entertainment. Resourceful in their psy-chological meaning and shifting in commentary, they were to move the image of Blacks farther away from the stereotype of the earlier period. Song titles give us a clear picture of this difference. "When the Saints Go Marching In," "Dark-town Strutters' Ball," "Where Did You Stay Last Night," and "I Ain't Gonna Tell Nobody" all suggest a new feeling of worth and a deeper involvement in self-identification.

IMAGES IN "THE BLUES"

Performers moved away from the two-beat march flow of ragtime toward a driving four-beat pulsation. The energy of improvised melodic lines above a chordal structure of traditional tunes established greater freedom. The blues represented a further pilgrimage to the inner self. They represented a view of self-revelation, usually between a man and a woman, and displayed an emotional consciousness of poetic optimism.

An illustration of traditional blues text follows.

> I'm blue, high as a Georgia Pine
> I'm blue, high as a Georgia Pine
> Someday I'm gonna find a woman
> And make her mine.[1]

In these blues lines, we see the simple form (AAB) that proved to be both popular and enduring. Through a simple harmonic vocabulary of three chords (I IV V), this structure has shown the ability to expand expression and adaptability based on the unique personality of its performers. Without question, the blues have become one of the most influential contributions of Black Americans to twentieth century music. From the early days of country blues with its free rhythm of a guitar accompanying a solo vocal line to the great classical blues era with the birth of recorded music and significant Black female singers, the music dem-onstrated a capacity for popularity. The key in those days as in contemporary times was the solo performer. Blacks moved from Blind Lemon Jefferson and Lightnin' Hopkins to Ma Rainey and Bessie Smith. Later, with larger numbers of Blacks moving into the urban environment, the electric blues of B. B. King and Muddy Waters were to take over. This period took place simultaneously with Joe Williams and Jimmy Rushing's performances of blues lyrics with the great Count Basie band.

While the text of the blues did have a significance, these performers and many others created a style through gestures, quality of voice, stage presence, and insight. To this day, these experiences from the folk tradition continue to inspire both audience and performers. Of special interest is *Downhome Blues Lyrics:*

An Anthology from the Post-World War II Era (1981) by Jeff Todd Titon. Texts of blues lyrics composed and sung by Black Americans during that period appear here. Titon's introduction is useful for its historical perspective on this art form. For contemporary insight into the blues, refer to *Blues People: Negro Music in White America* (1963) by Amiri Baraka. "Race records" directed specifically to the Black audience were issued beginning in 1922. Paul Oliver's scholarly survey with transcription of a number of songs on this subject was published under the title *Songsters and Saints: Vocal Traditions on Race Records* (1984). The work includes blues along with other examples of musical forms. Oliver, an authority on the blues, has authored other books on the subject including *Blues off the Record: Thirty Years of Blues Commentary* (1985). A collection of essays and articles, this book covers a wide range of topics about the blues.

Valuable perspectives into this art form can also be found in James Cone's *The Spirituals and the Blues: An Interpretation* (1972) and Albert Murray's *The Omni-Americans: Some Alternatives to the Folklore of White Supremacy* (1970). Because they give a particular perspective and commentary on attitudes, biographies are worthy of examination. *His Eye Is on the Sparrow: An Autobiography* (1951) by Ethel Waters and *Lady Sings the Blues* (1956), the autobiography of Billie Holiday, are excellent examples.

GOSPEL MUSIC

Another important development in Black American image building has been gospel music. Like the Negro spirituals, it is rooted in Biblical traditions. Again, the personal statement as in the blues was important. Verbal imagery in the presentation of these songs and songs composed by practitioners in the gospel style all added up to a music which had its own history. From solo performer to gospel quartets and choruses, these musicians have been able to "witness" in an unrestricted way. Horace Clarence Boyer has identified three important periods in gospel history: the first, from 1900 to 1920, in which the Negro spiritual was paramount in its literature; the second, from 1920 to 1945, when the music moved from the South to the North; and the third, from 1945 to 1970, when the style became international (Boyer 1). Just as the blues depended on the performance for its sense of communication, gospel music also has a great performing tradition. Thomas Andrew Dorsey, the great teacher and composer of "Precious Lord, Take My Hand," Mahalia Jackson, Reverend James Cleveland, Roberta Martin, and Clara Ward were all ground-swelling developers of this type. Their works are being followed up by Edwin Hawkins, Bill Moss, and Andrae Crouch. A continuation of personal testimony to bear witness has enabled this religious music to continue in its development. The revivals from rural religion to urban storefront churches to large churches with an audience that claps its hands and stomps its feet are now international in scope and are beginning to influence other musical expressions. In the solo performance of Sam Cooke with his falsetto, Aretha Franklin and her improvisation, or James

Cleveland and the voice of the Tabernacle Choir, the tradition lives on. For different approaches to gospel music, the researcher will want to examine *The Gospel Sound: Good News & Bad Times* (1985) by Anthony Heilbut and *Black Gospel: An Illustrated History of the Gospel Sound* (1985) by Viv Broughton.

IMAGES IN JAZZ

In the late 1930s, the big jazz band movement presented a number of songs to Black audiences. These bands, which had started out approximately ten years earlier, expanded from about twelve pieces to as many as twenty musicians. With a saxaphone section, brass section, and rhythm section, the bands performed in ballrooms, nightclubs, stageshows, and cabarets. A large core of the song literature was composed by white musicians such as Cole Porter, George Gershwin, Jerome Kern, and Richard Rodgers. For a general history of popular music in America, one should consult David Ewen's *Panorama of American Popular Music* (1957). Ewen acknowledges the contributions of Black music with this statement:

The techniques and idioms, moods, and atmospheres, personality, and idiosyncrasies of Negro songs have formed the bone and tissue of our popular musical expression (Ewen 63).

Black composers who were also orchestra leaders were writing music as well: Count Basie, Cab Calloway, Benny Carter, Duke Ellington, Erskine Hawkins, Andy Kirk, Jimmy Lunceford, Don Redmon, Thomas "Fats" Waller, and Chick Webb. Of this group, Duke Ellington proved to be the master creator of Black images through songs. Works like "Mood Indigo," "Sophisticated Lady," "Don't Get Around Much Anymore," "I Got It Bad and That Ain't Good," "Solitude," "Do Nothin' till You Hear from Me," "Satin Doll," and "It Don't Mean a Thing If It Ain't Got That Swing" grew out of the Black aesthetic. The leading descendants of this tradition are George Russell with his Living Time Orchestra and the bands of Miles Davis. They capture the nuance of Black talk and extend the attitudes of creative people to a much larger audience, which is diverse in its makeup.

In recent times, the term "jazz" has provoked considerable comment. David Ewen quotes the following: "Its influence is as harmful and degrading to civilized races as it always has been among the savages from whom we borrowed it" (Ewen 63). This remark, from an anonymous source, continues to fuel the controversy. Eubie Blake objected to the term "jazz" because of its early association with the word "sex." He once said the expression "I jazzed that woman" had reference to a man and woman having intercourse. Billy Taylor has referred to jazz as "America's classical music." This position has been strongly supported by the jazz community. However, one would suspect that the attitudes toward Black achievement would be the same regardless of what the music is called. While there have been strong white supporters of jazz, such as John Hammond, Lewis Porter, Gunther Schuller, and Martin Williams, the general view of the popular society toward jazz has been rooted in the sociological status of Black people. Gunther Schuller's *Early Jazz: Its Roots and Musical Development* (1968) is an important source because the emphasis is placed on the music.

Stepping back from vocal music with texts, we now look at instrumental music. During the slave era, music was played by Blacks on the fiddle, French horn, fife, whistle, and other early instruments found in America. The literature was for white entertainment, and most of the musicians were taught by white musicians, or they acquired the skills of observation. It was not until the jazz era after the turn of the nineteenth century that a Black instrumental style became most meaningful. With New Orleans jazz being mostly an instrumental art form, we begin to see titles which reflected Black life. While some of these tunes may have had texts, they were favorite vehicles for instrumentalists.

Without question, the central figure of New Orleans jazz was Louis Armstrong. A cursory examination of his literature would show titles rooted in everyday Black lifestyles. Such titles as "Struttin and Some Barbecue," "Don't Jive Me," "Get Up off Knees," "SOL Blues" (the reader can determine the meaning of the letters), and "What Did I Do to Be Born So Black and Blue" were not only in the repertoire of his band but were standard pieces of the time performed by most bands. Again, as we have seen with Duke Ellington, the self-awareness of Black life formed a contrast to the earlier period. The images projected a prolongated picture of what was fashionable within the Black community: reflection of a culture. Many titles were quotations and paraphrases of street talk which served to communicate the essence of day-to-day life. In the 1940s a whole new vernacular was introduced. It featured Dizzy Gillespie, Thelonious Monk, Charlie Parker, and Max Roach, all contributors and developers in a jargon popularly known as bebop. In its title, one can see the accent of strong and weak beats (be-bop). Like Armstrong earlier, the image of Gillespie was one of fun and humor. The profundity of this music transformed the culture; it influenced the design and wearing of eyeglasses, hats, and other clothing as well as the language spoken during the time.

There are a number of references available on jazz. Outstanding among them are Martin Williams' *The Jazz Tradition* (1983); Rudi Blesh's *Shining Trumpets: A History of Jazz* (1958), an examination of the influences of several well-known jazz artists; and Frank Driggs and Harris Lewine's attractive *Black Beauty, White Heat: A Pictorial History of Classic Jazz, 1920–1950* (1982). In this area, biographies and autobiographies provide invaluable insights. To name a few, there are Louis Armstrong's *Satchmo: My Life in New Orleans* (1954), Willie Smith's *Music on My Mind: The Memoirs of an American Pianist* (1964), Stanley Dance's *The World of Duke Ellington* (1970), A. B. Spellman's *Black Music: Four Lives in the Bebop Business* (1970), Paul S. Machlin's *Stride: The Music of Fats Waller* (1985), and Dizzy Gillespie's autobiography, *to Be or not to*

Bop: Memoirs (1979). For further research, there is Len Lyons' comprehensive discography and commentary *The 101 Best Jazz Albums: A History of Jazz on Records* (1980).

PROTEST SONGS

Protest songs have always been a part of Black musical expression. Traditional songs of complaint with lines such as "times don't get no better here down the road I'm gone," or the Negro spiritual, "Oh Freedom" and the text "before I'd be a slave I'd be buried in my grave and go home to my lord and be free" exemplify these feelings. During the civil rights era of the 1960s, Black people expressed their protests through freedom songs. "We Shall Overcome" proved a national rallying cry. Bernice Johnson Reagon's contribution in the area of protest music, particularly during the civil rights era, must not go unnoticed. Of interest is her 1975 Ph.D. dissertation at Howard University, "Songs of the Civil Rights Movement, 1955–1965." Popular music of today is worthy of scrutiny because its source continues to protest. James Brown, the "Godfather of soul" with his constant "getup" proved a model for many entertainers, and today's generation finds Stevie Wonder at the forefront of social consciousness.

A suggested reference in the area of popular music is Arnold Shaw's *Black Popular Music in America: From the Spirituals, Minstrels and Ragtime to Soul, Disco, and Hi-Hop* (1986). This book gives a comprehensive account and includes a discography and extensive bibliography.

ART MUSIC

Another important aspect of image relates to art songs by Black composers. When the poets Sterling Brown, Countee Cullen, Langston Hughes, and Melvin B. Tolson were reflecting pride in self-image, Black composers were putting to pen musical compositions that sent the Black spiritual message to future generations. Margaret Bonds, Harry T. Burleigh, William Dawson, R. Nathaniel Dett, Undine Smith Moore, Florence Price, William Grant Still, and John Work, Sr., made substantial contributions. Unlike the generation before, these composers had classical training and were able to incorporate the European art song into their general message. Their styles were strongly influenced by the nineteenth-century classical music of Germany. Yet, within their compositions, one can see a glimpse of the Negro spiritual, folk blues tradition, or jazz influence. This generation has been followed by a group of composers who went deeper into Black culture for their resources. The names of Ulysses Kay, Thomas Kerr, Hale Smith, Howard Swanson, and George Walker come to mind. Further efforts in this direction can be seen in the songs of Leslie Adams, David Baker, Noel Da Costa, Anthony Davis, Wendell Logan, Coleridge-Taylor Perkinson, Billy Taylor, and Olly Wilson. These songs started from a religious base and expanded to engulf the total stream of Black consciousness.

General sources mentioned at the beginning of this chapter will be helpful in locating information on images reflected by Black composers of art music and opera. In addition, the work done at Indiana University by Dominique-René deLerma and David N. Baker on contemporary musicians deserves attention. Composers speak in their own words in the Baker et al. work *The Black Composer Speaks* (1977). Among deLerma's publications on Black music is *Reflections on Afro-American Music* (1973).

IMAGES IN OPERA

The field of opera has been dominated by America's love affair with George Gershwin's *Porgy and Bess*. While the work is without question a major contribution to operatic literature, it nevertheless perpetuates the stereotypical images found in minstrels. In contrast, operas by Black composers have focused on positive hero developments—Kay's *Frederick Douglass* (1985), Joplin's *Treemonisha* (1911), Still's *Highway 1, U.S.A.* (1962), Anderson's *Soldier Boy, Soldier* (1982), and Anthony Davis' "X" (1986) are examples.

THE BLACK AMERICAN IDENTITY

In *Worlds of Music*, ed. Jeff Titon, the following quotation appears:

Music of work, music of worship, music of play: the traditional music of black people in the United States has a rich and glorious heritage, embracing generations of the black experience. Neither African nor European, it is fully a Black American music, changing through the centuries to give voice to changes in black people's ideas of themselves. Yet despite the changes it retains its Black American identity, with a stylistic core of ecstasy and improvisation that transforms the regularity of everyday life into the freedom of expressive artistry. Spirituals, the blues, jazz—to Europeans, these unusual sounds are considered America's greatest (some would say her only) contribution to the international music world.

Of course, modern black music does not sound unusual to Americans, and that is because in this century the black style transformed popular music in America—the music of the theatre, movies, radio, and television. Today, country music, rock, disco, reggae, and, tellingly, advertising jingles owe a great debt to the black sound (*Worlds of Music* 105).

If one considers this statement, it should become apparent that the general characteristics of what has been identified as "American music" is obviously deeply indebted to the Black musical experience in the United States. Regardless of images portraying Blacks, what we now define as American music is really possessed by dominant features from Black musical culture.

NOTE

1. Source unknown. I first heard the beginning line of this text when it was sung by Danny Richmond. Richmond, Jackie McLean, and I had a band together in Greensboro, N.C., in the 1950s.

SELECTED BIBLIOGRAPHY

Abdul, Raoul. *Blacks in Classical Music: A Personal History*. New York: Dodd, Mead, & Co., 1977.

Anderson, T. J. *Minstrel Man for Bass Trombone, Bass Drum, and Hi-Hat Cymbals*. Music and text by T. J. Anderson. New York: American Composer's Alliance, 1982.

————. *Thomas Jefferson's Minstrels: An Evening of Entertainment for Baritone Soloist and Male Glee Club, and Jazz Band*. Music and text by T. J. Anderson. New York: American Composer's Alliance, 1982.

Armstrong, Louis. *Satchmo: My Life in New Orleans*. New York: Prentice-Hall, 1954.

Baker, David, Lida M. Belt, and Herman C. Hudson. *The Black Composer Speaks*. Metuchen, N.J.: Scarecrow Press, 1977.

Ballantine, Christopher. *Music and Its Social Meaning*. New York: Gordon and Breach Science Publications, 1984.

Baraka, Amiri [LeRoi Jones]. *Black Music*. New York: Morrow, 1968.

————. *Blues People: Negro Music in White America*. New York: Morrow, 1963.

Berlin, Edward A. *Ragtime: A Musical and Cultural History*. Berkeley: University of California Press, 1980.

Black Music Research Journal, 1980-.

Black Perspective in Music. Ed. Eileen Southern. Cambria Heights, N.Y.: The Foundation for Research in Afro-American Creative Arts, Inc. Published semiannually.

Blesh, Rudi. *Shining Trumpets: A History of Jazz*. 2d ed. New York: Knopf, 1958.

Blesh, Rudi, and Harriet Janis. *They All Played Ragtime*. 4th ed. New York: Poole, Dorset, 1985.

Boyer, Horace Clarence. "Gospel and Concert Music: A New Marriage." *Con Brio: National Black Music Caucus of M.E.N.C.*, April 1985: 1.

Brooks, Tilford. *America's Black Musical Heritage*. Englewood Cliffs, N.J.: Prentice-Hall, 1984.

Broughton, Viv. *Black Gospel: An Illustrated History of the Gospel Sound*. Poole, Dorset (England): Blandford Press, 1985.

Brown, Marion. *Recollections: Essays, Drawings, Miscellanea, Etc*. Frankfurt-Am-Main: Jurgen A. Schmitt, 1984.

Burleigh, Harry T. *Plantation Melodies, Old and New*. New York: G. Schirmer, 1901.

Carawan, Guy, and Cindy Carawan. *We Shall Overcome: Songs of the Southern Freedom Movement*. New York: Oak, 1963.

Cayer, David A. "Black and Blue and Black Again; Three Stages of Racial Imagery in Jazz Lyrics." *Journal of Jazz Studies* 1 (1974):38–71.

Charosh, P. "Slander in Song; Coon or Negro Songs." *Listen* 1 (December 1963):3–7.

Classic Rags and Ragtime Songs. Conducted by T. J. Anderson. Smithsonian Collection

N001 CBSm Inc. Brochure Notes: "Pine Apple Rag." Words by Joe Snyder. Music by Scott Joplin.

Coleridge-Taylor, Samuel. *Twenty-Four Melodies, Op. 59*. Boston, Mass.: Oliver Ditson, 1905.

Cone, James H. *The Spirituals and the Blues: An Interpretation*. New York: Seabury Press, 1972.

Critchley, MacDonald, and R. A. Henson, eds. *Music and the Brain*. London: William Heinemann Medial Books Ltd., 1977.

Dance, Stanley. *The World of Duke Ellington*. New York: C. Scribner's Son, 1970.

deLerma, Dominique-René. *Bibliography of Black Music*. 4 vols. Westport, Conn.: Greenwood Press, 1981–1984.

————. *Reflections on Afro-American Music*. Kent, Ohio: Kent State University Press, 1973.

Dennison, Sam. *Scandalize My Name: Black Imagery in American Popular Music*. New York: Garland Publishing Co., 1982.

Dett, R. Nathaniel. *Religious Folk-Songs of the Negro as Sung at Hampton Institute*. Hampton, Va.: Hampton Institute Press, 1927.

Driggs, Frank, and Harris Lewine. *Black Beauty, White Heat: A Pictorial History of Classic Jazz, 1920–1950*. New York: William Morrow & Co., 1982.

Epstein, Dena. *Sinful Tunes and Spirituals: Black Folk Music to the Civil War*. Urbana: University of Illinois Press, 1977.

Ewen, David. *Panorama of American Popular Music*. Englewood Cliffs, N.J.: Prentice-Hall, 1957.

Floyd, Samuel A., Jr. *Black Music Biography: An Annotated Bibliography*. White Plains, N.Y.: Kraus, 1987.

Floyd, Samuel A., Jr., and Marsha J. Reisser. *Black Music in the United States: An Annotated Bibliography of Selected Reference and Research Materials*. New York: Kraus International Publications, 1983.

Gilbert, Douglas. *Lost Chords: The Diverting Story of American Popular Songs*. New York: Cooper Square Publishers, 1942.

Gillespie, Dizzy, with Al Fraseer. *to Be or not to Bop: Memoirs*. Garden City, N.Y.: Doubleday & Co, 1979.

Green, Archie. *Only a Miner*. Urbana: University of Illinois Press, 1972.

Green, Mildred Denby. *Black Women Composers: A Genesis*. Boston, Mass.: Twayne, 1983.

Handy, W. C. *Father of the Blues: An Autobiography*. New York: Macmillan Co., 1955.

Hare, Maud Cuney. *Negro Musicians and Their Music*. 1936. Reprint. New York: Da Capo Press, 1974.

Heilbut, Anthony. *The Gospel Sound: Good News & Bad Times*. New York: Limelight Editions, 1985.

Holiday, Billie. *Lady Sings the Blues*. New York: Avon, 1956.

Hughes, Langston, and Milton Meltzer. *Black Magic: A Pictorial History of the Negro in American Entertainment*. Englewood Cliffs, N.J.: Prentice-Hall, 1967.

Jackson, George Pullen. *White and Negro Spirituals*. New York: J. J. Augustin, 1943.

Johnson, James Weldon. *Along the Way: The Autobiography of James Weldon Johnson*. New York: Viking Press, 1938. 151–52.

————. *The Book of American Negro Spirituals*. New York: Viking Press, 1925.

Katz, Bernard, ed. *The Social Implications of Early Negro Music in the United States.* New York: Arno Press and *New York Times*, 1969.

Keil, Charles. *Urban Blues.* Chicago: The University of Chicago Press, 1966.

Levine, Lawrence. *Black Culture and Black Consciousness—Afro-American Folk Thought from Slavery to Freedom.* New York: Oxford University Press, 1977.

Levy, Lester S. *Grace Notes on American History: Popular Sheet Music from 1820 to 1900.* Norman: University of Oklahoma Press, 1967.

Lomax, John A. *American Ballads and Folk Songs.* New York: Macmillan, 1934.

Lovell, John, Jr. *Black Song: The Forge and the Flame.* New York: Macmillan Co., 1972.

Lyons, Len. *The 101 Best Jazz Albums: A History of Jazz on Records.* New York: William Morrow & Co., 1980.

Machlin, Paul S. *Stride: The Music of Fats Waller.* Boston, Mass.: Twayne, 1985.

Marsh, J. B. T., and F. J. Loudin. *The Story of the Jubilee Singers.* Cleveland, Ohio: Cleveland Printing and Publishing Co., 1892.

Maultsby, P. K. "Soul Music: The Sociological and Political Significance in American Popular Culture." *Journal of Popular Culture* 17, 2 (1983):51–60.

Merriam, Alan P. *The Anthropology of Music.* Evanston, Ill.: Northwestern University Press, 1964.

Miller, Wayne Charles. *A Comprehensive Bibliography for the Study of American Minorities.* 2 vols. New York: New York University Press, 1976.

Murray, Albert. *The Omni-Americans: Some Alternatives to the Folklore of White Supremacy.* New York: Outerbridge & Dienstfrey, 1970.

Music in America: An Anthology from the Landing of the Pilgrims to the Close of the Civil War, 1620–1865. Comp. and ed. W. Thomas Marrocco and Harold Gleason. New York: W. W. Norton, 1964.

The Music Index. Ed. Florence Kretzschmar. Detroit, Mich.: Information Coordinators, 1950–. Published monthly.

The Negro and His Folklore in Nineteenth-Century Periodicals. Ed. with an introduction by Bruce Jackson. Austin: University of Texas Press, 1967.

The Negro Caravan: Writings by American Negroes. Selected and ed. Sterling A. Brown, Arthur P. Davis, and Ulysses Lee. New York: The Dryden Press, 1941.

Oakley, Giles. *The Devil's Music: A History of the Blues.* New York: Taplinger, 1977.

Oliver, Paul. *Blues off the Record: Thirty Years of Blues Commentary.* Turnbridge Wells, Kent (England): The Baton Press, 1985.

———. *Songsters and Saints: Vocal Traditions on Race Records.* Cambridge: Cambridge University Press, 1984.

Paskman, Dailey. *"Gentlemen Be Seated": A Parade of American Minstrels.* Rev. ed. New York: C. N. Potter, 1976.

Popular Music: An Annotated Index of American Popular Songs. Ed. Nat Shapiro. New York: Adrian Press, 1950–.

Reagon, Bernice. "Songs of the Civil Rights Movement, 1955–1965." Ph.D. diss., Howard University, 1975.

Roach, Hildred. *Black American Music: Past and Present.* (vol. I) Boston, Mass.: Crescendo Publishing Co., 1973.

———. *Black American Music: Past and Present.* vol. II, *Pan-African Composers Thenceforth and Now.* Malabar, Fla.: Robert E. Krieger Publishing Co., 1985.

Schuller, Gunther. *Early Jazz: Its Roots and Musical Development*. New York: Oxford University Press, 1968.

Shaw, Arnold. *Black Popular Music in America: From the Spirituals, Minstrels and Ragtime to Soul, Disco, and Hi-Hop*. New York: Schirmer, 1986.

Sidran, Ben. *Black Talk*. New York: Holt, Rinehart & Winston, 1971.

Smith, Willie. *Music on My Mind: The Memoirs of an American Pianist*. New York: Da Capo, 1964.

Southern, Eileen. *Biographical Dictionary of Afro-American and African Musicians*. Westport, Conn.: Greenwood Press, 1982.

————. *The Music of Black Americans: A History*. 2d ed. New York: W. W. Norton, 1983.

————, comp. and ed. *Readings in Black American Music*. 2d ed. New York: W. W. Norton, 1983.

Spellman, A. B. *Black Music: Four Lives in the Bebop Business*. New York: Schocken Books, 1970.

Stowe, Harriet Beecher. *Uncle Tom's Cabin; or Life Among the Lowly*. Boston: Jewett & Co., 1964. Many editions have been published.

Titon, Jeff Todd. *Downhome Blues Lyrics: An Anthology from the Post-World War II Era*. Boston, Mass.: Twayne, 1981.

Toll, Robert C. *Blacking Up: The Minstrel Show in 19th Century America*. New York: Oxford University Press, 1974.

Trotter, James M. *Music and Some Highly Musical People*. Boston, Mass.: Lee and Shepard, 1878.

Waldo, Terry. *This Is Ragtime*. New York: Hawthorn Books, 1976.

Warrick, Mancel, Joan R. Hillsman, and Anthony Manno. *The Progress of Gospel Music: From Spirituals to Contemporary Gospel*. New York: Vantage Press, 1977.

Waters, Ethel. *His Eye Is on the Sparrow: An Autobiography*. Garden City, N.Y.: Doubleday & Co., 1951.

Williams, Martin. *The Jazz Tradition*. New & rev. ed. New York: Oxford University Press, 1983.

Wittke, Carl. *Tambo and Bones*. Durham, N.C.: Duke University Press, 1930.

Work, John W. *American Negro Songs: A Comprehensive Collection of Religious and Secular Folk Songs for Mixed Voices*. Philadelphia, Pa.: Theodore Presser, 1940.

————. "The Negro Spirituals." *Hymn Society of America* 24 (1962):17–27.

Worlds of Music: An Introduction to the Music of the World's Peoples. Gen. ed. Jeff Todd. New York: Schirmer Books, 1984.

Literary Criticism and Black Imagery

It would be difficult to cite a more pervasive topic in the study of Black literature than "images." As a result, an initial warning has to be that these remarks provide only an introduction. The reader interested in a specific author, period, genre, or theme needs to consult the references noted here as starting points. This chapter limits the topic by concentrating on literary criticism. Attention is also given to primary sources frequently discussed in terms of images. Although some works necessarily belong in more than one category, the following types of resources supply a useful outline for exploring the subject: (1) studies which themselves survey several periods, genres, and themes; (2) studies of specific, recurring images; (3) studies of images of women; and (4) studies of types of literature, periods, or highly germane authors.

I emphasize initially, as well, that the enormity of the topic stems less from aesthetic consideration than from the context of racism in which the literature has been created. To be concerned with images of people usually means a study of those considered outsiders in a culture. Highly unlikely titles, for example, are "Images of Whites in American Literature" and "Images of Anglo-Saxon Protestant Males in American Literature." Such clearly reverse (or perverse) examples point out the extreme—even ludicrous—broadness of any attempt to cover images of an entire group of people placed together only on the basis of race, itself a problematic term. If one assumes, as most often has been the case, that whites, especially descendants of English immigrants, *are* American liter-ature, then it is inappropriate to see such white characters as merely "in" the literature. Tom Sawyer's Aunt Sally makes the point tellingly in the often quoted passage in *Huckleberry Finn*. After Huck says the steamboat had an accident, Aunt Sally cries, " 'Good gracious! anybody hurt?' " When Huck replies, " 'No'm, killed a nigger,' " her comment is " 'Well, it's lucky because sometimes people do get hurt.' '"[1] In a society that has not always considered Blacks "people," attention to image is crucial indeed.[2]

Aunt Sally's remark thus goes a long way in explaining why much of the discussion of images of Blacks in literary works has been in the context of basically polemic questions: Are the images positive or negative? stereotypical? realistic? archetypal? idealized? Such questions may well include a consideration of craft: How well have the images been developed? In a broad sense, any matter bearing on the effectiveness or ineffectiveness of characterization is relevant. Within such a framework, virtually all literature depicting Blacks deserves consideration. The implications are overwhelming for a single chapter in a volume covering many other fields as well. Although this overview could limit its attention to works which merely survey images, some very insightful criticism would be omitted as a result. For example, Henry Louis Gates, Jr.'s " 'The Blackness of Blackness': A Critique of the Sign and the Signifying Monkey'' (1983) does not focus on the question of images. The essay explores narrative techniques and the interplay of texts within Black literature, including material from the oral tradition. In the process, Gates illuminates the uses that Blacks themselves make of images.

It is clear in any case that a concern with images of Blacks in American literature remains just as timely now as it was in 1926 when Langston Hughes published "The Negro Artist and the Racial Mountain," which concluded with the often quoted passage:

We younger Negro artists who create now intend to express our individual dark-skinned selves without fear or shame. If white people are pleased we are glad. If they are not, it doesn't matter. We know we are beautiful. And ugly too. . . . If colored people are pleased we are glad. If they are not, their displeasure doesn't matter either.[3]

Sixty years later, though the terminology has changed most often from "colored" and "Negro" to "Black" and "Afro-American," the artist's freedom to present a variety of images without concern for audience reaction remains an issue. Discussions surrounding Alice Walker's *The Color Purple* (1982) have supplied an example. One needs to look at this book, as any book, on its own terms, but larger cultural questions are also important. Whatever one's approach, the topic of images is by no means passé.

CRITICAL WORKS COVERING SEVERAL PERIODS, GENRES, AND THEMES

Blacks in America: Bibliographical Essays (1971) edited by James M. McPherson and others is a handy capsulization of literary history and recommended critical studies. Many of the chapters focus on images in literature, including "Black and Negro as Image, Category, and Stereotype," "Racial Themes in the Writing of Poe and Melville," "Black Literature before the Civil

War,'' and "Blacks in American Culture, 1900–1970.'' *Blacks in America* thus provides comprehensive guidance for delving into the topic.

For more detailed discussion of authors and periods, Sterling Brown's works are excellent sources. His "A Century of Negro Portraiture in American Literature" (1966) draws on and updates several of his previous studies. In a highly informative essay, Brown writes with the verve and wit that characterize his own poetry. "A Century" surveys writers from the mid-nineteenth century to the 1960s. Many other critics refer to Brown's works when they discuss stereotypes found in pre–Civil War literature, especially in fiction by whites. Brown identifies (1) the contented slave/the wretched freedman (these two often occur in pairs), (2) the comic minstrel, (3) the persecuted victim, (4) the noble savage, (5) the submissive Christian, and (6) the tragic octoroon. Looking at post–Civil War fiction, again especially that by whites, he adds (7) the brute Negro and (8) the tragic mulatto.[4]

Brown also assesses critical works. John Herbert Nelson's *The Negro Character in American Literature* (1926) receives due acknowledgement as one of the earliest full-length studies, for example, with Brown noting further that the work reflects stereotypical assumptions. Brown's previous works cited in "A Century" are "Negro Character as Seen by White Authors" (1933) and *The Negro in American Fiction* (1937). His *Negro Poetry and Drama* (1937) remains a sound introduction to some of the early images in those genres. Despite the time that has passed since the publication of "A Century," Brown's analyses are not outdated for the periods they cover.

Images of the Negro in American Literature (1966) edited by Seymour L. Gross and John Edward Hardy, also supplies a comprehensive overview of the topic. Gross's well-documented introduction "Stereotype to Archetype: The Negro in American Literary Criticism" covers the beginning of criticism through (then) LeRoi Jones. Gross includes attention to the contributions of Benjamin Brawley and William Stanley Braithwaite, Black critics whose work in the early decades of the twentieth century stressed the need for positive images of Blacks. The first section of *Images*, "Traditions," consists of essays covering periods of American literature from colonial times to the twentieth century. Tremaine McDowell's "The Negro in the Southern Novel Prior to 1850" (first published in 1926) is probably the most dated interpretation. The second part of *Images* has essays on Herman Melville, Harriet Beecher Stowe, Mark Twain, Langston Hughes, Eudora Welty, Richard Wright, James Baldwin, Ralph Ellison, and William Faulkner. Although more recent studies need to be consulted by any researcher, the Gross and Hardy collection remains an excellent resource. Its extensive bibliography includes studies of many individual authors as well as general critical works.

Images of the Negro in America: Selected Source Materials for College Research Papers (1965), coedited by Darwin T. Turner and Jean M. Bright, is useful not only for students doing research papers, but for anyone interested in the topic. Its selections range from the early 1900s to the 1960s. The introduction to *The Book of Negro Folklore* (1958), coedited by Arna Bontemps and Langston Hughes, is included for the attention that it gives to the oral tradition. Overviews of literature are supplied in Blyden Jackson's chapter "The Negro's Image of the Universe as Reflected in His Fiction" and in Turner's article "The Negro Dramatist's Image of the Universe, 1920–1960." Jackson provides a brief discussion of attitudes conveyed in the works of writers from William Wells Brown to John O. Killens; most of the attention is given to Wright's *Native Son*, Ellison's *Invisible Man*, and Ann Petry's *The Street*. Noting that that stereotypical views of Blacks (largely outsiders' views) do not allow for any irony, Jackson points out that Black authors use irony extensively, starting with the titles of their works. Turner considers dramas which depict a variety of themes from the "noble savage" to educated Blacks. Finding a movement from idealization of characters as a response to caricature through explicit defensiveness of negative tendencies to objective appraisals, he also shows that characters become individualized in the later plays instead of being merely representative of certain types. On the whole, Turner and Bright's *Images* gives more attention to the works of Blacks themselves than do the works cited here thus far.

Self-definition and pride receive great emphasis in the bulk of criticism published since the mid–1960s. Herbert Aptheker's "Afro-American Superiority: A Neglected Theme in Literature" (1970) traces the theme of pride beginning with the earliest folk materials. As a major spokesman for the concept of the Black aesthetic (see also in this chapter "The 1960s and Beyond"), Addison Gayle, Jr., evaluates the impact of audience on image making as he discusses Black fiction from its beginning to the 1970s in *The Way of the New World: The Black Novel in America* (1976). Gayle's edited volumes, *Black Expression: Essays by and about Black Americans in the Creative Arts* (1969) and *The Black Aesthetic* (1971), also focus on the nature of images in different periods and genres.

Catherine J. Starke's *Black Portraiture in American Fiction: Stock Characters, Archetypes, and Individuals* (1971), based on her 1963 dissertation, relies somewhat heavily on plot summary. This tendency occurs in many such studies in part because the works discussed are no longer widely read. Starke examines works by both Black and white authors, and her treatment of categories of images is clear and comprehensive. Her work can thus serve as a helpful introduction.

In 1974, under the leadership of Stephen E. Henderson, the Institute for the Arts and Humanities at Howard University sponsored a national conference of Afro-American writers on "The Image of Black Folk in American Literature." Unfortunately, the proceedings of the conference are available only in part and that part not very widely. (See the bibliography section "General Studies, Fiction, and More Than One Genre" for a listing of individual papers.) John O. Killens' keynote address, "The Image of Black Folk in American Literature," is accessible through its publication in *The Black Scholar* (1975). Killens succinctly criticizes Stowe, Twain, and Faulkner. He also lists many themes needing exploration; several involve the depiction of Black women, to whom, as can be seen, the studies noted thus far give scant attention. (Black women critics were themselves beginning to address this need; see "Women" in this chapter.) Killens also called for an evaluation of the 1960s, attention to the significance of naming, and further consideration of the role of the Southern experience in characterizing Blacks.

Another highly pertinent resource is Sherley Anne Williams' *Give Birth to Brightness: A Thematic Study in Neo-Black Literature* (1972). Concentrating on Amiri Baraka (formerly LeRoi Jones), James Baldwin, and Ernest Gaines, she examines Black literature as a whole in illuminating these writers' contexts. All the chapters focus on heroes. Examples include "The Heroic Tradition in Black America," "Rebel and Streetman in Black Literature," and "The Black Musician: The Black Hero as Law Breaker."

A poet herself, Williams is included among the authors cited in Dellita Martin's "In Our Own Black Images: Afro-American Literature in the 1980s" (1981). Martin also considers Alice Walker, Toni Morrison, and Michael S. Harper. As the title suggests, such writers are found to be freer than those before them of the problems of being "in" someone else's literature.

There are many other works—pre- and post–1960—which could be cited as basic introductions to Black literature and which, as a result, include much applicable discussion. This overview has limited itself to a selection of the post–1960 works that most explicitly address the topic of images. Again, the citations are leads, not ends.

THEMATIC STUDIES: BOOKS ABOUT FICTION

As noted above, in a broad sense, any study of characterization bears on a consideration of images. Many analyses of fiction, in which characterization is presented in depth, are especially relevant.[5] Indeed, several works noted in the previous section concentrate solely on fiction. Although all of the sources discussed above touch on issues to follow, the studies noted here are more specialized. They provide a sampling of themes explored.

Studies of the mulatto are prominent. Further, the theme of color consciousness often relates to works by and about Black women, a result of society's associations of color with beauty. Many of the works identified in the section below on women thus address this theme. For example, Barbara Christian's chapter on Jessie Redmon Fauset, Nella Larsen, and Zora Neale Hurston in *Black Women Novelists: The Development of a Tradition, 1892–1976* (1980) is entitled "The Rise and Fall of the Proper Mulatta." Judith R. Berzon's *Neither White nor Black: The Mulatto Character in American Fiction* (1978), based on her 1974 dissertation, looks at both male and female characters and works by both Black and white authors. Recently, more attention has been given to the larger theme of miscegenation (see the work of William L. Andrews [1979] and James Kinney [1985]).

Phyllis R. Klotman's *Another Man Gone: The Black Runner in Contemporary Afro-American Literature* (1977) looks mainly at fiction, but it starts with slave narratives and includes the drama of Douglas Turner Ward. Klotman places the depictions of the man who leaves society in the context of other American literature as well.

Trudier Harris' *Exorcising Blackness: Historical and Literary Lynching and Burning Rituals* (1984) gives thorough and insightful attention to how Black authors including Richard Wright, John Edgar Wideman, Toni Morrison, and David Bradley treat the fact of lynching in the context of art. Inextricably tied to the question of image, the impact of lynching is explored in its historical context without the study's being a mere cataloging of examples. Harris' *From Mammies to Militants: Domestics in Black American Literature* (1982) draws on oral tradition for another excellently conceived and executed study.

WOMEN

Beginning in the 1970s, increased recognition of women writers brought more attention to their works. As a result, many studies and bibliographies focus on the image of women. (For additional discussion of this theme, see chapter 7.) Barbara Christian's *Black Women Novelists* (1980), already mentioned, is one of the first full-length studies to address the topic comprehensively. Harris' *From Mammies to Militants*, just cited, also explores primarily images of women since most domestic workers have been women.

Several collections of essays survey the literature chronologically. *Sturdy Black Bridges: Visions of Women in Literature* (1979), edited by Roseann P. Bell and others, includes brief but highly relevant essays such as Mary Burger's "Images of Self and Race in the Autobiographies of Black Women" and Gloria T. Hull's "Black Women Poets from Wheatley to Walker." *Bridges* encompasses not only depictions of women but also the views of Black women artists themselves on all topics. A select but basic bibliography concludes the volume.

All the Women Are White, All the Blacks Are Men, but Some of Us Are Brave: Black Women's Studies (1982), edited by Gloria T. Hull and others, includes many pedagogical guides for women's studies programs. " 'Necessary Bread': Black Women's Literature" focuses on theory, individual authors, and classroom approaches. Much of the volume's bibliographical chapter covers major literary genres.

Black Women Writers (1950–1980): A Critical Evaluation (1983), edited by Mari Evans, features perspectives on fifteen writers in all major genres. Evans is herself appropriately one of the fifteen. There are statements by each artist, two critical essays about that artist, and biographical highlights with a selected bibliography. The essays are stimulating, and the work as a whole is a most welcome resource.

Conjuring: Black Women, Fiction, and Literary Tradition (1985), edited by Marjorie Pryse and Hortense J. Spillers, also contains informative essays on individual authors. The essays cover works from slave narratives to the twentieth century. The editors' framing essays address links and differences among the authors covered.

Home Girls: A Black Feminist Anthology (1983), edited by Barbara Smith, features much recent creative literature. Critical essays include "The Black Lesbian in American Literature" by Ann Allen Shockley and "A Cultural Legacy Denied and Discovered: Black Lesbians in Fiction by Women" by Jewell L. Gomez. Shockley's essay appeared previously as well in *Conditions: Five/The Black Women's Issue* (1979), coedited by Lorraine Bethel and Barbara Smith. *Conditions* also contains much creative literature along with several articles on images of lesbians.

Many of the primary sources by women are being combined into anthologies for the first time, and the introductions to such collections often discuss images. Erlene Stetson's *Black Sisters: Poetry by Black American Women, 1746–1980* (1981) is an example. For analysis of fiction, one should not miss Mary Helen Washington's introductions to *Black-Eyed Susans: Classic Stories by and about Black Women* (1975) and *Midnight Birds: Stories of Contemporary Black Women Writers* (1980). Washington's essay " 'Taming All That Anger Down': Rage and Silence in Gwendolyn Brooks's *Maud Martha*" (1983) discusses the work's handling of negative images of Black women. The essay also has a wider application through Washington's documentation of male critics' inadequate attention to Brooks' work. Washington also includes attention to other Black women writers.

Claudia Tate's *Black Women Writers at Work* (1984) consists of interviews with fourteen contemporary writers. It is highlighted here because many of the artists reject the depiction of Black women as victims, finding that such an image does not reflect the reality they seek to convey in their works.

The studies discussed above, which consider more than one period, a theme across many periods, or the treatment of women in different periods, all touch on the categories to be discussed below as well. In what follows, the references become even more specialized and follow a rough chronological framework. "Rough" needs to be emphasized because, for example, folklore both precedes and continues simultaneously with the written literature. Studies of images in slave narratives are often treated in books which go beyond that period as well.

In addition to suggesting some of the basic critical sources, the sections below also briefly identify images prominent during the period in selected primary sources. The researcher is thus alerted to some of the individual authors whose works are especially relevant.

FOLKLORE

Sterling Stuckey's "Through the Prism of Folklore: The Black Ethos in Slavery" (1968) draws on folk forms such as spirituals and tales to show that Blacks viewed themselves much more positively than the white-imposed stereotypes tried to convey. Lawrence W. Levine's *Black Culture and Black Consciousness: Afro-American Folk Thought from Slavery to Freedom* (1977) also uses materials from folklore to explore the images slaves had of themselves. The last chapter in particular, "A Pantheon of Heroes," gives examples of how figures such as the trickster and the "bad nigger" provide balance against the images of Blacks as ignorant fools and shuffling victims. *Mother Wit from the Laughing Barrel: Readings in the Interpretation of Afro-American Folklore* (1973), edited by Alan Dundes, contains several essays in the section on folk narratives which treat the image of the trickster and the strong man. As Dundes points out, Beardsley's article on "The Ba-ad Nigger" dates from 1939 and reflects many Southern whites' attitudes of that time.

As noted previously, the introduction to *The Book of Negro Folklore* offers a brief discussion of images in folk material. This work and the other folklore resources look at the significance of animal tales. Slaves and their descendants could readily identify with Brer Rabbit, a figure whose survival was accomplished through cunning and strategic retreats. Brer Rabbit in Black folklore could often be cruel and a wielder of power. Such tales are very different from those made accessible in literature through Joel Chandler Harris' work in the late nineteenth century. Harris presents domesticated or tamed versions of the stories as harmless entertainment. (See also chapter 6 and the bibliography on Harris at the end of this chapter.)

Tales about preachers are also prominent in the folklore, a sign of their importance, even when they are the victims of their own faults.

In addition to the sources listed above, the works of J. Mason Brewer (*American Negro Folklore*, 1968) and Zora Neale Hurston (*Mules and Men: Negro Folktales and Voodoo Practice in the South* (1935) are good basic ones. More recently, Daryl C. Dance's collection *Shuckin' and Jivin': Folklore from Contemporary Black Americans* (1978) identifies and provides examples of a variety of images.

SLAVE NARRATIVES AND OTHER AUTOBIOGRAPHICAL LITERATURE

Written slave narratives, both antebellum and postbellum, were designed to appeal to white audiences. Antebellum narratives in particular often stressed images of victimization to arouse sympathy, although there were also usually examples of slaves who refused to be treated as oppressed. The latter images were important as a part of stressing that slaves were indeed people, not just totally brutalized objects of oppression.

Frances Smith Foster's *Witnessing Slavery: The Development of Ante-bellum Slave Narratives* (1979) provides a thorough overview of the genre. Especially pertinent is the chapter "Racial Myths in Slave Narratives." Two of Foster's subsequent essays pinpoint differences between narratives by women and those by men.

7. Slave narrative. Courtesy of Special Collections, Fisk University Library. Photo by Vando Rogers.

LUNSFORD LANE;

OR,

ANOTHER HELPER FROM NORTH CAROLINA.

BY

THE REV. WILLIAM G. HAWKINS, A. M.
AUTHOR OF "THE LIFE OF HAWKINS."

BOSTON:

CROSBY & NICHOLS,

117 WASHINGTON STREET.

1864.

Also addressing differences between narratives by men and women is "The Problematic of Self in Autobiography: The Example of the Slave Narrative" by Annette Niemtzow in *The Art of Slave Narrative: Original Essays in Criticism and Theory* (1982), edited by John Sekora and Darwin T. Turner. Niemtzow focuses on Frederick Douglass and Harriet Jacobs. Houston Baker, Jr.'s chapter "Figurations for a New American Literary History: Archeology, Ideology, and

Afro-American Discourse'' in *Blues, Ideology, and Afro-American Literature: A Vernacular Theory* (1984) shows how economic realities led to different survival strategies for male and female slave narrators. In addition to considering Douglass and Jacobs, Baker discusses Olaudah Equiano whose narrative *The Life of Olaudah Equiano or Gustavus Vassa* (1789) includes his African past. *The Art of Slave Narrative*, cited above, concentrates primarily on narrative strategies. Many of the essays indicate in the process how ex-slaves manipulated images others had of them. A notable example is Lucinda H. Mackethan's "Metaphors of Mastery in the Slave Narratives."

The collection *The Slave's Narrative* (1985), edited by Charles T. Davis and Henry Louis Gates, Jr., includes many relevant essays. Among them are Charles H. Nichols' "The Slave Narrators and the Picaresque Mode: Archetypes for Modern Black Personae" and James Olney's " 'I Was Born': Slave Narratives, Their Status as Autobiography and as Literature.''[6]

William L. Andrews' "The First Century of Afro-American Autobiography: Theory and Explication" in *Black American Prose Theory* (1984), edited by Joe Weixlmann and Chester Fontenot, draws on speech act theory to explain the narrators' choices and restrictions in presenting self. Andrews' *To Tell a Free Story: The First Century of Afro-American Autobiography, 1760–1865* (1986) further exemplifies his mastery of the material and the importance of his approach.

Older studies such as Charles H. Nichols' *Many Thousand Gone: The Ex-Slaves' Account of Their Bondage and Freedom* (1963) and Marion Starling's *The Slave Narrative: Its Place in American History* (first published in 1981; dissertation, 1946) established the solid historical groundwork which has assisted many of the later more literary analyses. Similarly, historian John W. Blassingame's studies look at the slaves' own responses, including narratives. See *The Slave Community: Plantation Life in the Antebellum South* (1972; revised and enlarged edition 1979).

Several full-length studies begin with slave narratives and consider later autobiographical literature as well. Stephen Butterfield's *Black Autobiography in America* (1974) is one such example. Throughout, Butterfield analyzes how the narrators define themselves. Robert B. Stepto's *From behind the Veil: A Study of Afro-American Narrative* (1979) explores the question of authorial control in slave narratives and then moves to later works. Stepto identifies the quest for literacy and freedom as central in shaping Afro-American literary texts.

In general, autobiographical writing is indeed a most important component of Black literature. Such works often reveal a triumph over adversity via character and art.

PRE–CIVIL WAR, CREATIVE LITERATURE

Of works by whites, Stowe's *Uncle Tom's Cabin* (1852) has often been discussed in terms of its images. The work has not received extensive attention since the 1960s, especially from Black critics. Killens in "The Image of Black

8. *Uncle Tom's Cabin.* Courtesy of Special Collections, Fisk University Library. Photo by Vando Rogers.

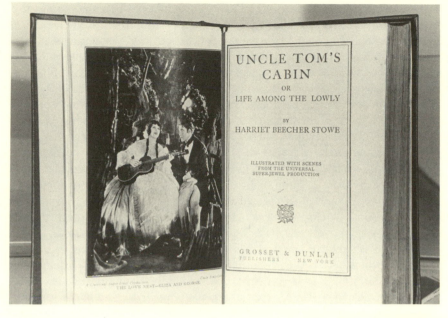

Folk" finds that Stowe "created more black stereotypes than any literature ever written."[7] One example, as many other readers have noted as well, is that only the mulatto slaves are rebellious. Stowe meant Tom to be a symbol of Christian forbearance and his mistreatment to arouse sympathy from white readers.

Jean Fagan Yellin's *The Intricate Knot: Black Figures in American Literature, 1776–1863* (1972) features sensitive discussions of Jefferson, James Kirke Paulding, John Pendleton Kennedy, William Gilmore Simms, Richard Hildredth, Stowe, and Melville (*Benito Cereno*). Yellin's study also provides balance through attention to Douglass, William Wells Brown, Nat Turner, and Martin Delany.

POST–CIVIL WAR LITERATURE THROUGH THE EARLY 1900s

Twain is perhaps the major white author discussed frequently with reference to images of Blacks. Most analyses center on *Huckleberry Finn* or *Puddn'head Wilson.* A noteworthy resource is the Fall 1984 issue of *The Mark Twain Journal.* Thadious M. Davis served as guest editor for the special issue "Black Writers on *Adventures of Huckleberry Finn* One Hundred Years Later." (See bibliography, under Clemens, for individual articles.) The critics illuminate Twain's ambivalence and contradictions, especially in the depiction of Jim. The most negative attitude toward the novel is presented by Julius Lester in "Morality and the *Adventures of Huckleberry Finn.*" In addition to pointing out the contradictions between slave reality and Twain's depiction of it, Lester criticizes the escapist philosophy of "lighting out for the territory" as detrimental to an understanding of responsible adulthood. Such a point has been made before, as by Leslie Fiedler, but arguments about the book's possible negative influence on young minds more often remain tied to the race issue. (See also chapter 6.)

As noted previously, the image of the "brute Negro" became especially prominent in much of the literature by whites in this period. Another emphasis in the works of white authors was the plantation tradition, a nostalgic look back at the "good old days before the war." Thomas Dixon's novels, including *The Leopard's Spots* (1902) and *The Clansman* (1905), helped establish the image of the brute Negro. In serving as bases for D. W. Griffith's film *Birth of a Nation* (1915), Dixon's novels played a major role in the very wide dissemination of such an image. Thomas Nelson Page's fiction exemplifies the plantation tradition through novels such as *In'Ole Virginia* (1887) and *Red Rock* (1898).

George Washington Cable depicts more of the complexities of conflicts stemming from societies stratified by racial distinctions. Cable's *The Grandissimes* (1880) explores the effects of caste-based society in New Orleans. The novel includes the character Bras Coupé, an especially powerful and noble African.

In poetry, white writers such as Irwin Russell perpetuated a minstrel stage image of Blacks as dialect-speaking, shuffling, ignorant "coons." Russell's images of happy-go-lucky Blacks merely updated images of contented slaves.

In countering the negative images of the time, Black authors employed a variety of approaches. W. E. B. Du Bois' *The Souls of Black Folk* (1903), in its title, gives an answer to those who saw Blacks as soulless beasts. Du Bois articulates the dual and conflicting nature of Blacks' lives: "One ever feels his two-ness—an American, a Negro; two souls, two thoughts, two unreconciled strivings; two warring ideals in one dark body, whose dogged strength alone keeps it from being torn asunder."[8] *Souls* also pays tribute to the images of dignity, beauty, and faith expressed in the spirituals or "sorrow songs," as Du Bois characterizes them.

Major Black writers who concentrated on creative writing were often oblique in their protests. Paul Laurence Dunbar and Charles Waddell Chesnutt are examples. Dunbar's "We Wear the Mask" clearly refers to Blacks in general who play the role of the happy-go-lucky "darky" while hiding pain and hatred. The poem also captures his own dilemma as an artist, presenting images of such seemingly happy Blacks and most often doing so in dialect poetry. Though he would have preferred to write less often in dialect, Dunbar's path was prescribed when William Dean Howells sanctioned such an emphasis. Dunbar does show how the mask can be used effectively, most notably perhaps in his poem "An Ante-bellum Sermon." The Black preacher speaks in dialect, but he is not contented. He uses the Moses story to get across a message of freedom even while denying he has done so. In calling it "An Ante-bellum Sermon," Dunbar himself escapes being accused of seditious sentiments in his own time, an added mask of the message.

Dunbar's short stories and novels deal only indirectly with images of Blacks. Of most relevance is the novel *The Sport of The Gods* (1902), which contains an example of the faithful Black servant, one who suffers unjustly as a result. The novel also shows contrasts between life for Blacks in the North and in the South.

Chesnutt's short stories collected in *The Conjure Woman* (1899) contain an alternative image from Joel Chandler Harris' Uncle Remus, who tells tales of Brer Rabbit. Chesnutt's character Uncle Julius tells stories in dialect to naive whites from the North. The stories usually enable Julius to get his own way, even though the whites continue to treat him condescendingly. Julius' mask makes him a Janus-like figure who illustrates Dunbar's poem once again. As a trickster, Julius is shrewd and effective even while he plays the role of being harmless and stupid. Chesnutt's *The Marrow of Tradition* (1901) provides one of the first fictional examples of a literally Black (as opposed to mulatto) militant rebel in Josh Green, who prefigures the sentiments of Claude McKay's "If We Must Die" (1919).

James Weldon Johnson, an immediate precursor of the Harlem Renaissance, published works prior to, during, and after the peak of the Renaissance. Johnson pays tribute to the images linked to oral tradition, including preachers in *God's Trombones: Seven Negro Sermons in Verse* (1927) and to creators of spirituals in his poem "O Black and Unknown Bards." His fictional work *The Autobiography of an Ex-Colored Man*, first published anonymously (1912), treats the theme of passing, a topic intimately tied to identity and self-image. Johnson's "Saint Peter Relates an Incident" (1930) exposes the ridiculousness of prejudice when the symbol of patriotism, the unknown soldier, turns out to be a "nigger" (*Saint Peter Relates an Incident: Selected Poems by James Weldon Johnson*, 13–21).

THE 1920s

The topic of images received extensive discussion during the 1920s, usually termed "The Harlem Renaissance." Some writers stressed the "best foot forward," which Richard Wright later criticized as a part of trying to "prove" that Blacks are human (See "Blueprint for Negro Literature"). Other writers depicted less highly educated folk or presented a range of characters. White authors in many cases depicted Blacks as exotic or primitive, an embodiment of the hedonism associated with the Jazz Age. (The term Jazz Age itself reflects the application of a Black image to the wider culture.)

We have already noted Hughes' declaration of artistic freedom in "The Negro Artist and the Racial Mountain" (1926). The major manifesto of the period is the anthology *The New Negro: An Interpretation* (1925), edited by Alain Locke.

Locke's own essays in that volume, "The New Negro" and "Negro Youth Speaks," articulate the view that the young writers would express their own self-concepts rather than be defined from the outside. *The New Negro* contains samples of selections in all literary genres and gives attention to music and folklore.

From March through November 1926, *The Crisis* published responses from many major writers and publishers to the survey "The Negro in Art: How Shall He Be Portrayed?" The prescriptive implication—how *shall* the Negro be portrayed?—indicates that the racial mountain stood high indeed. Almost all respondents attested to the need for artistic freedom in addressing the first question: "When the artist, black or white portrays Negro characters is he under any obligations or limitations as to the sort of character he will portray?" Remaining questions are loaded in the direction of calling for focus on educated, middle-class Blacks. The survey's concluding questions are examples:

Is not the portrayal of the sordid, foolish and criminal convincing the world that this and this alone is really and essentially Negroid, and preventing white artists from knowing any other types and preventing black artists from daring to paint them? . . . Is there not a real danger that young colored writers will be tempted to follow the popular trend in portraying Negro characters in the underworld rather than seeking to paint the truth about themselves and their own social class?[9]

Edited by W. E. B. Du Bois and the official journal of the NAACP, *The Crisis* was a logical place to work against negative images in the wider culture. At the same time, the questions almost rhetorically answer themselves.

Not surprisingly, the answers reflect the respondent's own orientations. For example, Jessie Redmon Fauset, whose novels are about such people, advocated emphasizing the most educated Blacks. Langston Hughes noted that those who write about either the "high" or the "low" are correct and concluded: "It's the way people look at things, not what they look at that needs to be changed." Carl Van Vechten, white patron of the Renaissance, often called its godfather, wrote: "The squalor of Negro life, the vice of Negro life offer a wealth of novel, exotic, picturesque material to the artist." Van Vechten's own novel *Nigger Heaven* (1925) received much negative criticism; the title itself often initiated the reaction. In addition to objecting to the title, DuBois felt that the work focused too much on cabaret life.[10]

Indeed, white writers of the period generally presented Blacks as primitives or exotics. Sterling Brown points out that Eugene O'Neil's *The Emperor Jones* (1920) depicts Blacks with some improvement over earlier images, but that the work relies heavily on "tomtoms and atavism."[11] The works of Julia Peterkin and DuBose Heyward illustrate a similar slight improvement, although their Black characters are often romanticized as sensual and unencumbered by Western society's repressions.

As noted, Blacks themselves often wrote about middle-class characters. Narratives about "passing" added to the literature on the tragic mulatto. Both of Nella Larsen's novels, *Quicksand* (1928) and *Passing* (1929), feature light-skinned heroines. The tragedy was not so much that the heroines could not be white, but that they could not live full lives as *themselves*. The effects of color consciousness within the race received explicit treatment, as in Wallace Thurman's *The Blacker the Berry* (1929). The theme had appeared earlier, of course; Chesnutt's *The Wife of His Youth and Other Stories of the Color Line* (1899) supplies examples.

Another recurring image in 1920s Black writing was the American Black dispossessed from an African heritage. Waring Cuney's "No Images," for example, laments the separation of Blacks from a sense of their past. A Black woman should see her beauty, but "dishwater gives back no images."[12] Cullen's "Heritage" addresses the same dispossession. The images of Africa are generalized and romantic—palm trees are often mentioned. The primitive imagery emphasized by whites thus had a version in Black writing as well. However, images used by Blacks evoked a more pastoral, Edenic quality rather than the animalistic sensual characteristics often stressed by whites.

Langston Hughes' work is an exception to the theme of alienation from Africa. Starting with "I've Known Rivers," Hughes articulates the continuity of the Afro-American with the African heritage. Hughes also celebrates struggling Black citizens who have fun and remain whole despite society's battering. "Laughing to keep from crying" delineates a survival technique and capsulizes another statement of the mask delineated by Dunbar. Though he created Simple in the 1940s, Hughes captures through that Harlem sage many of the emphases present in the Hughes canon from the 1920s.

A physician as well as an author of fiction, Rudolph Fisher created a range of characters, rather than only those associated with the middle class. The novels of Claude McKay, such as *Home to Harlem* (1928) and *Banjo* (1929), explore the lines of those who must fight for their survival against the realities of harsh city life.

Jean Toomer's *Cane* (1923) offers contrasts between Black life in the North and South, with Southern life generally seen as more vibrant, even if more violent. Although he depicts a variety of male and female characters, Toomer associated women of the South with land, sensuality, and emotion.

Women writers of the Renaissance supply their own perspectives as well. The works of previously cited Jessie Redmon Fauset and Nella Larsen are highly pertinent. Zora Neale Hurston's *Their Eyes Were Watching God* is a 1937 publication, but Hurston was actively involved with the 1920s writers. Long neglected, *Eyes* has been recognized as a seminal work exploring themes related to images of women.

The Renaissance also featured more images than had been seen previously of militant, dissatisfied Blacks speaking up about their plight. Some of Claude McKay's sonnets are examples, but the works of almost all poets have some expressions of bitterness and frustration. Although known primarily for her love poems, for example, Georgia Douglas Johnson criticizes the absence of brave, strong men. In "Courier," she calls those stymied by prejudice "pygmies" (*Crisis*, November 1926). Her poem is an example of a Black writer talking to a Black audience in exploring the images that do exist.

Several critical works give overviews of the period. Primarily a historical study, Nathan Huggins' *Harlem Renaissance* (1971) discusses literature in the process, especially in the chapters "The New Negro" and "Art: The Black Identity." George E. Kent's "Patterns of the Harlem Renaissance" identifies major emphases concisely yet comprehensively. Kent's essay appears in *The Harlem Renaissance Remembered* (1972), edited by Arna Bontemps. An important author who began his career during the Renaissance, Bontemps introduces the volume with a memoir of the period. Other essays in *Remembered*, which grew out of a seminar Bontemps led at Yale, cover most major and minor writers.

THE 1930s, 1940s, AND 1950s

Of course, many of the writers of the 1920s continued to publish in subsequent decades. Hurston and Hughes have already been cited. Bontemps' *Black Thunder* (1936), a novel based on Gabriel Prosser's 1880 slave revolt, incorporates historical detail in bringing that time to life.

Sterling Brown's poems in *Southern Road* (1932) speak in the voice of the folk and celebrate many heroes, from the rascally Slim Greer to Ma Rainey to an unnamed cotton farmer. Poets Gwendolyn Brooks, Margaret Walker, Robert Hayden, and Melvin Tolson began to publish in the 1940s. Their poetry, as Brown's, displays virtuosity of craft and, in the process, they also pay tribute to Black heroes, famous and not famous. Key fiction writers, at least those given extensive critical attention, are Wright, Ellison, Baldwin, and Faulkner. Dorothy West's *The Living is Easy* (1948) is an example of a less frequently discussed work which deserves consideration. The novel features fully drawn characters in engrossing situations, with problems stemming from character flaws as well as from the environment.

George Schuyler's *Black No More* (1931) satirizes the effects of color consciousness. By exploring the question "What if there were no more Blacks?," Schuyler uses an imaginative premise to expose the impact of racial distinctions. This question was also later satirized in Douglas Turner Ward's short play *Day of Absence* (1966), which also posits a hypothetical disappearance of Blacks. The play demonstrates with biting humor how whites need certain images of Blacks and how Blacks themselves succeed through their knowledge of whites' limited perceptions. Ward's companion play *Happy Ending* (1966) has a more realistic premise, but it makes a similar point.

Richard Wright illustrates a change in images within his own work. His collected volume of short stories, *Uncle Tom's Children* (1940), features fiction which, for the most part, shows Blacks as victims of harsh Southern brutality.

Wright found that the stories aroused sympathy from Northern liberals who could feel superior to Southern racists. In *Native Son* (1940), however, Bigger Thomas illustrates how Northern whites have not escaped complicity in creating an alienated murderer. Bigger has kinship with the "brute Negro," except that Wright makes it clear that society itself has created Bigger. Wright's protagonists, including Cross Damon in *The Outsider* (1953), are antiheroes, but not because they are inherently evil.

Ellison's *Invisible Man* (1954) includes a range of images. Even though characters suggest certain types—Mary, a mother figure; Bledsoe, a self-aggrandizing, hypocritical "leader"; Ras, a West Indian radical—none of these characters is merely a type. The protean nature of existence, which the narrator experiences throughout the novel, makes Rinehart, the man of several identities, an appropriate emblem for the significance of dynamic and often contrasting images.

Baldwin's collected essays analyze perceptively the nature and impact of images. Examples include *Notes of a Native Son* (1955), *Nobody Knows My Name* (1961), and *The Fire Next Time* (1963). In novels and plays as well, Baldwin delineates the perspectives of many whites and the impact of positive and negative self-images on Blacks themselves.

The development of Jones/Baraka, prolific as a poet and dramatist, also illustrates how an individual artist's work evolves. In the 1950s, Jones was often published with "Beatnik" poets, the outsiders of the time in their use of forms and themes beyond the more conservative approaches to poetry. In this context, Jones' poetry often focused on the outsider, though not specifically on the Black as an outsider. In the 1960s, the poems became much more explicit in calling for Blacks to assert themselves and to reject whites' images of them.

Wright, Ellison, Baldwin, Jones, and Hughes are the five authors covered in *Five Black Writers* (1970), edited by Donald Gibson. Many of the collected essays pertain to images. Sherley Ann Williams' *Give Birth to Brightness*, already cited as a good general source, examines Baldwin and Baraka extensively. Dudley Randall's "The Black Aesthetic in the Thirties, Forties, and Fifties" offers a brief overview of major authors and themes (in Gayle, ed., *The Black Aesthetic*). Lorraine Hansberry's *A Raisin in the Sun* (1959) should not be overlooked in reviewing the period. The drama features effectively realized characters who reflect a wider Black situation but who are not themselves stereotypical.

Of white writers, Faulkner has perhaps received the most discussion.[13] Ellison in "Twentieth Century Fiction and the Black Mask of Humanity" finds Faulkner's attitude toward Blacks "mixed" (*Shadow and Act*, widely reprinted, including Gross and Hardy). Killens in "Images" is less optimistic about Faulkner's final "liberalness." Charles Nilon's *Faulkner and the Negro* (1965) focuses to a great extent on *The Bear* and *Intruder in the Dust*. Nilon concludes that Faulkner succeeds in creating Black characters who are individuals rather than stereotypes. Providing in-depth analysis of novels with emphasis on *The Sound and the Fury, Light in August*, and *Absalom, Absalom*, Thadious M. Davis shows how a concept of "the Negro" is central to Faulkner's artistic aims and achievements in *Faulkner's "Negro": Art and the Southern Context*, 1983. As a result, Davis grounds her study in cultural reality but keeps the emphasis on the art of the novels. George Kent's articles (*Phylon* 1974 and 1975) conclude that Faulkner's characterizations of Black women are not complex. One reason for this, Kent points out, is that Faulkner (wisely, most critics agree) does not try to speak from a Black point of view.

THE 1960s AND BEYOND

The term characterizing the 1960s and the critical outlooks stressed from that time include "the Black aesthetic" and "the Black Arts Movement." These phrases accompanied the political slogan "Black power" and the related assertion "Black is beautiful!" The beauty of blackness had been noted before, but it had not been stated so openly, so often, so loudly, and by so many. The new mood more often celebrated blackness and expressed identity, as opposed to a defensive posture. Nevertheless, polemics and protest did not automatically disappear. A major difference between the 1960s and the 1920s, the previous most intense time of attention to images, was a more direct connection in the 1960s to larger audiences. In addition, the later Black writers stressed separatism more often than racial integration; the latter was an emphasis—or at least a hope—of many 1920s writers.

The writers of the 1960s have many characteristics in common with the literature of the "New Negro" forty years earlier, however.[14] Examples of continuity include the celebration of Africa as a part of reaffirming identity and the celebration of Black heroes including ordinary, hardworking Blacks. As a brief comparative example of the first theme, Nikki Giovanni's "Ego-Tripping" can be seen as an upbeat, hyperbolic parallel to Hughes' reflective "I've Known Rivers." The moods and tones differ, but each poem sees the continuity in an African heritage and the richness of the African world. Even though Hughes' poem meditates on the fact rather than flaunts it, each poem asserts the superiority of the speaker as a result of this connection with the past.

Two Black heroes especially celebrated by the poets of the 1960s are musician John Coltrane and activist Malcolm X. Julius Lester's title captures the importance of both in his poem "On the Birth of My Son, Malcolm Coltrane." Recognizing the musician as an important image did not originate in the 1960s— Sterling Brown's tribute to Ma Rainey in the 1930s is a forerunner, as is Langston Hughes' use of the blues stanza and blues lyrics. But in the 1960s, poets more often use the model of jazz sounds as a basis for poetic form. In this way, too, the poets recognized that the voice of the masses, as LeRoi Jones pointed out in *Blues People* (1963), is found more often in music than in literary forms. The assertive, earthy language of the poems refuted the image of docility. See Stephen Henderson, *Understanding the New Black Poetry: Black Speech and Black Music as Poetic References* (1973).

As does Ossie Davis in his prose tribute, many poems written after the assassination of Malcolm X emphasize Malcolm's being a *man*.[15] Examples include "At That Moment (For Malcolm X)" by Raymond R. Patterson and "Malcolm X—an Autobiography" by Larry Neal. (In *Soulscript: Afro-American Poetry*, edited by June Jordan, 1970.)

Women chosen for celebration along with singers such as Billie Holiday and Aretha Franklin include the older, usually not famous, mother figure. (See also chapter 7.) An example is Carolyn Rodgers' "It Is Deep," the source for the title of *Sturdy Black Bridges*, edited by Bell and others.

The satirical dramas of Douglas Turner Ward noted previously illustrated one variety of the unapologetic mood of the 1960s. *Dutchman* (1964) by LeRoi Jones demonstrated the explosive results of whites' images of Blacks. In general, directness was the key element in the many plays which explored the effects of racism on both whites and Blacks. The section on drama in *The Black Aesthetic*, edited by Gayle, is a good starting point for identifying some of the additional playwrights prominent in the period.

Novels of the 1960s and beyond are even more difficult to categorize. The difficulty may itself be a good sign: Categories are especially inadequate since authors write on a variety of themes in a variety of ways. Only a few especially pertinent authors and works can be noted here. Again, these citations should lead to other works by these authors and to other writers.

William Styron's *The Confessions of Nat Turner* (1967) raised a storm of controversy. Much of the criticism stresses that Styron's image of Nat Turner distorts what is known from historical accounts. See especially *William Styron's Nat Turner: Ten Black Writers Respond*, edited by John Henrik Clarke, 1968.

John O. Killens and John A. Williams are among the eminent creative writers and scholars who critiqued Styron's novel. Their own novels reflect the greater militancy of the 1960s. For example, Killens' *And Then We Heard the Thunder* (1962) explores pressures on Black soldiers in a segregated World War II army unit. Williams' *The Man Who Cried I Am* (1960) examines efforts of whites in the literary and political power structure to manipulate and eradicate Blacks.

Chester Himes creates a range of characters, starting much before the 1960s with *If He Hollers, Let Him Go* (1945). He also wrote several novels featuring Harlem detectives Coffin Ed and Grave Digger. Perhaps the most widely known of these is *Cotton Comes to Harlem* (1964, 1965).

William Melvin Kelley's *A Different Drummer* (1969) treats the theme of whites' need for Blacks even if only as scapegoats. The novel also depicts a strong African, seen earlier in the slave narratives and in *The Grandissimes*.

Ishmael Reed's works, including poetry and essays as well as novels, especially defy brief characterization. Like his other novels, *Mumbo Jumbo* (1972) shows his ability to make readers examine both past and present with a fresh eye.

A storyteller par excellence, Ernest Gaines creates memorable characters—individuals whose history and environment shape but do not overpower them.

One of his novels, *The Autobiography of Miss Jane Pittman* (1971), draws on the traditions of the slave narratives. The characters of Jane, Ned, and Jimmy illustrate the continuity of Black protest; the story of Mary Agnes and Tee Bob, the effect of caste and color on sexual relations. Gaines' Louisiana settings make the presence of Creole society a significant part of his work.

Margaret Walker's epic novel *Jubilee* (1966) draws on her own past and on the broader history of slavery in showing the resiliency of many of its survivors.

Toni Morrison's *The Bluest Eye* (1970) is a sensitive exploration of Black girls' lives. Morrison's later novels, *Sula* (1974), *Song of Solomon* (1977), and *Tar Baby* (1981), include many examples of characters who define themselves rather than let the larger society do so.

The works of Paule Marshall, including *Brown Girl, Brown Stones* (1959) and *Praise Song for the Widow* (1984), feature brilliantly realized characterizations. The novels also show the grounding of Black culture in an African and Caribbean past as well as in the American context.

Attention to images of women in recent literature would not be complete without citing the works of Gloria Naylor, starting with *The Women of Brewster Place* (1980, 1982). Also highly pertinent are the works of Ntozake Shange, starting with *for colored girls who have considered suicide/when the rainbow is enuf* (1975). *For colored girls* raised a controversy because many felt that it stresses images of Black men. Defenders of the work counter that its main point is that Black women need to nourish self-images.

As indicated at the outset of this survey, a similar controversy emerged in discussions of *The Color Purple*, especially as a result of the filmed version. Some have objected to the book and the film on the grounds that the images of the male characters are particularly negative. Another position is that such a problem is beyond the novel if readers mistakenly take the book or film to categorize all Black men. For a clear statement of the issues, see Trudier Harris' "On *The Color Purple*, Stereotypes and Silence," (*BALF*, 1984).

Walker's previous fiction includes *The Third Life of Grange Copeland* (1970), *Meridian* (1976), and *In Love and Trouble* (short stories, 1967–75). These works also have much to offer in any consideration of imagery. *Grange* contains one of the most unredeemed characters in Black literature, for example, in Grange's son Brownfield. The novel shows how Brownfield came to be that way and Grange's development from a similar character to one who is changed greatly for the better.

The list of additional writers could go on and on. Ronald Fair, Leon Forrest, John McCluskey, Toni Cade Bambara, and Gayl Jones are a few examples. One could add Black writers of science fiction, Samuel Delany and Octavia Butler.

The variety of the literature makes it necessary to stress again that this overview suggests emphases, but nuances are significant as well. The best of the literary criticism pays attention to those nuances and to a much longer list of writers than could be noted here.

NOTES

1. Samuel Langhorn Clemens (Mark Twain), *Adventures of Huckleberry Finn* (1885; reprinted, New York: Rinehart & Co., 1956), 222.

2. Two historical studies which document the contexts of whites' attitudes toward Blacks are Winthrop D. Jordan's *White over Black: American Attitudes toward the Negro, 1550–1812* (Baltimore: Penguin Books, 1968) and George M. Frederickson's *The Black Image in the White Mind: The Debate on Afro-American Character and Destiny, 1817– 1914* (New York: Harper and Row, 1971). Although these works have little to say about literature per se, they explain the background of predominant attitudes at different periods in U.S. history.

3. In Addison Gayle, Jr., ed., *The Black Aesthetic* (Garden City, N.Y.: Doubleday, 1972), 172. Originally published in *The Nation* 122 (June 24, 1926):692–94.

4. "A Century of Negro Portraiture in American Literature," ed. Abraham Chapman, in *Black Voices: An Anthology of Afro-American Literature* (New York: New American Library [Mentor]), 567, 569. The distinctions in the terms octoroon (one-eighth "Negro blood") as opposed to mulatto (half white and half black) were not always rigidly maintained in the literature. Octoroons, more nearly white, were distinguished in caste-oriented societies such as nineteenth-century New Orleans, where octoroon women were given a certain status as the mistresses of white men.

5. The same could be said of drama, of course. Works of fiction are more widely accessible than performed dramas. As the bibliography on drama below illustrates, attention to image is equally important in that criticism.

6. Olney's essay originally appeared in *Callaloo* 7, 1(Winter 1984):46–73.

7. John O. Killens, "The Image of Black Folk in American Literature," *The Black Scholar* 6(June 1975):49.

8. W. E. B. DuBois, *The Souls of Black Folk*, 1903; Reprinted. Millwood, N.Y.: Kraus-Thomson, 1973. Ed. Herbert Aptheker.

9. *The Crisis* 31(March 1926):219.

10. Fauset, *The Crisis* 32(June 1926):71–72; Hughes, *The Crisis* 31(April 1926):278; Van Vechten, *The Crisis* 31(March 1926):219; DuBois on *Nigger Heaven*, *The Crisis* 33(December 1926):80–81.

11. "A Century of Negro Portraiture in American Literature," ed. Abraham Chapman, in *Black Voices* (New York:New American Library, 1968), 574.

12. Arna Bontemps, ed., *American Negro Poetry* (New York: Hill and Wang, 1963), 99.

13. Although Faulkner's novels date from the 1920s, he is noted here because many of the major novels, ones also bearing on the treatment of Blacks, were published in the 1930s and 1940s. *The Sound and the Fury* (New York: Random House, 1929) is also very close to the decades noted here.

14. Even though the term "Black" largely replaces "Negro," critics and writers of the 1960s recognized the continuity of attitudes with those who may have used different terminology previously. Nevertheless, the change from "Negro" to "Black" is linked to the topic of images. "Black" often denotes self-awareness and pride at a very high level.

15. Ossie Davis, "On Malcolm X," in *The Autobiography of Malcolm X* (New York: Grove Press, 1964), 457. Also as "Why I Eulogized Malcolm X," in *Black on Black:*

Commentaries by Black Americans from Frederick Douglass to Malcolm X, ed. Arnold Adoff (New York: The Macmillan Co., 1968), 190–93.

SELECTED REFERENCES

Sources

The emphasis here is on criticism published since 1966, the date of Gross and Hardy's *Images of the Negro*. That work's bibliography remains an excellent compilation.

In continuing to locate references, the researcher can be aided by many resources. The following journals regularly feature bibliographical updates and have been especially useful in developing this listing: *Black American Literature Forum, Black Scholar, Callaloo, College Language Association Journal, Freedomways, MELUS, Mississippi Quarterly*, and *Phylon*. *Phylon* and the *College Language Association Journal* pioneered in keeping readers abreast of literary works about Blacks as *The Crisis* and *Opportunity* had done earlier. (Unlike *Opportunity*, the journal of the National Urban League, *The Crisis* is still being published. Its focus is of course wider than literature.) Although it is no longer published, *Black World* (formerly *Negro Digest*) provided extensive coverage of matters related to images, especially as discussed in the 1960s and 1970s.

Since 1975, very helpful essays devoted solely to Black literature have been included in *American Literary Scholarship* (Duke University Press). Volumes for previous years do include Black authors (and, of course, whites who depict Blacks in their works), but in a scattered manner.

Other resources used in compiling the citations which follow include *Afro-American Poetry and Drama, 1760–1975: A Guide to Information Sources*, edited by Geneviève Fabre and others (Detroit: Gale, 1979); M. Thomas Inge, Maurice Duke, and Jackson R. Bryer, *Black American Writers: Bibliographic Essays*, 2 vols. (New York: St. Martin's, 1978); Edward Margolies and David Bakish, *Afro-American Fiction, 1853–1976: A Guide to Information Sources* (Detroit: Gale, 1979); the *MLA International Bibliography*; and *Southern Literature, 1968–1975: A Checklist of Scholarship*, compiled by Jerry T. Williams (Boston: G. K. Hall, 1978).

Along with *Dissertation Abstracts*, sources for dissertations cited include James Woodress, *Dissertations in American Literature, 1891–1966* (Durham, N.C.: Duke University Press, 1968); Jack D. Wages and William L. Andrews, "Southern Literary Culture: 1969–1975," *Mississippi Quarterly* 32 (Winter 1978–1979): 14–215; and Janet Sims-Wood, "African-American Women Writers: A Selected Listing of Masters Theses and Doctoral Dissertations," *Sage: A Scholarly Journal on Black Women* II (Spring 1985): 69–70. (Recently founded, *Sage* has already contributed substantially to research on Black women.) "Images" has been and remains a popular dissertation topic; only a few dissertations are included below.

Many of the basic reference sources for the study of Black literature are listed compactly in the section "Afro-American Literature" in Margaret C. Patterson's *Literary Research Guide*, 2d ed. (New York: Modern Language Association, 1984).

A less widely known but very valuable research resource is Carolyn Fowler's *Black Arts and Black Aesthetics: A Bibliography* (Atlanta, Ga.: First World Foundation, 1976, 1981). The bibliography has over 2,000 entries as well as an excellent introduction, "By Way of Preface: Balancing on the Brink," v–xxxi. Fowler also rates the quality of a majority of the entries.

Organization and Scope

As indicated at the outset, the focus is on works of literary criticism. A few bibliographies are included, but space limitations prevent a comprehensive listing. Some anthologies of primary sources are cited if the works' introductions discuss images. Other primary sources cited in chapter 5 also appear below.

It is also important to remember that the canon of primary works is itself still growing, not just by additions from current authors but also through discoveries and wider dissemination of past works. Henry Louis Gates' republication (1983) of Harriet E. Wilson's *Our Nig; or, Sketches from the Life of a Free Black* (1859; Reprinted, New York: Random House, 1983) is an example. The critical evaluation of images of Blacks will need to continue to be updated as a result. It is especially significant that *Our Nig* is by a woman, for many of the unemphasized perspectives now being researched are those of women.

The main sections of the bibliography are as follows:

1. General studies, fiction, and more than one genre (including general studies of women)

2. Poetry

3. Drama

4. Folklore

5. Slave narratives and other autobiographical literature

6. Themes (cross-listed from other sections)

    (a) Mulatto, miscegenation

    (b) Soldier

    (c) Preacher

7. Individual authors (selected), in alphabetical order.

Only a few of the general articles (1–5) in the first bibliographical sections are cross-listed to individual authors, especially in the case of authors such as Baldwin, Ellison, Toomer, and Hughes, who are discussed in almost all comprehensive general studies.

Not all relevant individual authors could be included, but most are. Those which seem to be omissions, such as Lillian Smith, are covered in general studies cited in the overview. General studies also provide leads for finding material on earlier authors such as Frances E. W. Harper and more recent ones such as Lucille Clifton, June Jordan, Ethridge Knight, Gloria Naylor, Leon Forrest, and John Edgar Wideman.

Key to Abbreviations

The following are used prior to the entry when appropriate:

*The work is cited in the preceding chapter

**Primarily bibliographical

(BA) Black Arts Movement

(HR) Harlem Renaissance

(W) Women

More than one category may apply to an individual work. If so, the letters appear in alphabetical order, hyphenated, e.g., (HR-W).

Categories are omitted from the individual author listings, except in cases where the work might otherwise be missed. The works about Alice Walker are not further designated with a (W), for example. A work about women among the entries on James Baldwin, on the other hand, is so designated.

Frequently cited works are as follows:

Collected Essays	(full reference given in General Studies)
Anger and Beyond.	Hill, Herbert, ed.
BA	*The Black Aesthetic.* Gayle, Addison, ed.
BAP	*Black American Poets between Worlds.* Miller, R. Baxter, ed.
BE	*Black Expression.* Gayle, Addison, ed.
BF	*Black Fiction.* Lee, Robert A., ed.
Black and White	Chametzky, Jules and Sidney Kaplan, eds.
BWW	*Black Women Writers.* Evans, Mari, ed.
Conjuring	Pryse, Marjorie and Hortense Spillers, eds.
FBW	*Five Black Writers.* Gibson, Donald B., ed.
Gross and Hardy	*Images of the Negro in American Literature.*
SBB	*Study Black Bridges.* Bell, Roseann P., et al., eds.

In addition, any work frequently cited in an individual author's entry is so designated with the shortened form at the beginning of the author's listing.

The following abbreviations are used for journals:

AL	*American Literature*
BALF	*Black American Literature Forum*
CLAJ	*College Language Association Journal*
MR	*Massachusetts Review*
NALF	*Negro American Literature Forum* (predecessor to *BALF*)
PMLA	*Publications of the Modern Language Association*
SLJ	*Southern Literary Journal*

General Studies, Fiction, and More than One Genre

Andrews, William L. "Miscegenation in the Late Nineteenth Century Novel." *Southern Humanities Review* 13 (1979): 13–24.

*Aptheker, Herbert. "Afro-American Superiority: A Neglected Theme in Literature."
    Phylon 31(Winter 1970): 336–43. Reprinted in *Black Life and Culture in the
    United States*. Ed. Rhoda L. Goldstein. New York: Thomas Y. Crowell Company,
    1971.

Baker, Donald G. "Black Images: The Afro-American in Popular Novels, 1900–1945."
    Journal of Popular Culture 7(Fall 1973): 327–46.

*Baker, Houston A., Jr. *Blues, Ideology, and Afro-American Literature: A Vernacular
    Theory*. Chicago, Ill.: The University of Chicago Press, 1984.

————. *The Journey Back: Issues in Black Literature and Criticism*. Chicago, Ill.: The
    University of Chicago Press, 1980.

————. *Long Black Song: Essays in Black American Literature and Culture*. Charlottes-
    ville: University of Virginia Press, 1972.

————. *Singers of Daybreak: Studies in Black American Literature*. Washington, D.C.:
    Howard University Press, 1974. Paperback reprint, 1983.

[Baraka, Imamu Amiri] Jones, LeRoi. "Myth of a Negro Literature." In *Home: Social
    Essays*. New York: William Morrow & Co., 1966.

*(W) Bell, Roseann, P., Betty J. Parker and Beverly Guy-Sheftall. *Sturdy Black Bridges:
    Visions of Women in Literature*. New York: Doubleday (Anchor Books), 1979.

Berghahn, Marion. *Images of Africa in Black American Literature*. Totowa, N.J.: Row-
    man and Littlefield, 1977.

Berzon, Judith R. *Neither White nor Black: The Mulatto Character in American Fiction*.
    New York: New York University Press, 1978.

*Bethel, Lorraine, and Barbara Smith, eds. *Conditions: Five/The Black Women's Issue*.
    Brooklyn, N.Y.: Conditions, 1979.

Bigsby, C. W. E., ed. *The Black American Writer*. 2 vols. Deland, Fla.: Everett Edwards,
    1969.

————. *The Second Black Renaissance: Essays in Black Literature*. Westport, Conn.:
    Greenwood Press, 1980. Starts with Wright.

Billingsley, R. G. "Forging New Definitions: The Burden of the Hero in Afro-American
    Literature." *Obsidian* 1 (Winter 1975): 5–21; *Black World* 25 (December 1975):
    38–45, 66–73.

Bone, Robert. *Down Home: A History of Afro-American Short Fiction from its Beginnings
    to the End of the Harlem Renaissance*. New York: G. P. Putnam, 1975.

————. *The Negro Novel in America*. New Haven, Conn.: Yale University Press, 1958;
    revised edition, 1965.

(HR) Bontemps, Arna. "The Black Renaissance of the Twenties." *Black World* 20
    (November 1970): 5–9. See also Herbert Hill, ed., *Anger and Beyond*.

*(HR) Bontemps, Arna, ed. *The Harlem Renaissance Remembered*. New York: Dodd,
    Mead and Co., 1972.

Braithwaite, William Stanley. "The Negro in Literature." *The Crisis* 28 (1924): 204–
    10; also essentially the same: "The Negro in American Literature," in Alain
    Locke, ed., *The New Negro*.

Brawley, Benjamin. *The Negro Genius: A New Appraisal of the Achievements of the
    American Negro in Literature and the Fine Arts*. New York: Dodd, Mead and
    Co., 1937. Reprinted. New York: Biblo and Tannen, 1966.

————. *The Negro in Literature and Art*. New York: Duffield and Co., 1918.

Brown, Lloyd. "The West Indian as an Ethnic Stereotype in Black American Literature."
    NALF 5 (Spring 1971): 8–14.

*Brown, Sterling. "A Century of Negro Portraiture in American Literature." *MR* 7, 1 (Winter 1966): 73–96. Reprinted in *Black and White*, 333–59; also in Abraham Chapman, ed., *Black Voices*, 564–89.

*————. "Negro Character as Seen by White Authors." *Journal of Negro Education* 2 (April 1933): 179–203.

*————. *The Negro in American Fiction*. Port Washington, N.Y.: Kennikat Press, 1937. Reissued 1968.

*————. *Negro Poetry and Drama*. Washington, D.C.: Associates in Negro Folk Education, 1937.

Burt, Della. "The Legacy of the Bad Nigger." *Journal of Afro-American Issues* 5, 2 (Second Quarter 1977): 111–24.

Butcher, Margaret Just. *The Negro in American Culture*. New York: Alfred A. Knopf, 1956.

Chametzky, Jules and Sidney Kaplan. *Black and White in American Culture: An Anthology from the Massachusetts Review*. Amherst: University of Massachusetts Press, 1959–1969.

Chandonia, Ronald P. "The New South in Black and White: Afro-American Fiction from the End of Reconstruction until the First World War." Ph.D. diss., Emory University, 1974. Discusses Chestnutt, DuBois, Dunbar, Sutton E. Griggs, and J. W. Johnson.

*Chapman, Abraham, ed. *Black Voices: An Anthology of Afro-American Literature*. New York: New American Library (Mentor), 1968.

(W)Childress, Alice. "The Negro Woman in American Literature." *Freedomways* 6 (1966): 14–19, 75–80.

*(W)Christian, Barbara. *Black Women Novelists: The Development of a Tradition, 1892– 1976*. Westport, Conn.: Greenwood Press, 1980.

(BA-HR)Collier, Eugenia W. "Heritage from Harlem." *Black World* 20 (November 1970): 52–59.

**(W)Collins, L. M. *Images of the Afro-American Woman: A Bibliographic Profile*. With an introduction by Nikki Giovanni. Nashville, Tenn.: Fisk University Press, 1980.

Cook, Mercer and Stephen Henderson. *The Militant Black Writer in Africa and the United States*. Madison: University of Wisconsin Press, 1969.

Cooke, Michael G. *Afro-American Literature in the Twentieth Century: The Achievement of Intimacy*. New Haven, Conn.: Yale University Press, 1984.

————, ed. *Modern Black Novelists: A Collection of Critical Essays*. Englewood Cliffs, N.J.: Prentice-Hall, 1971.

Couch, William, Jr. "The Image of the Black Soldier in Selected American Novels." *CLAJ* 20 (1976): 176–84. Discusses Styron, *The Long March*; McKay, *Home to Harlem*; and Killens, *And Then We Heard the Thunder*.

(W)Dance, Daryl C. "Black Eve or Madonna? A Study of the Mother in Black American Literature." *SBB*, 123–32.

Daniel, Walter C. *Images of the Preacher in Afro-American Literature*. Lanham, Md.: University Press of America, 1981.

Davis, Arthur P. *From the Dark Tower: Afro-American Writers from 1900 to 1960*. Washington, D.C.: Howard University Press, 1974.

(BA)————. "Novels of the New Black Renaissance (1960–1977): A Thematic Survey." *CLAJ* 21 (June 1978): 457–90.

Davis, Charles T. *Black Is the Color of the Cosmos: Essays on Afro-American Literature*. Ed. Henry Louis Gates, Jr. New York: Garland Publishing, 1982.

Davis, Vivian. "Black American Literature: A Cultural Interpretation." *MELUS* 8 (1981): 13–21.

(BA)Dickstein, Morris. "The Black Aesthetic in White America." *Partisan Review* 38 (Winter 1971–1972): 376–95.

Doughty, Anaelia S. "Realistic Negro Characterization in Post-Bellum Fiction." *NALF* 3 (1969): 57–62.

*Du Bois, W. E. B. *The Souls of Black Folk*. 1903. Reprinted. Millwood, N.Y.: Kraus-Thomson, 1973. Ed. Herbert Aptheker.

Durham, Frank. "The Reputed Demise of Uncle Tom; or, The Treatment of the Negro in Fiction by White Southern Authors in the 1920's." *Southern Literary Journal* 2 (Spring 1970): 26–50. Discusses T. S. Stribling, H. A. Shands, DuBose Heyward, and Julia Peterkin.

Ellison, Curtis W. "Black Adam: The Adamic Assertion and the Afro-American Novelist." Ph.D. diss., University of Minnesota, 1970. Discusses William Wells Brown, James Weldon Johnson, Jean Toomer and Richard Wright.

Ellison, Ralph Waldo. *Shadow and Act*. New York: Random House, 1964.

Erno, Richard B. "The Image of the Negro in Ante-Bellum Southern Diaries." Ph.D. diss., University of Minnesota, 1961.

*(W)Evans, Mari. *Black Women Writers (1950–1980): A Critical Evaluation*. Garden City, N.Y.: Doubleday (Anchor Books), 1983.

(BA)Fenderson, Lewis H. "The New Breed of Black Writers and Their Jaundiced View of Tradition." *CLAJ* 15 (September 1971): 18–24.

Fiedler, Leslie. *Love and Death in the American Novel*. Rev. ed. New York: Dell Publishing Co., 1966.

Fisher, Dexter, and Robert B. Stepto, eds. *Afro-American Literature: The Reconstruction of Instruction*. New York: Modern Language Association, 1978.

(W)Fisher, Jerilyn. "From under the Yoke of Race and Sex: Black and Chicano Women's Fiction in the Seventies." *Minority Voices* 2 (Fall 1978): 1–12. Discusses Toni Cade Bambara, Gayl Jones, and Alice Walker.

Ford, Nick Aaron. *The Contemporary Negro Novel: A Study in Race Relations*. Boston, Mass.: Edward K. Meador, 1936. Reprinted. Wilmington, N.C.: McGrath Publishing Co., 1968.

**(BA)Fowler, Carolyn. *Black Arts and Black Aesthetics: A Bibliography*. Atlanta, Ga.: First World Foundation, 1976, 1981. (Order directly from the author, Afro-American Studies Department, Atlanta University, Atlanta, Ga. 30314)

*Frederickson, George M. *The Black Image in the White Mind: The Debate on Afro-American Character and Destiny, 1817–1914*. New York: Harper and Row, 1971. More historical than literary, but it gives brief attention to Cable, Dixon, J. C. Harris, and Stowe.

Frisby, James R. "New Orleans Writers and the Negro: George Washington Cable, Grace King, Ruth McEnery Stuart, Kate Chopin, and Lafcadio Hearn, 1870–1900." Ph.D. diss., Emory University, 1972.

Fuller, Hoyt W. "Identity, Reality and Responsibility: Elusive Poles in the World of Black Literature." *Journal of Negro History* 57 (1972): 83–98.

Gallagher, Brian. "Explorations of Black Identity from *The New Negro* to *Invisible Man*." *Perspectives on Contemporary Literature* 8 (1982): 1–9.

*Gates, Henry Louis, Jr. " 'The Blackness of Blackness': A Critique of the Sign and the Signifying Monkey." In *Black American Prose Theory*. Eds. Joe Weixlmann and Chester J. Fontenot, 1984, 129–81. An abbreviated version of this essay was published previously in *Critical Inquiry* 9 (June 1983): 685–723; also in Gates, ed., *Black Literature and Literary Theory*, 285–322.

———. *Figures in Black: Words, Signs, and the Racial Self*. New York: Oxford University Press, 1986.

———, ed. *Black Literature and Literary Theory*. New York: Methuen, 1984.

———, ed. " 'Race,' Writing, and Difference." *Critical Inquiry* 12 (Autumn 1985): 1–300. See Du Bois and Hurston for essays on Black American authors.

Gayle, Addison, Jr. "Cultural Hegemony: The Southern White Writer and American Letters." *Amistad 1: Writings in Black History and Culture*. Eds. Charles F. Harris and John A. Williams. New York: Random House (Vintage), 1970. 1–24.

(HR-BA)———. "The Harlem Renaissance: Toward a Black Aesthetic." *Midcontinent American Studies Journal* 11 (Fall 1970): 78–87.

*———. *The Way of the New World: The Black Novel in America*. Garden City, N.Y.: Doubleday and Co. (Anchor), 1976.

*———, ed. *The Black Aesthetic*. Garden City, N.Y.: Doubleday and Co., 1971.

*———, ed. *Black Expression: Essays by and about Black Americans in the Creative Arts*. New York: Weybright and Talley, 1969.

Gibson, Donald. *The Politics of Literary Expression*. Westport, Conn.: Greenwood Press, 1981.

*———, ed. *Five Black Writers: Essays on Wright, Ellison, Baldwin, Hughes and LeRoi Jones*. New York: New York University Press, 1970.

Glicksberg, Charles I. "The Negro Cult of the Primitive." *Antioch Review* 4 (Spring 1944): 47–55.

Gloster, Hugh M. *Negro Voices in American Fiction*. Chapel Hill: University of North Carolina Press, 1948.

Godbold, E. Stanly, Jr. "A Battleground Revisited: Reconstruction in Southern Fiction, 1895–1905." *South Atlantic Quarterly* 73 (Winter 1974): 99–116. Discusses Cable, Dixon, Glasgow, J. C. Harris, Page, and John S. Wise.

Graham, Mary Emma. "The Shaping of a Cause: American Romanticism and the Black Writer." *CLAJ* 24 (September 1980): 16–25.

*Gross, Seymour L. and John Edward Hardy, eds. *Images of the Negro in American Literature*. Chicago, Ill.: The University of Chicago Press, 1966.

Gross, Theodore. *The Heroic Ideal in American Literature*. New York: The Free Press, 1971.

———. "Idealism of Negro Literature in America." *Phylon* 30 (Spring 1969): 5–10.

Gwin, Minrose C. *Black and White Women of the Old South: The Peculiar Sisterhood in American Literature*. Knoxville: University of Tennessee Press, 1985.

Gysin, Fritz. *The Grotesque in American Negro Fiction: Jean Toomer, Richard Wright, and Ralph Ellison*. Berne, Switzerland: A. Francke AG Verlag, 1975.

(W)Harley, Sharon, and Rosalyn Terborg-Penn, eds. *The Afro-American Woman: Struggles and Images*. Port Washington, N.Y.: Kennikat Press, 1978.

Harper, Michael S., and Robert B. Stepto. *Chant of Saints: A Gathering of Afro-American Literature, Art, and Scholarship*. Urbana: University of Illinois Press, 1984.

*Harris, Trudier. *Exorcising Blackness: Historical and Literary Lynching and Burning Rituals*. Bloomington: Indiana University Press, 1984.

*(W)————. *From Mammies to Militants: Domestics in Black American Literature*. Philadelphia, Pa.: Temple University Press, 1982.

————. "Three Black Women Writers and Humanism: A Folk Perspective." *Black American Literature and Humanism*. Ed. R. Baxter Miller. Lexington: The University Press of Kentucky, 1981. 50–74. Discusses Sarah E. Wright's, *This Child's Gonna Live*; Alice Walker's *The Third Life of Grange Copeland*, and Paule Marshall's *The Chosen Place, The Timeless People*.

Harris, Trudier, and Thadious Davis, eds. *Afro-American Fiction Writers after Nineteen Fifty-Five*. Detroit: Gale, 1984.

Hill, Herbert. ed. *Anger and Beyond: The Negro Writer in the United States*. New York: Harper, 1966.

*(HR)Huggins, Nathan. *Harlem Renaissance*. New York: Oxford University Press, 1971.

*Hughes, Langston. "The Negro Artist and the Racial Mountain." *Nation* 122 (June 24, 1926): 692–94. Reprinted (selected) (BA), 167–72, Charles F. Harris and John A. Williams, eds. *Amistad* 1. New York: Random House (Vintage Books), 1970: 305–6.

(HR)————. "The Twenties: Harlem and Its Negritude." *African Forum* 1 (Spring 1966): 11–20.

*Hull, Gloria, Patricia Bell Scott and Barbara Smith, eds. *All the Women Are White, All the Blacks Are Men, But Some of Us Are Brave: Black Women's Studies*. Old Westbury, N.Y.: The Feminist Press, 1982.

(HR)Ikonne, Chidi. *From DuBois to Van Vechten: The Early New Negro Literature, 1903–1926*. Westport, Conn.: Greenwood Press, 1981.

*"The Image of Black Folk in American Literature." Proceedings of the National Conference of Afro-American Writers, presented by the Howard University Institute for the Arts and the Humanities. Directed by Stephen E. Henderson. Typescript, limited ed. May be read at the Howard University Afro-American Studies Resource Center. Contents: John O. Killens, "The Image of Black Folk in American Literature" (see also Killens, *Black Scholar* 6 (June 1975): 45–52; A. The Non-Fiction Panel: John Henrik Clarke, "The Black American Writer in Crisis"; Samuel F. Yette, "Black Hero Dynamics and the White Media." B. The Literature for Young Readers Panel: Sharon Bell Mathis, "Black Writers and Children: Lessons in Black Love"; Lorenz Graham, "The Task of Image Makers"; June Jordan, "Towards a Survival Literature for Afrikan-Amerikan Children"; John Steptoe, "On Writing Children's Literature." C. The Playwriting Panel: (1) Clay Goss, "The Creative Team"; Alice Childress, "Image and the Contradictions of Black Experience"; J. E. Franklin, "Common Theological Questions in Black Literature"; Ron Milner, "The '60's: Myth or Reality"; Eugene Perkins, "Black Theater as Image Maker"; Richard Wesley, "New Directions for the 70's."

Isalni, Mukhtar A. "The Exotic and Protest in Earlier Black Literature: The Use of Alien Setting and Character." *Studies in Black Literature* 5 (Summer 1974): 9–14. Discusses W. W. Brown and also refers to Arna Bontemps, J. W. Johnson, and Albery Whitman.

Jackson, Blyden. "The Ghetto of the Negro Novel: A Theme with Variations." In *The Waiting Years: Essays on American Negro Literature*. Baton Rouge: Louisiana State University Press, 1976. 179–88.

*————. "The Negro's Image of the Universe as Reflected in His Fiction." *CLAJ* 4

(September 1960): 22–31. Reprinted in Turner and Bright, eds., *Images*, 85–90; Jackson, *The Waiting Years*, 92–102.

Jahn, Janheinz. *Neo-African Literature: A History of Black Writing*. New York: Grove Press, 1968.

(W)Johnson, Beulah V. "The Treatment of the Negro Woman as a Major Character in American Novels, 1900–1950." Ph.D. diss., New York University, 1955.

(HR)Johnson, Charles S. "The Negro Renaissance and Its Significance." *The New Negro Thirty Years Afterward*. Ed. Edward Rayford Logan. Washington, D.C.: Howard University Press, 1955. 80–88.

*Johnson, James Weldon. *Saint Peter Relates an Incident: Selected Poems by James Weldon Johnson*. New York: Viking, 1935.

Jones, LeRoi. See Baraka, Imamu Amiri.

*Jordan, June, ed. *Soulscript: Afro-American Poetry*. New York: Doubleday (Zenith Books), 1970.

*Jordan, Winthrop D. *White over Black: American Attitudes toward the Negro, 1550–1812*. Baltimore: Penguin Books, 1968. This source is primarily historical.

Kent, George. *Blackness and the Adventure of Western Culture*. Chicago, Ill.: Third World Press, 1972.

*(HR)———. "Patterns of the Harlem Renaissance." *Black World* 21 (June 1972): 13–24, 76–80. Also in Bontemps, ed., *The Harlem Renaissance Remembered*, 27–50.

*Killens, John O. "The Image of Black Folk in American Literature." *The Black Scholar* 6 (June 1975): 45–52. See also "The Image of Black Folk," Howard University conference.

Kinney, James. *Amalgamation! Race, Sex, and Rhetoric in the Nineteenth Century American Novel*. Westport, Conn.: Greenwood Press, 1985.

*Klotman, Phyllis R. *Another Man Gone: The Black Runner in Contemporary Afro-American Literature*. Port Washington, N.Y.: Kennikat Press, 1977. Includes slave narratives, Baldwin, Barry Beckham, Claude Brown, George Davis, Ellison, William Melvin Kelley, Douglas Turner Ward, John A. Williams, and Wright.

Lamplugh, George R. "The Image of the Negro in Popular Magazine Fiction, 1875–1900." *Journal of Negro History* 57 (April 1972): 177–89.

Lee, Don L. See Madhubuti, Haki.

Lee, Robert A., ed. *Black Fiction: New Studies in the Afro-American Novel Since 1945*. London: Vision Press Limited, 1980. Includes Essays on Baldwin, Ellison, Hughes, LeRoi Jones, Petry, Ishmael Reed, and Wright and briefly refers to others.

(W)Lewis, Vashti Crutcher. "The Mulatto as Major Character in Novels by Black Women, 1892–1937." Ph.D. diss., University of Iowa, 1981.

Littlejohn, David. *Black on White: A Critical Survey of Writing by American Negroes*. New York: Grossman, 1966.

*Locke, Alain, ed. *The New Negro: An Interpretation*. New York: Albert and Charles Boni, 1925. Reprinted. Arno Press, 1968.

(HR)Lomax, Michael L. "Fantasies of Affirmation: The 1920's Novel of Negro Life." *CLAJ* 16 (December 1972): 232–46. Discusses Cullen, Fauset, Fisher, Larsen, and Walter White.

***McPherson, James M., Laurence B. Holland, James M. Banner, Jr., et. al., eds. *Blacks in America: Bibliographical Essays*. Garden City, N.Y.: Doubleday (Anchor), 1971.

Madhubuti, Haki. [Don L. Lee] "Directions for Black Writers." *Black Scholar* 12 (December 1969): 53–57.

Margolies, Edward. "The Image of the Primitive in Black Letters." *Midcontinent American Studies Journal* 11 (Fall 1970): 67–77.

———. *Native Sons: A Critical Study of Twentieth-Century Negro American Authors.* Philadelphia: J. B. Lippincott, 1968. Includes attention to Chesnutt, Ellison, J. W. Johnson, Toomer, and Wright.

*Martin, Dellita L. "In Our Own Black Images: Afro-American Literature in the 1980s." *MELUS* 8 (Summer 1981): 65–71.

Mellard, James M. "Racism, Formula, and Popular Fiction." *Journal of Popular Culture* 5 (Summer 1971): 10–37.

Miller, R. Baxter, ed. *Black American Literature and Humanism.* Lexington: The University Press of Kentucky, 1981.

Mootry, Maria K. "Studies in Black Pastoral: Five Afro-American Writers." Ph.D. diss., Northwestern University, 1974. Includes DuBois, Dunbar, Ellison, Larsen, McKay, Toomer, and Wright.

Muraskin, William. "An Alienated Elite: Short Stories in *The Crisis*, 1910–1950." *Journal of Black Studies* 1 (December 1971): 282–305.

Murray, Albert. "Literary Implications of the Blues: The Hero as Improviser." *Quadrant* 16 (November/December 1972): 34–38.

Musgrave, Marian E. "Patterns of Violence in Pro-Slavery and Anti-Slavery Fiction." *CLAJ* 16 (June 1973): 426–37.

*"The Negro in Art: How Shall He Be Portrayed?" *Crisis* 31–33 (March, April, May, June, August, September, November 1926).

*Nelson, John Herbert. *The Negro Character in American Literature.* Lawrence: University of Kansas Press, 1926. Reprinted. New York: AMS Press, 1968.

(W)Noble, Jeanne. *Beautiful Also, Are the Souls of My Black Sisters: A History of the Black Woman in America.* Englewood Cliffs, N.J.: Prentice-Hall, 1978. See especially chapter 4, "Dishwater Images," which speaks mainly of the mammy figure and chapter 7, "Speak Truth to the People."

Palosaari, Ronald G. "Images of the Black Minister in the Black Novel from Dunbar to Baldwin." Ph.D. diss., University of Minnesota, 1970.

Payne, Ladell. *Black Novelists and the Southern Literary Tradition.* Athens: University of Georgia Press, 1981.

**(HR)Perry, Margaret. *The Harlem Renaissance: An Annotated Bibliography.* New York: Garland Publishing, 1982.

———. *Silence to the Drums: A Survey of the Literature of the Harlem Renaissance.* Westport, Conn.: Greenwood Press, 1976.

*(W)Pryse, Marjorie, and Hortense J. Spillers, eds. *Conjuring: Black Women, Fiction, and Literary Tradition.* Bloomington: Indiana University Press, 1985.

Rose, Alan H. "The Evolution of the Image of the Negro as Demon in Southern Literature." Ph.D. diss., Indiana University, 1970. Includes Faulkner, G. H. Harris, Henry Clay Lewis, and Mark Twain.

Rosemond, Sarah L. "The Mythic Black Hero: From Slavery to Freedom." Ph.D. diss., Florida State University, 1984.

Rosenblatt, Roger. *Black Fiction.* Cambridge, Mass.: Harvard University Press, 1974.

Roy, Ratna. "The Marginal Man: A Study of the Mulatto in American Fiction." Ph.D. diss., University of Oregon, 1972.

Rubin, Louis D., Jr. "Southern Local Color and the Black Man." *Southern Review* 6 (Autumn 1970): 1011–30.

**(W)Rushing, Andrea B. "An Annotated Bibliography of Images of Black Women in Black Literature." *CLAJ* 25 (December 1981): 234–62; revises and updates Andrea B. Rushing, "An Annotated Bibliography of Images of Black Women in Black Literature." *CLAJ* 21 (March 1978): 435–42. (See also Rushing, in the poetry bibliography below.)

(W)Schultz, Elizabeth. " 'Free in Fact and at Last': The Image of the Black Woman in Black American Fiction." In *What Manner of Woman: Essays on English and American Life and Literature.* Ed. Marlene Springer. New York: New York University Press, 1977. 316–44. Includes attention to W. W. Brown, Chesnutt, Gaines, Himes, Hurston, Killens, Toomer, and Alice Walker.

Scott, Nathan A., Jr. "Judgment Marked by a Cellar: The American Negro Writer and the Dialectic of Despair." In *The Shapeless God: Essays on Modern Fiction.* Ed. Harry J. Mooney, Jr., and Thomas F. Staley. Pittsburgh: University of Pittsburgh Press, 1969. 139–69. Appeared previously in *University of Denver Quarterly* 2 (Summer 1967): 5–35.

Sieben, John K. "The Presentation of the Negro Character in the Best Selling Novels of the Postwar Period 1946 through 1965 in the United States." Ph.D. diss., New York University, 1971. Discusses Ellison, Faulkner, Harper Lee, Reynolds Price, Styron, Warren, and Wright.

(HR)Singh, Amritjit. *The Novels of the Harlem Renaissance: Twelve Black Writers, 1923–1933.* University Park: The Pennsylvania State University Press, 1976. The twelve writers are Bontemps, Cullen, DuBois, Fauset, Fisher, Hughes, Larsen, McKay, Schuyler, Thurman, Toomer, and White.

*(W)Smith, Barbara, ed. *Home Girls: A Black Feminist Anthology.* New York: Kitchen Table; Women of Color, 1983.

Smith, James F., Jr. "Primitives and Saviors: Cultural Images of Blacks in the 1920's." *Minority Voices* 1 (Spring 1977): 53–61.

Smitherman, Geneva. *Talkin' and Testifyin': The Language of Black America.* Boston: Houghton Mifflin Co., 1977.

*Starke, Catherine J. *Black Portraiture in American Fiction: Stock Characters, Archetypes, and Individuals.* New York: Basic Books, 1971.

(W)Sterling, Dorothy, ed. *We Are Your Sisters: Black Women in the Nineteenth Century.* New York: W. W. Norton & Co., 1984. See the brief introduction.

*(W)Tate, Claudia, ed. *Black Women Writers at Work.* New York: The Continuum Publishing Corp., 1984.

Taylor, Clyde. "Black Writing as Immanent Humanism." *The Southern Review* 21 (Summer 1985): 790–800.

Tischler, Nancy. *Black Masks: Negro Characters in Modern Southern Fiction.* University Park: The Pennsylvania State University Press, 1969.

———. "The Negro in Southern Fiction: Stereotype and Archetype." *NALF* 2 (Spring 1968): 3–6.

(HR)Turner, Darwin T. "The Harlem Renaissance: One Facet of an Unturned Kaleidoscope." In *Toward a New American Literary History: Essays in Honor of Arlin Turner.* Eds. Louis J. Budd, Edwin H. Cady and Carl L. Anderson. Durham, N.C.: Duke University Press, 1980: 195–210.

———. *In a Minor Chord: Three Afro-American Writers and Their Search for Identity.*

Carbondale: Southern Illinois University, 1971. Discusses Cullen, Hurston, and Toomer.

————. "Southern Fiction, 1900–1910." *Mississippi Quarterly* 21 (Fall 1968): 281–85.

*————, and Jean M. Bright, eds. *Images of the Negro in America: Selected Source Materials for College Research Papers*. Boston, Mass.: D. C. Heath and Co., 1965.

(BA)Wade, Melvin, and Margaret Wade. "The Black Aesthetic in the Black Novel." *Journal of Black Studies* 2 (June 1972): 391–408.

Wander, P. C. "The Savage Child: The Image of the Negro in the Pro-Slavery Movement." *Southern Speech Communication* 37 (Summer 1972): 335–60.

Waniek, Marilyn N. "The Space Where Sex Should Be: Toward a Definition of the Black American Literary Tradition." *Studies in Black Literature* 6 (Fall 1975): 7–13.

(W)Washington, Mary Helen. "Black Women Image Makers." *Black World* 23 (August 1974): 10–18.

*(W)————. " 'Taming All That Anger Down': Rage and Silence in Gwendolyn Brooks' *Maud Martha*." See Individual Authors section for complete entry.

*————, ed. "In Pursuit of Our Own History." Introduction to *Midnight Birds: Stories of Contemporary Black Women Writers*. Garden City, N.Y.: Doubleday (Anchor Books), 1980.

*(W)————, ed. Introduction to *Black-Eyed Susans: Classic Stories by and about Black Women*. Garden City, N.Y.: Doubleday (Anchor Books), 1975.

Watkins, Floyd. *The Death of Art: Black and White in the Recent Southern Novel*. Mercer University Lamar Memorial Lectures, no. 13. Athens: University of Georgia Press, 1970.

Weixlmann, Joe, and Chester J. Fontenot. *Black American Prose Theory*. Vol. 1, *Studies in Black American Literature*. Greenwood, Fla.: The Penkevill Publishing Co., 1984.

Whitlow, Roger. *Black American Literature: A Critical History*. Totowa, N.J.: Littlefield, Adams, & Co., 1973.

Williams, John A. "The Crisis in American Letters." *Black Scholar* 6 (June 1975): 67–71.

*(BA)Williams, Sherley Anne. *Give Birth to Brightness: A Thematic Study in Neo-Black Literature*. New York: The Dial Press, 1972.

*Wright, Richard. "Blueprint for Negro Literature." (1937) In *Amistad 2: Writings on Black History and Culture*. Eds. Charles F. Harris and John A. Williams. Random House (Vintage Books), 1971. 3–20.

Yarborough, Richard. "The Depiction of Blacks in the Early Afro-American Novel." Ph.D. diss., Stanford University, 1980.

*Yellin, Jean F. *The Intricate Knot: Black Figures in American Literature, 1776–1863*. New York: New York University Press, 1972.

Young, James O. *Black Writers of the Thirties*. Baton Rouge: Louisiana State University Press, 1973.

Poetry

Baker, Houston A., Jr., ed. *A Dark and Sudden Beauty: Two Essays in Black American Poetry*. Philadelphia: Afro-American Studies Program, University of Pennsylvania, 1977.

Barksdale, Richard K. "Trends in Contemporary Poetry." *Phylon* (1958): 408–16.

Bell, Bernard W. *The Folk Roots of Afro-American Poetry*. Detroit, Mich.: Broadside Press, 1974.

(BA)Brooks, A. Russell. "The Motif of Dynamic Change in Black Revolutionary Poetry." *CLAJ* 15 (September 1971): 7–17. Includes references to Nikki Giovanni, Don L. Lee, and Sonia Sanchez.

*Brown, Sterling. *Negro Poetry and Drama*. 1937. Reprinted with *The Negro in American Fiction*. New York: Atheneum, 1969.

(BA)Davis, Arthur P. "The New Poetry of Black Hate." *CLAJ* 14 (June 1970): 382–91. Also in *Modern Black Poets*, ed. Donald B. Gibson.

Gibson, Donald B., ed. *Modern Black Poets: A Collection of Critical Essays*. Englewood Cliffs, N.J.: Prentice-Hall, 1973.

*(BA)Henderson, Stephen. "The Form of Things Unknown." Introduction to *Understanding the New Black Poetry: Black Speech and Black Music as Poetic References*. New York: William Morrow & Co., 1973. 1–69.

Jackson, Blyden, and Louis D. Rubin, Jr. *Black Poetry in America: Two Essays in Historical Interpretation*. Baton Rouge: Louisiana State University Press, 1974.

Miller, R. Baxter, ed. *Black American Poets between Worlds, 1940–1960*. Tennessee Studies in Literature, vol. 30. Knoxville: University of Tennessee Press, 1986. Includes essays on Melvin B. Tolson, Robert Hayden, Dudley Randall, Margaret Danner, Margaret Walker, and Gwendolyn Brooks.

Redding, Jay Saunders. *To Make a Poet Black*. 1939. Reprinted. Great Neck, N.Y.: Core Collection Books, 1978.

(W)Rushing, Andrea Benton. "Images of Black Women in Afro-American Poetry." *The Black Woman Cross Culturally*. Ed. Filomina Chioma Steady. Cambridge, Mass.: Schenkman Books, 1981. Also in *The Afro-American Woman: Struggles and Images*, eds. Sharon Harley and R. Terborg-Penn (see general section above); based on a September 1975 *Black World* essay.

(BA)Sheffey, Ruthe. "Wit and Irony in Militant Black Poetry." *Black World* 22 (June 1973): 14–21.

(BA)Smitherman, Geneva. "The Power of the Rap: The Black Idiom and the New Black Poetry." *Twentieth Century Literature* 19 (October 1973): 259–74.

(W)Stetson, Erlene. Introduction to *Black Sisters: Poetry by Black American Women, 1746–1980*. Bloomington: Indiana University Press, 1981.

Tyms, James D. "The Black Poet and a Sense of Self—The Praise of Famous Men." *Journal of Religious Thought* 32 (Spring-Summer 1975): 22–35.

Wagner, Jean. *Black Poets of the United States: From Paul Laurence Dunbar to Langston Hughes*. Urbana: University of Illinois Press, 1973. Trans. Kenneth Douglas. First published in French in 1962 as *Les poètes negrès des Etats-Unis: le sentiment racial et religieux dans la poésie de P. L. Dunbar à L. Hughes (1890–1940)*. Paris: Librairie Istra, 1963 [c1962].

Williams, Sherley Anne. "The Blues Roots of Contemporary Afro-American Poetry." *Afro-American Literature: The Reconstruction of Instruction*. Eds. Dexter Fisher and Robert Stepto. New York: Modern Language Association, 1978: 72–87. Reprinted. *Chant of Saints*: 123–35.

Drama

Abramson, Doris E. *Negro Playwrights in the American Theatre, 1925–1959*. New York: Columbia University Press, 1969.

(W)Anderson, Mary Louise. "Black Matriarchy: Portrayals of Women in Three Plays." *NALF* 10 (Fall 1976): 93–95. Includes plays by James Baldwin, Hansberry, and Alice Childress.

**Arata, Esther Spring, and Nicholas Rotoli. *Black American Playwrights 1800 to the Present: A Bibliography*. Metuchen, N.J.: Scarecrow Press, 1976.

Archer, Leonard C. *Black Images in the American Theater*. Brooklyn, N.Y.: Pageant-Poseidon, 1973.

Bigsby, C. W. E. "Black Drama in the Seventies." *Texas Quarterly* 3 (Spring 1971): 10–20.

————, ed. *The Black American Writer*. See general section above, vol. 2.

Bradley, Gerald. "Goodbye Mr. Bones: The Emergence of Negro Themes and Character in American Drama." *Drama Critique* 7 (Spring 1964): 79–86.

Brooks, A. Russell. "The Comic Spirit and the Negro's New Look." *CLAJ* 6 (September 1962): 35–43.

Brown, Lloyd W. "The Cultural Revolution in Black Theatre." *NALF* 8 (Spring 1974): 159–64.

*Brown, Sterling. *Negro Poetry and Drama*. See poetry section above.

Bullins, Ed. "Theatre of Reality." *Negro Digest* 18 (April 1969): 60–66.

Couch, William, Jr. "The Problem of Negro Character and Dramatic Incident." *Phylon* 11 (June 1950): 127–33.

Craig, E. Quita. *Black Drama of the Federal Theatre Era*. Amherst: University of Massachusetts Press, 1980.

(W)Flowers, Saundra Hollins. "*Colored Girls*: Textbook for the Eighties." *BALF* 15 (Summer 1981): 51–54.

Green, Alan W. C. " 'Jim Crow', 'Zip Coon': The Northern Origins of Negro Minstrelsy." *MR* 9 (Spring 1970): 385–97.

**Hatch, James. *Black Image on the American Stage: A Bibliography of Plays and Musicals, 1770–1970*. New York: DBS Publications, 1970.

Hay, Samuel A. "The Image of the Black Man as Projected by Representative White American Dramatists, 1900–1963." Ph.D. diss., Cornell University, 1971.

Hill, Errol, ed. *The Theatre of Black Americans*. 2 vols. Englewood Cliffs, N.J.: Prentice-Hall, 1980.

Kaplan, Sidney. "*The Octoroon*: Early History of the Drama of Miscegenation." *Journal of Negro Education* 20 (Fall 1951): 547–57.

McIlrath, Patricia. "Stereotypes, Types, and Characters in Drama." *Educational Theatre Journal* 7 (March 1955): 1–10.

(W)Miller, Jeanne-Marie A. "Images of Black Women in Plays by Black Playwrights." *CLAJ* 20 (June 1977): 494–507.

Mitchell, Loften. *Black Drama: The Story of the American Negro in the Theatre*. New York: Hawthorn Books, 1967.

(BA)Neal, Larry. "Black Art and Black Liberation." *Ebony* 24 (August 1969): 54–58.

Pawley, Thomas. "The First Black Playwrights." *Black World* 21 (April 1972): 16–24.

(W)Potter, Vilma R. "New Politics, New Mothers." *CLAJ* 16 (December 1972): 247–55.

Teer, Barbara Ann. "Needed: A New Image." *The Black Power Revolt: A Collection of Essays*. Ed. Floyd B. Barbour. Boston, Mass.: Porter Sargent, 1968, 263–68.

Thompson, Larry. "The Black Image in Early American Drama, 1760–1930." *Black World* 26 (April 1975): 54–69.

Turner, Darwin T. "Visions of Love and Manliness in a Blackening World: Dramas of Black Life from 1953–1970." *Iowa Review* 6 (1975): 82–99.
(W)Turner, S. H. Regina. "Images of Black Women in the Plays of Black Women Playwrights, 1950–1975." Ph.D. diss., Bowling Green State University, 1982.
Wilkerson, Margaret B., and Vèvè A. Clark, guest eds. "Black Theatre Traditions." *Black Scholar* 10 (July-August 1979): 3–88.
Williams, Mance. *Black Theatre in the 1960s and 1970s: A Historical-Critical Analysis of the Movement.* Westport, Conn.: Greenwood Press, 1985.

Folklore

*Bontemps, Arna, and Langston Hughes, eds. *The Book of Negro Folklore.* New York: Dodd, Mead & Co., 1958. See Introduction.
Brewer, J. M. "American Negro Folklore." *Phylon* 6 (Fourth Quarter 1945): 354–61.
*———. *American Negro Folklore.* Chicago: Quadrangle Books, 1968.
*Dance, Daryl C. *Shuckin' and Jivin': Folklore from Contemporary Black Americans.* Bloomington: Indiana University Press, 1978.
Dickson, Bruce D. "The 'John and Old Master' Stories of the World of Slavery: A Study of Folktales and History." *Phylon* 35 (December 1974): 418–29.
*Dundes, Alan. *Mother Wit from the Laughing Barrel: Readings in the Interpretation of Afro-American Folklore.* Englewood Cliffs, N.J.: Prentice-Hall, 1973.
*Hurston, Zora Neale. *Mules and Men: Negro Folktales and Voodoo Practice in the South.* 1935. Reprinted. New York: Harper and Row, Perennial Library, 1970.
*Levine, Lawrence. *Black Culture and Black Consciousness: Afro-American Folk Thought from Slavery to Freedom.* New York: Oxford University Press, 1977.
McGhee, Nancy B. "The Folk Sermon: A Facet of the Black Literary Heritage." *CLAJ* 13 (September 1969): 51–61.
*Stuckey, Sterling. "Through the Prism of Folklore: The Black Ethos in Slavery." *MR* 9 (Summer 1968): 172–91. Also in *New Black Voices*, ed. Abraham Chapman. New York: New American Library, 1972, 439–57. Also in *Black and White*.

Slave Narratives and Other Autobiographical Literature

*Andrews, William L. "The First Century of Afro-American Autobiography: Theory and Explication." *Black American Prose Theory*, Vol. I, *Studies in Black American Literature.* 1984. Eds. Joe Weixlmann and Chester Fontenot. 4–42.
———. *To Tell a Free Story: The First Century of Afro-American Autobiography.* Urbana: University of Illinois Press, 1986.
Baker, Houston A., Jr. "The Problem of Being: Some Reflections of Black Autobiography. *Obsidian* 1 (Spring 1975): 18–30.
Barton, Rebecca Chambers. *Witnesses for Freedom: Negro Americans in Autobiography.* Oakdale, N.Y.: Dowling College Press, 1969.
(W)Blackburn, Regina. "In Search of the Black Female Self: African-American Women's Autobiography and Ethnicity." In *Women's Autobiography: Essays in Criticism.* Ed. Estelle C. Jelinek. Bloomington: Indiana University Press, 1980. 133–48.
*Blassingame, John. *The Slave Community: Plantation Life in the Antebellum South.* New York: Oxford University Press, 1972. Rev. and enl. ed. Oxford, 1979.

(W)Braxton, Joanne M. "Autobiography by Black Women: A Tradition within a Tradition." Ph.D. diss., Yale University, 1984.

**Brignano, Russell C. *Black Americans in Autobiography: An Annotated Bibliography of Autobiographies and Autobiographical Books Written Since the Civil War*. Rev. and exp. ed. Durham, N.C.: Duke University Press, 1984.

Burger, Mary. "Black Autobiography: A Literature of Celebration." Ph.D. diss., Washington University, 1973.

*———. "Images of Self and Race in the Autobiographies of Black Women." *SBB*, 107–22.

*Butterfield, Stephen. *Black Autobiography in America*. Amherst: University of Massachusetts Press, 1974.

Dance, Daryl C. "Wit and Humor in the Slave Narratives." *Journal of Afro-American Issues* 5 (2d quarter 1977): 125–33.

*Davis, Charles, and Henry Louis Gates, Jr., eds. *The Slave's Narrative*. New York: Oxford University Press, 1985.

(W)Foster, Francis Smith. "Adding Color and Contour to Early American Self-Portraiture: Autobiographical Writings of Afro-American Women." *Conjuring*: 25–38.

———. " 'In Respect to Females . . . ': Differences in the Portrayals of Women by Males and Females." *BALF* 15 (Summer 1981): 66–70.

*———. *Witnessing Slavery: The Development of Ante-bellum Slave Narratives*. Westport, Conn.: Greenwood Press, 1979.

Hedin, Raymond. "The American Slave Narrative: The Justification of the Picaro." *AL* 53 (January 1982): 630–45.

Johnson, Paul D. " 'Goodbye to Sambo': The Contribution of the Slave Narrative to the Abolitionist Movement." *NALF* 6 (Fall 1972): 79–84.

Minter, David. "Conceptions of Self in Black Slave Narratives." *American Transcendental Quarterly* 24 (Fall 1974, part 1): 62–68.

*Nichols, Charles H. *Many Thousand Gone: The Ex-Slaves' Account of Their Bondage and Freedom*. Bloomington: Indiana University Press, 1963.

Schultz, Elizabeth. "To Be Black and Blue: The Blues Genre in Black American Autobiography." In *The American Autobiography: A Collection of Critical Essays*. Ed. Albert E. Stone. Englewood Cliffs, N.J.: Prentice-Hall, 1981. 109–32.

*Sekora, John, and Darwin T. Turner, eds. *The Art of Slave Narrative: Original Essays in Criticism and Theory*. Macomb: Western Illinois University, 1982.

"The First Fifty Years of the Slave Narrative, 1760–1810," William L. Andrews; "Strategies of Form in the American Slave Narrative," Raymond Hedin; "The Slave Narrative and the Black Literary Tradition," Martha K. Cobb; "Tryin' to Get Over: Narrative Posture in Equiano's Autobiography," Chinosole; Metaphors of Mastery in the Slave Narratives," Lucinda H. Mackethan; "We Wear the Mask: Deceit as Theme and Style in Slave Narratives," Keith Byerman; "The Slave Narratives as Rhetorical Art," Mary Ellen Doyle, S.C.N.; "The Problematic of Self in Autobiography: The Example of the Slave Narrative," Annette Niemtzow; "Point of View in the Afro-American Slave Narratives: A Study of Narratives by Douglass and Pennington," Lillie Butler Jugurtha; "The Slave Narrative: Prototype of the Early Afro-American Novel," Marva J. Furman; Appendix One: "Uses of the Ante-bellum Slave Narrative in Collegiate Courses in Literature," Darwin T. Turner; Appendix Two: "Black Slave Narratives—A Selected Checklist of Criticism," Gregory S. Sojka.

Smith, Sidonie. *Where I'm Bound: Patterns of Slavery and Freedom in Black American Autobiography*. Westport, Conn.: Greenwood Press, 1974.

*Starling, Marion. *The Slave Narrative: Its Place in American History*. Boston, Mass.: G. K. Hall, 1981.

*Stepto, Robert. *From behind the Veil: A Study of Afro-American Narrative*. Urbana: University of Illinois Press, 1979.

Themes (selected; cross-listed from other sections)

1. Mulatto, Miscegenation. *General*: Andrews; Berzon; Brown, Sterling; Kinney; Lewis; Roy. (As noted earlier, almost all comprehensive general studies give attention to the theme.) See also *Drama*: Kaplan; *Hughes, Langston*: Davis; *Hurston, Zora Neale*: Lewis.
2. Soldier. *General*: Couch.
3. Preacher. *General*: Daniel; Palosaari.

Individual Authors (selected)

Angelou, Maya

O'Neale, Sondra. "Reconstruction of the Composite Self: New Images of Black Women in Maya Angelou's Continuing Autobiography." *BWW*: 25–36.

Baldwin, James

Cowan, Kathryn O. "Black/White Stereotypes in the Fiction of Richard Wright, James Baldwin, and Ralph Ellison." Ph.D. diss., St. Louis University, 1972.

Hagopian, John V. "James Baldwin: The Black and the Red-White-and-Blue." *CLAJ* 7 (December 1963):133–40. Reprinted in *James Baldwin: A Critical Evaluation*. Ed. Therman B. O'Daniel. Washington, D.C.: Howard University Press, 1977. Cited hereafter as *JB*.

(W)Harris, Trudier. *Black Women in the Fiction of James Baldwin*. Knoxville: University of Tennessee Press, 1985.

———. "The South as Woman: Chimeric Images of Emasculation in *Just Above My Head*." In *Black American Prose Theory*. Eds. Joe Weixlmann and Chester J. Fontenot. 88–110.

Hernton, Calvin C. "Blood of the Lamb: The Ordeal of James Baldwin." *Amistad 1*. Eds. Charles F. Harris and John A. Williams. N.Y.: Random House. 183–225. The essay's final section considers other authors, such as LeRoi Jones, William Melvin Kelley, and John A. Williams.

Levin, David. "Baldwin's Autobiographical Essays: The Problem of Negro Identity." *MR* 5 (Winter 1964):239–47. Reprinted in *Black and White*: 372–79.

O'Daniel, Therman B., ed. *James Baldwin: A Critical Evaluation*. (See Hagopian, above this section.)

(W)Orsagh, Jacqueline E. "Baldwin's Female Characters—A Step Forward?" *JB*: 56–68.

Pratt, Louis H. *James Baldwin*. Boston, Mass.: G. K. Hall (Twayne's United States Author Series), 1978.

Reilly, John M. " 'Sonny's Blues': James Baldwin's Image of Black Community."
    NALF 4 (July 1970): 56–60. Reprinted *JB*: 163–69.
Schrero, Elliott M. "*Another Country* and the Sense of Self." *Black Academy Review*
    2 (Spring-Summer 1971):91–100.
**Standley, Fred L., and Nancy V. Standley. *James Baldwin: A Reference Guide*. Boston,
    Mass.: G. K. Hall, 1979.
See also General: *FBW*; Drama: Anderson.

Bambara, Toni Cade

Hull, Gloria. " 'What It Is I Think She's Doing Anyhow': A Reading of Toni Cade
    Bambara's *The Salt Eaters*." *Conjuring*:216–32.
See also General: Fisher, Jerilyn.

Baraka, Imamu Amiri

Benston, Kimberly W. *Baraka, the Renegade and the Mask*. New Haven, Conn.: Yale
    University Press, 1976.
————, ed. *Imamu Amiri Baraka (LeRoi Jones): A Collection of Critical Essays*. En-
    glewood Cliffs, N.J.: Prentice-Hall, 1978.
Brown, Lloyd. *Amiri Baraka*. Boston, Mass.: Twayne, 1980.
Costello, Donald P. "Black Man as Victim." *Commonweal* 88 (June 28, 1968): 436–
    40. Reprinted *FBW*: 206–14.
Harris, William J. "Militant Singers: Baraka, Cultural Nationalism and Madhubuti."
    Minority Voices 2 (Fall 1978):29–34.
Hudson, Theodore. *From LeRoi Jones to Amiri Baraka: The Literary Works*. Durham,
    N.C.: Duke University Press, 1973.
Lacey, Henry C. *To Raise, Destroy, and Create: The Poetry, Drama, and Fiction of
    Imamu Amiri Baraka*. Troy, N.Y.: Whitston, 1982.

Bontemps, Arna

**Fleming, Robert E. *James Weldon Johnson and Arna Bontemps: A Reference Guide*.
    Boston, Mass.: G. K. Hall, 1978.
See also works on the Harlem Renaissance in the General section under (HR).

Brooks, Gwendolyn

Andrews, Larry R. "Ambivalent Clothes Imagery in Gwendolyn Brooks's 'The Sundays
    of Satin-Legs Smith.' " *CLAJ* 24 (December 1980):150–63.
Davis, Arthur P. "The Black and Tan Motif in the Poetry of Gwendolyn Brooks." *CLAJ*
    6 (December 1962):90–97.
————. "Gwendolyn Brooks: A Poet of the Unheroic." *CLAJ* 7 (December 1963):114–
    25.
Gayle, Addison, Jr. "Gwendolyn Brooks: Poet of the Whirlwind." *BWW*: 70–87.
Guy-Sheftall, Beverly. "The Women of Bronzeville." *SBB*: 157–70.
Kent, George E. "Aesthetic Values in the Poetry of Gwendolyn Brooks." In *Black
    American Literature and Humanism*. Ed. R. Baxter Miller. 75–94.
————. "Gwendolyn Brooks' Poetic Realism: A Developmental Survey." *BWW*: 88–
    105.

**Miller, R. Baxter. *Langston Hughes and Gwendolyn Brooks: A Reference Guide*. Boston, Mass.: G. K. Hall, 1978.

*Washington, Mary Helen. " 'Taming All That Anger Down': Rage and Silence in Gwendolyn Brooks' *Maud Martha*." *MR* 24 (Winter 1983):453–66. Reprinted in *Black Literature and Literary Theory*. Ed. Henry Louis Gates, Jr.: 249–62. An earlier version entitled "Plain, Black, and Decently Wild: The Heroic Possibilities of *Maud Martha*" appeared in *Voyage In: Fictions of Female Development*. Eds. Elizabeth Abel and others. Hanover, N.H.: University Press of New England, 1983:270–86.

See also *BAP*.

Brown, Sterling (for critical works by Brown, see the general bibliography)

Gabbin, Joanne V. *Sterling A. Brown: Building the Black Aesthetic Tradition*. Westport, Conn.: Greenwood Press, 1985.

Harper, Michael S. *The Collected Poems of Sterling A. Brown*. New York: Harper and Row (Colophon), 1980. See introduction by Sterling Stuckey, pp. 3–15.

**O'Meally, Robert. "An Annotated Bibliography of the Works of Sterling A. Brown. *CLAJ* 19 (December 1975):268–79.

———. "Game to the Heart: Sterling Brown and the Badman." *Callaloo* 5, 1–2 (February-May, 1982):43–54. Entire issue, pp. 11–105, devoted to Brown.

Brown, William Wells (and Martin Delaney)

Ellison, Curtis W., and E. W. Metcalf. *William Wells Brown and Martin R. Delaney: A Reference Guide*. Boston, Mass.: G. K. Hall, 1978.

See also Autobiographical Literature: Sekora and Turner, eds. *The Art of Slave Narrative*; other general references.

Butler, Octavia

Govan, Sandra Y. "Connections, Links, and Extended Networks: Patterns in Octavia Butler's Science Fiction." *BALF* 18 (Summer 1984):82–87.

Salvaggio, Ruth. "Octavia Butler and the Black Science-Fiction Heroine." *BALF* 18 (Summer 1984):78–81.

Shinn, Thelma K. "The Wise Witches: Black Women Mentors in the Fiction of Octavia E. Butler." *Conjuring*:203–15.

Cable, George Washington

Campbell, Michael L. "The Negro in Cable's *The Grandissimes*." *Mississippi Quarterly* 27 (Spring 1974):165–68.

Rubin, Louis D., Jr. "The Division of the Heart: Cable's *The Grandissimes*." *SLJ* 1 (Spring 1969):27–47.

See also General: Frisby, Godbold.

Chesnutt, Charles Waddell

Andrews, William L. "The Significance of Charles Waddell Chesnutt's 'Conjure Stories.' " *SLJ* 7 (Fall 1974):78–99.

Baldwin, Richard E. "The Art of *The Conjure Woman*." *AL* 43 (November 1971):385–98.

Dixon, Melvin. "The Teller as Folk Trickster in Chesnutt's *The Conjure Woman*." *CLAJ* 18 (December 1974):186–97.

**Ellison, Curtis W., and E. W. Metcalfe, Jr. *Charles W. Chesnutt: A Reference Guide*. Boston, Mass.: G. K. Hall, 1975.

Taxel, Joel. "Charles Waddell Chesnutt's Sambo: Myth and Reality." *NALF* 9 (Fall 1975):104–8.

Childress, Alice

See Drama: Anderson.

Chopin, Kate

Potter, Richard H. "Negroes in the Fiction of Kate Chopin." *Louisiana History* 12 (Winter 1971):41–58.

See also General: Frisby.

Clemens, Samuel

Browdin, Stanley. "Blackness and the Adamic Myth in Mark Twain's *Pudd'nhead Wilson*." *Texas Studies in Literature and Language* 15 (Spring 1973):167–76.

Chellis, Barbara A. "Those Extraordinary Twins: Negroes and White." *American Quarterly* 21 (Spring 1969):100–112.

*Davis, Thadious M., guest ed. "Black Writers on *Adventures of Huckleberry Finn* One Hundred Years Later." *Mark Twain Journal* 22 (Fall 1984):2–52. David L. Smith, "Huck, Jim, and American Racial Discourse"; Charles H. Nichols, " 'A True Book with Some Stretchers': *Huck Finn Today*"; Richard K. Barksdale, "History, Slavery, and Thematic Irony in *Huckleberry Finn*"; Charles H. Nilon, "The Ending of *Huckleberry Finn*: 'Freeing the Free Negro' "; Rhett S. Jones, "Nigger and Knowledge: White Double-Consciousness in *Adventures of Huckleberry Finn*"; Kenny J. Williams, "*Adventures of Huckleberry Finn*; Or, Mark Twain's Racial Ambiguity"; Julius Lester, "Morality and *Adventures of Huckleberry Finn*"; Arnold Rampersad, "*Adventures of Huckleberry Finn* and Afro-American Literature."

Fiedler, Leslie. " 'Come Back to the Raft Ag'in, Huck Honey!' " *Partisan Review* 15 (June 1948):664–71. Reprinted in Fielder's *An End to Innocence*. Boston, Mass.: Beacon Press, 1955.

Gibson, Donald B. "Mark Twain's Jim in the Classroom." *English Journal* 57 (February 1968):196–99, 202.

Hansen, Chadwick. "The Character of Jim and the Ending of *Huckleberry Finn*." *MR* 5 (Autumn 1963):45–66.

Hoffman, Daniel G. *Form and Fable in American Fiction*. New York: Oxford University Press, 1961. Hoffman's chapter entitled "Black Magic—and White—in *Huckleberry Finn*" is reprinted in *Mark Twain: A Collection of Critical Essays*. Ed. Henry Nash Smith. Englewood Cliffs, N.J.: Prentice-Hall, 1963. Also in the Norton Critical Edition of *Huckleberry Finn* (1961–62). Eds. Sculley Bradley, Richmond Croom Beatty, and E. Hudson Long. 396–409.

Schonhorn, Manuel. "Mark Twain's Jim: Solomon on the Mississippi. *Mark Twain Journal* 14 (Winter 1967–1968):9–11.

Wysong, Jack P. "Samuel Clemens' Attitude toward the Negro as Demonstrated in *Pudd'nhead Wilson* and *A Connecticut Yankee in King Arthur's Court*." *Xavier University Studies* 7 (July 1968):41–57.

Cullen, Countee

Davis, Arthur P. "The Alien-and-Exile Theme in Countee Cullen's Racial Poems." *Phylon* 14 (Winter 1953):390–400.

See also General: works on the Harlem Renaissance (HR).

Delany, Samuel R.

Govan, Sandra Y. "The Insistent Presence of Black Folk in the Novels of Samuel R. Delany." *BALF* 18 (Summer 1984):43–56. The same issue includes other essays and bibliographical information on Delaney as well.

Dixon, Thomas

Gallagher, Brian. "Racist Ideology and Black Abnormality in *The Birth of a Nation*." *Phylon* 43 (March 1982):68–76. On the role of *The Leopard's Spots* and *The Clansman* in the 1915 film.

Kinney, James. "The Rhetoric of Racism: Thomas Dixon and the 'Damned Black Beast.' " *American Literary Realism, 1870–1910* 15 (Autumn 1982):145–54.

See also General: Godbold.

Douglass, Frederick

Andrews, William L. "Frederick Douglass, Preacher." *AL* 54 (December 1982):592–97.

Stepto, Robert B. "Storytelling in Early Afro-American Fiction: Frederick Douglass's 'The Heroic Slave.' " *Georgia Review* 6 (Summer 1982):355–68. Reprinted. *Black Literature and Literary Theory*. Ed. Henry Louis Gates, Jr. 175–86.

Stone, Albert E. "Identity and Art in Frederick Douglass's *Narratives*." *CLAJ* 17 (December 1973):192–213.

Watson, Charles S. "Portrayals of the Black and the Idea of Progress: Simms and Douglass." *Southern Studies* 20 (Winter 1981):339–50.

See also General: Fisher and Stepto, eds. *Afro-American Literature* for studies of the 1845 *Narrative* by O'Meally, Stepto, and Gates.

Du Bois, W. E. B.

Andrews, William L. *Critical Essays on W. E. B. Du Bois*. Boston, Mass.: G. K. Hall, 1980.

Appiah, Anthony. "The Incompleted Argument: Du Bois and the Illusion of Race." *Critical Inquiry* 12 (Autumn 1985):21–37.

Rampersad, Arnold. *The Art and Imagination of W. E. B. Du Bois*. Cambridge, Mass.: Harvard University Press, 1976.

Stewart, James B. "Psychic Duality of Afro-Americans in the Novels of W. E. B. Du Bois." *Phylon* 44 (June 1983):93–107.

Dunbar, Paul Laurence

Martin, Jay. *A Singer in the Dawn*. New York: Dodd, Mead, 1975.
See also General: Gayle, *The Way of the New World*, especially pp. 48–57; Houston
Baker, *Blues, Ideology, and Afro-American Literature*, "The 'Limitless' Freedom
of Myth: Paul Laurence Dunbar's *The Sport of the Gods* and the Criticism of
Afro-American Literature." 114–38. An earlier version of Baker's essay appeared
in *The American Self: Myth, Ideology, and Popular Culture*. Ed. Sam B. Girgus.
Albuquerque: University of New Mexico Press, 1981. 124–43.

Ellison, Ralph

Baker, Houston A., Jr. "To Move without Moving: An Analysis of Creativity and
Commerce in Ralph Ellison's Trueblood Episode." *PMLA* 98 (October 1983):828–
45. Reprinted. *Black Literature and Literary Theory*. Ed. Henry Louis Gates, Jr.
221–48. See also Baker, *Blues, Ideology, and Afro-American Literature*. 172–
203.
Crewdson, Arlene J. "Invisibility, a Study of the Works of Toomer, Wright, and Ellison."
Ph.D. diss., Loyola University of Chicago, 1974.
O'Daniel, Therman B. "The Image of Man as Portrayed by Ralph Ellison." *CLAJ* 10
(June 1967):272–84. Reprinted *FBW*: 105–115.
O'Meally, Robert G. *The Craft of Ralph Ellison*. Cambridge, Mass.: Harvard University
Press, 1980.
Reilly, John M., ed. *Twentieth Century Interpretations of Invisible Man: A Collection
of Critical Essays*. Englewood Cliffs, N.J.: Prentice-Hall, 1970.
(W)Sylvander, Carolyn. "Ralph Ellison's *Invisible Man* and Female Stereotypes." *NALF*
9 (Fall 1975):77–79.
See also General: Gibson, *Politics*; Murray, Albert: Freeman.

Faulkner, William

*Davis, Thadious M. *Faulkner's "Negro": Art and the Southern Context*. Baton Rouge:
Louisiana State University Press, 1983.
Denniston, Dorothy L. "Faulkner's Image of the Black Man in *Go Down Moses*." *Phylon*
44 (Spring 1983):33–43.
Jackson, Blyden. "Faulkner's Depiction of the Negro." *University of Mississippi Studies
in English*. 15 (1978):33–47.
———. "Two Mississippi Writers: Wright and Faulkner." *University of Mississippi
Studies in English*. 15 (1978):49–59.
Jenkins, Lee. *Faulkner and Black-White Relations: A Psychoanalytic Approach*. New
York: Columbia University Press, 1981.
*Kent, George E. "The Black Woman in Faulkner's Works with the Exception of
Dilsey." Part I. *Phylon* 35 (December 1974):430–41; Part II. *Phylon* 36 (March
1975):55–67.
*Nilon, Charles H. *Faulkner and the Negro*. New York: Citadel Press, 1965.
Taylor, Walter. "Faulkner: Nineteenth Century Notions of Racial Mixture and the Twen-
tieth Century Imagination." *South Carolina Review* 10 (1977):57–68.
Turner, Darwin T. "Faulkner and Slavery." In *The South and Faulkner's Yoknapataw-
pha: The Actual and the Aprocryphal*. Eds. Evans Harrington and Ann J. Abadie.
Jackson: University Press of Mississippi, 1977.

Werner, Craig. "Tell Old Pharoah: The Afro-American Response to Faulkner." *Southern Review* 19 (October 1983):711–35.

Fauset, Jessie Redmon

McDowell, Deborah E. "The Neglected Dimension of Jessie Redmon Fauset." *Conjuring*:86–104.

Sylvander, Carolyn Wedin. *Jessie Redmon Fauset: Black American Writer.* Troy, N.Y.: Whitston Publishing Co., 1981.

Fisher, Rudolph

Deutsch, Leonard J. " 'The Streets of Harlem': The Short Stories of Rudolph Fisher." *Phylon* 40 (Summer 1979):159–71.

Gaines, Ernest

Andrews, William L. " 'We Ain't Going Back There': The Idea of Progress in *The Autobiography of Miss Jane Pittman. BALF* 11 (Winter 1977):146–49.

McDonald, Walter R. " 'You Not a Bum, You a Man.': Ernest J. Gaines's *Bloodline.*" *NALF* 9 (Summer 1975):47–49.

Rowell, Charles H. "The Quarters: Ernest Gaines and the Sense of Place." *The Southern Review* 21 (Summer 1985):733–50.

Giovanni, Nikki

See Madhubuti, Haki.

See General: works which discuss the Black Arts Movement (BA); and Poetry: Brooks.

Griggs, Sutton

Moses, Wilson J. "Literary Garveyism: The Novels of Reverend Sutton E. Griggs." *Phylon* 40 (Fall 1979):203–16.

Hansberry, Lorraine

(W)Barthelemy, Anthony. "Mother, Sister, Wife: A Dramatic Perspective." *The Southern Review* 21 (Summer 1985):770–89.

Discusses *A Raisin in the Sun* and Theodore Ward's *Big White Fog.*

Carter, Steven R. "Images of Men in Lorraine Hansberry's Writing." *BALF* 19 (Winter 1985):160–62.

Farrison, W. Edward. "Lorraine Hansberry's Last Drama." *CLAJ* 16 (December 1972):188–97.

Wilkerson, Margaret B. "The Sighted Eyes and Feeling Heart of Lorraine Hansberry." *BALF* 17 (Spring 1983):8–13.

See also Drama: Anderson.

Harris, Joel Chandler

Bickley, R. Bruce, ed. *Critical Essays on Joel Chandler Harris.* Boston, Mass.: G. K. Hall, 1981.

Flusche, Michael. "Joel Chandler Harris and the Folklore of Slavery." *Journal of American Studies* 9 (December 1975):347–63.

Glazier, Lyle. "The Uncle Remus Stories: Two Portraits of American Negroes." *Journal of General Education* 22 (April 1970):71–79.

Hedin, Raymond. "Uncle Remus: Puttin' On Ole Massa's Son." *SLJ* 15 (Fall 1982):83–90.

Rubin, Louis D., Jr. "Uncle Remus and the Ubiquitous Rabbit." *The Southern Review* 10 (Autumn 1974):787–804.

Turner, Darwin T. "Daddy Joel Harris and His Old-Time Darkies." *SLJ* 1 (Autumn 1968):20–41.

Wolfe, Bernard. "Uncle Remus and the Malevolent Rabbit." In *Mother Wit from the Laughing Barrel*. Ed. Alan Dundes. 524–40. Listed in Folklore.

See also General: Godbold.

Hayden, Robert

Fetrow, Fred M. " 'Middle Passage': Robert Hayden's Anti-Epic." *CLAJ* 22 (June 1979):304–18.

See also *BAP*.

Himes, Chester

Reckley, Ralph. "The Use of the Doppelganger or Double in Chester Himes' *Lonely Crusade*." *CLAJ* 20 (June 1977):448–58.

Hopkins, Pauline

Tate, Claudia. "Pauline Hopkins: Our Literary Foremother." *Conjuring*:53–66.

See also General: Christian.

Hughes, Langston

Blake, Susan L. "Old John in Harlem: The Urban Folktales of Langston Hughes." *BALF* 14 (Fall 1980):100–104.

(W)Dandridge, Rita B. "The Black Woman as Freedom Fighter in Langston Hughes' *Simple's Uncle Sam*." *CLAJ* 18 (December 1974):273–83.

Davis, Arthur P. "The Tragic Mulatto Theme in Six Works of Langston Hughes." *FBW*: 167–77.

Jackson, Blyden. "A Word about Simple." *CLAJ* 11 (June 1968):310–18. Reprinted. *FBW*: 183–89. Also in Jackson, *The Waiting Years*, 70–80 (listed in General) and in O'Daniel, *Langston Hughes, Black Genius* (listed below), 110–19.

(W)Miller, R. Baxter. " 'No Crystal Stair': Unity, Archetype, and Symbol in Langston Hughes's Poems on Women." *NALF* 9 (Winter 1975):109–14.

**O'Daniel, Therman B. "Langston Hughes: An Updated Selected Bibliography." *BALF* 15 (Fall 1980):104–7.

———, ed. *Langston Hughes, Black Genius: A Critical Evaluation*. New York: William Morrow, 1971.

Rampersad, Arnold. *The Life of Langston Hughes, Vol. I, 1902–1941, I, Too, Sing America*. New York: Oxford University Press, 1986.

Hurston, Zora Neale

**Dance, Daryl C. "Zora Neale Hurston. In *American Women Writers: Bibliographic Essays*. Ed. Maurice Duke, Jackson Bryer, and M. Thomas Inge. Westport, Conn.: Greenwood Press, 1983. 321–51.

Johnson, Barbara. "Thresholds of Difference: Structures of Address in Zora Neale Hurston." *Critical Inquiry* 12 (Autumn 1985):278–89.

Lewis, Vashti Crutcher. "The Declining Significance of the Mulatto Female as Major Character in the Novels of Zora Neale Hurston." *CLAJ* 28 (December 1984):127–49.

Rayson, Ann L. "The Novels of Zora Neale Hurston." *Studies in Black Literature* 5 (Winter 1974): 1–9.

Walker, S. J. "Zora Neale Hurston's *Their Eyes Were Watching God*: Black Novel of Sexism." *Modern Fiction Studies* 20 (Winter 1974–1975):519–27.

For discussions of images of Hurston herself see also the essays by Mary Helen Washington and Alice Walker in *I Love Myself When I Am Laughing . . . And Then Again When I Am Looking Mean and Impressive: A Zora Neale Hurston Reader*. Ed. Alice Walker. Old Westbury, N.Y.: The Feminist Press, 1979.

Johnson, James Weldon

Faulkner, Howard. "James Weldon Johnson's Portrait of the Artist as Invisible Man." *BALF* 19 (Winter 1985):147–51.

Long, Richard A. "The Weapon of My Song: The Poetry of James Weldon Johnson." *Phylon* 32 (Winter 1971):374–82.

For bibliography see Bontemps, Arna: Fleming, *James Weldon Johnson and Arna Bontemps*.

Jones, Gayl

Ward, Jerry W., Jr. "Escape from Trublem: The Fiction of Gayl Jones." *Callaloo* 5 (October 1982):95–104.

See also General: Fisher, Jerilyn.

Jones, LeRoi (See Baraka, Imamu Amiri)

Kelley, William Melvin

Weyant, Jill. "The Kelley Saga: Violence in America." *CLAJ* 19 (December 1975):210–20.

Kennedy, John Pendleton

Rose, Alan H. "The Image of the Negro in the Pre–Civil War Novels of John Pendleton Kennedy and William Gilmore Simms." *Journal of American Studies* 4 (February 1971):217–31.

Killens, John O.

See General: Couch; also most general studies of fiction.

Lanier, Sidney

Simms, L. Moody. "A Note on Sidney Lanier's Attitude toward the Negro and toward Populism." *Georgia Historical Quarterly* 52 (September 1968):305–7.

Lee, Don L. (See Madhubuti, Haki)

McKay, Claude

(W)Pyne-Timothy, Helen. "Perceptions of the Black Woman in the Works of Claude
    McKay." *CLAJ* 19 (December 1975):152–64.
Stoff, Michael B. "Claude McKay and the Cult of Primitivism." In *The Harlem Ren-
    aissance Remembered*. Ed. Arna Bontemps. 126–46.
See also General: Couch; also studies of the Harlem Renaissance (HR).

McPherson, James Alan

(W)Blicksilver, Edith. "The Image of Women in Selected Short Stories by James Alan
    McPherson." *CLAJ* 22 (June 1979):390–401.

Madhubuti, Haki

Giddings, Paula. "From a Black Perspective: The Poetry of Don L. Lee." *Amistad 2*.
    Ed. John A. Williams and Charles F. Harris. New York: Random House (Vintage),
    1971. 297–318.
Palmer, R. Roderick. "The Poetry of Three Revolutionists: Don L. Lee, Sonia Sanchez,
    and Nikki Giovanni." *CLAJ* 15 (September 1971):25–36.
See also Poetry: Brooks; General and Poetry listings, Black Arts Movement (BA).

Marshall, Paule

Spillers, Hortense J. "*Chosen Place, Timeless People*: Some Figurations on the New
    World." *Conjuring*: 151–75.

Melville, Herman

Altschuler, Glenn C. "Whose Foot on Whose Throat? A Re-examination of Melville's
    Benito Cereno." *CLAJ* 18 (March 1975):383–93.
Margolies, Edward. "Melville and Blacks." *CLAJ* 18 (March 1975):364–71.

Morrison, Toni

Miner, Madonne M. "Lady No Longer Sings the Blues: Rape, Madness, and Silence in
    The Bluest Eye." *Conjuring*: 176–91.
Pinsker, Sanford. "Magic Realism, Historical Truth, and the Quest for a Liberating
    Identity: Reflections on Alex Haley's *Roots* and Toni Morrison's *Song of Solo-
    mon*." In *Studies in Black American Literature*. Ed. Weixlmann and Fontenot.
    183–98.
Smith, Valerie. "The Quest for and Discovery of Identity in Toni Morrison's *Song of
    Solomon*." *The Southern Review* 21 (Summer 1985):721–32.

Murray, Albert

Freeman, Alma S. *Black Culture and Black Identity: Albert Murray's Train Whistle
    Guitar and Ralph Ellison's Invisible Man in Alabama*. Troy, Ala.: Troy State
    University Press, 1978.

O'Connor, Flannery

Byrd, Turner F. "Ironic Dimensions in Flannery O'Connor's 'The Artificial Nigger.' "
Mississippi Quarterly 21 (Fall 1968):243–51.
Williams, Melvin G. "Black and White: A Study in Flannery O'Connor's Characters."
BALF 10 (Winter 1976):130–32.

Page, Thomas Nelson

Rubin, Louis D., Jr. "The Other Side of Slavery: Thomas Nelson Page's 'No Haid
Pawn.' " *Studies in the Literary Imagination* 7 (Spring 1974):95–99.
See also General: Brown Sterling: also other sources identified earlier as overviews in
this chapter.

Petry, Ann

Bell, Bernard W. "Ann Petry's Demythologizing of American Culture and Afro-American
Character." *Conjuring*: 105–31.

Reed, Ishmael

Musgrave, Marian E. "Ishmael Reed's Black Oedipus Cycle." *Obsidian* 6 (Winter
1980):60–67.
**Settle, Elizabeth A., and Thomas A. Settle. *Ishmael Reed: A Primary and Secondary
Bibliography*. Boston, Mass.: G. K. Hall, 1982.
See also General: Gates, " 'The Blackness of Blackness' "; Lee, *Black Fiction*.

Roth, Philip

Gross, Barry. "American Fiction, Jewish Writers, and Black Characters: The Return of
'The Human Negro' in Philip Roth." *MELUS* 2 (Summer 1984):5–22.

Russell, Irwin

Simms, L. Moody, Jr. "Irwin Russell and Negro Dialect Poetry: A Note on Chronological
Priority and True Significance." *Notes on Mississippi Writers* 2 (Fall 1969):67–
73.

Sanchez, Sonia

See Poetry: Brooks; also Madhubuti, Haki: Palmer; also General and Poetry sections,
Black Arts Movement (BA).

Simms, William Gilmore

See Douglass, Frederick: Watson; also Kennedy, John Pendleton: Rose.

Stowe, Harriet Beecher

Baldwin, James. "Everybody's Protest Novel." In *Notes of a Native Son*. Boston, Mass.:
Beacon Press, 1955. 13–23.
Furnas, J. C. *Goodby to Uncle Tom*. New York: William Sloan Associates, 1956.
Hirsch, Stephen A. "Uncle Tom's Companions: The Literary and Popular Reaction to
Uncle Tom's Cabin." Ph.D. diss., State University of New York, Albany, 1975.
See also General: Killens.

Styron, William

Amis, Harry D. "History as Self-Serving Myth: Another Look at Styron's *The Confessions of Nat Turner*." *CLAJ* 22 (December 1978):134–46.

Cannon, Patricia R. "Nat Turner: God, Man, or Beast?" *Barat Review* 6 (Summer 1971):25–28. Other essays in this issue focus on the topic as well.

*Clarke, John H., ed. *William Styron's Nat Turner: Ten Black Writers Respond*. Boston, Mass.: Beacon Press, 1968. "Nat's Last White Man," Lerone Bennett, Jr.; "*The Confessions of Nat Turner* and the Dilemma of William Styron," Alvin F. Poussaint; "You've Taken My Nat and Gone," Vincent Harding; "The Confessions of Willie Styron," John Oliver Killens; "The Manipulation of History and of Fact: An Ex-Southerner's Apologist Tract for Slavery and the Life of Nat Turner; or, William Styron's Faked Confessions," John A. Williams; "The Failure of William Styron," Ernest Kaiser; "William Styron's Nat Turner—Rogue-Nigger," Loyle Hairston; "Our Nat Turner and William Styron's Creation," Charles V. Hamilton; "Back with the Wind: Mr. Styron and the Reverend Turner," Mike Thelwell; Appendix: the text of *The Confessions of Nat Turner*, as reported by Thomas R. Gray (1831).

Gross, Seymour L., and Eileen Bender. "History, Politics and Literature: The Myth of Nat Turner." *American Quarterly* 23 (October 1971):487–518.

Holder, Alan. "Styron's Slave: *The Confessions of Nat Turner*." *South Atlantic Quarterly* 68 (Spring 1969):167–80.

Ratner, Marc L. "Styron's Rebel." *American Quarterly* 21 (Fall 1969):596–608.

Sitkoff, Harvard, and Michael Wreszin. "Whose Nat Turner?: William Styron vs. the Black Intellectuals." *Midstream* 14 (November 1968):10–20.

See also General: Couch.

Tolson, Melvin B.

Farnsworth, Robert M. *Melvin B. Tolson, 1898–1966: Plain Talk and Poetic Philosophy*. Columbia: University of Missouri Press, 1984.

Russell, Mariann. *Melvin B. Tolson's Harlem Gallery: A Literary Analysis*. Columbia: University of Missouri Press, 1980.

See also *BAP*.

Toomer, Jean

(W)Chase, Patricia. "The Women in *Cane*." *CLAJ* 14 (March 1971):259–73.

(W)Clark, J. Michael. "Frustrated Redemption: Jean Toomer's Women in *Cane*." *CLAJ* 22 (June 1979):319–34.

McKay, Nellie Y. *Jean Toomer, Artist: A Study of His Life and Work, 1894–1936*. Chapel Hill: University of North Carolina Press, 1984.

See also Ellison, Ralph: Crewdson.

Twain, Mark (See Clemens, Samuel L.)

Updike, John

Jackson, Edward M. "Rabbit Is Racist." *CLAJ* 28 (June 1985):444–51.

Walker, Alice

Christian, Barbara. "The Contrary Women in Alice Walker: A Study of *In Love and Trouble.*" *Black Scholar* 12 (March-April 1981):21–30, 70–71.
*Harris, Trudier. "On *The Color Purple*, Stereotypes and Silence." *BALF* 18 (Winter 1984):155–61.
Pryse, Marjorie. "Introduction: Zora Hurston, Alice Walker and the 'Ancient Power' of Black Women." *Conjuring*: 1–24.
Washington, Mary Helen. "An Essay on Alice Walker." *SBB*: 133–49.

Walker, Margaret

Gwin, Minrose C. "Jubilee: The Black Woman's Celebration of Human Community." *Conjuring*: 132–50.
Miller, R. Baxter. "The 'Etched Flame' of Margaret Walker: Biblical and Literary Recreation in Southern History." *Tennessee Studies in Literature* 26 (1981):157–72.
See also *BAP*.

Wheatley, Phyllis

**Robinson, William H. *Phyllis Wheatley: A Bio-bibliography*. Boston, Mass.: G. K. Hall, 1981.
————. *Phyllis Wheatley and Her Writings*. New York: Garland Publishing, 1983.
————, ed. *Critical Essays on Phyllis Wheatley*. Boston, Mass.: G. K. Hall, 1982.

Williams, John A.

Cash, Earl. *John A. Williams: The Evolution of a Black Writer*. New York: Third Press Review of Books, 1974.
Munro, C. Lynn. "Culture and Quest in the Fiction of John A. Williams." *CLAJ* 22 (December 1978):71–100.
Walcott, Ronald. "The Early Fiction of John A. Williams." *CLAJ* 16 (December 1972): 198–213.
See also Baldwin, James: Hernton.

Wright, Richard

Abcarian, Richard, ed. *Richard Wright's Native Son: A Critical Handbook*. Wadsworth Guides to Literary Study. Belmont, Calif.: Wadsworth Publishing Co., 1970.
Baker, Houston A., Jr. *Twentieth Century Interpretations of Native Son*. Englewood Cliffs, N.J.: Prentice-Hall, 1972.
Brown, Lloyd W. "Stereotypes in Black and White: The Nature of Perception in Wright's *Native Son.*" *Black Academy Review* 1 (Fall 1970):35–44.
Hakutani, Yoshinobu, ed. *Critical Essays on Richard Wright*. Boston, Mass.: G. K. Hall, 1982.
(W)Mootry, Maria K. "Bitches, Whores, and Woman Haters: Archetypes and Typologies in the Art of Richard Wright." In Richaard Macksey and Frank E. Moorer, eds. *Richard Wright: A Collection of Critical Essays*. Englewood Cliffs, N.J.: Prentice-Hall, 1984.

Reilly, John M., ed. *Richard Wright: The Critical Reception*. New York: Burk, Franklin, 1978.

(W)Timmer, John. "Trust and Mistrust: The Role of the Black Woman in Three Works by Richard Wright." *Studies in the Twentieth Century* 10 (Fall 1972):38–48.

See also Baldwin, James: Cowan; Ellison, Ralph: Crewdson.

Images of Blacks in Children's Books

"After all, the white folks always did get the best of everything. You took it for granted."[1]

The culture of America is multiethnic and multiracial. It is the nature of American culture to accord to the most recently arrived minority groups the bottom round of the economic and social ladder: poorest housing, unequal employment opportunities, disparity in education. Many have owned little except themselves. The Black race had the greatest handicap of all. They were the only people who began life in America not even owning themselves. They had no choice in where they would live. Sold apart from others who spoke their language, they had to survive by learning the speech of the white masters. They faced laws forbidding their learning to read and write and were not permitted to travel freely about the area in which they lived. Forced separation of families destroyed the family structure and was a deterrent to the transmittal of culture, heritage, and family relationships through generations. Much of the nation consciously attempted to mold the Black mentality into one self-image—that of a slave.

With deliberate, structured efforts to restrict social, educational, and economic development, Blacks had little chance to learn history, to establish self-identity, or to formulate satisfying self-images. The concentration on studies of Black history and Black literature in the 1960s and 1970s was a necessary measure because there was much to learn and many emotional weaknesses needed to be strengthened. However, Black Americans are not only a part of Black America; they are an integral part of total America. As such, Black children, while still retaining the identity, individuality, and understanding of their own race, must expand their reading into the concept of a world whose people are drawing closer through faster transportation, advanced communications media, and mutual need for continued survival of the planet earth. Children must read about all ethnic groups, or they will lack the knowledge and understanding of others that are so acutely necessary for living in the world today.

The focus of this chapter is on images of Blacks in children's books: images that were, images that are, and images of the times that lie in between. It is about children growing up in a land reading that "all men are created equal," a land of opportunity for all, a country viewed as a model of what can be accomplished in a democracy in two brief centuries. It is about children being told that their people have no culture, no history except slavery, no ambition; that they are an inferior race and therefore are not entitled to a good life, jobs, better housing, legal justice, and education. It is about children who have been taught to see things through white eyes by being exposed to white readers and fairy tales, white dolls and paperdolls, white television programs, white beauty standards, and total orientation to white rightness. Yet, at the same time, they were indoctrinated with the understanding, "That's not for us; that's for the white people." These are children who have experienced the bitterness of looking at picture books and not even seeing themselves as one token face in the crowd. The few Black images which appeared in books written by white authors inspired shame and embarrassment rather than pride. They were caricatures which did injustice to both Black and white children, for these stereotypes of stupidity, ineptitude, and other negative values fostered hatred and lack of understanding. The images that were portrayed reinforced in the white child the belief that he or she was superior. On the other hand, the images led the Black child to lack confidence and self-respect, and to develop a negative self-image.

The reader of this chapter should consider two terms and their definitions, which have special relevance here. As a term that is an important indication of the changing cultural image, we first consider "Black" as it has changed from a noun synonymous with "slave" or a derogatory adjective to a more favorable connotation. The road was long from "Black *but* comely" of the Biblical song of Solomon to "Black is Beautiful" of the Black Power conferences.[2] Along the way, many names with negative images were used in derision by the white race: darky, coon, shine, and numerous others. "Negro," the term used in the early twentieth century, was shared with the other acceptable term, "colored." Later, "African American" or "Afro-American" came into use. During the protest period of the 1960s, young people made their own decision and, although never conceded by some older members of the race, "Black" came into general usage. The changes in terminology have been reflected in children's books, in the media, and in other aspects of our culture.

The second term that the reader should consider is "culture." No race is devoid of culture. Culture is the total of all that constitutes a lifestyle; it is passed on as a heritage of the people. It includes many facets: food, religion, art, music, dance, language and speech, folklore, and games. It includes family style, interpersonal relationships, and rites of passage from child to adult. One of the most important areas of culture is literature because (1) literature is communication between peoples through the ages as well as in the present; (2) it is a means of passing knowledge and culture to succeeding generations; and (3) it encompasses all other areas of culture.

Literature for children has special importance. It involves the presentation of both factual and creative material to motivate and stimulate minds still in the formative stages of development. The adult brings to reading his or her life experience and a foundation for evaluation of the material read. The adult reader has consciously or unconsciously formed guidelines for accepting or rejecting the information presented. Young readers are still in the process of fulfilling the basic needs for information, security, relationships with others, and coming to terms with self. Literature is important in establishing positive feelings of self-identity and human relationships. It affects a child's view of himself, of other people of his own race, and of other races. This is a critical issue in the future of our young people. If they are ill-prepared for adulthood by exposure to racist or other detrimental images in reading material, children will experience difficulty in coming to terms with themselves and their identities, and they will experience problems in interpersonal relationships. Thus, those who write, publish, or select materials for children are challenged to see that books give accurate and honest characterizations and portrayals of life and are devoid of individual bias and racism.

This chapter traces the trends noted in children's literature about Black people during the years since juvenile literature has been accorded separate attention in the United States, and it correlates the portrayal of Blacks in these books with the reality of social, cultural, and historical changes in our country. Works of fiction provide an intercultural exchange for young readers—something that is not derived from nonfiction. Fiction provides more images to the reader, and even when the setting is in a different time frame, it reflects the ideas and attitudes of the period in which it is written. For these reasons, this survey is limited to works of fiction. Titles mentioned provide merely a sampling of books published in any period and by various authors and illustrate the trends of that time. Some titles are mentioned because they are true landmarks in the progression from earlier years to the present time. Not all books included are Black literature; that designation is reserved for those works by Black writers. Each title referenced in the chapter is listed at the end of this chapter alphabetically under the heading "Bibliography of Children's Books." References that require some explanatory note are listed also under "Notes."

EARLY IMAGES IN PUBLISHED WORKS

The earliest literary images presented to Black people in America came from the Bible. Each Sunday, the white preacher on the plantation admonished his gathering: "Children, obey your parents; slaves, obey your masters." This placed the Biblical stamp of reverential authority upon the Black servile position. Children were taught to accept rather than to think, and through the years they continued to pay homage to a blond Jesus image—an image of one who would wash away Black sins leaving them whiter than snow. Children had images of white angels with snowy wings. The devil was presented as Black, as was all else that was evil. Black people were viewed as inhuman, incapable of thinking, learning, or loving. The institution of slavery in America fostered the image of Black racial inferiority. Blacks were considered a race with no heritage, no ambition, no culture. In a more or less subtle form of brainwashing, these ideas became indelible on the minds of Black people. Black parents helped this image to survive as they encouraged their children to keep a low profile and to be conciliatory in order to survive in a white world. The very fact that no slave rebellions found their way into early history books caused Black children of a later era to consider their own image negatively as they questioned, ''Why didn't the slaves revolt? Why did they tolerate such treatment?''

Prior to the 1920s there were no Black history books for children. With the appearance of Carter G. Woodson's *The Negro in Our History* (1922) and Arthur H. Fauset's *For Freedom* (1927)[3] the first Black history textbooks were published. Except in their role as slaves, Black people were omitted from white history and white textbooks. By the time most Black children learned of the slave rebellions of Nat Turner, Denmark Vesey, and Gabriel Prosser, their courageous ancestors, the children themselves had grown to find their own way to revolt. The Black child could well have denied the existence of Black inventors, explorers, or any other worthwhile Black achievers. Histories and textbooks that were available reinforced the negative image of the Black race for Black and white children.

Children's books are latecomers to the field of literature. Thoughts of early years of books about Black children bring to mind books now out of print, but preserved in juvenile historical collections and in the minds of older adults who read them as children. Books written by white authors were directed to a white reading audience, with no thought that any non-white child might read them and without concern for the sensitivities of the non-white reader.

Three books published in the late nineteenth century are memorable: *Ten Little Niggers* (1869), *Diddie, Dumps, and Tot* (1882), and *Little Black Sambo* (1899). A picture book of a nursery rhyme, *Ten Little Niggers* was inspired by the English version, *Ten Little Nigger Boys* (1868). It appeared in the United States as *Ten Little Injuns*, but soon reverted to *Ten Little Niggers* and many versions were published.[4] *Diddie, Dumps, and Tot* by Louise-Clark Pyrnelle tells of the happy life on a plantation shared by three little white children and three little slave children. The story insidiously impresses upon the young reader the inferiority of the slave children, Dilsey, Chris, and Riar, and perpetuates the myth of the good master and the happy plantation life.

At the turn of the century, Helen Bannerman, a Scottish woman, wrote a book that has remained controversial until the present: *Little Black Sambo*. At the time of its publication in 1899 and in the decades immediately following, children enjoyed the story. Although the images are of the southern plantation, Sambo was created during the author's thirty-year stay in India. The original edition by Stokes was devoid of dialect and was not termed condescending. It is a children's fantasy picture book story of a child who, frightened by a tiger, appeases him by giving the beast articles of his clothing, one by one. Children found the idea of the tiger melting into butter for pancakes delightful and humorous. Character portrayals and illustrations have made the book unappealing to Black people as they eventually related to the book only through the ridicule the image brought to them from the white race. For a brief time in the 1930s, an Indian version of the book was published, but the original was still considered a childhood classic by many librarians and classroom teachers. The book has been critically evaluated from all aspects, and it has even been considered one with sexist overtones and racist undercurrents. The name "Sambo" has been one of the most frequent derogatory epithets. It was the name of the ventriloquist's little black dummy, the stupid buffoon in the minstrel show, a demeaning name to call a servant or a shoeshine boy.

A suitable companion book for *Little Black Sambo* was *Epaminondas and His Auntie* by Sarah Cone Bryant (1907). The story is a traditional chain-of-sequences nursery tale, but the illustrations are the fat, bandana-headed mammy figure and a pigtail-haired, thick-lipped pickaninny boy. The book was republished in 1938 at about the same time as *Sambo and the Twins*.

Within the late nineteenth century, two books appeared by an author who was a literary legend in his own time: Samuel Langhorne Clemens, whose pseudonym was Mark Twain. The first, *The Adventures of Tom Sawyer* (1876), is still enjoyed by children, but the second, *The Adventures of Huckleberry Finn* (1884), is without doubt one of the most discussed, acclaimed, maligned, and censored books of all time. Mark Twain was not a children's author, yet, like many other works that appeared prior to a real advent of literary output for children (for example, *The Merry Adventures of Robin Hood*, *Gulliver's Travels*, and *Arabian Nights*),[5] his books were adopted by children. That *The Adventures of Huckleberry Finn* is still a point of contention among parents, librarians, educators, and literary critics is illustrated in Nat Hentoff's recent book, *The Day They Came to Arrest the Book* (1982), which tells of a confrontation between a principal and a Black parent over the image of the character Jim and the use of the word "nigger" in *Huckleberry Finn*. The situation which developed brought national notoriety to the town. The fictional plot of Hentoff's book has its counterpart in many cases of censorship. Many parents who, outraged by the repetition of the offensive word, seek to ban the book from school reading lists without reading the work before asserting their complaints. *Huckleberry Finn* should be read objectively and evaluated in the light of Mark Twain's philosophy, the period of the story, and the authenticity of the language. The first person narrative by Huck, despite his vacillation and indecision about right and wrong, results in neither an immoral nor a racist book. At times, Twain sacrifices character credibility for humorous effect. However, the reader should note that the author's real concern is not that of presenting Black readers with an image of Jim to which they can relate, but to present the tale from Huck's point of view; to show the precarious balance in the development of the character of the young white boy as he acknowledges the humanity of the slave on the one hand and struggles against the attitudes of his upbringing and environment on the other. The significance of the book lies not in the image of the Black character, Jim, but in the understanding afforded the reader of Huck's white mind and the times in which he lived.

Joel Chandler Harris' collections of Black folk stories (1882) are still included in folklore collections today. The dialect portraying the plantation speech of the slave era was planned to preserve in original form and speech pattern the folktales of Black people. The tales as Harris presented them are difficult for children to read, but there are more readable versions available today that retain the flavor of the original tales.[6] As seen in the spirituals or slave songs which in various periods were rejected by Blacks as being degrading and nonrepresentative of a serious, dignified image, the folktales of Black America survive as the earliest American literary creation other than the Native American myths and legends. Like the Anansi tales from Africa and the Caribbean, Harris' Brer Rabbit character portrays the image of the little guy winning over the big ones through wit and ingenuity, a philosophy similar to the "John" tales which also have roots in African culture.[7] The Uncle Remus tales carry a strong sense of African humor as well as plantation humor; the two are not identical. Brer Rabbit's ability to cope despite adverse circumstances was the key to his survival, as it is true of the Black American today. In later years, there would be folktale collections by Blacks—Langston Hughes, Arna Bontemps, Zora Neale Hurston, Julius Lester, and others—but the folklore tradition survived in Black culture through the oral tradition, or family storytelling.

EARLY TWENTIETH-CENTURY WORKS

Books by White Authors

The early 1920s were not good years for positive images of Blacks in children's books. In 1920, Lippincott published the first of a twelve-book series: *The Story of Doctor Dolittle* by Hugh Lofting, an English veterinarian. Translated into twelve languages, it was later made into a movie. Doctor Dolittle himself an exemplification of a white racist, chauvinist, paternalist, is one major problem of the series, but an even greater objection to Black readers is the depiction of the African characters as objects of ridicule and humor. Prince Bumpo is portrayed as a stupid, ignorant, inferior person who would do anything to become white in order to marry the Sleeping Princess, who rejected him because he was Black. This is possible only superficially and temporarily, but Bumpo believes he has been changed to white. The second book, *The Voyages of Doctor Dolittle* (1922) won the 1923 Newbery Award presented by the Children's Services Division of the American Library Association as "the most distinguished contribution to American literature for children."[8] In this book, Bumpo attends

9. *The Story of Doctor Dolittle.* Courtesy of Special Collections, Fisk University Library.

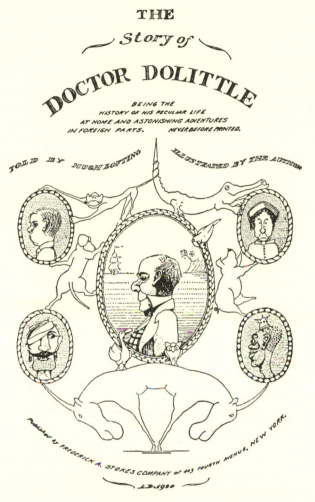

THE

Story of

DOCTOR DOLITTLE

BEING THE
HISTORY OF HIS PECULIAR LIFE
AT HOME AND ASTONISHING ADVENTURES
IN FOREIGN PARTS.   NEVER BEFORE PRINTED.

TOLD BY HUGH LOFTING   ILLUSTRATED BY THE AUTHOR

PUBLISHED BY FREDERICK A. STOKES COMPANY at 443 FOURTH AVENUE, NEW YORK.

Oxford University, but he remains incapable of any job except that of cook on a voyage. The Doctor Dolittle stories reinforce for children the concept of Africa as a dark continent, peopled by ignorant, man-eating savages. Even the animals in the story flaunt their superiority by tossing insults at the Black characters. The Dolittle books with their objectionable images and support of racism have appeared on many recommended book lists. *Dr. Dolittle, A Treasury*, published by Lippincott in 1967, contains excerpts from two-thirds of the Doctor Dolittle titles and deletes Prince Bumpo completely.[9]

In considering the images of Blacks presented in children's books, the early twentieth century cannot be passed without reference to Francis Boyd Calhoun's

Miss Minerva and William Green Hill (1909) and Booth Tarkington's *Penrod* (1914) and its sequels. The principal characters of these books were white, but the Black supporting characters and the interpersonal, interracial relationships were strongly objectionable for the Black child reader. In the chapter "Changing the Ethiopian" in Calhoun's book, a Black mother rejoices as she believes the Lord is turning her child white after the little boys have dyed the baby's hair yellow. The fact that the scenes involved humorous incidents created appeal. The effect on Black children was subtle, for they laughed at the bullying of Tarkington's Herman and Verman by Penrod and Sam without realizing the influence on their own self-image. Unknowingly, they identified with the white characters as they ridiculed and degraded the Black characters, just as Black children identified with white cowboys and with Tarzan in films. Black children reading Tarkington books in an integrated class in the North have found *Penrod* and its sequels considerably less enjoyable than Black children in segregated classrooms of the South. The taunting and teasing of white classmates brought home to them the realization of the image of their race—that of being once removed from an uncivilized Africa and some degree less than human. Through the medium of innocent child's play, dialogue, and situation comedy, the author manages to convey a portrayal of Black people as gullible, lazy, unattractive in appearance, undependable, mentally inferior, and unpredictably violent. The feat is accomplished in a happy, good-natured style, planned to leave the reader laughing.

The migration of southern Blacks to the North during and following World War I brought many talented Black Americans together in New York City, specifically in Harlem. This paved the way for the Negro Renaissance of the 1920s (or the Harlem Renaissance, as it was called), an awakening of Black art, music, and literature which brought Black writers into prominence along with Black artists, musicians, and other entertainers. It also brought to white America some recognition of Black talent and ability. Prior to that time, Black poetry had meant to most people Phillis Wheatley in the eighteenth century and later Paul Laurence Dunbar. The Harlem Renaissance brought to light Langston Hughes, Countee Cullen, Claude McKay, and many others who, in addition to songs of Black life, wrote of freedom from oppression and proclaimed that freedom from the slave status was not enough.

Black Writers and Publishing

Works by Black writers of this era were not easily published. The failure of white publishers to accept these works forced Black poets and writers to find ways to print and sell their own books. Langston Hughes toured the South reading and selling his poetry. Carter G. Woodson, who in 1915 organized the Association for the Study of Negro Life and History (since 1972, the Association for the Study of Afro-American Life and History), formed his own publishing company, Associated Publishers, in order to help reach the public with authentic accounts of Negro history and culture. Among the titles that he published were *The Negro in Our History* (1922) and an elementary school textbook, *African Myths* (1928). *Opportunity* magazine, under the editorship of Charles S. Johnson, and the NAACP magazine, *The Crisis*, edited by W. E. B. Du Bois, gave visibility to many new Black writers through contests, provided a voice for the New Negro movement in literature, and were forerunners of the later Black magazines and periodicals. One importance of the Harlem Renaissance was that creative Black people found support in each other. They were able to unite and find others who appreciated their work for its worth, and they achieved a wider measure of success among other Americans. The momentum generated at that time might have continued, but the decade closed with the beginning of the Great Depression. The literary surge weakened before it encompassed Black children's books.

WORKS IN SERIES

With the unsatisfactory presentations of white authors on Black themes and the lack of Black juvenile literature, children read the works of Black poets and adult writers such as Jessie Redmon Fauset, who wrote novels of Negro family life. They learned from Black magazines and newpapers that it was possible to read something written by people of their own race about people like themselves. Slowly the literary image was beginning to change. The Black person was being presented by Black writers in a more accurate, credible manner than by white writers of the past.

With the advent of Black writers came a significant change in the language used. Prior to this time, most of the speech of Black characters and much of the poetry had been in dialect. As a spoken expression rather than a written one, the material was usually difficult to read. Black poets of this period successfully made the change from the plantation or minstrel type dialect deemed acceptable in early writings to the common, everyday, colorful speech of Blacks in some phases of real life. This was a change which would continue to evolve in dialogue until it later was termed "Black English."

The increase in numbers of Black writers and the resulting change in literary style prompted some white authors to realize the need to portray a different picture of Black life in America. As early as 1936, Friendship Press began accepting material on Blacks. The status of Blacks in children's fiction improved very little. Blacks in most books written by whites were still relegated to the role of stereotyped supporting characters.

The most popular type of book for children at this time was the series book. The *Elsie Dinsmore* series by Martha Finley of the later nineteenth century was outdated and no longer read, but the prevailing image of Blacks in the servant's role continued in books of the Edward Stratemeyer syndicate. Beginning in 1899 and including as many as sixty-five series under forty-six pseudonyms, these followed the path of the earlier *Horatio Alger* dime store novels[10] in popularity as well as in adventurous style. Written for entertainment, they provided many of their young readers with the only image they had of Black people. Many adult readers remember "The Rover Boys," "The Bobbsey Twins," "Tom Swift," "Honey Bunch," "The Motor Boys," and similar series. Following Stratemeyer's death, the syndicate was carried on by his daughter, Harriet Stratemeyer Adams, who was responsible for the continuation of "The Hardy Boys" and "Nancy Drew."[11] After the initial years, the products were all written to formula by "hack" writers. Rejected for purchase by many libraries because of poor literary quality (not because of their racism), they were inexpensive enough to be purchased prolifically by children. The books were thoroughly predictable not only in plot, but also in the portrayal of minority race characters (Black, Jewish, and foreign), which suffered from extreme negative stereotyping.[12]

THE POST-DEPRESSION YEARS

The trend for white authors to display insensitivity toward Black character portrayal or to ignore the existence of Blacks completely persisted until more books written by Black writers were published. One of the most distasteful images of Blacks came from an English author, Pamela Travers. *Mary Poppins* (1934), a fantasy, featured a prim, proper, and magical English nursemaid who continually equated misbehavior with Black or foreign people in her reprimands of the children. The chapter "Bad Tuesday" included a trip to Africa complete with watermelon-eating plantation stereotypes.

Mary White Ovington, one of the founders of the NAACP, was one of the first white authors to present a more positive image of Black people in books. *Zeke* (1931) and an earlier title about his mother, *Hazel* (1913), contained main characters with career goals and education. The Nicodemus books (1932–1935), a series of twelve books written by Inez Hogan for younger children, failed the attempt to write a convincing story of farm life. In a later book, however, *Nappy Has a New Friend* (1947), the author managed to use a theme of friendship and cooperation with more appealing illustrations. Arna Bontemps was one of the most outstanding Black writers of this period for adults as well as for children. If the illustrations in *You Can't Pet a Possum* (1934) and *Sad Faced Boy* (1937) seem to resemble the stereotypes shown in white authors' books, the reader must remember that there was still the white publisher with which to contend, and books by Blacks had to conform to the then current acceptability in order to be purchased. As Bontemps stated in a letter written to me dated on March 7, 1972 on the subject, " . . . it helped to plough the field. I only regret that so many of the young adults of today can't even imagine the sweat and blood and casualties our generation suffered during this plowing."

Many of the books about Blacks in the 1930s were plantation or farm life stories not too far removed from the images in some of the Lucy Fitch Perkins twin books.[13] Ellis Credle wrote a twin story on plantation life, *Across the Cotton Patch* (1935), with twins named Atlantic and Pacific. This book and her following one, *Little Jeemes Henry* (1936), were a continuation of the happy plantation stories.

A few books depicted city life. A Black writer, Ellen Tarry, wrote *Hezekiah Horton* (1942), a picture book of a city boy who loved automobiles. The character was drawn from a real child the author knew when she was the "Story Lady" in a Harlem community center. Eleanor Frances Lattimore wrote *Junior, a Colored Boy of Charleston* (1938), but apparently white authors were too unfamiliar with Black life to write convincingly. Their books persisted in being fairly one dimensional, with little stereotypes creeping in despite the author's sincere efforts to write an unbiased book.

With so few titles available to offer Black children, the American Library Association decided that a bibliography on that subject was needed. The first widely circulated list of recommended titles was appended to an article on "Library Service for Negro Children" in the *ALA Children's Library Yearbook* of 1932.[14] Seventeen titles were listed. Three were books by Erick Berry (pseudonym for Allena Best) and one a work by Herbert Best, all set in Africa; three were Mary White Ovington's works; three were collective biographies; and three were *Uncle Remus* collections. *The Life and Works of Paul Laurence Dunbar* (1896), Langston Hughes' *The Dream Keeper* (1932), and two additional books for younger children, A. V. Weaver's *Frawg* (1930) and *Little Black Sambo*,[15] completed the list.

ILLUSTRATED WORKS AND PICTURE BOOKS

Illustrations play an important role in children's books. This is true in nonfiction as well as in fiction, but it is especially true of picture books and books on an elementary reading level. Among the first books with text and illustrations suitable for young children to read alone were the books by Eva Knox Evans: *Araminta* (1935), in which a little city girl visits relatives in the country, and *Jerome Anthony* (1936), in which Araminta's friend from the country visits the city. These books were welcomed because of the scarcity of elementary level books about Black children engaged in normal, everyday life situations. One of the first integrated picture books was *Small Rain* (1943), a collection of Bible verses selected by Jessie O. Jones, illustrated by Elizabeth Orton Jones and chosen as a Caldecott Honor book in 1944. The following year, the Caldecott Award for the most distinguished American picture book for children was awarded to Elizabeth Orton Jones for her illustrations in *Prayer for a Child* (1944) written by Rachel Field.[16] Both books included Black children in normal roles in the pictures.

Two large photographic picture books in black and white were forerunners of the photographic picture books which later became very popular. They were a relief from the many unrealistic illustrations of that period. *Tobe* (1939) by Stella Sharpe Gentry, shows the life of a Black boy on a farm in the South. *My Happy Days* (1944) by Jane Shackelford[17] gives an equally good portrayal of the daily activities of a middle-class Black family in an urban setting. These books and Ellen Tarry and Marie Hall Ets' *My Dog Rinty* (1946)[18] compare favorably to later photographic picture books.

A book still in print, *Two Is a Team* (1945) by Lorraine and Jerrold Beim, was the first racially balanced picture book and the forerunner of modern integrated books. It is significant that teamwork rather than race is stressed. Although the two friends are of different races, the reader learns this through the pictures rather than in the text.

WORKS FOR OLDER CHILDREN

A number of the books for older children about Black people focused on African life, but Florence Crannell Means in *Shuttered Windows* (1938) points out differences in Black lifestyles in the United States as a northern Black girl goes to live with a grandmother on a South Carolina Sea Island. This work and others that Means wrote later portray goal- or career-oriented Blacks, but they have sometimes been criticized for the limited horizons of the characters. One must remember, however, that these works were written during the time when career opportunities for Black children were limited.

All American by John Tunis (1942), a white sports book author, was among the first sports stories with an interracial theme. The football story unveils the tense situations brought about by social attitudes. Duane Decker, another sports author, wrote the first integrated baseball story two years after Jackie Robinson broke the baseball color barrier. *Hit and Run* (1949) deals with racial discrimination in sports using a Black supporting character.

LATER STEREOTYPING

Cultural images from 1940 to 1950 still leaned toward portraying the life of segregation. Some books showed Blacks adjusting to life as it was in the segregated South; others capitalized on the paternalistic factor: kind, understanding whites helping Blacks who were well behaved and deserving. Blacks were still presented as achieving the breakthrough by athletic ability or musical talent, and there was no balanced cross-cultural relationship with whites in the books. Stereotypes prevailed, although they were beginning to be less obvious in illustration and language. However, the Caldecott Award winner, *The Rooster Crows*, by Maude and Miska Petersham (1945) contained "four pages showing Negro children with great buniony feet, coal black skin and bulging eyes (in the distance, a dilapidated cabin with a black, gun-toting barefoot adult)."[19] The images were not deleted until the 1964 edition, which completely eliminated Black children from the book.

CHANGING IMAGES

Georgene Faulkner's *Melindy's Medal* (1945), a story of a little Black girl in a Boston housing project who wants to follow the male family tradition of winning a medal, is similar to *Araminta*, by Eva Knox Evans. While Faulkner's work is less episodic in plot, both of these works provide a picture of everyday life. Like *Araminta*, it is followed by a sequel which takes place in a different setting, *Melindy's Happy Summer* (1949), in which Melindy visits the country as a part of a cross-cultural exchange vacation program. Despite the author's intent and the purpose of the program, Melindy's self-image suffers throughout the summer. She cuts her hair to wear a blonde wig to perform in the closing play. In *Bright April* (1946) by Marguerite De Angeli, a Philadelphia middle-class Black family becomes conscientiously involved in racial image as April joins an integrated Brownie Scout troop. Frieda Friedman's *A Sundae with Judy* (1949) was one of the earliest conscious efforts to integrate Black and Asian ethnic children into a contemporary work of fiction.

Among picture books of that period, one little book by Margaret Rey, *Spotty* (1945), a story about rabbits, emerged as an integrated work which sought to approach prejudice on a picture book level. The storm of criticism it drew in the South had no equal for an animal story book until the 1958 picture book by Garth Williams, *The Rabbit's Wedding*, in which a brown rabbit and a white rabbit are married.

Jesse Jackson, a Black author, led into the period of stories about crisis situations in integration with *Call Me Charley* (1945), the first book with a direct racial conflict. In many cases of fiction dealing with Black life, the paternalistic factor remained, as in *Lady Cake Farm* (1952) by Mabel Hunt. Here white neighbors show kindness to a Black family moving a house. Florence Crannell Means wrote *Great Day in the Morning* (1946) about a Sea Island girl's experience with career decisions at Tuskegee Institute in Alabama. This is one of the first juvenile books to reveal in the dialogue of the characters the animosity of Black people toward whites and double standards of judging Black and white behavior and goals.

The list of books accepted by publishers from Black authors between 1940 and 1960 was still very limited. Many who were writing books which could have been valuable in presenting a true picture of Black life continually encountered frustration as they tried to sell their manuscripts. After a nine-year effort, Lorenz Graham succeeded in finding a publisher for his work, *South Town* (1958). The story was too bold in realism for its time; violence was included with Blacks defending themselves with guns against white southern oppression. The story is continued in sequels.[20]

Some revisions were made to improve books already published. *Nancy Drew* and *The Hardy Boys* were revised, and the dialect was changed to standard English. Even so, most contemporary articles about the revision stressed modernization of the white characters in dress, hair style, and activities. In 1962 a new edition of the English classic *Mary Poppins* was published by Harcourt, Brace, Jovanovich revising the objectionable chapter "Bad Tuesday," but it did not completely eliminate the stereotyping of minority groups.

Change was not readily accepted by all publishers. As late as 1960, *A Summer to Share* by Helen Kay with a theme similar to that in *Melindy's Happy Summer* (1949) ran into a "color me white" situation. Due to the editor's response to negative reaction of salespersons, the Black child was changed into a white child, eliminating the integrated cast.[21] However, more books were published with Black characters, showed greater variety of theme and plot, and were becoming less objectionable in characterization and illustration. The gain was more noticeable in fiction and nonfiction than in picture books.

THE DESEGREGATION YEARS

The years between 1950 and 1960 brought unexpected and sudden developments in the racial climate of America. Discrimination was denounced, the Supreme Court acted on school desegregation (1954), and the Montgomery bus boycott (1955) launched the more visible phase of the civil rights movement.[22] It is interesting to note that *A Cap for Mary Ellis* (1953) by Hope Newell, a story of the experiences of two Black students in a previously all-white nursing school, appeared a year before the Supreme Court decision.[23]

Laws for school integration brought new themes for children's books. *Tender Warriors* (1958) by Dorothy Sterling, a white author who has written excellent nonfiction books on Black history, was the first book on school integration after the court decision. Sensitively and accurately written, based on interviews with Black students involved, it encountered opposition and was termed "a commercial failure" by its author, as few copies reached school or public libraries.[24] Sterling's *Mary Jane* (1959), drawn from the experience of the interviews, was the most outstanding fiction book in regard to school integration. Written five years after the Supreme Court decision, it was followed by other books such as *Classmates by Request* (1964) by Hila Colman, *The Empty Schoolhouse* (1965) by Natalie Carlson, *Lions in the Way* (1966) by Bella Rodman, and *Tessie* (1968) by Jesse Jackson, to name a few. *Where Were You That Year?* (1965) by Margaret Strachan deals with the experience of a northern white high school girl working with the voter registration drive in Mississippi. *Tolliver* (1963) by Florence Crannell Means tells of Black college students' participation in the Freedom Bus rides for equal rights. *Dead End School* (1968), by psychiatrist Robert Cole, deals with the controversy surrounding the busing of Black children to white schools to achieve integration. Louis Shotwell's *Roosevelt Grady* (1963) recounts the problems of a Black migrant family. Commended by many reviewers, it was criticized by others for the passive submissiveness of the family and for its limited goals.

Many books were written to deal with a current issue; characters were sometimes more one dimensional than convincing. In contrast to all of the books on contemporary topics, one of the most outstanding works of that decade was a historical novel by a Black author, Ann Petry: *Tituba of Salem Village* (1964). This was the story of a slave from Barbados who maintained dignity and strength of character under the pressure of accusation in the Salem witchcraft trials.

The trend in writing was changing as authors began to regard Black characters as significant persons contributing to the action of the story. Black people became leading characters as well as supporting ones, and supporting Black characters were more the substance of real life people.

One segment of teenage reading remained unchanged. The junior romance novel, popular among teenage girls, was still white suburbia America oriented with no images of Blacks. Only one author, Betty Cavanna in *A Time for Tenderness* (1962), acknowledged a Black character in a romantic involvement. Set in Brazil, a white girl from North Carolina and a Brazilian boy form an intimate friendship. Although they are equal in social level, caste and color prejudice terminate the romance.

By 1960 two factions were at work within the Black race which were alternately affecting Black identity. A growing militancy existed among one segment of Blacks and a movement toward securing rights through non-violence existed in the other. Each had its own effect upon the changing images of Blacks in America. Martin Luther King, Jr., captured the attention of whites as well as Blacks in the speech he made at the Washington Freedom March on August 28, 1963, making a profound impression upon the nation and the world. He stated:

The Negro lives on a lonely island of poverty in the midst of a vast ocean of material prosperity . . . and finds himself in exile in his own land. . . . It would be fatal for the nation to overlook the urgency of the moment and to underestimate the determination of the Negro. This sweltering summer of the Negro's legitimate discontent will not pass until there is an invigorating autumn of freedom and equality. There will be neither rest nor tranquility in America until the Negro is granted his citizen rights.[25]

The emotional impact of the "I have a dream" portion of King's speech, prophesying future integration and brotherhood for his children, the sons of former slaves, and the sons of former slaveowners fired the hearts of long tolerant Black people. It would have been well had the nation heeded the warning of the previous paragraph, for those words contained the prophesy for the immediate future.

The assassination of King, following that of John F. Kennedy, was the catalyst that caused many urban areas in major cities to explore the violence of racial riots. The *U.S. Riot Commission Report* (commonly called the "Kerner Report") compiled by a special commission authorized by President Lyndon B. Johnson in 1967 made this statement:

Despite these complexities, certain fundamental matters are clear. Of these, the most fundamental is the racial attitude and behavior of white Americans toward Black Americans. Race prejudice has shaped our history decisively in the past; it now threatens to do so again. White racism is essentially responsible for the explosive mixture which has been accumulating in our cities since the end of World War II.

The report further states:

Powerful forces of social and political inertia are moving the country steadily along the course of existing policies toward a divided country (and that a serious consequence is that) this course would lead to the permanent establishment of two societies: one predominately white and located in the suburbs, in smaller cities and in outlying areas, and one largely Negro, located in central cities.[26]

The 1960s were a period of unrest, revolt, and protest against all that needed to change in the lives of Black Americans. With the traumatic events of the past few years fresh in all minds, it was obvious that steps had to be taken to preserve a unified nation. Antagonism, resentment, and anger were aroused in some whites; others displayed enormous guilt complexes and a desire to rectify past wrongs committed by unknown white ancestors. Blacks, on the other hand, varied from increased militancy in demands for reparations to sincere attempts to improve racial relations by cooperative planning toward change. The need for greater understanding between races was obvious; or, as predicted by the report, polarization would indeed be the result of the course present then.

Books are a means of expression and communication. Realizing that meaningful communication leads to better understanding, the nation turned to books as one means of achieving this end. New titles on Black themes published for juveniles and adults increased in number, and books published earlier were reissued or updated. Federal funds were made available to purchase books and to strengthen school and public libraries. Publishers printed catalogs of minority booklists, and the book industry flourished as the demand for Black titles on all levels and themes mushroomed. Many librarians and teachers found themselves dealing with entirely new and unfamiliar areas of books in which they totally lacked selection experience; consequently, the need for critically evaluative lists of Black titles was glaring.

The 1941 booklist entitled *We Build Together*, edited by Charlemae Rollins to meet the need of a good list for selection by adults working with children, had been greatly needed. Too few books had offered a true picture of Negroes in contemporary life—"Books that Negro children could enjoy without self-consciousness, books with which they could identify satisfactorily, books that white children could read and so learn what Negro people and families were like."[27] Only 200 satisfactory titles had been found. The 1945 edition had 500 titles. The 1967 edition (reprinted in 1974) found many titles from which to choose. There was a noticeable change in the presentation of the Black image in the more recent books, with less dialect, more realistic relationships between Blacks and whites, better balance of jobs, and Blacks being shown in all roles of society. The cast of supporting Black characters created by white authors improved, as seen in Zilpha

Snyder's *The Egypt Game* (1967) and E. L. Konigsberg's *Jennifer, Hecate, Macbeth, William McKinley and Me, Elizabeth* (1967); both books have white leading characters and a story told from the white child's point of view. In *A Wonderful Terrible Time* (1967) by Mary Stolz, two little Black girls share an unexpected trip to summer camp with different reactions.

The Black cultural image of the picture books of the 1960s shows up well in the total perspective. Some of the most endearing and enduring picture books appeared during this decade. A Caldecott winner, *The Snowy Day* (1962) by Ezra Jack Keats, introduced the technique of collage with illustrations of a Black child who could be a child of any race having fun playing in the snow. Other books by Keats about Peter, his family, and his dog, Willie, follow the behavior and emotions of real, true to life children. *Sam* (1967) by Ann Herbert Scott, *Becky* (1966) by Julia Wilson, and Mary Jo in *What Mary Jo Shared* (1966) by Janice Udry are all favorite friends of the picture book crowd. City children are able to relate to these books just as they are able to identify with the child's need for a corner of his own in *Evan's Corner* (1967) by Elizabeth Starr Hill. *J. T.* (1969), a photographic book by Jane Wagner and photographer Gordon Parks, also introduced children in urban settings. This trend was continued into the decade of the 1970s.

A new reader series with integrated characters, the "Bank Street Readers" replaced the white suburban oriented Dick and Jane type readers in many areas where Blacks were involved. These readers portrayed family life patterns and scenes to which city children could relate. Another innovation on this level was the Harper *I Can Read* beginning reading series. Crosby Bonsall's mysteries are solved by a fun-loving little integrated group of children; Joan Lexau's books are in similar vein. By 1970, several historical *I Can Read* books had also appeared, many helping the youngest reader to relate to Black history. Crowell's *Let's Read and Find Out* science series includes Augusta Goldin's *Straight Hair, Curly Hair* (1966), Paul Showers' *Look At Your Eyes* (1962) and *Your Skin and Mine* (1965), all books which help the younger reader to understand racial differences and to appreciate his or her own image.

For over half a century the majority of books about Black people had been written by white authors. Since such authors bring a different cultural perspective to their work, the white author has difficulty convincing the reader that he or she is sincere or knowledgeable about the subject. Publishers finally accepted this fact, and Black writers were in the vanguard of that consciousness which came as an aftermath of the civil rights movement. Publishers were searching for books which would meet the demands of Black readers' need for identity as well as white readers' interest in increasing their own understanding of the racial problem. The late 1960s and 1970s gave birth to many nonfiction books as librarians tried to fill neglected gaps in collections. As noted earlier, publishers printed special catalogs and promoted series on minority books such as the Doubleday Zenith books (introduced by Black editor and historian John Hope Franklin) which covered areas of Black history back to the African heritage.

The *Golden Legacy* format books from Fitzgerald Publishing Company told of Black history and the contributions of Black people. While not heralded as great literary works, they served to interest many reluctant readers to become involved in learning more about their own history and culture. Children found enjoyment in the first Black children's monthly magazine, *Ebony, Jr.*, first issued in May 1973, published by Johnson Publishing Company in Chicago. *Wee Pals*, a comic strip in some daily newspapers, produced by Morrie Turner, was the first syndicated cartoon to feature Black children. It first appeared in 1964 in the *Chicago Defender*.

During this period in literature, there was a resurgence among Blacks seeking more information about Black culture, digging into previously unrecorded history, collecting anthologies of poetry, folklore, and fairy tales ranging from African traditional to modern. Sometimes one had difficulty determining what was relevant and authentic and what was not. Black children were finally given a key to their past. As Black children learned that Africa had been civilized long before countries in Europe and the Western world, a new Black pride was born in them.

INCREASE IN NONFICTION AND REALISM

In the area of biography, previously written about only two or three historical people and a few sports figures whose demand had declined while the books were still new on library shelves, there were now stories of public figures, politicians, artists, musicians, and scientists of the past as well as of that period. Biographies of women increased. There were histories on all age levels, from Lucille Clifton's *The Black BC's* (1970), an illustrated easy-level book on contributions to American life, to Julius Lester's *To Be a Slave* (1968), a poignant history of slavery in the words of slaves. There were accounts of Black pioneers, Black explorers, Black cowboys, and Black soldiers. Nonfiction books in science, recreation, and sports displayed integrated illustrations that were not the "color me black" variety of the earlier awareness period. New terms became familiar in talking and writing of Black city life—inner city, ghetto, disadvantaged, culturally deprived. These were prevalent key words in material designed to meet the current need. Sometimes the very terms intended to help improve social conditions were as demeaning in relation to self-image as some of the earlier terms.

The Way It Is (1969) by John Holland and *The Other City* (1969) by Ray Vogel, compilations of photographs and commentary by junior and senior high school boys of Brooklyn, New York, are visually excellent, but both have been criticized for failing to give children positive feedback about their own environment. *It's Wings That Make Birds Fly* (1968) by Sandra Weiner, another photograph book and one which tells the story in a boy's own words about his life and environment, is taken from tapes made by the author. An appended note tells was killed not long afterward crossing the street. A 1968 book by John Neufeld, *Edgar Allan*, gives a thirteen-year-old son's account of the adoption of a Black baby by a white minister's family and the pressure of the community attitudes that forced them to give him up. Readers were beginning to face the realism of unhappy endings in stories of racial relationships. A fact that Black children already knew was being verbalized in books; they do not "all live happily ever after."

The work of over-eager publishers and an increase in conflicting opinions of many titles were balanced by more critical reviewing of the works published. The term "controversial" was applied to more than the average number of books, including some award winners. Even Black authors failed to escape criticism by other Blacks.

IMAGES IN CONTROVERSIAL BOOKS

The issue of questionable images in controversial books lends itself to lengthy discussion; however, the comments in this chapter are limited to a few books which the reader may wish to examine to draw his or her own conclusions. One of these is William Armstrong's *Sounder* (1969), a fable of oppression and brutality to Blacks, and a vaguely remembered tale which a white man was told by a Black man (only the dog has a name); the movie version has a happier ending. *Sourland* (1971), a sequel, shows the boy from *Sounder* grown into manhood and spending his time teaching the white man's children. What motivates the main character is difficult to understand. Like *Sounder*, the story has an unhappy ending. *The Slave Dancer* (1973) by Paula Fox tells of the evils of slavery as seen through the eyes of a white boy who was shanghaied to a slave ship to provide music for the slaves' exercise. The main criticism of this work is that the author fails to point out the moral evil and degradation of slavery for clear interpretation by young people, and the effect upon the boy, Jessie, is inadequate for the trauma of the experience. In *Charlie and the Chocolate Factory* (1964) by Roald Dahl, the oompa loompas from darkest Africa are brought to work in the chocolate factory, but they were not regarded as people and their lives were expendable. This was an extremely popular book that led many teachers to refute the sadistic, capitalistic, and racial overtones. The oompa loompas were changed from black to green in the movie version, but this made no noticeable improvement in the story. A revised edition in 1973 portrays the oompa loompas with rosy white skin and long, golden brown hair, wearing deerskin or leaves. *Harriet and the Promised Land* (1968), an outstanding art book by Black artist Jacob Lawrence, was unfavorably criticized when, due to its format, it was evaluated as a picture book. Parental interpretation is required for younger children to appreciate and understand properly this unusual book about freedom fighter Harriet Tubman. *Black Folk Tales* (1969) by Black author Julius Lester was cited by the more conventional, conservative reviewers for lack of reverence and religious respect. *O Lord, I Wish I Was a Buzzard* (1968) by Polly Greenberg was based on the author's memory of a story told to the author about a southern Black childhood. The work has been criticized because some of the animals the child envies as she labors picking cotton—a snake, a dog, and a buzzard—contribute to low self-esteem. *The Cay* (1969) by Theodore Taylor returns to the loyal servant image as the young white boy for whom the old Black sailor gives his life actually relates to the Black only in terms of his use to the boy.

For an in-depth study of Black images in fiction between the years 1827 and 1967, the reader is encouraged to consult *Images of the Black in Children's Fiction* by Dorothy Broderick (1973). This critical analysis, based on the author's doctoral thesis, pinpoints specific instances of racism, attitudes, and images portrayed in different subject areas of children's fiction.

SELECTION TOOLS OF THE 1960s AND 1970s

In 1965 the Council on Interracial Books for Children was founded. It was one of the earliest organizations to fight for equality in books for Black children, and it was dedicated to the promotion of antiracism and antisexism in literature and instructional material for children. The council publishes the *Bulletin* (at that time called *Interracial Books for Children*), which became a constructive tool for reviews and which gives guidelines and criteria for evaluating Black children's literature. Later, the focus expanded to encompass other minorities including Native Americans, third-world peoples, women, the handicapped, and ageism.

The 1974 edition of the New York Public Library's *The Black Experience in Children's Books* selected by Barbara Rollock, Coordinator of Children's Services, differed greatly in appearance from the 1957 pamphlet by Augusta Baker, *Books about Negro Life for Children*. Baker's work consisted of twenty-four pages of titles carefully chosen and unbiased, giving an accurate account of Negro life and considering standards of language, theme, and illustration. Although just as carefully chosen, the 1974 book list was a 122-page bibliography consisting of books of all types and on all levels. Like the 1971 edition, it received monies from the Federal Library Services and Construction Act funds. Original guidelines for content still held true, but one new factor was noted in the 1974 edition. While dialect and colloquialism had been a concern in earlier books, in the 1970s, Black English in dialogue and narration had become an issue. The subject of its validity as a language is still controversial.

NEW TRENDS

John Steptoe's *Stevie* (1969), a story of a child's mixed emotions of jealousy and love for a younger playmate, created a new trend. The child's thoughts were expressed in street idiom accompanied by bold, vigorous, full-color illustrations. The author was only seventeen years old when he wrote and illustrated *Stevie*; this was followed by *Uptown* (1970), *Train Ride* (1971), and other works. Books by authors who sought to offer children a greater sense of self-identity by writing in the vernacular to which they were accustomed include *na-ni* (1973) by Alexis De Veaux, *The Dragon Takes a Wife* (1972) by Walter Dean Myers, and on an older level, *His Own Where* (1971) by June Jordan. Picture books by Lucille Clifton such as *My Brother Fine with Me* (1975) and *The Times They Used To Be* (1974), and Eloise Greenfield's *She Come Bringing Me That Little Baby Girl* (1974) are all written in Black English with warm understanding of a Black child's emotions and culture.

Muriel Feelings chose a theme based on her experience in East Africa for her book, *Zamani Goes to Market* (1970), an African boy's first trip to market. *Moja Means One: Swahili Counting Book* (1972) and *Jambo Means Hello: Swahili Alphabet Book* (1974) by the same author also contribute to the child's understanding of cultural heritage. All three books are illustrated in soft lithographs by Black illustrator Tom Feelings.

Arnold Adoff, who compiled *The Poetry of Black America* (1973) and other poetry anthologies, crossed a racial frontier in picture books when he wrote *Black Is Brown Is Tan* (1973). The story about love in a biracial family is based on his own. The author is married to Black author Virginia Hamilton. Children of interracial marriages will be able to identify with this book. *Me Day* (1971) by Joan Lexau tells of a small boy's fear of losing his father as a result of his parents' divorce, and the reassurance that his father gives him.

As libraries became multimedia centers, the wider availability of filmstrips and films, and more recently videotapes, influenced children's reading and the images that they encountered. These media present ready-made images with bad as well as good effects. Films and filmstrips, like television, without conscious coalition on the part of children, impress upon young minds the images and ideas which the producer wishes to convey. Positive images of Black children are presented in many films and filmstrips made from children's books. *Evan's Corner* and *The Case of the Elevator Duck* both show warm human relationships within an urban community.

In 1970 a song which since 1900 had been an inspirational part of Black culture but was less familiar to second- and third-generation northern children was published in an illustrated juvenile book with piano arrangement. *Lift Every Voice and Sing*, by James Weldon Johnson and set to music by his brother, J. Rosamond Johnson, is generally known to Black people as ''The Negro National Anthem.'' The heritage of the past as well as the hope for the future expressed in the lyrics have done much for Black pride and self-image. In 1974 the cultural tradition of the spirituals was renewed by Ashley Bryan in *Walk Together Children*, an outstanding book illustrated with unusual woodcuts.

During the 1960s and 1970s many authors attempted to deal with current issues in children's fiction, particularly in books directed to teenagers. Writers sought to express, explain, and solve problems, or at least to give meaning to them. Bibliotherapy, the use of books to help solve personal problems, grew as a recommended tool for psychiatry in helping young people.

Frank Bonham, a white author, wrote books dealing with California ghetto life: *Durango Street* (1965), *Mystery of the Fat Cat* (1968), *The Nitty Gritty* (1968), and *Hey Big Spender* (1972) to name a few. Favorably accepted at first, these works later drew criticism for showing only the negative side of city life and unfavorable images of Blacks. Robert Lipsyte's *The Contender* (1967) and Barbara Rinkoff's *Member of the Gang* (1968) were two other stories by white authors on the inner city locale. Kristin Hunter, a Black author who has written several very successful adult books, wrote *The Soul Brothers and Sister Lou* (1968) about an inner city girl's search for identity and *Guests in the Promised Land* (1972), a collection of short stories reflecting the bitterness of Black adolescence. Sharon Bell Mathis' books *Teacup Full of Roses* (1972), about drug addition, and *Listen for the Fig Tree* (1974), whose central character is a sixteen-year-old Black blind girl, lend depth to the portrayal of the seamier side of Black inner city life. *Sidewalk Story* (1971) by the same author is written for younger children and tells a happier story of a nine-year-old who helps her friend during the family's eviction from their home.

Plots in books for older children became more innovative and diversified. Louise Fitzhugh's *Nobody's Family Is Going to Change* (1974) is the story of a middle-class Black family with a daughter, overweight Emma, who wants to be a lawyer and brother Willie, who wants to be a tap dancer. In *Sister* by Eloise Greenfield (1974), a young Black girl's diary highlights her preteen years and her relationship to an older sister. Rosa Guy's *The Friends* (1973) is about prejudice against a West Indian girl shown by Harlem classmates. Walter Dean Myers and Alice Childress broke new ground by portraying father figures differently from those usually found in children's books. In *A Hero Ain't Nothin' but a Sandwich* by Childress (1973), a mother's boyfriend tries to save her son, a thirteen-year-old heroin addict; this portrays a father figure who is not a relative. In Myers' *It Ain't All for Nothin'* (1978), a twelve-year-old, after his aged grandmother is consigned to a nursing home, must cope with living with a father who is on the wrong side of the law and who forces his son to follow the pattern. Adrienne Jones' *So Nothing Is Forever* (1974) tackles the situation of three orphaned children of an interracial marriage determined to make their home with a white grandmother who does not welcome them. *Reggie and Nilma* by Louise Tanner (1971) tells of changing relationships between a wealthy white girl and a boy from the ghetto.

WORK OF ORGANIZATIONS

Works published during the years covered in this chapter have been limited to a few, but enough are included to give the reader a general idea of the maturing trend of topics handled and the honest approach to real life. Many books published in the 1970s contain Black and white young people in some type of positive relationship. Publishers of this period realized that racism seen in children's books of the past should be avoided, and many of them established policies for accepting manuscripts to ensure that racism and sexism were avoided. Recognizing the importance of books in intercultural relations, organizations such as the NAACP launched protests against racist materials in libraries. The National Council of Teachers of English created a task force on racism and bias in the teaching of English which brought forth a statement of criteria for teaching literature. The statement was adopted in 1970. In 1972 the Children's Services Division of the American Library Association adopted a statement for critical reevaluation of children's materials to weed out books no longer relevant to current societal conditions, attitudes, and relationships, thereby releasing a storm over censorship, with the Intellectual Freedom Committee taking up the opposing challenge. The ALA subsequently drew up a Resolution on Racism and Sexism Awareness, which was adopted in 1976. The Foundation for Change and the National Council of Christians and Jews have produced and distributed literature and booklists for the promotion of human rights. The Council on Interracial Books for Children in 1974 published a brochure, ''10 Quick Ways to Analyze Children's Books for Racism and Sexism.'' Two other publications, *Racism and Sexism in Children's Books* and *Stereotypes, Distortions and Omissions in U.S. History Textbooks*, are useful in learning about racism and stereotypes.[28]

Near the end of the 1970s the tide of children's books published began to recede. Inflation and rising costs caused publishers to limit production. The demand for works on other minorities meant that publishers would limit the number of books published on Blacks and other groups. Without the stimulus of federal funds, interest in Black publications began to wane.

AWARDS

One important breakthrough, which occurred in the seventies, was the winning of the Newbery Award for the most distinguished contribution to American literature for children by the first Black recipient, Virginia Hamilton. The award was given for *M. C. Higgins, the Great* (1974). Mayo Cornelius (M. C.) and his family provide insight into an extraordinary lifestyle, yet one which can provide the means for young Black children to come to terms with themselves and their own problems. Virginia Hamilton's first book, *Zeely* (1967), recounts a summer vacation when a farm girl who resembles a Watusi princess helps a little girl to understand her own identity. *The House of Dies Drear* (1968), possibly the most popular of her books with children, is a Black heritage mystery which puts Black children in touch with the earlier history of their race. *The Planet of Junior Brown* (1971) transcends reality and enters the world of the mentally disturbed. With too many titles to mention individually, Hamilton is one of the most prolific and versatile contemporary authors of children's works. She has a state-of-the-art writing style which appeals to the above average reader who can relate to a more sophisticated, out of the ordinary plot. Yet, her substantial, factual biographies appeal to many age levels.

Bette Greene's *Philip Hall Likes Me, I Reckon Maybe*. (1973) was a Newbery

Awards Honor book in 1974.[29] Greene is a white author who writes about an eleven-year-old southern Black girl, Beth Lambert, and her efforts to win the affection of her classmate, Philip. The book received some criticism because no identifiable white characters were included.

The Newbery Award for 1977 was presented to Black author Mildred Taylor for her book, *Roll of Thunder, Hear My Cry*. This is an unforgettable saga of the struggle of the author's family to retain their land in Mississippi and the pride and dignity of their heritage. The beginning of this series was *Song of the Trees* (1975), a Council on Interracial Books for Children contest winner. Taylor tells her story in the first person from the viewpoint of the child, Cassie, relating family memories as vividly as though they were her own experiences. The cultural image is that of a Black family with a balance of normal, rural family activities, humor and tragedy, and a wealth of racial pride and concern for the events of the period.

Caldecott Awards for 1975 and 1976 were won by illustrators Leo and Diane Dillon, an integrated team, for *Why Mosquitoes Buzz in People's Ears*, an African folktale, and *Ashanti to Zulu*, an African heritage alphabet book. The 1979 Newbery Award was won by a white author, Ellen Raskin, for *The Westing Game*, an unusual mystery which a Black woman judge helps to solve.

The Newbery Award was established in 1922, the Caldecott Award in 1938. A chronological reading of the books which received the awards reveals the extent to which they reflect the ideas and values of their times. Many of the earlier titles are guilty of racism and, for that reason, would have difficulty meeting the standards of today's books. The first national children's award won by a Black author was the Jane Addams Children's Book Award. Recipient Arna Bontemps won the award in 1956 for *Story of the Negro*. The Women's International League for Peace and Freedom established the award in 1953 to encourage publication of books for children which are of literary merit and contain constructive themes. The first national children's fiction award won by a Black author was given to Lorenz Graham for *South Town* in 1959. It was the Child Study Association of America/Wel-Met Children's Annual Award for a book that relates to problems and realities in children's lives.[30]

Of the numerous awards offered for children's books through the years, many have not been books to which Black children could relate. Three awards which have best provided images and identity for Black children are unique in purpose. In 1968 the Council on Interracial Books for Children established an award for unpublished Afro-American writers of children's books whose manuscripts were judged to be outstanding and met the criteria for antiracism, antisexism, and positive values. The contest expanded to five ethnic minority categories. No awards were given if a manuscript failed to meet the criteria. The contest was discontinued after 1979. Most of the winners and runner-ups have continued to produce other outstanding works. To facilitate identification of the winners, a chronological list is given later in this chapter.

The Coretta Scott King Award, since its inception in 1970, has been presented to a Black author and, since 1979, a Black illustrator for a fiction or nonfiction children's and young adults' book published in the preceding year. Selection criteria state that "The book must portray people, places, things, and events in a manner sensitive to the true worth and value of all beings."[31] A chronological list of award winners is given later in this chapter.

The Carter G. Woodson Book Award, established in 1974, was intended to "encourage the writing, publishing and dissemination of outstanding social science books for young readers which treat topics related to ethnic minorities and race relations sensitively and accurately."[32] It was sponsored by the National Council for the Social Studies. Winners include Eloise Greenfield, Jesse Jackson, and Dorothy Sterling.

WORKS OF THE EIGHTIES

Although over 2,000 titles were published in 1984, only about 100 new titles were added to the 1984 edition of *The Black Experience in Children's Books*. Increased publishing costs, restructuring of some publishing companies with a cutback in children's divisions, and priorities determined by the buying market all have affected children's book production. Conservative trends in social thought replaced the liberal wave that followed the civil rights movement, resulting in less attention to Black people and their concerns. Current economic and governmental priorities have led to the end of federal subsidies for publishing books on minorities, forcing publishers to operate within their own budgets. The cost of children's books, even the very popular paperbacks, is a deterrent which limits retail sales. Like publishing companies, libraries have automated their services, restructured staffs, and merged collections thereby eliminating or decreasing specialists in children's work. All of these factors have affected the children's book field.

The new books by Black authors and illustrators are fresh and vital in their portrayal of the Black image, and high standards are maintained. Trends are toward greater realism and more explicit sex included in implication, language, and act, necessitating more parental awareness of content and style when selecting books for younger children. Changing moral values nationwide also affect images in children's books. Young adult and even younger children's books continue to offer themes of current concern: broken homes, divorce, single parents, alcoholism and drugs, premarital sex, sexuality, women's rights, adjustment to aging and death. These themes reflect young people's concerns and life's problems.

Walter Dean Myers in writing *Won't Know Till I Get There* (1982) uses a diary technique and a theme of intergeneration relationships. When a thirteen-year-old boy with a police record is adopted into a family, a graffiti incident results in the sentence of four teenagers to work in a senior nursing home for the summer. Virginia Hamilton continues to bring new innovations of plot, this time with a psychic twist. In 1980 *The Gathering* completes her Black ESP fiction trilogy begun with *Justice and Her Brother* (1978) and continued in *Dustland* (1980). In *Sweet Whispers, Brother Rush* (1982), the ghost of fourteen-year-old Tree's uncle helps her to relive events of her family's past as a means of understanding the present. *The Magical Adventures of Pretty Pearl* (1983) delves into the backgrounds of Afro-American history, folklore, mythology, and legend and weaves them into an unusual heritage fantasy. The reader never finds duplication of plot or theme in Hamilton's books.

Kristin Hunter continues the story of *The Soul Brothers and Sister Lou* in *Lou in the Limelight* (1981). After a distressing and almost disastrous stage tour in New York and Las Vegas, Lou on a down home tour of Georgia finds her family and her identity and comes to terms with her life. The powerful saga of the Logan family is continued by Mildred Taylor in *Let the Circle Be Unbroken*, the Newbery Award winner of 1982. She deals realistically and frankly with mature topics such as Black legal justice in Mississippi, Black and white relations in the South, and family and community reactions to interracial marriage.

The trend in picture books also turns toward new and creative ideas and illustrations. Marcia Brown's *Shadow* inspired by her African travels is a collage picture book which won the 1983 Caldecott Award. Claudia Zaslavsky's *Count on Your Fingers, African Style* (1980), illustrated with pencil drawings of the African market place, gives African words for counting and can be used with the African culture books of Muriel and Tom Feelings. In the 1983 title of Lucille Clifton's series about a small boy and his everyday life and family relationships, *Everett Anderson's Goodbye*, a child comes to terms with his grief over his father's death in one of the best books on coping with death ever written for children. Arnold Adoff has added another book to help the child of an interracial marriage realize identity. *All the Colors of the Race* (1982) expresses in poems a young girl's thoughts on having a Black mother and a white father. Jeanette Caines' *Just Us Women* (1982), illustrated by Pat Cummings, a new Black illustrator, describes a delightful car trip to North Carolina with no men, no boys, just a little girl and her favorite aunt. The book is a joy to the picture-book-age feminist. Continuing the presentation of Black American spirituals, Ashley Bryan adds a second illustrated volume, *I'm Going to Sing* (1982).

The *Jafta* series by Hugh Lewin, originally published in England (1981), introduced the young reader to the life of a Black boy in apartheid South Africa in beautiful sepia and cream picture books without the violent aspects that are the reality of life in some areas today. Peter Magubane, a Black South African photographer, was the winner of the 1983 Coretta Scott King Award with *Black Child*, a photographic portrayal of Black children in South Africa compiled with realism for older children and adults.

The importance of the illustration of children's books to the cultural image presented should not be underestimated. Front covers of paperbacks or book jackets or trade books present visual images even to the casual viewer. Illustrations today exhibit many styles and techniques, and more innovative and artistic ways of bringing pages to life appear each year. Many outstanding picture books are available to teach Black children their heritage and to help them begin their reading experiences with positive racial images. The 1984 edition of *The Black Experience in Children's Books* will be especially valuable in identifying Black authors and illustrators through a separate section given in its appendix.

In retrospect, one has a different perspective of the books of earlier years and a broader view of the entire spectrum. As earlier noted, this chapter concentrates on the literature for children that was published between the 1920s and the early 1980s. This span of years corresponds to the years of the author's own involvement with children's books from childhood to the present. It is interesting to compare the style of recent books to the earlier titles. The Black English or "street talk" that appears in some of the books of the 1980s differs from the dialect of the past in purpose, use, and expression; however, some of it is no more easily understood by the uninitiated. The new trend of raw realism in language and plot exemplified by Alice Childress, Walter Dean Myers, and Kristin Hunter pulls no punches on single parenthood, extramarital sex, and language to an extent not found in previous children's literature. The hairstyles that were a source of embarrassment and censure in earlier times are now worn with pride and are illustrated in books of African heritage. *Cornrows* (1979) by Camille Yarborough is a testimony to the tradition of the hairstyle as the beautiful heritage of Black people is poetically explained.

In the current decade, some of the apathy of earlier years of children's literature, including the reluctance of publishers to chance new writers, appears to be returning. The output of Black children's literature has diminished in recent years, and many Black books published since 1965 are now out of print. Nevertheless, one of the greatest changes over the years has been the quantity of books available. In contrast to the days when few books recognized the existence of Blacks and Black bibliographies included some mediocre titles because they were the most acceptable of those available, many titles have been published within the time span of the past ten years alone. The child seeking to find expression and identity through poetry can choose *Ego Tripping* (1973) by Nikki Giovanni, *Daydreamers* (1981) by Tom Feelings and Eloise Greenfield, or *Bronzeville Boys and Girls* (1956) by prizewinner Gwendolyn Brooks. The folklore enthusiast can enjoy the modern style of Julius Lester in *Black Folk Tales* (1969) or find a folk hero in *John Henry, an American Legend* (1965) by Ezra Jack Keats. Black histories are available, and Black biographies and illustrations in all categories of nonfiction books include Black people in relevant roles.

EXPANSION OF CHILDREN'S FICTION

Children's fiction by Black writers has expanded into more general themes. The emphasis is no longer confined to writing books oriented to Black concerns alone, but on universalism and creativity of individual thought. The fact of Blackness has been achieved. America has been led to accept Black culture as a truth, a state of being. There is in children's literature an expression of acceptance of self as a person as well as acceptance as a Black person. The Black author is competing on a wider basis to write a good book, not just a good Black book.

The images of Black America in children's books are still in the process of change. The 1931 preface to the revised issue of James Weldon Johnson's *Book of American Negro Poetry* (1922) states that the best poems of the American Negro up to that time had been about race. He further states:

Assuredly the time will come when he will know other things as well as he knows ''race'' and will, perhaps, feel them as deeply; or to state this another way, the time will come when he will not have to know ''race'' so well or feel it so deeply. But even now, he can escape the sense of being hampered if, standing on his racial foundation, he strives to fashion something that rises above mere race and reaches out to the universal in truth and beauty.[33]

This, then, is the positive thing that has occurred following the concentrated emotions of Black people of the militant 1960s. Rather than wearing Blackness as a factor to be overcome, there is recognition of Blackness as an innate, positive quality as writers reach toward their full potential.

Have those of us who work with children changed as much as the trends in books have changed? I hope and believe that in many ways we have. I believe we have grown more honestly evaluative and understanding of the need to include all lifestyles, all races, and all types of people in children's books as a true reflection of life. I believe we have grown in respect for each other's sensitivities, young and old, Black and white. We recognize changing morals and lifestyles. We accept the need to realize that the child readers live in today's world and seek books with characters with whom they can identify rather than idealistic imitations of life. We hold fast to the true values which are important to the growth and proper development of the child's mind.

CHARTING THE FUTURE

What are the needs and responsibilities of the future of literature for Black children? There is a need for high standard, quality books that portray accurate images and actions. Writers should avoid contrived plots, distortions, and misrepresentations. Editors and publishers must be selective and evaluative. Just as authors must write thoughtful, intelligent books for children, publishers must continue to provide excellent children's books for all segments of American society. When this occurs, at least for a while each child can walk briefly in the worlds of his or her friends and associates and understand more fully the various peoples who make America what it is today.

In nonfiction we recognize the need to accept history as it was and not to disregard some phase of it which we resent or prefer to reject. We respect the right to interpret today's events in the light of yesterday's history, but also to interpret yesterday's events in the perspective brought by the knowledge of today. History cannot be rewritten to coincide with the way we would like to have had it happen. Some conditions did exist; some attitudes were prevalent among both Blacks and Whites. Prejudices did and do exist. We respect the child's right to know.

We see the need for biographical images of Blacks developed with honesty and truth in portrayal for young people as well as in adult biographies. Good and bad elements are a part of all personalities; honest images of biographical figures enable children to cope with their own weaknesses and aid in character building.

We reserve the right to disagree with each other on individual books published, both contemporary and historical, as we seek to avoid witch-hunts for racism and stereotypes. We realize that there will always be books such as *The Slave Dancer*, *Sounder*, and *The Cay*, sometime written with good intent and becoming winners of coveted awards, yet falling into the realm of controversial books.

We have a duty to protect children's freedom to read just as we have a responsibility to provide children with worthwhile books to read. Rather than censor books from children's shelves and reading lists, it is important to teach children to select wisely, to avoid accepting all printed words as documented truth either from Black or white authors, and to know that biased views from any author are possible. Children should be led to seek reliable sources, to exercise sound judgement, and to practice clear thinking. In fiction, one should be able to recognize untruths masquerading as truths, to identify stereotypes no matter how cleverly presented, and to learn to accept what is good and to discard what is harmful to one's mental image.

Black writers and artists, teachers and librarians, have a responsibility to younger generations to help them to know the Black American experience of difficult years, the struggles that have brought Black people to the point where they now stand. Many battles are yet to be won; there is much to be accomplished and many goals to be attained. In forgetfulness lies the danger of cultural reversal and loss of contact with one's real roots and culture. Knowledge and use of good literature for Black children can bring to the present generation true identity and racial pride. Children's literature can be a bridge for understanding between cultures, but it can also be a bridge for understanding and communication among Black people.

Mildred Taylor in her acceptance speech for the Newbery Award for *Roll of Thunder, Hear My Cry* stated:

It is my hope that these books, one of the first chances to mirror a Black child's hopes and fears from childhood innocence to awareness to bitterness and disillusionment will one day be instrumental in teaching children of all colors the tremendous influence that Cassie's generation—my father's generation—had in bringing about the great Civil Rights movement of the fifties and sixties. . . . If they can identify with the Logans, who are representative not only of my family, but of the many Black families who faced adversity and survival, and understood the principles by which they lived, then perhaps they can better understand and respect themselves and others.[34]

What can be said for the future outlook of the image of Blacks in American culture where books for children are concerned? With the strong foundations for values and guidelines well formulated by dedicated librarians of the past such as Charlemae Rollins and Augusta Baker, who stood fast to principles in the early years; with roots in the writings of Arna Bontemps, Lorenz Graham, and Jesse Jackson; and with the excellent current Black writers such as Virginia Hamilton, Mildred Taylor, Walter Dean Myers, Lucille Clifton, and many, many others, we are moving into a new age of Black children's literature—an age for positive images and true cultural identity.

NOTES

1. Florence Crannell Means, *Great Day in the Morning* (Boston, Mass.: Houghton Mifflin, 1946), 61.

2. *Ebony Pictorial History of Black America*, vol. III (Chicago, Ill.: Johnson Publishing Co., 1971), 86.

3. Carter G. Woodson, *The Negro in Our History* (Washington, D.C.: Associated Publishers, 1922); Arthur Huff Fauset, *For Freedom* (Philadelphia: Franklin Publishing Co., 1927).

4. The nursery rhyme "Ten Little Injuns" originally was written by Septimus Winters as a song for an American minstrel show of the 1860s. It was followed in England by the similar and equally popular "Ten Little Nigger Boys" written by Frank Green. (William Baring-Gould and Cecil Baring-Gould, *The Annotated Mother Goose* (New York: Clarkson N. Potter, 1962). See also *Interracial Books for Children Bulletin* 1, no. 7 (1979): 4, which lists the author as Septimus Winners, according to *The Oxford Dictionary of Nursery Rhymes* by Iona and Peter Opie, Oxford, 1969.

5. The edition of *Robin Hood* that children read is Howard Pyle, *The Merry Adventures of Robin Hood of Great Renown in Nottinghamshire* (New York: Scribner, 1883, 1946). The original story is derived from ballads dating back to 1495. Jonathan Swift's *Gulliver's Travels* (Dublin: Faulkner, 1735) contains satires on social and political life which children read as fanciful tales. *Arabian Nights or The Thousand and One Nights* was first written in Arabic; the tales reached Europe in about the 1700s.

6. The Black folk stories of Joel Chandler Harris (b. 1848, d. 1908), a white author and journalist in Georgia, who was the first person to collect American Negro folktales, are still an active part of folklore collections today. His best known characters are Brer Rabbit, Brer Fox, Brer Bear, and Brer Wolf. A favorite among children is the "Tar Baby" story in which Brer Rabbit is tricked by Brer Bear and Brer Fox and his own curiosity into getting all four paws stuck fast to the tar figure. Richard Chase, ed., *The Complete Tales of Uncle Remus* (Boston: Houghton Mifflin, 1955) includes seven collections and illustrations from editions dating from 1896 to 1918. *Brer Rabbit*, adapted by Margaret Wise Brown (New York: Harper, 1941) and *The Favorite Uncle Remus*, eds. George Van Santvoord and Archibald Coolidge (Boston: Houghton Mifflin, 1948) have simplified the dialect and are more easily read by children.

7. Anansi, the folk hero of the Ashanti in West Africa, appears in African and in Jamaican folktales sometimes as a spider and sometimes as a man. He is endlessly occupied in tricking the other creatures, but he is sometimes tricked himself. He is also a source of explanation for folktales of natural creation and natural phenomenon. See Philip Sherlock, *Anansi the Spider Man* (New York: Crowell, 1954); Harold Courlander, *The Hat-Shaking Dance and Other Ashanti Tales from Ghana* (New York: Harcourt Brace Jovanovich, 1957); and Gerald McDermott, *Ashanti the Spider; a Tale from the Ashanti* (New York: Holt, 1972), a picture book.

The John tales, generated in slave times in the United States, moved all of the cleverness and trickery of the African animal tales into the person of John, a slave who had an unending battle of wits with "ol' master," other slaves, and sometimes even the devil. The culture hero High John the Conqueror was the epitome of strength, the symbol of courage, and the fantasy of escape for the slaves. When no longer needed, he receded into the earth as the High John the Conqueror root. See Zora Neale Hurston, "High John de Conqueror," *The American Mercury* 57, 238 (October 1943): 454–55.

8. Established in 1921 by Frederick Melcher, an American publisher, the Newbery Award is presented by the Association for Library Services to Children (ALSC, formerly the Children's Services Division) of the American Library Association to the author of the most distinguished contribution to American children's literature during the previous year.

9. Isabelle Suhl, "The 'Real' Doctor Dolittle," *Interracial Books for Children*, vol. II, nos. 1 and 2 (1969); reprinted in Donnarae McCann and Gloria Woodard, eds., *The Black American in Books for Children: Readings in Racism* (Metuchen, N.J.: Scarecrow Press, 1972), 78–88.

10. Horatio Alger published 123 original titles, all on the "rags to riches" theme (although this was never one of his titles). Best known titles are *Tom the Bootblack*, originally titled *The Western Boy* (New York: G. K. Carleton, 1878–1880) and *Ragged Dick* (Boston: Lorin, 1868). A short verse made of names of some of his titles and frequently used by him for autograph books was expressive of his themes:

> Strive to succeed, The World's temptations flee.
> Be Brave and Bold! And Strong and Steady be!
> Shift for yourself and prosper then you must,
> Win fame and fortune while you try and trust.

See Ralph D. Gardner, *The Bibliography of the Works of Horatio Alger* (Mendota, Ill.: Wayside Press, rev. 1971), 63.

11. First title of the Hardy Boys series was *The Tower Treasure* (New York: Grossett and Dunlap, 1927). Leslie McFarland was the actual author of the first twenty-two books. Franklin Dixon was the Stratemeyer syndicate pseudonym. The first title of the Nancy Drew series was *Secret of the Old Clock* (New York: Grossett and Dunlap, 1930). Author pseudonym was Carolyn Keene.

12. Ruth Langdon Inglis, "Children's Literature Today: Changing Patterns," *A Time to Learn: A Guide for Parents to the New Theories in Early Childhood Education* (New York: Dial, 1973), 216–19.

13. Lucy Fitch Perkins, *The American Twins of the Revolution* (Boston: Houghton, 1926); *The Pickaninny Twins* (Boston: Houghton, 1931).

14. Barbara Bader, *American Picturebooks from Noah's Ark to the Beast Within* (New York: Macmillan Publishing Co., 1976), 373.

15. A. V. Weaver, *Frawg* (New York: Frederick Stokes, 1930); a happy plantation type story in which Frawg is pictured singing and eating watermelon throughout the book. Unflattering and derogatory illustrations.

16. Established by Frederick G. Melcher in 1937, the award is given by the Association of Library Services to Children (formerly Children's Services Division) of the American Library Association to the illustrator of the most distinguished American picture book for children during the previous year.

17. Jane Shackelford, an Indiana teacher, also published an elementary history, *The Child's Story of the Negro* (Washington, D.C.: Associated Publishers, 1938).

18. Bader, *American Picturebooks*, 378. The authenticity of the characters is brought to one's attention when one learns that the photographs include Spencer Shaw, a recently retired (1986) professor at the University of Washington School of Library Science, as the man reading picture books downstairs and Augusta Baker, the retired Coordinator of Children's Services, New York Public Library, as the Story Lady upstairs.

19. Nancy Larrick, "The All White World of Children's Books," *Saturday Review* (September 11, 1965); reprinted in McCann and Woodard, eds., *The Black American in Books for Children*, 156–68. This was one of the first articles to speak out on the subject of discrimination and racism in children's books.

20. The story is continued in Lorenz Graham, *North Town* (New York: Crowell, 1965), *Whose Town?* (New York: Crowell, 1969), and *Return to South Town* (New York: Crowell, 1976).

21. Nancy Larrick, "The All White World of Children's Books," in *The Black American in Books for Children*, McCann and Woodard, eds., 156–68.

22. Gilbert Ware, author of *William Hastie: Grace under Pressure* (New York: Oxford University Press, 1985), points out that the civil rights revolution was begun in the early 1930s by William Hastie, Charles Hamilton Houston, Thurgood Marshall, and other lawyers who carried out the NAACP plan with strong support from Howard University Law School (Philadelphia *Inquirer*, August 16, 1985).

23. *Steppin and Family* (New York: Oxford University Press, 1940) was the first book about the Steppins family. The series continues in *Mary Ellis Student Nurse* (New York: Harper & Row, 1958).

24. Dorothy Sterling, "Negroes and the Truth Gap," *Interracial Books for Children* 1, 2–3 (Winter 1967): 1–4.

25. Martin Luther King, Jr., "I Have a Dream" speech, in *The Negro in American History*, vol. 1, "Black Americans" (Chicago: Encyclopedia Brittanica Corp., 1928–71, 1969–72), 225–26.

26. *Report of the National Advisory Committee on Civil Disorders*, *New York Times* edition (1968): 203, 396.

27. Charlemae Rollins, *We Build Together*, Introduction (Urbana, Ill.: National Council of Teachers of English, 1941), ix.

28. First appeared in Council for Interracial Books for Children, *Bulletin* V, 2 (1974). A free catalog of resources to counter racism, sexism, and other forms of bias is available from the Racism and Resource Center, a division of the CIBC.

29. The sequel is Bette Greene, *Get on out of Here, Philip Hall* (New York: Dial, 1981).

30. Children's Book Council, *Awards and Prizes*. The award is now known as the Child Study Book Committee at Bank Street College Award.

31. Children's Book Council, *Awards and Prizes*.

32. Coretta Scott King Award, Fact Sheet (1985).

33. James Weldon Johnson, *Book of American Negro Poetry* (New York: Harcourt, Brace, 1931), 7.

34. Mildred D. Taylor, Newbery Award Acceptance Speech, *Top of the News* 33, 4 (Summer 1977): 311–17.

CORETTA SCOTT KING AWARD WINNERS

The Council of the American Library Association at its annual conference in 1982 passed a resolution declaring the Coretta Scott King Award an official ALA unit award. The award is administered by the Social Responsibilities Round Table.

When the illustrator is listed first below, the award was given to the illustrator.

1970 Patterson, Lillie. *Dr. Martin Luther King, Jr., Man of Peace*. Champaign, Ill.: Garrad, 1969.

1971 Rollins, Charlemae. *Black Troubador; Langston Hughes*. Chicago, Ill.: Rand, 1970.

1972 Fax, Elton. *17 Black Artists*. New York: Dodd, 1971.

1973 Duckett, Alfred. *I Never Had It Made: The Autobiography of Jackie Robinson*. New York: Putnam, 1972.

1974 Mathis, Sharon Bell, and George Ford. *Ray Charles*. New York: Crowell, 1973.

1975 Robinson, Dorothy, and Herbert Temple. *The Legend of Africania*. Chicago, Ill.: Johnson, 1974.

1976 Bailey, Pearl. *Duey's Tale*. New York: Harcourt, Brace, Jovanovich, 1975.

1977 Haskins, James. *The Story of Stevie Wonder*. New York: Lothrop, Lee and Shepard, 1976.

1978 Greenfield, Eloise. *Africa Dream*. Illus. Carole Byard. New York: Crowell, 1977.

1979 Davis, Ossie. *Escape to Freedom*. New York: Viking, 1978.
Feelings, Tom, illustrator. Words by Nikki Grimes. *Something on My Mind*. New York: Dial, 1978.

1980 Myers, Walter Dean. *Young Land Lords*. New York: Viking, 1979.
Byard, Carole, illustrator. Yarbrough, Camille. *Cornrows*. New York: Coward, McCann & Geoghegan, 1979.

1981 Poitier, Sidney. *This Life*. New York: Alfred Knopf, 1980.
Bryan, Ashley, illustrator and author. *Beat the Story Drum, Pum Pum*. New York: Atheneum, 1980.

1982 Taylor, Mildred. *Let the Circle be Unbroken*. New York: Dial, 1981.
Steptoe, John, illustrator. Diop, Birago. *Mother Crocodile-Maman-Caiman*. New York: Delacorte, 1981.

1983 Hamilton, Virginia. *Sweet Whispers, Brother Rush*. New York: Philomel, 1982.
Mugubane, Peter, photographer and author. *Black Child*. New York: Knopf, 1982.

1984 Clifton, Lucille. *Everett Anderson's Goodbye*. Illus. Ann Grifalconi. New York: Holt, Rinehart and Winston, 1983.
Cummings, Pat, illustrator. Walter, Mildred Pitts. *My Mama Needs Me*. New York: Lothrop, Lee and Shepard, 1983.

1985   Boyd, Candy Dawson. *The Circle of Gold*. Englewood Cliffs, N.J.: Apple Pa-
       perback, Scholastic, 1984.
       Myers, Walter Dean. *Motown and Didi*. New York: Viking, 1984.
       Honorable Mention: Hamilton, Virginia. *A Little Love*. New York: Philomel,
       1984.
1986   Hamilton, Virginia. *The People Could Fly, American Black Folktales*. New York:
       Knopf, 1985.
       Pinkey, Jerry, illustrator. Flournoy, Valerie. *Patchwork Quilt*. New York: Dial,
       1985.

COUNCIL ON INTERRACIAL BOOKS FOR CHILDREN AWARD WINNERS

In 1970 the award was changed from age level categories to ethnic groups: Afro-
American, Native American, Asiatic American, Puerto Rican American, and Chicano
American. The list below includes only the Afro-American category winners for all the
years given. The contest was discontinued in 1979. Not all award books were successful
in being published.
1968   Hunter, Kristen. *The Soul Brothers and Sister Lou*. New York: Scribner, 1968.
       Myers, Walter Dean. *Where Does the Day Go*. Illus. Leo Carty. Bergenfield,
       N.J.: Parents, 1969.
1969   Mathis, Sharon Bell. *Sidewalk Story*. Illus. Leo Carty. New York: Viking, 1971.
       Cox, Virginia. *ABC: The Story of the Alphabet*. Not published.
       Webb, Margot S. *Letters from Uncle David, Underground Hero*. Not published.
1970   Shepard, Anthony. *Sneakers*. New York: Dutton, 1973. (Original title: *Warball*)
1971–72   Maxwell, Florenz Webbe. *The Rock Cried Out*. Not published.
       Runner-up: Johnson, Brenda A. *Between the Devil and the Sea*. Not published.
1973–74   Taylor, Mildred. *Song of the Trees*. Illus. Mahiri Fufuka. New York: Dial,
       1975. (Original title: *Year of the Trees*)
1975   Abdullah, Aisha S. *Simba, Midnight (The Stallion of the Night)*, *Mweusi*. Not
       published.
       Runner-up: Musgrove, Margaret. *Ashanti to Zulu, African Traditions*. Illus. Leo
       and Diane Dillon. New York: Dial, 1976. (Original title: *Traditional Sketches of
       African Peoples*)
       Additional runners-up: Caldwell, Bill. *The Adventures of Tip, the Dog with the
       Yellow Spots*; Cardy, Leo. *Anton's First Winter*; Peters, Janice. *"A Morning, A
       Night"* and *Three Months Come, Three Months Go*. Not published.
1976–77   No award in the Afro-American category.
1978   No award in the Afro-American category.

BIBLIOGRAPHY OF CHILDREN'S BOOKS

The titles discussed throughout the text of this chapter are listed in alphabetical order
by author in this section. Many authors have written other works; however, only those
in the essay are given. Books no longer listed in *Books in Print* are indicated "o.p.;"
however, many of these can still be found in libraries and in used book stores. Dates for
recent revisions or reprints are given when known.

Aardema, Verna. *Why Mosquitoes Buzz in People's Ears*. Illus. Leo and Diane Dillon. New York: Dial, 1974.

Adoff, Arnold. *All the Colors of the Race*. New York: Lothrop, 1982.

———. *Black Is Brown Is Tan*. New York: Harper and Row, 1973.

Adoff, Arnold, ed. *The Poetry of Black America*. New York: Harper and Row, 1973.

Armstrong, William H. *Sounder*. New York: Harper and Row, 1969.

———. *Sour Land*. New York: Harper and Row, 1971.

Bannerman, Helen. *Little Black Sambo*. New York: Stokes, 1899. New York: Harper, 1923. New York: Platt, 1978.

Beim, Lorraine, and Jerrold Beim. *Two Is a Team*. New York: Harcourt Brace Jovanovich, 1945.

Berends, Polly. *The Case of the Elevator Duck*. New York: Random House, 1973.

Berry, Erick. *Black Folk Tales*. New York: Harper, 1928.

———. *Girls in Africa*. New York: Macmillan, 1928.

———. *Mom du Jos: The Story of a Little Black Doll*. New York: Doubleday, 1931.

Best, Herbert. *Garram the Hunter, a Boy of the Hill Tribes*. New York: Doubleday, 1930.

Black, Irma Simonton, ed. Bank Street Readers. New York: Macmillan, 1965. Series includes:

———. *In the City*. Preprimer. 1965.

———. *People Read*. Preprimer. 1965.

———. *Around the City*. Primer. 1965.

———. *Uptown, Downtown*. First reader. 1965.

———. *Green Light Go*. Second reader. 1965.

———. *My City*. Second reader. 1965.

———. *City Sidewalks*. Third reader. 1965.

———. *Round the Corner*. Third reader. 1965.

Bonham, Frank. *Durango Street*. New York: Dutton, 1965.

———. *Hey Big Spender*. New York: Dutton, 1972.

———. *Mystery of the Fat Cat*. New York: Dutton, 1968.

———. *The Nitty Gritty*. New York: Dutton, 1968. o.p.

Bontemps, Arna. *Golden Slipper, an Anthology of Negro Poetry*. New York: Harper, 1941. o.p.

———. *Sad Faced Boy*. Boston: Houghton Mifflin, 1937. o.p.

———. *Story of the Negro*. New York: Alfred A. Knopf, 1956. Rev. 1969.

———. *You Can't Pet a Possum*. New York: Morrow, 1934. o.p.

Brooks, Gwendolyn. *Bronzeville Boys and Girls*. New York: Harper, 1956.

Brown, Marcia. *Shadow*. New York: Scribner, 1982.

Bryan, Ashley. *I'm Going to Sing: Black American Spirituals*. Vol. II, New York: Atheneum, 1982.

———. *Walk Together Children: Black American Spirituals*. New York: Atheneum, 1974.

Bryant, Sarah Cone. *Epaminondas and His Auntie*. 1907. Boston: Houghton, 1938. o.p.

Burroughs, Edgar Rice. *Tarzan of the Apes*. Chicago: McClurg, 1914. New York: Random House, 1982.

Caines, Jeanette. *Just Us Women*. Illus. Pat Cummings. New York: Harper, 1982.

Calhoun, Francis Boyd. *Miss Minerva and William Green Hill*. Chicago: Reilly and Britton, 1909. o.p.

Carlson, Natalie. *The Empty Schoolhouse*. New York: Harper and Row, 1965.

Cavanna, Betty. *A Time for Tenderness*. New York: Morrow, 1962. o.p.

Childress, Alice. *A Hero Ain't Nothin' but a Sandwich*. New York: Coward, 1973.

Clemens, Samuel L. *The Adventures of Huckleberry Finn*. Webster, 1884. New York: Dodd, Mead, 1984.

————. *The Adventures of Tom Sawyer*. Hartford, Conn.: American, 1876. New York: Grossett and Dunlap, 1978.

Clifton, Lucille. *The Black B C's*. New York: Dutton, 1970. o.p.

————. *Everett Anderson's Goodbye*. New York: Holt, Rinehart and Winston, 1983.

————. *My Brother Fine With Me*. New York: Holt, Rinehart and Winston, 1975.

————. *The Times They Used to Be*. New York: Holt, Rinehart and Winston, 1974.

Cole, Robert. *Dead End School*. Boston, Mass.: Little, Brown, 1968. o.p.

Colman, Hila. *Classmates by Request*. New York: Morrow, 1964. o.p.

Credle, Ellis. *Across the Cotton Patch*. Nashville, Tenn.: Thomas Nelson, 1935. o.p.

————. *Little Jeemes Henry*. Nashville, Tenn.: Thomas Nelson, 1936. o.p.

Dahl, Roald. *Charlie and the Chocolate Factory*. New York: Knopf, 1964. Rev. 1973.

De Angeli, Marguerite. *Bright April*. New York: Doubleday, 1946. o.p.

Decker, Duane. *Hit and Run*. New York: Morrow, 1949.

Deveaux, Alexis. *na-ni*. New York: Harper, 1973.

Dunbar, Paul Laurence. *The Life and Works of Paul Laurence Dunbar*. 6 vols. Dayton, Ohio: Press of United Brethren Pub. House, 1893–97.

Evans, Eva Knox. *Araminta*. New York: Putnam, 1935. o.p.

————. *Jerome Anthony*. New York: Putnam, 1936. o.p.

Faulkner, Georgene. *Melindy's Happy Summer*. New York: Messner, 1949. o.p.

————. *Melindy's Medal*. New York: Messner, 1945. o.p.

Feelings, Muriel. *Jambo Means Hello*. Illus. Tom Feelings. New York: Dial, 1974.

————. *Moja Means One*. Illus. Tom Feelings. New York: Dial, 1972.

————. *Zamani Goes to Market*. Illus. Tom Feelings. New York: Seabury, 1970. o.p.

Feelings, Tom, and Eloise Greenfield. *Daydreamers*. New York: Dial, 1981.

Field, Rachel. *Prayer for a Child*. Illus. Elizabeth Orton Jones. New York: Macmillan, 1944. o.p.

Finley, Martha (Martha Farquharson). *Elsie Dinsmore*. New York: Dodd, 1867. Reprinted Laguna Beach, Calif.: Buccaneer, 1974–1981.

Fitzhugh, Louise. *Nobody's Family Is Going to Change*. New York: Farrar, Straus and Giroux, 1974.

Fox, Paula. *The Slave Dancer*. Scarsdale, N.Y.: Bradbury, 1973.

Friedman, Frieda. *A Sundae with Judy*. New York: Morrow, 1949. o.p.

Gentry, Stella Sharpe. *Tobe*. Chapel Hill: University of North Carolina Press, 1939. o.p.

Giovanni, Nikki. *Ego Tripping*. Illus. George Ford. Westport, Conn.: Lawrence Hill, 1973.

Goldin, Augusta. *Straight Hair, Curly Hair*. New York: Crowell, 1966.

Graham, Lorenz. *North Town*. New York: Crowell, 1965. o.p.

————. *Return to South Town*. New York: Crowell, 1976.

————. *South Town*. Chicago: Follett, 1958. Reprinted 1976.

————. *Whose Town?* New York: Crowell, 1969.

Green, Frank. "*Ten Little Nigger Boys*". In *The Annotated Mother Goose*. Eds. William Baring-Gould and Cecil Baring-Gould. New York: Clarkson N. Potter, 1962.

————. *Ten Little Niggers*. *The Annotated Mother Goose*. William Baring-Gould, and

Cecil Baring-Gould. New York: Clarkson N. Potter, 1962. Various editions of this work have been published by McLoughlin Bros.

Greenberg, Polly. *O Lord, I Wish I Was a Buzzard*. New York: Macmillan, 1968.

Greene, Bette. *Get on out of Here, Philip Hall*. New York: Dial, 1981.

——. *Philip Hall Likes Me, I Reckon Maybe*. Illus. Charles Lilly. New York: Dial, 1973.

Greenfield, Eloise. *She Come Bringing Me That Little Baby Girl*. Philadelphia: Lippincott, 1974.

——. *Sister*. Illus. Moneta Barnett. New York: Crowell, 1974.

Guy, Rosa. *The Friends*. New York: Holt, Rinehart and Winston, 1973.

Hamilton, Virginia. *Dustland*. New York: Greenwillow, 1980.

——. *The Gathering*. New York: Greenwillow, 1980.

——. *The House of Dies Drear*. New York: Macmillan, 1968.

——. *Justice and Her Brothers*. New York: Greenwillow, 1978.

——. *A Little Love*. New York: Putnam, 1984.

——. *The Magical Adventures of Pretty Pearl*. New York: Harper, 1983.

——. *M. C. Higgins, the Great*. New York: Macmillan, 1974.

——. *The Planet of Junior Brown*. New York: Macmillan, 1971.

——. *Sweet Whispers, Brother Rush*. New York: Philomel, 1982.

——. *Zeely*. New York: Macmillan, 1967.

Harris, Joel Chandler. *The Complete Tales of Uncle Remus*. Ed. Richard Chase. Boston: Houghton Mifflin, 1955.

——. *Favorite Uncle Remus*. Eds. George Van Santvoord and Archibald Coolidge. Boston: Houghton Mifflin, 1948.

——. *Uncle Remus, His Songs and Sayings*. New York: Appleton, 1880.

Hentoff, Nat. *The Day They Came to Arrest the Book*. New York: Delacorte, 1982.

Hill, Elizabeth Starr. *Evan's Corner*. New York: Holt, Rinehart and Winston, 1967.

Hogan, Inez. *Nappy Has a New Friend*. New York: Dutton, 1947. o.p.

——. *Nicodemus* (series). New York: E. F. Dutton, 1932–1935. o.p.

Holland, John. *The Way It Is*. New York: Harcourt, 1969. o.p.

Hughes, Langston. *The Dream Keeper*. New York: Knopf, 1932. o.p.

Hunt, Mabel. *Lady Cake Farm*. Philadelphia: Lippincott, 1952. o.p.

Hunter, Kristin. *Guests in the Promised Land*. New York: Scribner, 1972.

——. *Lou in the Limelight*. New York: Scribner, 1981.

——. *The Soul Brothers and Sister Lou*. New York: Scribner, 1968.

Jackson, Jesse. *Call Me Charley*. New York: Harper, 1945.

——. *Tessie*. New York: Harper and Row, 1968. o.p.

Johnson, James Weldon. *Book of American Negro Poetry*. New York: Harcourt Brace, 1922. Reprinted 1931.

Johnson, James Weldon, and J. Rosamond Johnson. *Lift Every Voice and Sing*. New York: Hawthorne, 1970.

Jones, Adrienne. *So, Nothing Is Forever*. Boston: Houghton, Mifflin, 1974.

Jones, Jessie O. *Small Rain*. Illus. Elizabeth Orton Jones. New York: Macmillan, 1942. o.p.

Jordan, June. *His Own Where*. New York: Crowell, 1971.

Kay, Helen. *A Summer to Share*. New York: Hastings House, 1960. o.p.

Keats, Ezra Jack. *John Henry, an American Legend*. New York: Pantheon, 1965.

——. *The Snowy Day*. New York: Viking, 1962.

Konigsberg, E. L. *Jennifer, Hecate, Macbeth, William McKinley and Me, Elizabeth*. New York: Atheneum, 1967.

Lattimore, E. F. *Junior, a Colored Boy of Charleston*. New York: Harcourt Brace, 1938. o.p.

Lawrence, Jacob. *Harriet and the Promised Land*. New York: Simon and Schuster, 1968.

Lester, Julius. *Black Folk Tales*. Illus. Tom Feelings. Woodbury, N.Y.: Baron, 1969.

————. *Long Journey Home, Stories from Black History*. New York: Dial, 1972.

————. *To Be a Slave*. Illus. Tom Feelings. New York: Dial, 1968.

Lewin, Hugh. *Jafta* (series). Minneapolis, Minn.: Carolrhodas, 1983. Eng. publ. 1981.

Lexau, Joan. *Me Day*. New York: Dial, 1971. o.p.

Lipsyte, Robert. *The Contender*. New York: Harper and Row, 1967.

Lofting, Hugh. *Dr. Dolittle, A Treasury*. Philadelphia: Lippincott, 1967.

————. *The Story of Dr. Dolittle*. New York: Stokes, 1920.

————. *The Voyages of Dr. Dolittle*. New York: Stokes, 1922. Philadelphia: Lippincott, 1922. o.p.

Magubane, Peter. *Black Child*. New York: Knopf, 1983.

Mathis, Sharon Bell. *Listen for the Fig Tree*. New York: Viking, 1974.

————. *Sidewalk Story*. Illus. Leo Carty. New York: Viking, 1971. o.p.

————. *Teacup Full of Roses*. New York: Viking, 1972.

Means, Florence Crannell. *Great Day in the Morning*. Boston, Mass.: Houghton Mifflin, 1946. o.p.

————. *Shuttered Windows*. Boston, Mass.: Houghton Mifflin, 1938. o.p.

————. *Tolliver*. Boston, Mass.: Houghton Mifflin, 1963. o.p.

Musgrove, Margaret. *Ashanti to Zulu: African Traditions*. Illus. Leo and Diane Dillon. New York: Dial, 1976.

Myers, Walter Dean. *The Dragon Takes a Wife*. Indianapolis: Bobbs Merrill, 1972.

————. *It Ain't All for Nothin'*. New York: Viking, 1978.

————. *Won't Know Till I Get There*. New York: Viking, 1982.

Neufeld, John. *Edgar Allan*. New York: S. G. Phillips, 1968. o.p.

Newell, Hope. *A Cap for Mary Ellis*. New York: Harper. 1953.

Ovington, Mary White. *Hazel*. New York: Crisis Publishing, 1913. o.p.

————. *Zeke*. New York: Harcourt Brace, 1931. o.p.

Perkins, Lucy Fitch. *The American Twins of the Revolution*. Boston, Mass.: Houghton, 1926. o.p.

————. *The Colonial Twins of Virginia*. Boston, Mass.: Houghton, 1924. o.p.

————. *The Pickaninny Twins*. Boston, Mass.: Houghton, 1931. o.p.

Petersham, Maude, and Miska Petersham. *The Rooster Crows*. New York: Macmillan, 1945. Reprinted 1969.

Petry, Ann. *Tituba of Salem Village*. New York: Harper, 1964.

Pyrnelle, Louise-Clark. *Diddie, Dumps, and Tot*. New York: Harper, 1882. o.p.

Raskin, Ellen. *The Westing Game*. New York: Dutton, 1978.

Rey, Margaret. *Spotty*. New York: Harper and Row, 1945. o.p.

Rinkoff, Barbara. *Member of the Gang*. Illus. Harold James. New York: Crown, 1968.

Rodman, Bella. *Lions in the Way*. Chicago: Follett, 1966. Avon, 1967. o.p.

Scott, Ann Herbert. *Sam*. New York: McGraw-Hill, 1967.

Shackleford, Jane. *The Child's Story of the Negro*. Washington, D.C.: Associated Publishers, 1938. o.p.

————. *My Happy Days*. Washington, D.C.: Associated Publishers, 1944. o.p.

Shotwell, Louise. *Roosevelt Grady*. New York: World, 1963.

Showers, Paul. *Look at Your Eyes*. New York: Crowell, 1962.

————. *Your Skin and Mine*. New York, Crowell, 1965.

Snyder, Zilpha. *The Egypt Game*. New York: Atheneum, 1967.

Steptoe, John. *Stevie*. Illus. by author. New York: Harper and Row, 1969.

————. *Train Ride*. New York: Harper and Row, 1971.

————. *Uptown*. New York: Harper and Row, 1970.

Sterling, Dorothy. *Mary Jane*. New York: Doubleday, 1959.

————. *Tender Warriors*. New York: Hill, 1958. o.p.

Stolz, Mary. *A Wonderful Terrible Time*. New York: Harper, 1967.

Strachan, Margaret. *Where Were You That Year?* New York: Washburn, 1965. o.p.

Stratemeyer, Edward (series books)

———— [Victor Appleton]. *Tom Swift*. New York: Grossett and Dunlap, 1910–1961.

———— [Frank Dixon]. *The Hardy Boys*. New York: Putnam, Wanderer, 1925–. New York: Grossett & Dunlap, 1927–.

———— [Laura Lee Hope]. *The Bobbsey Twins*. New York: Mershon, 1904. New York: Grosset and Dunlap, 1913–1977. o.p.

———— [Helen Louise Thorndyke]. *Honey Bunch*. New York: Grosset and Dunlap, 1923–1930.

————[Arthur M. Winfield]. *The Rover Boys*. New York: Mershon, 1899–1925. New York: Grosset & Dunlap, 1925. o.p.

————[Clarence Young]. *The Motor Boys*. New York: Cupples, 1906–1924.

Stratemeyer, Harriet [Carolyn Keene]. *Nancy Drew*. New York: Putnam, Wanderer, 1935–. (First title, 1930; New York: Grossett & Dunlap, 1930)

Tanner, Louise. *Reggie and Nilma*. New York: Farrar, Straus and Giroux, 1971. o.p.

Tarkington, Booth. *Penrod*. New York: Doubleday, 1914. o.p.

Tarry, Ellen. *Hezekiah Horton*. Illus. Oliver Harrington. New York: Viking, 1942. o.p.

Tarry, Ellen, and Marie Hall Ets. *My Dog Rinty*. New York: Viking, 1946. o.p.

Taylor, Mildred. *Let the Circle Be Unbroken*. New York: Dial, 1981.

————. *Song of the Trees*. Illus. Jerry Pinkney. New York: Dial, 1975.

Taylor, Theodore. *The Cay*. New York: Doubleday, 1969.

Travers, Pamela. *Mary Poppins*. New York: Harcourt, 1962.

Tunis, John. *All American*. New York: Harcourt, 1942.

Udry, Janice. *What Mary Jo Shared*. Chicago, Ill.: Whitman, 1966.

Vogel, Ray. *The Other City*. New York: David White, 1969. o.p.

Wagner, Jane. *J.T.* Photos, Gordon Parks, Jr. New York: Van Nostrand Reinhold, 1969. New York: Dell, paperback, 1971.

Weaver, A. V. *Frawg*. New York: Frederick Stokes, 1930. o.p.

Weiner, Sandra. *It's Wings That Make Birds Fly*. Illus. Gordon Parks, Jr. New York: Pantheon, 1968. o.p.

Williams, Garth. *The Rabbit's Wedding*. New York: Harper and Row, 1958. o.p.

Wilson, Julia. *Becky*. Illus. John Wilson. New York: Crowell, 1966. o.p.

Winters, Septimus. "*Ten Little Injuns*". In *The Annotated Mother Goose*. Eds. William Baring-Gould and Cecil Baring-Gould. New York: Clarkson N. Potter, 1962.

Woodson, Carter G. *African Myths*. Washington, D.C.: Associated Publishers, 1928.

————. *The Negro in Our History*. Washington, D.C.: Associated Publishers, 1922.

————. *Negro Makers of History*. Washington, D.C.: Associated Publishers, 1928. Reprinted 1945.

Yarbrough, Camille. *Cornrows*. Illus. Carole Byard. New York: Coward, McCann & Geoghegan, 1979.
Zaslavsky, Claudia. *Count On Your Fingers, African Style*. Illus. Jerry Pinkney. New York: Crowell, 1980.

GENERAL BIBLIOGRAPHY

References and Related Readings

Adler, Mortimer, J., et al., eds. *The Negro in American History*. 3 vols. Chicago: Encyclopedia Brittanica Corp., 1969, 1972.
Arbuthnot, Mae Hill, and Zena Sutherland. *Children and Books*. 4th ed. Glenview, Ill.: Scott, Foresman, 1972. See also entry under Sutherland.
Austin, Mary C., and Esther C. Jenkins. *Promoting World Understanding through Literature, K–8*. Littleton, Colo.: Libraries Unlimited, 1983.
Bader, Barbara. "Negro Identification, Black Identity." *American Picturebooks from Noah's Ark to the Beast Within*. New York: Macmillan Publishing Co., 1976, 373–82.
Baker, Augusta. *Books About Negro Life for Children*. New York, The New York Public Library, 1957.
———. "The Changing Image of the Black in Children's Literature." *Horn Book Magazine* 51, 1 (February 1975): 79–88.
———. "Guidelines for Black Books: An Open Letter to Juvenile Editor." *Publishers' Weekly* 196, 2 (July 14, 1969): 131–33. Reprinted in McCann and Woodard, *The Black American in Books for Children*, 50–56.
Birtha, Jessie M. "Portrayal of the Black in Children's Literature." *PLA Bulletin* (July 1969): 187–97. Reprinted in ALA *Top of the News* (June 1970); excerpted in McCann and Woodard, *The Black American in Books for Children*, 63–71, 153–54.
Black History Museum Committee, ed. *Sunaru: A Multimedia Guide for the Black Child*. Philadelphia, Pa.: Black History Museum UXUM Publishers, 1979.
Broderick, Dorothy M. *Image of the Black in Children's Fiction*. New York: R. R. Bowker, 1973.
Carpenter, Humphrey, and Mari Pritchard. *The Oxford Companion to Children's Literature*. New York: Oxford University Press, 1984.
Children's Book Council. *Awards and Prizes*. New York: 1976.
Comer, James P., and Alvin F. Poussaint. *Black Child Care: How to Bring Up a Healthy Black Child in America: A Guide to Emotional and Psychological Development*. New York: Simon and Schuster, 1975.
Cornelius, Paul. "Interracial Children's Books: Problems and Progress." *Library Quarterly* 41, 2 (April 1971): 106–27.
Council on Interracial Books for Children. "10 Quick Ways to Analyze Children's Books for Racism and Sexism." *Bulletin* 5, 3 (1974).
———. "Children of Interracial Families." *Bulletin* 5, 6 (1984).
———. *Human and Anti-Human Values in Children's Books: A Content Rating Instrument for Educators and Concerned Parents*. New York: CBIC, 1976.
———. *Racism and Sexism in Children's Books*. New York: CBIC, 1979.

————. *Stereotypes, Distortions and Omissions in U.S. History Textbooks.* New York: CBIC, n.d.

Ebony, Jr. Chicago: Johnson Publishing Co. Monthly magazine for children.

Ebony Pictorial History of America. 4 vols. Chicago, Ill.: Johnson Publishing Co., 1971.

Fauset, Arthur. *For Freedom.* Philadelphia: Franklin Publishing Co., 1927.

Fitzgerald, Bertram A., Jr. *Golden Legacy: Illustrated History Magazine.* St. Albans, N.Y.: Fitzgerald Publishing Co., 1967.

Fraser, James. "Black Publishing for Black Children." *School Library Journal* 20, 3 (November 1973): 19–24.

Harrison, Phyllis, and Barbara Wyden. *The Black Child: A Parent's Guide.* New York: McKay, 1973.

Huck, Charlotte S., and Doris Young. *Children's Literature in the Elementary School.* New York: Holt, Rinehart and Winston, 1961. 3rd ed., 1979.

Hunter, Kristin. "The Soul Brothers: Background of a Juvenile." *Publishers' Weekly* 193, 22 (May 27, 1968): 30–31.

Inglis, Ruth Langdon. "Children's Literature Today: Changing Patterns." In *A Time to Learn: A Guide for Parents to the New Theories in Early Childhood Education.* New York: Dial Press, 1973, 205–34.

Larrick, Nancy. "The All-White World of Children's Books." *Saturday Review* 48, 37 (September 11, 1965): 63–85.

————. *A Parent's Guide to Children's Reading.* 5th ed. New York: Bantam Books, 1982.

McCann, Donnarae, and Gloria Woodard, eds. *The Black American in Books for Children: Readings in Racism.* Metuchen, N.J.: Scarecrow Press, 1972. 2nd ed. 1986.

————. *Cultural Conformity in Books for Children; Further Readings in Racism.* Metuchen, N.J.: Scarecrow Press, 1977.

McLaughlin, Clara. *The Black Parent's Handbook: A Guide to Healthy Pregnancy, Birth and Child Care.* New York: Harcourt, Brace, Jovanovich, 1976.

Parks, Carole A. "Goodbye, Black Sambo." *Ebony* 28, 1 (November 1972): 60–70.

Ploski, Harry A., and Warren Marr, comps., eds. *The Negro Almanac: A Reference Work on the Afro-American.* 4th ed. New York: John Wiley, 1983.

Rollock, Barbara. "Where Has All the Beauty Gone?—A Discussion on the Black Experience in Children's Books." *The Book Mark.* University of the State of New York, Fall, 1984. Issue on Children's Library Service.

Rudman, Masha Kabakov. *Children's Literature, An Issues Aprroach.* Lexington, Mass.: D. C. Heath and Co., 1976.

Sadker, Myra Pollock, and David Miller Sadker. *Now Upon a Time: A Contemporary View of Children's Literature.* New York: Harper, 1977.

Shockley, Ann Allen, and Sue P. Chandler. *Living Black American Authors: A Biographical Directory.* New York: R. R. Bowker, 1973.

Suhl, Isabelle. "The 'Real' Doctor Dolittle." *Interracial Books for Children* 2, 1–2 (1969). Reprinted in McCann and Woodard, *The Black American in Books for Children: Readings in Racism,* 1972; 78–88.

Sutherland, Zena, and Mae Hill Arbuthnot. *Children and Books.* 5th ed. Glenview, Ill.: Scott, Foresman and Co., 1977.

Thernstrom, Stephan, ed. "Afro-Americans." *Harvard Encyclopedia of American Ethnic Groups.* Boston, Mass.: Harvard University Press, 1980, 5–23.

Thompson, Judith, and Gloria Woodard. "Black Perspective in Books for Children."
    Wilson Library Bulletin 44, 4 (December 1969): 416–24.
Tucker, Nicholas. *Suitable for Children? Controversies in Children's Literature*. Berke-
    ley: University of California Press, 1976, 184–91.
U.S. Riot Commission. *Report of the National Advisory Commission on Civil Disorders*.
    New York Times ed. New York: Dutton, 1968.
Walter, M. P., and J. Voic. "What's Ahead for the Black Writer?" *Publishers' Weekly*
    218, 4 (July 25, 1980): 90–92.
Weiss, Jacqueline Shacter. *Prizewinning Books for Children: Themes and Stereotypes in
    U.S. Prizewinning Prose Fiction for Children*. Lexington, Mass.: D. C. Heath,
    1983.
Yuille, Phyllis J. *Little Black Sambo: A Closer Look*. New York: Council on Interracial
    Books for Children, 1976.

Annotated Bibliographies of Children's Books

American Library Association. Office for Library Service to the Disadvantaged. *Multi-
    Ethnic Media—Selected Bibliographies in Print*. Chicago, Ill.: American Living
    Association, 1975.
Baker, Augusta. *Books about Negro Life for Children*. New York: New York Public
    Library, 1949. Reprinted 1957.
Buttlar, Louis, and Lubomyr R. Wynar. "Black Americans." In *Building Ethnic Col-
    lections: An Annotated Guide for School Media Centers and Public Libraries*.
    Littleton, Colo.: Libraries Unlimited, 1977, 111–64.
Dreyer, Sharon Spredemann. *The Bookfinder: A Guide to Children's Literature about
    the Needs and Problems of Youth Aged 2–15*. Circle Pines, Minn.: American
    Guidance Service, 1977.
Hunt, Mary Alice, ed. *A Multimedia Approach to Children's Literature, A Selective List
    of Films and Video Cassettes, Filmstrips, and Recordings Based upon Children's
    Books*. 3rd ed. Chicago, Ill.: American Library Association, 1983.
Johnson, Harry A. *Multimedia Materials for Afro-American Studies*. New York: R. R.
    Bowker, 1971.
Keating, Charlotte Matthews. *Building Bridges of Understanding between Cultures*. Tuc-
    son, Ariz.: Palo Verde Publishing Co., 1971.
Latimer, Bettye, ed. *Starting out Right, Choosing Books about Black People for Young
    Children, Pre-School through Third Grade*. Washington, D.C.: Day Care and
    Child Development Council of America, 1972.
McWhirter, Mary Esther. *Books for Friendship*. Philadelphia, Pa.: American Friends
    Service Committee, 1968. (Former editions, *Books are Bridges*)
Meacham, Mary. *Information Sources in Children's Literature, A Practical Reference
    Guide for Children's Librarians, Elementary School Teachers and Students of
    Children's Literature*. Westport, Conn.: Greenwood Press, 1978.
Mills, Joyce White, ed. *The Black World in Literature for Children: A Bibliography of
    Print and Non Print Materials*. Atlanta, Ga.: Atlanta University School of Library
    Service, vols. 1–4, 1975–1979 (copyright 1984). Vol. 5 will include 1980 through
    1984.
National Conference of Christians and Jews. *Books for Brotherhood*. Published annually.

New York Public Library, Office of Children's Services. *The Black Experience in Children's Audio Visual Materials.* 1973.

Reid, Virgina, ed. *Reading Ladders for Human Relations.* 6th ed. Washington, D.C.: American Council on Education, 1981.

Rollins, Charlemae, ed. *We Build Together: A Reader's Guide to Negro Life and Literature for Elementary and Junior High School Use.* Urbana, Ill.: National Council of Teachers of English, 1941.

————. *We Build Together.* 3rd rev. ed. National Council of Teachers of English, 1967. (Second printing 1974, but no revision)

Rollock, Barbara, sel. *The Black Experience in Children's Books.* New York: New York Public Library, 1974, 1979, 1984.

Schmidt, Nancy J. *Children's Books on Africa and Their Authors: An Annotated Bibliography.* New York: Africana Publishing Co., 1975.

————. *Children's Literature and Audio Visual Materials in Africa.* Buffalo, N.Y.: Conch Magazine, 1977.

Schmidt, Velma E., and Earldene McNeill. *Cultural Awareness: A Resource Bibliography.* Washington, D.C.: National Association for the Education of Young Children, 1978.

Space, George. *Good Reading for the Disadvantaged Reader: Multi-Ethnic Resources.* Champaign, Ill.: Garrard, 1975.

The Black Female: Mammy, Jemima, Sapphire, and Other Images

The image of Blacks has been one of distortions and misconceptions, and the image of Black women has been especially stereotyped. Several studies have been done on the portrayal and images of Black men and women in the media. In 1967, Royal D. Colle conducted dissertation research at Cornell University. His study of "The Negro Image and the Mass Media" examined the depiction of Blacks in mass media (newspapers, film, radio, magazines, and television) and the efforts of each medium to effect change in the portrayed images of Blacks. In 1976, Karen Sue Warren Jewell studied the development and perpetualization of stereotypes in mass media for her doctoral dissertation, "An Analysis of the Visual Development of a Stereotype: The Media's Portrayal of Mammy and Aunt Jemima as Symbols of Black Womanhood." Her claim was that the mass media had historically developed and portrayed Black women as mammy and Aunt Jemima, and that these images ran myths and stereotypes that are generalized to all Black women irrespective of social class or age. She stated further that the rationale for the media's portrayal of mammy and Aunt Jemima is deeply embedded in the very fabric of American society. According to Jewell, this rationale dates back to early conceptions of the value and worth of Black women as human beings. These images of Black women suggest that they are lacking in beauty, femininity, attractiveness, and the other attributes generally associated with womanhood. In addition, the images suggest that Black women are satisfied with their lives and want nothing better for themselves or their families.

Sharon Harley and Rosalyn Terborg-Penn's 1978 anthology, *The Afro-American Woman: Struggles and Images*, gives an overview of the many historical experiences of Black women from the early nineteenth century to the 1970s. They document the work experience of Black women, the discrimination they faced in the women's movement, their struggle for equality in the South, and their images in both music and poetry. Dorothy Porter notes in her introduction to the book that "we now have a more accurate image of the Afro-American woman and her place in history and in the cultural development of our society" (Harley and Terborg-Penn viii).

Visual images, unlike the written word, constantly portray mammy and Aunt Jemima from a negative perspective. These characters are usually pictured as obese, in unattractive or tattered clothing, and bossy and stern while at the same time somewhat comical. On the other hand, literature generally depicts the mammy and Aunt Jemima as loving, caring, productive, and vital in society. Many poems and literary works note with deep sentiment the accomplishments and the need for mammy in American society. So deeply entrenched was the mammy image in American society that, in the early 1920s, a group of Southern white women proposed a project to erect a bronze monument in honor of the "Black Mammy." This caused an outrage in the Black community which did not want to glorify a tradition that belittled the Black woman and was also a symbol of white southern aristocracy. The Black community wanted a monument in honor of the Black mother who worked and sacrificed to raise her children ("The Black Mammy Monument," *New York Age*, January 6, 1923: 4).

Since the media have been the main conveyors and perpetuators of the negative stereotypes of Black women, this chapter examines the images of Black women in literature, in films, and on television. The reader should also consult sections of the other chapters in this book that discuss Black women, particularly the chapters on art, literature, film, and the television media.

THE BLACK WOMAN IN LITERATURE

Images of Black women in literature have been varied. Mary Helen Washington's article on "Black Women Image-Makers" lists the tragic mulatto, the hot-blooded exotic whore, and the strong Black mammy as sexist and racist stereotypes of Black women. She calls Beulah, Sapphire, and Pinky white fantasies and encourages the reading of powerful and realistic images by writers such as Gwendolyn Brooks, Paule Marshall, Alice Walker, Maya Angelou, Ann Petry, Toni Morrison, and Toni Cade Bambara (Washington 10–18).

One of the most comprehensive essays on the images of Black women in literature is Elizabeth Schultz's "Free in Fact and at Last: The Image of the Black Woman in Black American Literature" in *What Manner of Woman* (1977). Schultz contrasts white stereotypes of females with Black stereotypes, and she finds the white woman weak and the Black woman strong. She examines what Mary Helen Washington has called "the intimidation of color" in dark protagonists like Pecola in Toni Morrison's *The Bluest Eye* and Emma Lou in Wallace Thurman's *The Blacker the Berry*, the fair-skinned females like Vyry in Margaret Walker's *Jubilee*, and the sexually promiscuous female such as Sula in Morrison's book by that title. Schultz examines the rites-of-passage novels such as

10. Mammy stage prop, wood, as example of the female image. Courtesy of Joyce Cross. Photo by Vando Rogers.

Walker's *The Third Life of Grange Copeland* and Louise Meriwether's *Daddy Was a Number Runner* and speculates that the most liberated Black woman is the older character such as Aunt Hager in Langston Hughes' *Not Without Laughter* and Miss Jane in Ernest Gaines' *The Autobiography of Miss Jane Pittman*.

Barbara Christian describes in detail in *Black Women Novelists: The Development of a Tradition, 1892–1976* (1980) the various images of Black women in literature from the late nineteenth century to the present time. Christian feels that each image of the Black woman was created to keep a particular image about white women in tact. The breaking of any of these images was seen as a threat to the entire system (Christian 11).

The mammy was the mainstay among the characters of white antebellum and Reconstruction novels. The mammy's physical characteristics are always the same: black, fat with enormous breasts, and a head covered with a kerchief to hide her kinky hair. She is strong to survive her white master, she is kind and loyal, she is sexless, and she is religious and superstitious (Christian, *Black Women Novelists* 11–12).

Christian further states in *Black Feminist Criticism: Perspectives on Black Women Writers* (1985) that the images of the white and Black women were interdependent. The white woman was frail, incapable of doing hard work, and in need of protection; the Black woman was strong, fat, and always working or nurturing white children. In the literature of the South, men had no need to fight duels or protect the honor of women who were busy cooking, cleaning, and caring for children, for only frail women needed this protection (Christian, *Black Feminist Criticism* 2).

The image of the Black mammy is prevalent in all types of literature. Andrea Rushing notes in "Images of Black Women in Afro-American Poetry" (1975) that Black mothers are the most prevalent images in Black poetry. Black attitudes toward mothers are extremely complex, but in almost all mother poems the mother is the perfect symbol of Black struggle, suffering, and endurance. Rushing cites poems such as Helen Johnson's "The Mother's Rock," Frances Ellen Watkins Harper's "Eliza Harris," John Wesley Holloway's "Black Mammies," and Jessie Redmond Fauset's "Oriflamme" as examples of Black mother poems. Some poets such as Sterling Brown ("When the Saints Go Ma'chin In") and Owen Dodson ("Black Mother Praying") use religion to express the deep emotion of the Black mother.

Daryl C. Dance in "Black Eve or Madonna? A Study of the Antithetical Views of the Mother in Black American Literature" (1975) examines the treatment of the Black mother by American writers. Some writers portray the mother as the "Black Eve" who has succumbed to the tempting allurements and wiles of the devil. Other writers pay tribute to the Black mother as a madonna who brings salvation to her children. Dance feels that many writers fail to understand that the Black mother has suffered rape, humiliation, and despair to help her children survive.

Gloria Wade-Gayles in "She Who Is Black and Mother: In Sociology and Fiction, 1940–1970" (1980) examines the mother image in several twentieth-century novels. She looks at Mrs. Thomas in Richard Wright's *Native Son*, Elizabeth Grimes in James Baldwin's *Go Tell It on the Mountain*, Sissie in John Williams' *Sissie*, and Momma Hawkins in Kristin Hunter's *Soul Brothers and Sister Lou*.

Mary Anderson in "Black Matriarchy: Portrayal of Women in Three Plays" (1976) has examined the mamma image in plays by three Black playwrights:

James Baldwin's *The Amen Corner*, Lorraine Hansberry's *A Raisin in the Sun*, and Alice Childress' *Wine in the Wilderness*. In the Baldwin and Hansberry plays, the mammas realize that the protection they are giving their men is emasculating them, and the Childress play shows how a Black man copes with the matriarchal stereotype.

Closely related to the mammy image is that of the Black domestic. Jeanne Noble's *Beautiful, Also, Are the Souls of My Black Sisters: A History of the Black Woman in America* (1978) discusses, among other topics, different types of domestics under the heading "Dishwasher Image." There is the mammy or "take charge" image of such women as the mammy in Margaret Mitchell's *Gone with the Wind*, the "Rock of Gibralter" domestic such as Dilsey in William Faulkner's *The Sound and the Fury*, the domestic who works to ensure her children's future such as Mamba in Dorothy Heyward's *Mamba's Daughters*, the domestic at wits end such as Maya Angelou in *I Know Why the Caged Bird Sings*, the domestic on the take such as Vi and Ellie in Douglas Turner Ward's *Happy Ending*, and the domestic who has her dream deferred such as Ruth in *A Raisin in the Sun* (Noble 75–79).

Trudier Harris noted in *From Mammies to Militants: Domestics in Black American Literature* (1982) that the maid, like the matriarch, the hot mama, and the tragic mulatto, is a stereotype of the Black woman. From Charles Waddell Chesnutt's *The Marrow of Tradition* to Toni Morrison's *The Bluest Eye*, Black writers, some of whom worked as maids themselves, have developed the stereotype to their advantage or to trick their oppressors (Harris, book jacket).

The mulatto image has existed since the beginning of the American novel. Unlike the abolitionists' literature of the antebellum period, the southern writers of literature wrote more about the mammy than the mulatto since they wanted to diminish the existence of miscegenation. When they did write about this image, they portrayed it as tragic. The mulatto is often shown as caught between two worlds as the result of the illicit relationship from which she was born. Unlike the white southern lady whose charm, beauty, and refinement bring her love and admiration, the ultimate result of miscegenation is tragedy (Christian, *Black Women Novelists* 15–16).

Then, too, the literature of the period portrays the heroine as beautiful and frail, with chastity and refinement. The Black woman could not fulfill these requirements since Black was not beautiful and refinement was a term applied to the upper class. Thus, the mulatto figure of the nineteenth and early twentieth centuries could be the only type of Black woman beautiful enough to be cast as the heroine and close enough to wealth (vis-à-vis her white father) to be well-bred (Christian, *Black Women Novelists* 24).

Several historical studies have been done on mulattoes; examples are Edward Reuter's *The Mulatto in the United States* (1918; 1969) and John G. Mencke's *Mulattoes and Race Mixture: American Attitudes and Images, 1865–1918* (1979).

One of the best resources on the mulatto image in literature is Penelope Bullock's 1944 master's thesis, "The Treatment of the Mulatto in American

Fiction from 1826–1902.'' Vashti Lewis' 1981 doctoral dissertation, ''The Mulatto Female as Major Character in Novels by Black Women Writers, 1892–1934'' covers the mulatto up through the depression years.

When one discusses the tragic mulatto, the subject of ''passing'' always emerges. Works such as Nella Larsen's two novels, *Quicksand* (1928) and *Passing* (1929) come to mind. Most of these works on passing have been critiqued in publications such as Robert Bone's *The Negro Novel in America* (1958), Arthur Davis' *From the Dark Tower* (1974), and Priscilla Ramsey's ''A Study of Black Identity in 'Passing' Novels of the Nineteenth and Early Twentieth Centuries'' (1976).

The mulatto has also been depicted in poetry. The first lines of Pauli Murray's ''The Mulatto's Dilemma'' (1938) adequately state the plight of the mulatto: ''I curse the summer sun that burned me thus to fateful recognition'' (Murray 180).

Barbara Christian notes that these images of the Black woman cannot be seen in a vacuum, for she is a necessary correlate to the lady. This holds true for the hot mama image. If the southern lady was to be chaste except for producing children, then it was also necessary to have another woman to be the object of the man's sexual desires. The image of the Black woman as impure and loose developed as a result of this need for a counter image for whites and also because of the general idea about the sexuality of Blacks. White society commonly felt that Black women craved sex daily and with anyone available (Christian, *Black Women Novelists* 12–13).

Like the other images, the loose Black woman or the hot mama has certain physical characteristics. She has brown skin rather than black, she is voluptuous rather than fat, she has an evil disposition that makes her more desirable sexually. She is good looking and passionate but not beautiful, for she ensnares men with her body rather than with her beauty. The image of the loose Black woman is always present in the diaries of southern white women who hate their husband's sexual freedom. It is also in the writings of the plantation owners as a means of explaining their wayward activities and of legitimizing the existence of those mixed-blood children of slave women. (Christian, *Black Women Novelists* 15).

Saundra Townes notes in ''The Black Woman as Whore: Genesis of the Myth'' (1974) that loose women are dominant characters in several novels of the twentieth century. She cites Bessie in *Native Son*, Sarah in Houston Baker's *Long Black Song*, Ruth in James Baldwin's *Come Out of the Wilderness*, and Ida Scott in Baldwin's *Another Country*.

The image of the conjure woman is barely recognizable in the literature. Barbara Christian felt that this image was elusive. On one hand, the conjure woman image related to the traditional African religions that the plantation owners felt were dark and evil. This was used to their advantage since beliefs about African religious ceremonies were the bases for their justification of slavery. On the other hand, the image of the conjure woman was treated with respect and awe. Many felt that those evil, incomprehensible forces did exist and had some power to affect the fortunes of men. Whatever their real power, Black women such as Marie LaVeau in New Orleans and Mary Ellen Pleasant in San Francisco used their knowledge of voodoo and the white man's fear of the supernatural to become real-life conjure women, wielding power over matters of state and politics (Christian, *Black Women Novelists* 16–17).

The many activities of Mary Ellen Pleasant can be found in the two biographies of her life written by Helen O'Connell Holdredge—*Mammy Pleasant* (1953) and *Mammy Pleasant's Partner* (1954).

An emerging and often overlooked image is that of the Black lesbian, or the homophobic image. Barbara Christian notes that a radical change in the fiction of the 1980s is the "overt exploration of lesbian relationships among Black women and how these relationships are viewed by the black communities." She relates how works by Audre Lorde, Gloria Naylor, Alice Walker, and Ntozake Shange have dominant lesbian characters (Christian, "No More Buried Lives: The Themes of Lesbianism in Audre Lorde's *Zami*, Gloria Naylor's *The Women of Brewster Place*, Ntozake Shange's *Sassafras, Cypress and Indigo*, and Alice Walker's *The Color Purple*").

In an earlier article, "The Black Lesbian in American Literature: An Overview," (1979) Ann A. Shockley discusses the stereotypical caricature of Black lesbians in the Black community. She notes that stereotypical caricatures abound in the Black community (the lesbian walks and looks mannish, likes sports, wears mannish clothes, and so on). Shockley felt that within the works depicting Black lesbians are undercurrents of hostility, trepidation, subtlety, shadiness, and, in some cases, ignorance, all bringing forth homophobic stereotypes.

Anthologies such as Barbara Smith's *Home Girls: A Black Feminist Anthology* (1983) have, to quote from the book, brought about a "breakthrough because of its original and positive portrayal of black lesbian relationships" (Smith liii). She notes that it is homophobia, not homosexuality, that poses a threat to the solidarity of the race.

J.R. Roberts notes in her bibliography, *Black Lesbians: An Annotated Bibliography* (1981), that "a body of literature exists, although it is often hidden or unidentified for reasons directly related to the social, political and economic realities of being Black, female, and lesbian" (Roberts xi).

The foregoing analysis of the image of Black women in the literature leads us to the need for Black feminist criticism and to an increased effort to introduce and integrate more courses on Black women into curricular programs in academic institutions.

The immediate concern of Black feminist critics must be to develop a fuller understanding of Black women writers who have yet to receive critical attention equal to that of Black men writers. On this note, Deborah McDowell's "New Directions for Black Feminist Criticism" (1980) asserts, "while insisting on validity, usefulness and necessity of contextual approaches to Black women's literature the Black feminist critic must not ignore the importance of rigorous textual analysis.'' This analysis involves isolating as many thematic, stylistic, and linguistic commonalities among Black women writers as possible (McDowell 156–57).

Beverly Guy-Sheftall has found a heightened interest in the writings of Black women and describes the two phases of this condition. She notes that the first phase is characterized by several efforts to document that such a tradition exists. One of the first works to document this existence was Frances Collier Durden's master's thesis "Negro Women in Poetry from Phyllis Wheatley to Margaret Walker" (1947).

The second phase was instituted by the publication of Mary Helen Washington's article "Black Image Makers" (*Black World* 1974). Washington argued that Black women writers are a distinct group not only because of their long history but also because unique themes recur in their writings. Alice Walker's essay "In Search of Our Mothers' Gardens: The Creativity of Black Women in the South" (*Ms*, May 1974) is one of the most poignant and eloquent accounts of Black women writers. Walker also designed the first course on Black women writers, which was taught at the University of Massachusetts in 1972 and at Wellesley College in 1977. Another publication of this second phase was *Sturdy Black Bridges: Visions of Black Women in Literature*, edited by Roseann P. Bell, Bettye J. Parker, and Beverly Guy-Sheftall (1979). This publication was credited as being the first book-length critical work devoted to minority women's literature.

Guy-Sheftall feels that this second phase is also distinguished by the emergence of Black feminist literary criticism. Notably the works of Barbara Smith and Deborah McDowell, as well as Barbara Christian's *Black Women Novelists: The Development of a Tradition, 1892–1976*, are the pioneering volumes in this subject area. The publication of Gloria Wade-Gayles' *No Crystal Stair: Visions of Race and Sex in Black Women's Fiction* (1984) adds to the publications of Black feminist critics who analyze the works of Black female writers from a feminist or political perspective. Wade-Gayles subjects the novels she examines to the "rigorous textual analysis" that Deborah McDowell argues is essential for the Black feminist critic (Guy-Sheftall, "Introduction," *No Crystal Stair* xv–xvi).

During the 1970s many courses were offered on Black women in universities throughout the country, and they introduced many students to the neglected writings by and about Black women. Among these courses were "Major Afro-American Writers: Alice Walker Seminar," taught by Barbara Christian at the University of California, Berkeley; "Black Women Writers," taught by Gloria Hull at the University of Delaware; and "The Images of Black Women in the Works of Black Women Writers," taught by Patricia Bell Scott and Gloria Johnson at the University of Tennessee ("Doing the Work: Selected Course Syllabi—Literature," *Some of Us Are Brave* 360–78).

Likewise, at least four journals have published special issues focusing on Black women writers. *Conditions: Five* (The Black Women Issue) (1979) includes poetry, prose, poems, fiction/autobiographical fiction, journals, essays, song lyrics, and reviews by and about Black women writers. *Black American Literature Forum* 4 (Winter 1980) published articles on three Black women writers: Ann Petry, Nella Larsen, and Jessie Redmond Fauset and also included Deborah McDowell's pioneering article on "New Directions for Black Feminist Criticism." *Sunbury 10: A Literary Magazine, Black Women Writers* issue (1981) includes poems, plays, biographical sketches, a self-interview, and book reviews. *Sage: A Scholarly Journal on Black Women* published "Women as Writers," vol. 2 (Spring 1985), which features articles on writers such as Toni Morrison and Alice Walker, on African writers Buchi Emecheta and Bessie Head, on bonding in West Indian novels, an analysis of plays by selected Black women, interviews with writers such as Dorothy West and Lucille Clifton, a photographic essay, excerpts from diaries and journals by Black women, reviews, and a listing of master's theses and doctoral dissertations on Black women writers.

Stephen Henderson comments in his introduction to Mari Evans' critical evaluation of Black women that

[t]he process of correcting the portrayal of Black women has involved both the creative writer and the scholar-critic, and oftentimes one person serves both functions. . . . These efforts have led to a reexamination of the history and the texts of Black literature. . . . Obviously, Black women did not begin their involvement with literature in the 1970s, and one of the refreshing aspects of the reevaluation mentioned above is not only the reappraisal of Phillis Wheatley or the rediscovery of Zora Neale Hurston, but also a deepening realization of the role that Black women, both known and unknown, have historically played in building the institution of Black literature (Henderson, "Introduction," *Black Women Writers (1950–1980): A Critical Evaluation).*

FILMS

The Black woman has always been addressed by popular culture but rarely in her own terms. Her physical characteristics, which markedly clashed with American society's standards of beauty, not only set her apart, but also drew attention to her. These descriptions have chained her to the earth by likening her to its qualities—dusky dame, charcoal, blossom—or referred to her in animalistic terms—fox, chick, filly. Her perceived sexual nature is likened to rich foods—brown sugar, hot chocolate, piece of dark meat. Her physical attributes and color have been described as redbone, pinky, high yaller, brickhouse, and hammer. She is described by the work she performs—laundry queen, nurse, mammy. These images and terminology are discussed in Patricia Bell Scott's article "The English Language and Black Womanhood: Low Blow to Self-Esteem" (1974). Additional information on images of Black women in films and television is given in chapter 3.

The sexual dimension of American racism is reflected in the motion picture portrayal of the Black woman, and her film image has been defined by others rather than by herself. Edward Mapp's article "Black Women in Films" presents this view and asserts further that, at that time, few black female writers or producers were employed in the film industry. The result is a tragic history of stereotyping and a steady procession of mammies, maids, miscegenists, matriarchs, madams, and prostitutes (Mapp 42).

Barbara Jones, an actress and an independent film producer, warns that the system is controlled by people who do not have the interests of Black women at heart. She notes that "decisions are made out of a purely monetary reality. Too many people live, breathe and die to be accepted in the industry." Jones objects to Black women becoming the willing accompanists in the industry's choice to project negative but lucrative images of Black women. She holds to blame Black actresses who perpetuate negative images of themselves by appearing in certain roles, as well as the writers, directors, and producers of these projects (Martin 76–77).

For the Black woman, there have been four basic film stereotypes: the tragic mulatto, the mammy, the innocent or ingenue, and the hot mama. The Black response to the negative or stereotypical images produced by the industry was to create its own counter images. Early independent film companies such as Reol Pictures and Lincoln Motion Pictures focused on the Black woman as if she were the same as the white woman—frail, in need of protection, and helpless. She also often looked white as seen in the female characters in early productions of *A Man's Duty* (1923) and *By Right of Birth* (1921). These actresses were fair skinned with straight hair, and their station in life did not permit them to work.

By contrast, Oscar Micheaux, who produced *The Homesteader* in 1918, brought women of a different social class on the screen. In *The Brute* (1921) he exposed the rackets and the inner conflicts of caste and color. His female leads were easy prey for gangsters. Pearl Bowser's "Sexual Imagery and the Black Woman in American Cinema" continues this discussion.

In describing the stereotypes, the tragic mulatto is seen as the poor woman who is lucky enough to be born fair skinned but Black all the same. She sometimes falls in love with a white man, but they are unable to marry because of her Black blood. Usually in the background is a loving mother who, although rejected, loves her daughter just the same. *Imitation of Life* (1934, 1958) is a prime example.

Mammies are usually large, sturdy Black women to whom everyone turns for strength, love, and advice. Again, *Imitation of Life* is a classic example of the first two stereotypes, and *Gone with the Wind* (1939) shows a major example of the mammy type. In fact, Hattie McDaniel did such a good job that she won an Oscar for best supporting actress in *Gone with the Wind*.

The innocent image is one that closely resembles the white female. She is good, well-mannered, and attractive. A prime example is the role Diahann Carroll played in *Paris Blues* (1961) in which she is on equal terms with the white female lead.

The hot mama image is probably the most demeaning. Dorothy Dandridge portrayed that image in her 1959 role in *Porgy and Bess*. She leaves her husband for another man. The films of the 1960s and 1970s did little to improve the hot mama image of the Black woman. Films such as *Putney Swope* (1969) and *Cotton Comes to Harlem* (1970) are excellent examples. In *Putney Swope*, Blacks take over an advertising agency, while Black women bear their breasts and bounce around in slow-motion ectasy. In *Cotton Comes to Harlem*, a Black woman plays the role of the girlfriend of a jive-time preacher. Although Ossie Davis directed this film, it is still full of stereotypes. The audiences nevertheless loved it, and it was highly successful (Gant 61, 72).

The advent of Black films in no way diminished the incidence of the Black woman as a sex object. The *Liberation of L. B. Jones* (1970) was a blatantly racist film which demeaned the Black male, in which the female used her own home for an illicit affair with a white policeman.

Black prostitutes were displayed blatantly in the 1960s and 1970s in films such as *The New Centurions* (1972), *Across 110th Street* (1972), *Sweet Sweetback's Baadass Song* (1971), and *The Hit Man* (1972). One film, *Heavy Traffic* (1973), even used animation to portray prostitution.

The 1970s also brought a new image—the docile damsel. She is a step above the sex object, but both are subservient. One such film was *Buck and the Preacher* (1972) in which the female lead risks personal danger to be with her man. Doglike loyalty is the unmistakable trait of the docile damsel. In the film *Melinda* (1972), the damsel is loyal to her lover even though he puts her down for someone else (Mapp 45).

Next came the super female image. Films such as *Coffy* (1973), *Cleopatra Jones* (1973), and *Foxy Brown* (1974) use a well-built, sexy female who goes around fighting criminals (drug pushers, pimps, and others) with brute strength ("Pam Grier: Why Are Black Women Fading From Films?" 58).

Donald Bogle's 1973 study *Toms, Coons, Mulattoes, Mammies and Bucks: An Interpretation of Blacks in American Films* further elaborates on most of these images of Black women in films. He looks at the early period of the tragic mulatto and mammy images. Next Bogle discusses the 1930s servant image and goes on to the 1940s and 1950s, the period of the glamourous entertainers such as Lena Horne, Dorothy Dandridge, and Hazel Scott. The study concludes with an examination of the early 1970s and shows how the Black exploitation movies hurt the female image.

By the mid–1970s Black actresses were beginning to examine their treatment and perception in the film industry. Actress Laura Greene noted in "Bring It Down Front: A Bad Image in Film" that "while film companies were cashing in on the new found black market, they were at the same time, reinforcing the Black stereotypical image of Blacks, especially Black women" (Greene 70).

In 1973, Boston University conducted a seminar and panel discussion on "Black Images in Film: Stereotyping, and Self-Perception as Viewed by Black Actresses." Seminar papers were published in *Proceedings of a Symposium on Black Images in Films, Stereotyping, and Self-Perception as Viewed by Black Actresses* (1974). The Black actresses who participated and told of their experiences in the film industry were Ruby Dee, Susan Batson, Beah Richards, Cynthia Belgrave, and Cicely Tyson. Dee told of the disrespectful treatment she received from film crews, and Tyson told of her hurt at being excluded from a Black film festival because of her color (Proceedings of a Symposium 4).

In an interview conducted by *Essence* magazine, Cicely Tyson explained how she received the role of Rebecca in *Sounder* (1972).

I felt Rebecca in every sinew of my body. I knew her. She was every Black woman throughout history: every Black woman that society forces into the role of protector when it either takes away, or threatens to take, her husband. She was the glue that held the family together; the glue and the guts. Hers was the love that made him, the head of the house, stand just a little bit taller. And this was what I had to be (Ebert 74).

Alyce Gullattee of Howard University feels that films have portrayed Black women as objects of pleasure who are oversexed. Hardly ever are they shown fulfilling other needs or as persons of warmth and strength. She feels that "the Black family has been omitted from films because of its potential threat to white society's security" (Kisner 59–60).

The recent film *She's Gotta Have It* (1986) is, in my opinion, just another version of the hot mama image. Spike Lee, an independent film producer, has given us yet another demeaning view of the Black female. The lead, Tracy Camilla Jones, plays Nola who is involved in sexual relationships with three different men. The steamy sex scenes earned it an "R" rating. In explaining why she made the film, Jones said,

I got the idea from hearing a lot of my male friends boast and brag about how many female friends they have. So I wanted to present a picture of an independent Black woman who is leading her life as a man as far as relationships go. Black people have literally been—and I include myself too—starving for a movie of this sort that presents a realistic portrayal of Black male-female relationships. The reason Nola has three men is because she hasn't been able to find one man at this particular point that possesses everything she needs and desires (Moore 54–56).

Beah Richards and Carlton Moss sum it up best in the proceedings of the Boston University symposium. According to Richards,

You don't dig those naked movies and all that crap, don't go to them. Don't. All of them should be picketed. That's where the attack ought to be. If they continue to make movies like that, don't just say that Black people don't do it. If the whites continue to do it, don't support them. That's where I think the attack should be. I think it will be like Rosa Parks. Rosa Parks was not a militant. Rosa Parks didn't see herself as a great leader of anything. But one day she sat down and all of Alabama sat down and all of Alabama got up and walked. And I think it's going to be as simple as that. One day some actor is going to say no, and he's going to say it so loud, and in such a definite way, that all the actors are going to say no (*Proceedings of a Symposium 64*).

Carlton Moss concluded that

The healthiest thing about all this trash that is coming out is that it is awakening people and minority people to the fact that these instruments exist. And that they are attainable. And once this grabs hold, you won't have to worry about who goes in the box office and who doesn't. And you won't have to worry about the consciousness of the Black community, which is what comes out of a long continuous struggle. You will not have to worry about that consciousness moving in, moving over into the realm of art and entertainment. And the same thing that happened in those communities that gave birth to the black studies program will happen. It'll change the movies (*Proceedings of a Symposium* 65–66).

BLACK WOMEN AND TELEVISION

Marilyn Fife writes in her essay on the image of Blacks in television during the 1950s and 1960s that television failed the minority viewer, especially the Black viewer. And since television was a new form of mass media, it simply reinforced the ideas and images already set forth by films, radio, and most publications. The Black person on television was usually cast in character roles. Fife states that

TV continued to reinforce white racist ideas, while further destroying a meaningful self image. The only "real people" the black viewer saw in dramas and comedies were synthetic whites, living out white roles, in white lives, totally removed from him, and fairly inaccessible (Fife 8).

"Amos 'n' Andy" was one of the most famous radio and later television shows. Today, it is commonly felt that the show negatively depicted the images of both Black males and Black females. The leading female characters, Sapphire and Mama, were portrayed as big, bossy, and emasculating women who ruled the roost with an iron fist. The male characters were always finding ways to outsmart their female counterparts (Rose 37).

Between 1950 and 1952, NBC booked 218 Black acts and individuals as a beginning effort to integrate television. The network began to eliminate racial stereotypes from old movies ("NBC's 'Talent Has No Color' Projects Negro Contributions to a New High in '52" 1, 34). The June 1950 issue of *Ebony* notes that

Of the countless acts tested on television, none proved more popular than the guest star appearance of celebrated Negro artists. So well have colored guest stars been received by TV fans that impresarios of the new medium's top shows, including Ed Sullivan, find it wise to use at least one colored star regularly in their telecast format ("Television: Negro Performers" 22).

In the early 1950s, television programs began to feature Black actors in character roles on weekly series. "Beulah" was one of the first shows to do this.

The show ran from 1950 to 1953. Beulah was a domestic who worked for a white family and who also had other domestic friends working in the same community. Several actresses played the role, including Ethel Waters, Louise Beavers, and Hattie McDaniel. Butterfly McQueen played Oriole, one of the other neighborhood domestics (Fife 9).

Robert Shayon's article "Living Color on TV" notes that the Committee on Integration of the New York Society for Ethnic Culture in 1962 conducted a two-week prime-time survey of how Blacks appeared on television. Of the 398 half-hour units of television viewing, there were no Blacks in 309 units. In the 89 units with Blacks, they were featured as singers, musicians, or dancers who appeared only occasionally on the programs, not as regulars. In a 1975 master's research project, Gloria Ferguson studied "From 'Amos 'n' Andy' to 'Sanford and Son': An Historical Survey and Critical Analysis of the Characteristics and Images of Blacks on American Network Television and Drama." She describes the changes in the characterizations and images of Blacks in American television comedy and drama series between 1944 and 1974. Ferguson found that there were no significant changes in the kinds of images portrayed. Blacks were either portrayed as extraordinarily white ("Julia" and "I Spy") or extraordinarily bad (hustlers, drug pushers, or hookers).

Diahann! An Autobiography (1986) relates the 1968 NBC introduction of the "Julia" show, events leading up to the series, and some of the controversy surrounding it. Her statement may well typify the dilemma of the Black actress who accepts a potentially controversial role on television or in film productions. On this matter, Diahann Carroll notes:

What captured my attention was Julia herself. From the first scene I understood her completely. Julia's conversations with her son reflected many of the same middle-class attitudes toward parenting I experienced in my own childhood. I could relate to Julia's desire to make a place for herself in the world. She wanted a good job. She wanted an apartment. She wanted to give her child a decent education (Carroll 136).

Many critics thought that "Julia" was a cop-out. Blacks did not live like Julia, and they questioned the lack of a father figure for the son in the series. Robert Lewis Shayon in 1968 published several articles about the show for *Saturday Review* (April 20 and May 25). He felt that the plush suburban setting for the series was a far cry from the bitter realities of Black life.

Responding to the criticism, Carroll noted that

The fact that I had no decision-making powers at all didn't seem to matter. I was still held responsible. I had endless meetings with psychologists, journalists and heads of organizations who were so concerned about the show's impact they felt compelled to discuss it with me personally.

Some of the questions asked were: Don't you realize you're letting the white community get away with murder by not insisting it address itself to the Black male? How do you reconcile Julia's lavish lifestyle with her nurse's salary? Is there any truth to the rumor that Julia's going to have a white boy friend? Don't you feel guilty about the show?

There was no question that Julia had the responsibility to set a positive example in the way it presented a black family. And it didn't take long to realize that it was largely up to me to try to make that happen. I began scrutinizing the scripts for blatant examples of racism or just plain ignorance (Carroll 146–47).

In 1975 Jean Carey Bond conducted a study of the television images of Black women, "The Media Image of Black Women." She noted that while the media has responded to Black demands for better representation on television, this increased visibility had led to the perpetuation of age-old stereotypes of Blacks (Bond 34–37).

One example of stereotypical portrayal is "The Autobiography of Miss Jane Pittman." Although the film seems to celebrate the strength and soulfulness of Black women, at the same time, it depicts the impenetrability of white male power by Black males. The film makes clever use of a "positive image" of Black women, yet it puts in their place Black people as a whole (Ramsey 31–36).

Another example of stereotypical imagery is "Get Christie Love." Jean Carey Bond's article on "The Media Image of Black Women" asserts that the sexism ingrained in the role of this policewoman was very blatant. Although Christie one-ups her coworkers and dazzles everyone with her sharp wit and super competence, the camera continually played on her glossy lips and swinging hips, and the script had constant sexual overtones to her professional relationships with her all-white male coworkers at the precinct. "Get Christie Love" lasted but one season. In the words of Richard Pinkham of the Ted Bates Advertising Agency, "the black woman heroine may be O.K. for urban movie audiences but it won't play in Heartland, U.S.A." (Dreyfuss K–5).

Then there were "Good Times" and "That's My Mama." These comical shows are so full of fun that one hardly notices the stereotypes: Each of the female leads portrays the myth of the Black matriarch.

"Good Times" portrayed a ghetto family who had three wise-cracking children, a mostly out-of-work father, and the strong mother who held it all together. Criticism of the show included the antics of the eldest son, J. J. The next protest came when the television network decided to drop the male parent role on the show making it the stereotypical female-headed family. Because of a conflict with certain roles in the series, the female lead, Esther Rolle, left the show. She was also upset that there were no Black writers for the series. (For a discussion of the series, see Louie Robinson, Les Brown, and "Esther Is Back.")

The mammy image was so strong in "That's My Mama" that protests were formed by feminist groups. Theresa Merritt, star of the show, denied that the show portrayed a negative image of Black women. The literature on this subject includes "National Black Feminist Organization Lists T.V. Complaints and

Protests 'That's My Mama' " and "Theresa Merritt Denied 'Black Mama' Image on TV."

The current "Gimme a Break" has been criticized also as negatively portraying the mammy image. Nell Carter stars as the housekeeper to a white family. Bebe Moore Campbell discusses this in the article "If You Ask Me: Fat, Funny, Fictitious."

Over the years since television became one of the most popular forms of entertainment, many Black women have appeared on the screen. The positive images include Thelma Carpenter in "The Eddie Cantor Show," Nichele Nicholas in "Star Trek," Denise Nicholson in "Room 222," Isabel Sanford and Roxie Roker in "The Jeffersons," Debbie Allen in "Fame," Gladys Knight in "Charlie & Co.," Melba Moore in "Melba," Marla Gibbs and Alaina Reed in "227," and Phylicia Rashad in "The Cosby Show." The negative images include Lillian Randolph in "The Great Gildersleeve," Ernestine Ward in "Amos 'n' Andy," Hattie McDaniel in "Beulah," LaWanda Page in "Sanford & Son," Shirley Hemphill in "What's Happening," and Jackee Harry in "227." Some of these roles may or may not be considered negative by viewing audiences; for example, Jackee Harry in "227." The other stereotypical images in the latter group cannot be debated.

Two miniseries that have been aired included "Backstairs at the White House," which tells of the lives of Lillian Parks and her daughter who worked there, and "A Woman Called Moses," which depicts the life of underground railroad conductor Harriet Tubman.

Richard B. Koiner concludes in his article on Black images on television that

[w]hile TV undoubtedly reflects prejudiced attitudes within our society, it is also capable of either helping maintain these attitudes or of helping eliminate them. Philosophically, broadcasters have chosen the latter, socially responsible course. As a result, the appearance of Blacks in non-stereotyped roles has made it easier for whites to accept Blacks in real life positions and professions once unthinkable (Koiner 20).

SUMMARY

In citing the need for Black women's studies, Gloria Hull and Barbara Smith note the four important issues for a consideration of the politics involved: "(1) the general political situation of Afro-American women and the bearing this has had upon the implementation of Black women's studies; (2) the relationship of Black women's studies to Black feminist politics and the Black feminist movement; (3) the necessity for Black women's studies to be feminist, radical, and analytical; and (4) the need for teachers of Black women's studies to be aware of our problematic political positions in the academy and of the potentially antagonistic conditions under which we must work" (Hull and Smith xvii).

It is hoped that more research can and will be done on Black women to help dispel some of the negative and stereotypical images that surround them, to foster more positive images of Black women throughout the world, and to encourage more publications and publicity of this research on the Black female experience. To this end, several research centers, publishers, and organizations have developed special projects and publication efforts to help document the research. For a listing of many of these resource groups, consult "Selected Resources on Women of Color" and "New Books and Selected Periodicals" in *Sage*, vol. 1, Premier Issue (Spring 1984), pages 26–28.

SELECTED BIBLIOGRAPHY

General

This bibliography represents only a small sample of the articles and books on the suject of images of Black women throughout history. While I have mainly concentrated on images in literature, on television, and in films, such general histories and anthologies of Black women as Toni Cade Bambara's *The Black Woman: An Anthology* (1970), Angela Davis' *Women, Race and Class* (1981), Joyce Ladner's *Tomorrow's Tomorrow: The Black Woman* (1971), Robin Morgan's *Sisterhood Powerful* (1970), and Mel Warkins' *To Be a Black Woman: Portraits in Fact and Fiction* (1970) will further document how the Black woman has been portrayed in all aspects of her life.

Bambara, Toni Cade. *The Black Woman: An Anthology*. New York: New American Library, 1970.

"The Black Mammy Monument." *New York Age*, January 6, 1923: 4.

Colle, Royal D. "The Negro Image and the Mass Media." Ph.D. diss., Cornell University, 1967.

Davis, Angela. *Women, Race and Class*. New York: Random House, 1981.

Dennison, Sam. *Scandalize My Name: Black Imagery in American Popular Music*. New York: Garland Publishing, 1982. Includes the changing image of Black women.

Harley, Sharon, and Rosalyn Terborg-Penn. *The Afro-American Woman: Struggles and Images*. New York: Kennikat Press, 1978.

Jewell, Karen Sue Warren. "An Analysis of the Visual Development of a Stereotype: The Media's Portrayal of Mammy and Aunt Jemima as Symbols of Black Womanhood". Ph.D. diss., Ohio State University, 1976.

Ladner, Joyce A. *Tomorrow's Tomorrow: The Black Woman*. New York: Doubleday, 1971.

Lerner, Gerda. *Black Women in White America: A Documentary History*. New York: Vintage, 1972.

Morgan, Robin. *Sisterhood Powerful*. New York: Vantage Books, 1970.

Sims, Janet L. *The Progress of Afro American Women: A Selected Bibliography and Resource Guide*. Westport, Conn.: Greenwood Press, 1980.

Snodgrass, J. William, and Gloria T. Woody, comps. *Blacks and Media: A Selected, Annotated Bibliography 1962–1982*. Tallahassee: University Presses of Florida, Florida A&M University Press, 1985.

Wallace, Michelle. *Black Macho and the Myth of the Superwoman*. New York: Dial, 1979.

Watkins, Mel. *To Be a Black Woman: Portraits in Fact and Fiction*. New York: William Morrow, 1970.

White, Deborah Gray. *Ar'nt I a Woman? Female Slaves in the Plantation South*. New York: Norton, 1985.

Literature

Anderson, Mary Louise. "Black Matriarchy: Portrayal of Women in Three Plays." *Black American Literature Forum* 10 (Fall 1976): 93–95.

Angelou, Maya. *I Know Why the Caged Bird Sings*. New York: Random House, 1969.

Baker, Houston. *Long Black Song: Essays in Black American Literature and Culture*. Charlottesville: University Press of Virginia, 1972.

Baldwin, James. *Another Country*. New York: Dial Press, 1962.

———. *Come Out of the Wilderness*. In *Black Short Story Anthology*. Ed. Woodie King. New York: Columbia University Press, 1972, 277–99.

———. *Go Tell It on the Mountain*. New York: Knopf, 1953.

Bell, Roseann P., Betty J. Parker, and Beverly Guy-Sheftall. *Sturdy Black Bridges: Visions of Black Women in Literature*. New York: Anchor Books, 1979.

Black American Literature Forum 4 (Winter 1980).

Bone, Robert. *The Negro Novel in America*. New Haven, Conn.: Yale University Press, 1965.

Bullock, Penelope. "The Treatment of the Mulatto in American Fiction from 1826–1902." Master's thesis, Atlanta University, 1944.

Christian, Barbara. *Black Feminist Criticism: Perspectives on Black Women Writers*. New York: Pergamon Press, 1985.

———. *Black Women Novelists: The Development of a Tradition, 1892–1976*. Westport, Conn.: Greenwood Press, 1980.

———. "No More Buried Lives: The Themes of Lesbianism in Audre Lorde's *Zami*, Gloria Naylor's *The Women of Brewster Place*, Ntozake Shange's *Sassafras, Cypress and Indigo*, and Alice Walker's *The Color Purple*." In *Black Feminist Criticism: Perspectives on Black Women Writers*, New York: Pergamon Press, 187–204.

Conditions: Five. (The Black Women Issue) 2 (Autumn 1979).

Dance, Daryl C. "Black Eve or Madonna? A Study of the Antithetical Views of the Mother in Black American Literature." *Perspectives on Afro-American Women*. Eds. Willa Johnson and Thomas Green. Washington, D.C.: ECCA Publications, 1975, 103–11.

Davis, Arthur. *From the Dark Tower*. Washington, D.C.: Howard University Press, 1974.

"Doing the Work: Selected Course Syllabi—Literature." In *All the Women are White, All the Blacks are Men, but Some of Us Are Brave: Black Women's Studies*. Ed. Gloria Hull and others. New York: The Feminist Press, 1982, 360–78.

Durden, Frances Collier. "Negro Women in Poetry from Phyllis Wheatley to Margaret Walker." Master's thesis, Atlanta University, 1947.

Faulkner, William. *The Sound and the Fury*. London: Chatto & Windus, 1931.

Gaines, Ernest J. *The Autobiography of Miss Jane Pittman*. New York: Dial Press, 1971.

Guy-Sheftall, Beverly. "Introduction." In Gloria Wade-Gayles, *No Crystal Stair: Visions of Race and Sex in Black Women's Fiction*. New York: Pilgrim Press, 1984, xv–xvi.

Gwin, Minrose C. *Black and White Women of the Old South: The Peculiar Sisterhood in American Literature*. Knoxville: University of Tennessee Press, 1985.

Hansberry, Lorraine. *A Raisin in the Sun*. New York: Random House, 1959.

Harris, Trudier. *From Mammies to Militants: Domestics in Black American Literature*. Philadelphia: Temple University Press, 1982.

Henderson, Stephen H. "Introduction." In *Black Women Writers (1930–1980): A Critical Evaluation*. Ed. Mari Evans. New York: Doubleday, 1984.

Heyward, Dorothy H. *Mamba's Daughters*. New York: Farrar & Rinehart, 1939.

Holdredge, Helen O'Connell. *Mammy Pleasant*. New York: Putnam, 1953.

————. *Mammy Pleasant's Partner*. New York: Putnam, 1954.

Hughes, Langston. *Not Without Laughter*. New York: Knopf, 1930.

Hull, Gloria, and Barbara Smith. "The Politics of Black Women's Studies." In *All the Women are White, All the Blacks are Men, but Some of Us Are Brave: Black Women's Studies*. Ed. Gloria Hull and others. New York: The Feminist Press, 1982; xvii.

Hull, Gloria, Patricia Bell Scott, and Barbara Smith, eds. *All the Women Are White, All the Blacks Are Men, but Some of Us Are Brave: Black Women's Studies*. New York: The Feminist Press, 1982.

Hunter, Kristin. *Soul Brothers and Sister Lou*. New York: Scribner, 1968.

Johnson, Beulah V. "The Treatment of the Negro Woman as a Major Character in American Novels, 1900–1950." Ph.D. diss., New York University, 1955.

Larsen, Nella. *Passing*. 1929. New York: Negro Universities Press, 1969.

————. *Quicksand*. 1928. New York: Negro Universities Press, 1969.

Lewis, Vashti. "The Mulatto Female as Major Character in Novels by Black Women Writers, 1892–1934." Ph.D. diss., University of Iowa, 1981.

McDowell, Deborah. "New Directions for Black Feminist Criticism." *Black American Literature Forum* 14 (Winter 1980): 156–57.

Martin, Odette. "Curriculum and Response: A Study of Images of the Black Women in Black Fiction." Ph.D. diss., University of Chicago, 1980.

Mencke, John G. *Mulattoes and Race Mixture: American Attitudes and Images, 1865–1918*. Ann Arbor, Mich.: UMI Research Press, 1979.

Meriwether, Louise. *Daddy Was a Number Runner*. Englewood Cliffs, N.J.: Prentice-Hall, 1970.

Mitchell, Margaret. *Gone with the Wind*. New York: The Macmillan Co., 1936.

Morrison, Toni. *The Bluest Eye: A Novel*. New York: Holt, Rinehart and Winston, 1970.

————. *Sula*. New York: Knopf, 1974.

Murray, Pauli. "The Mulatto's Dilemma." *Opportunity* 16 (June 1938): 180.

"New Books and Selected Periodicals." *Sage* 1 (Spring 1984): 28.

Noble, Jeanne. *Beautiful, Also, Are the Souls of My Black Sisters: A History of the Black Woman in America*. Englewood Cliffs, N.J.: Prentice-Hall, 1978.

————. "Dishwasher Image." In *Beautiful, Also, Are the Souls of My Black Sisters*. Englewood Cliffs, N.J.: Prentice-Hall, 1978, 75–89.

Parkhurst, Jessie W. "The Role of the Black Mammy in the Plantation Household." *Journal of Negro Education* 23 (July 1938): 349–69.

Ramsey, Priscilla. "A Study of Black Identity in 'Passing' Novels of the Nineteenth and Early Twentieth Centuries." *Studies in Black Literature* 7 (Winter 1976): 1–7.

Reuter, Edward. *The Mulatto in the United States*. 1918. New York: Negro Universities Press, 1969.

Roberts, J. R. *Black Lesbians: An Annotated Bibliography*. Tallahassee, Fla.: The Naiad Press, 1981.

Rushing, Andrea B. "An Annotated Bibliography of Images of Black Women in Black Literature." CLA *Journal* 25 (December 1981): 234–62.

———. "Images of Black Women in Afro-American Poetry." *Black World* 24 (September 1975): 18–30.

Sage: A Scholarly Journal on Black Women. vol. 1–, 1984–.

Schultz, Elizabeth. "Free in Fact and at Last: The Image of the Black Woman in Black American Literature." In *What Manner of Woman*. Ed. Marlene Springer. New York: New York University, 1977, 316–42.

"Selected Educational Resources on Women of Color." *Sage* 1 (Spring 1984): 26–27.

Shockley, Ann A. "The Black Lesbian in American Literature: An Overview." *Conditions: Five* (The Black Women's Issue) 2 (Autumn 1979): 133–42.

Smith, Barbara. *Home Girls: A Black Feminist Anthology*. New York: Kitchen Table, Women of Color Press, 1983.

Sunbury 10: A Literary Magazine. (*Black Women Writers*) 1981. Box 277, Bronx, N.Y. 10468.

Thurman, Wallace. *The Blacker the Berry*. 1929. New York: Arno Press, 1969.

Townes, Saundra. "The Black Woman as Whore: Genesis of the Myth." *The Black Position* 3 (1974): 39–59.

Varga-Coley, Barbara Jean. "The Novels of Black American Women." Ph.D. diss., State University of New York at Stony Brook, 1981.

Wade-Gayles, Gloria. *No Crystal Stair: Visions of Race and Sex in Black Women's Fiction*. New York: Pilgrim Press, 1984.

———. "She Who Is Black and Mother: In Sociology and Fiction, 1940–1970." In *The Black Woman*. Ed. LaFrances Rodgers-Rose. Beverly Hills, Calif.: Sage Publications, 1980, 89–106.

Walker, Alice. "In Search of Our Mothers' Gardens: The Creativity of Black Women in the South." *Ms* 2 (May 1974): 64–70.

———. *The Third Life of Grange Copeland*. New York: Harcourt Brace Jovanovich, 1970.

Walker, Margaret. *Jubilee*. Boston: Houghton Mifflin, 1966.

Ward, Douglas Turner. *Happy Ending and Days of Absence: Two Plays*. New York: Dramatists Play Service, Inc., 1966.

Ward, Hazel Mae. "The Black Woman as Character: Images in the American Novel, 1852–1953." Ph.D. diss., University of Texas, 1977.

Washington, Mary Helen. "Black Women Image-Makers." *Black World* 13 (August 1974): 10–18.

———. "New Lives and New Letters: Black Women Writers at the End of the Seventies." *College English* 43 (January 1981): 1–11.

Williams, John A. *Sissie*. New York: Farrar, Straus and Cudahy, 1963.

Wright, Richard. *Native Son*. New York: Harper & Row, 1940.

Films

Bogle, Donald. *Toms, Coons, Mulattoes, Mammies and Bucks: An Interpretation of Blacks in American Films*. New York: Viking Press, 1973.

Bowser, Pearl. "Sexual Imagery and the Black Woman in American Cinema." In *Black Cinema Aesthetics: Issues in Independent Filmmaking*. Ed. Gladstone L. Year-

wood. Athens, Ohio: Ohio University Center for Afro-American Studies, 1982,
42–51.

"Claudine: A Movie That Blacks Can Relate To." *Jet* (July 4, 1974): 56–59.

Ebert, Alan. "Inside Cicely." *Essence* 3 (February 1972): 41, 74, 80.

Gant, Liz. "Ain't Beulah Dead Yet? Or Images of the Black Woman in Film." *Essence*
4 (May 1973): 61, 72–73, 75.

Greene, Laura. "Bring It Down Front: A Bad Image in Films." *Essence* 4 (May 1973): 70.

Horton, Luci. "Battle among the Beauties: Black Actresses Vie for Top Movie Roles."
Ebony 29 (November 1973): 144–46, 148, 150.

"Judy Pace Wants Better Roles for Black Women." *Jet* (October 4, 1973): 86.

Kisner, Ronald E. "What Films Are Doing to Image of Black Women." *Jet* (June 29,
1972): 56–61.

Mapp, Edward. "Black Women in Films." *The Black Scholar* 4 (March/April 1973):
42–46.

Martin, Sharon Stockard. "The Invisible Reflection: Images and Self-Images of Black
Women on Stage and Screen." *The Black Collegian* 9 (May/June 1979): 74–81.

Moore, Trudy S. "Spike Lee: Producer, Director, Star Discusses Making of Film 'She's
Gotta Have It.' " *Jet* 71 (November 10, 1986): 54–56.

Null, Gary. *Black Hollywood: The Negro in Motion Pictures.* Secaucus, N.J.: The Citadel
Press, 1975.

"Pam Grier: Why Are Black Women Fading from Films?" *Jet* 59 (November 6, 1980):
58–61.

"The Passing of Beulah: Will Hattie McDaniels' Death Mark End of Long Era of 'Kitchen-
Comedy' Roles for Negroes on Radio and Screen?" *Our World* 8 (February 1953):
12–15.

*Proceedings of a Symposium on Black Images in Films, Stereotyping, and Self-Perception
as Viewed by Black Actresses.* Boston, Mass.: Boston University Afro-American
Studies and American Studies Program, 1974.

Scott, Patricia Bell. "The English Language and Black Womanhood: Low Blow to Self-
Esteem." *Journal of Afro-American Issues* 2 (Summer 1974): 218–25.

Taylor, Clyde. "The Screen Scene—A Review of the Movies: Shooting the Black
Woman." *The Black Collegian* 9 (May/June 1979): 94–95.

Television

Bond, Jean Carey. "The Media Image of Black Women." *Freedomways* (First Quarter
1975): 34–37.

Brown, Les. " 'Good Times' Will Drop Male Parent; Black Media Coalition Protest
Move." *New York Times*, June 7, 1976: 25.

Campbell, Bebe Moore. "If You Ask Me: Fat, Funny, Fictitious." *Washington Post*,
July 6, 1983: B5.

Carroll, Diahann, with Ross Firestone. *Diahann! An Autobiography.* Boston: Little,
Brown & Co., 1986.

Dreyfus, Joel. "Blacks and Television, Part 1: Television Controversy: Covering the
Black Experience." *Washington Post*, September 1, 1974: K–5.

"Esther Is Back." *Soulteen* 8 (December 1978): 30–31.

Ferguson, Gloria H. "From 'Amos 'n' Andy' to 'Sanford and Son': An Historical Survey
and Critical Analysis of the Characteristics and Images of Blacks on American

Network Television and Drama.'' Master's thesis. University of Southern California, 1975.

Fife, Marilyn Diane. "Black Image in American TV: The First Two Decades.'' *The Black Scholar* 6 (November 1974): 7–15.

Hill, George H., and Sylvia Saverson Hill. *Blacks on Television: A Selected Annotated Bibliography*. Metuchen, N.J.: Scarecrow Press, 1985.

Jackson, Harold. "From 'Amos 'n' Andy' to 'I Spy': A Chronology of Blacks in Prime Time Network Television Programming, 1950–1964.'' Ph.D. diss., University of Michigan, 1982.

Joseph, Gloria I. "The Media and Blacks—Selling It Like It Isn't.'' In *Common Differences: Conflicts in Black and White Feminist Perceptives*. Eds. Gloria Joseph and Jill Lewis. New York: Anchor Books, 1981, 151–65.

Koiner, Richard B. "Black Images on TV: Good Or Bad.'' In *Ebony Images: Black Americans and Television*. Ed. George H. Hill. Carson, Calif.: Daystar Publishing Co., 1986, 17–23.

MacKenzie, Robert. "Review—Gimme A Break.'' *TV Guide* 30 (January 9, 1982): 23.

"Marla Gibbs Sounds off on Whites Who Write Insensitive Roles for Blacks.'' *Jet* (November 25, 1985): 60–61.

Matabane, Paula. "Black Women on America's Commercial Television.'' *The Western Journal of Black Studies* 6 (Spring 1982): 22–25.

"National Black Feminist Organization Lists TV Complaints and Protests 'That's My Mama.' '' *Media Report to Women* (December 1, 1974): 16.

"NBC's 'Talent Has No Color' Projects Negro Contributions to New High in '52.'' *Variety* (March 18, 1952): 1, 34.

Northcott, Herbert C., et al. "Trends in the TV Portrayal of Blacks and Women.'' *Journalism Quarterly* 52 (Winter 1975): 741–44.

Ramsey, Alvin. "Through a Glass Whitely: The Television Rape of Miss Jane Pittman.'' *Black World* 23 (August 1974): 31–36.

Robinson, Louie. "Bad Times on the 'Good Times' Set.'' *Ebony* 30 (September 1975): 33–40.

Rose, A. M. "TV Bumps into the Negro Problem: A Sociologist Looks at the 'Amos 'n' Andy' Controversy.'' *Printer's Ink* 236 (July 20, 1951): 36–37, 78.

Sellers, Valita. "'Movin' On Up: Black Women on TV.'' *Wall Street Journal*, December 12, 1985: 23.

Shayon, Robert Lewis. "Julia: Breakthrough or Letdown?'' *Saturday Review* 51 (April 20, 1968): 49.

———. "Julia Symposium: An Opportunity Lost.'' *Saturday Review* 51 (May 25, 1968): 36.

———. "Living Color on TV.'' *Saturday Review* 46 (February 9, 1963): 25.

"Television: Negro Performers Win Better Roles in TV Than Any Other Entertainment Medium.'' *Ebony* 5 (June 1950): 22–24.

"There Are Stereotypes.'' *TV Guide* (January 30, 1983): A4.

"Theresa Merritt Denied 'Black Mama' Image on TV.'' *Jet* 46 (September 19, 1974): 61.

U.S. Commission on Civil Rights. *Window Dressing on the Set: Women and Minorities in Television*. Washington, D.C.: U.S. Commission on Civil Rights, August 1977.

Sambo and Other Male Images in Popular Culture

The last defiant act of Clifton in Ralph Ellison's powerful novel, *Invisible Man* (1947), as he hawked a jangling, grinning, orange-and-black tissue doll before being killed by a white policeman:

> Shake it up! Shake it up!
> He's Sambo, the dancing doll, ladies and gentlemen.
> Shake him stretch him by the neck and set him down,
> —He'll do the rest. Yes!
>
> He'll make you laugh, he'll make you sigh, si—igh.
> He'll make you want to dance, and dance—
> Here you are, ladies and gentlemen, Sambo.
> The dancing doll.
>
> Buy one for your baby. Take him to your girl friend,
>   and she'll love you, loove you!
> He'll keep you entertained. He'll make you weep sweet—
> Tears from laughing.
> Shake him, shake him, you cannot break him,
> For he's Sambo, the dancing, Sambo, the prancing Sambo, the entrancing,
>   Sambo Boogie Woogie paper doll.
> And all for twenty-five cents, the quarter part of a dollar . . .
> Ladies and gentlemen, he'll bring you joy, step up and meet him.
> Sambo the . . . (Ellison 373).

Sambo is one of the many dominant images of the Black male that has prevailed in American culture over the centuries. An examination of the culture and the forces that shaped the stereotype demonstrates not only the ways in which images affect behavior and policies, but also the power of images to withstand assault and protest.

Separation and contact, hostility and cooperation, miscegenation and marriage, confronting and gaming, riots and counterriots: a history of continuous and seemingly repetitious opposites has characterized the nature of race behavior in American society. Like the colors black and white, the interaction between the races in the United States has been marked by polarities. Living together/living apart has reflected the social order from the earliest contact between the African and English people. What was past remains hazily present; what was then yet affects us now.

A dominant thread connecting the entwined opposites was the "image." For the European, the ideology that propelled him revolved around the concept of the "individual" with the attendant features of industriousness and materialism: the epitome of the rational self. At its opposite end was the character affixed to the African male, a being either "Savage" or "Sambo": the epitome of the primitive self. While both perceptions were rooted in a concept of biological inferiority, the two reflected opposite sides of white anxieties and aspirations. With respect to the Savage, it was held that the Black man was endowed with violent and sexual impulses. It was argued, buttressed with quasi-scholarly data from mid-nineteenth to the later decades of the twentieth century, that dark-skinned people were stunted in their intellectual capacities. This myth gave rise to specific cultural traits ascribed to Black men: to their supposed *natural* rhythm, their *flashy* dress habits, their sexual *prowess*, and their *proneness* to rioting and fighting.

The Black male as brute was not always explicit in popular culture. (See the discussion of the "brute Negro" in chapter 5.) Nonetheless, many tracts, novels, and theatrical productions in the nineteenth century—particularly in the aftermath of the Nat Turner rebellion—directed attention to the Savage image.[1] Later in the century, in jokes, stories, anecdotes, and sexual comic books, the image often made subterranean appearances. Occasionally, a film focused on the Savage, as in D. W. Griffith's pioneering movie, *Birth of a Nation* (1915), which portrayed Black men as sexual violators and political ravagers. The film industry reinforced the image in dozens of *Tarzan* movies wherein a single white man and boy brought political order and a modicum of civility and justice to anarchistic and warring jungle tribes.

Yet, white society generally publicly downplayed the Savage role. This was in part due to their fear that to accentuate the image was to court its realization. Not desiring to encourage the image, white society turned rather to its polar side—and embraced Sambo. Sambo was to be *the* stereotype that would enrapture white society—and it became a device through which both slavery and segregation would be made the more palatable.

The very title itself applied to a particular personality type in American culture. Although the name Sambo was not always directly applied—though it was the most viable designation for the Black male during the decades from the 1880s to the 1930s—it was always explicit in the mass culture. Other folk names were fashionable: Tambo, Rastus, Sam, Pompey, and the ubiquitous Boy and Uncle. In popular songs, the Black American male was called ''Old Black Joe'' and ''Uncle Ned.'' In advertising, he was adorned on various products as ''Uncle Ben's Rice,'' the ''Cream of Wheat Man,'' and ''Ben, the Pullman Porter.'' In literature, the most extensive expression of the character was to be found in Joel Chandler Harris's ''Uncle Remus'' stories published in *Uncle Remus: His Song and Sayings*. In radio and in other films, the name given to the character was to be found in the roles of ''Stepin Fetchit'' and ''Rochester.'' These names and images will be discussed later in this chapter.

The personality type which Sambo represented consisted of enmeshing features. He was regarded as childish and comical, a natural slave and servant, nonviolent and humble, and, at all times, a natural entertainer. There would be variations of these themes, but in the main they held fast against protestations to the contrary by Afro-Americans and various changes in the socioeconomic order. As a particular type, Sambo can be traced to historical and indigenous causes. To a considerable extent, the system of servitude played a dominant role. The status of the slave apparently evoked powerful expressions of disdain and exacerbated a sense of superiority among whites. As long as the slave remained at the lowest level of society, he could barely hope to improve his position; unable to improve his status, he was powerless to overturn the image of him. Traits attributed to both the Savage and Sambo, moreover, were located in other slave cultures. In this connection, David B. Davis noted that

the white slaves of antiquity and the Middle Ages were often described in terms that fit the later stereotype of the Negro. Throughout history it has been said that slaves, though occasionally as loyal and faithful as good dogs, were for the most part lazy, irresponsible, cunning, rebellious, untrustworthy, and sexually promiscuous (Davis 59–60).

Thus, there was historical precedent for anticipating the image of the American Black male. At the same time, the indigenous culture added yet another dimension to the stereotype. In the case of the American slave and worker, he was accorded certain qualities within the range of humor. It was a dimension which was wholly unprecedented and proved to be extraordinarily complex in binding the Black male into a cultural straightjacket. He was, in sum, both slave *and* entertainer.

SAMBO'S STROPHE

Over the centuries, in his extremely lengthy stay in American culture, Sambo was the perfect stereotype. He symbolized mirth and merriment, the genuine comic in a society in which entertainment came to assume major proportions. Sambo's unique gift was a presumed inherent form of humor: the possessor of the uninhibited laugh, the initiator of natural comedy, and the recipient of derogatory jokes. It was an interlacing combination of humorous qualities which no other racial or ethnic group was saddled with, a corroboration of Walter Lippmann's seminal hypothesis of stereotypes in his classic work on the subject, *Public Opinion* (1922). Lippmann trenchantly observed that "the subtlest and most pervasive of all influences are those which create and maintain the repertory of stereotypes. We are told about the world before we see it. We imagine most things before we experience them" (Lippmann 89–90).

To this observation, historian H. R. Trevor-Roper, in his study of the witch-obsession of the sixteenth and seventeenth centuries, added that the stereotype becomes in effect "its own folklore" and "in itself a centralizing force." Thus, when disparate persons extend their illusions to the same imaginary fixture, they in turn make the pattern real to others. Consequently, a stereotype is strengthened and cultivated as different people lend credence to it (Trevor-Roper 190–91).

As a cultural device with the capacity to shape collective images, the stereotype's apparent plausibility enables it to withstand attacks against its credibility. Gordon Allport, in *The Nature of Prejudice* (1954), took note of this particularity. Because different social and class groups incorporate the stereotype into their belief system, "it is possible for the stereotype to grow in defiance of *all* evidence". [2]

So fixed was the image, in fact, that dislodging it from its preeminent place in American popular culture seemed, especially to Afro-Americans over the years, virtually impossible. Sambo would undergo slight changes in time—the image would reflect time and place and would eventually crack and partially disintegrate—but always he was what he started out to be in American culture, a comic performer par excellence.

Sambo's widespread popularity was due in large measure to repetition and accumulation of performances. Sambo appeared in virtually every component of popular culture and throughout all regions in towns and cities over several centuries.

The 1790s

The place is Baltimore, but it could be New York, Philadelphia, or Boston. City commissioners grant a license to a Black man "to Exhibit on the Slack Rope, Tumbling &c. for one month . . ." (Berlin 62). Roving young Black youths frolic in the streets for pitch money while Black men perform in circuses before white audiences, who are highly amused by the physical movement, the laugh, the gait. Blacks became recognized performers exhibiting a style that was strange, intriguing, and repulsive.

The 1840s

The place is a plantation in Georgia, but it could be any plantation, large or small, throughout the South. Visitors have arrived for a two-day stay. The white family, concerned about social amenities, has already arranged for after-dinner entertainment. Into the living room troop special slaves who sing and dance and spell yarns. It is a festive occasion. The whites are regaled by physical movement and by the stories and good humor which they repeat over and again to acquaintances in their travels.

The 1880s

The place is any living room anywhere in the country. It is bedtime. One of the parents reads aloud a children's story to three children. In the story a young Black boy confuses every request his mother makes to him. When she tells him to bring a package of butter to his aunt who lives down the road, for example, he places it atop his head under his hat. The hot sun melts the butter which drips down his head and face. His mother instructs him to dip it into the stream three times. On his next trip to his aunt he is given a young puppy, which he proceeds to dip into the stream three times. And on the story goes.

The 1900s

The place is any house or restaurant in any region of the country. A family is seated at the table for dinner. The tablecloth, in red and green against a white background, consists of happy scenes from a plantation. On the wall are several Currier & Ives prints from the Darktown Series. In one of them, the Darktown Fire Brigade, men dressed in brick red shirts and blue tattered pants drawn with exaggerated mouths, eyes, and arms attempt to save several women and a cat from a burning house. The scene is farcical: hoses leak, firemen run about, and a woman is about to be skewed on a pole as she topples from a ladder. The cat is jumping for its life. Beneath the picture is the caption, "Brace her up dar and catch her on de fly."

The 1920s

The place is any drug or stationery store. A man enters, goes to the penny postcard section, scans the selection, and decides on his purchase. It is one of a grinning Black man and woman in evening clothes, he in top hat and cutaway, she in wide-brimmed hat and long gown. The woman is carrying a parasol; the man is carrying a watermelon.

The 1940s

The place is virtually every home in the country with a radio. The most visible servant in America, a man with a raspy voice and cutting edge, addresses his "Boss," one of the most popular comedians in the country, a white man with a quizzical, hesitating demeanor. Typically, he is called by a single name, "Rochester," although along the way he has acquired the family moniker, "Van

Jones.'' His real name, known but to a few, is Eddie Anderson. All other members of the show are addressed by their given names. The audience responds vigorously to the humor, the relationship, even the protests that Rochester is getting paid too little by his ''Boss.''

The 1960s

The place is a nightclub in Chicago. The performer is a slightly built Black man doing a routine before a white audience. His repartee is quick and slicing, his jokes are about white society. ''I sat in at Kress for three days,'' he tells them, ''but they didn't have what I wanted.'' He threatens the Weather Bureau, declaring that he will picket them unless they name a hurricane after ''Beulah.'' He tells them that ''flesh-colored band-aids'' were not meant for him. He is introduced by his full name, first and last, Dick Gregory.

Such was the reach and power of Sambo, his imagery and connection to all facets of culture, and his demise.

HISTORICAL THREADS

The life of Sambo began with the earliest colonization in the seventeenth century, if not much earlier. In all probability, the American Sambo was conceived on the European continent, particularly in England, and drew its first life with the initial contact with West Africans during the slave trading period. Sambo was a concept long before it assumed a specific identity.

In Sambo's earliest appearances, at the turn of the nineteenth century in the streets of small eastern cities, he was a vaudevillian, circus performer, and street player. His counterpart on the stage was a white man who performed in theatrical drama in blackface, speaking in dialect and offering comical asides. Within decades, the Black performer was forced out by whites who developed the first indigenous American theatrical form, the minstrel. (See also discussions of the minstrel in chapters 2 and 4.) From the 1840s to the 1880s, the minstrel show dominated the popular theatre. Its attraction waned as burlesque and vaudeville commanded audiences from the end of the nineteenth and into the twentieth centuries; nevertheless, it continued to be staged in small theatres in towns, high schools, and even hospitals across the country well into World War II.

It was the minstrel which disseminated the stereotype to all sections of the country. Sambo became the quintessential comic performer in American culture, regaling audiences with song, jokes, and dance. Constant declarations from white actors that they were familiar, indeed, intimate, with Afro-Americans assured audiences that they were viewing the essential Black man. Undaunted, white actors donned blackface and gaudy costumes, stretched their mouths into a perpetual grin and rounded their eyes, and then proceeded to prance in songs and patter while delivering jokes and quips in dialect. Hundreds of minstrel compendiums were sold, and complete minstrel instructions were tailored, for

11. Ceramic cookie jar, © 1987 by Carol Gifford, depicting the stereotype of the Black male. From the editor's collection. Photo by Vando Rogers.

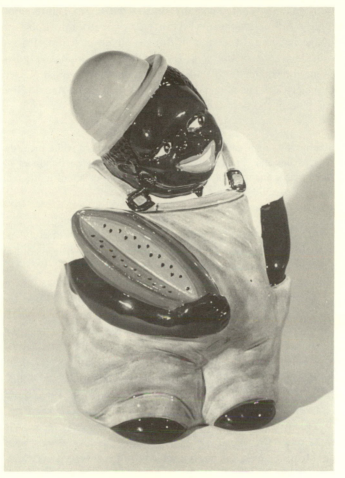

every group, trade, and profession in the country. Sambo's stage name was usually Jim Crow—he was supposedly representative of the plantation slave— and the song that bore his name became the most recognized one throughout the world. Many whites agreed with Mark Twain's assessment of the minstrel and of Jim Crow in particular: "Such natural gait!—such laugh!—and such a twitching-up of arm and shoulder! It was *the* Negro par excellence. Long live James Crow, Esquire" ("Tambo and Bones" 372).

The minstrel as a neighborhood production continued well into the 1950s and reached millions of persons who rarely had firsthand knowledge of Blacks. For the most part, immigrant groups who settled in the northern and midwestern urban areas and towns acquired knowledge of Afro-Americans through mass media and neighborhood theatre. The minstrel show was local fare throughout the twentieth century—and especially during the Great Depression when the Works Progress Administration (WPA) offered puppetry minstrels—and thereby kept the image in force. (Accounts of this are given in Joseph Boskin, *Sambo: The Rise and Demise of an American Jester*, 1986). In emphasizing Black dialect and in creating the vehicle for blackfaced buffoonery, the minstrel used language as well as imagery as signs of racial inferiority. Sociologist Arnold Rose assessed the damage done in the northern areas:

To the Northern white man, although seldom to the Southern white man, the speech of the Negro seems unusual. In fact, the "Negro dialect" is an important cause of the Northern white man's unconscious assumption that Negroes are of a different biological type from them (Rose 300–301).

By the latter decades of the nineteenth century, the commercial world replicated the minstrel performer for business and home use. Millions of Sambo items were sold as salt and pepper shakers, wooden spoons, whiskey pourers, and iron jockeys. Illustrations appeared in children's and adult books and on playing cards, dart boards, postcards, cartoons, and trading cards. Male figures were drawn on music sheet covers, almanacs, magazine covers, and posters. Sambo became, in short, a major advertising idiom. By the time the manufacturers needed an alluring attraction, particularly for household kitchen wares and parlor entertainment, they had a handy icon, the smiling Sambo. By that time, two distinct characters of minstrel show popularity had emerged—the plantation darky, nee Jim Crow, and the urban dandy, nee Zip Coon. Each represented the different classes of Black American culture; each was connected by the thread of comedy. One was portrayed in tattered clothing, overalls, and a battered farm straw hat; the other was drawn in luxuriant dress, cutaway coat, spats, and top hat. Physical features were the connection to the stereotype: kinky hair, extended red mouth, rounded white eyes, and elongated bodies appeared in books, posters, knick-knacks, cartoons, utensils, and figurines. (For additional information on these images and the artifacts and material in which they found full expression, see chapter 10.)

Subsequent discussion in this chapter is given to other stereotypical as well as positive images of the American male. While the names of positive, influential figures filtered through the culture, they were invisible in some part of that culture. The majority culture, for example, embraced the humorous image rather than highlight those whose personalities and energies contradicted the image. By emphasizing Sambo, for example, by focusing on the comical, whites undercut the Black male's intellect, dignity, and self-assertion. Harriet Martineau, the French traveller in the 1830s, insightfully noted this aspect of white behavior. Regarding the underpinning of the slave system, she observed:

12. Plaster string holder, depicting the Black male as redcap. From the editor's collection. Photo by Vando Rogers.

As long as the slave remains ignorant, docile and contented, [only then] he is taken care of, humoured, spoken of with a contemptuous, compassionate kindness. *But, from the moment he exhibits the attributes of a rational being,—from the moment his intellect seems likely to come into the most distant competition with that of whites, the most deadly hatred springs up;—not in the black, but in his oppressors.* It is a very old truth that he hates those whom he has injured.[3]

As noted earlier, Sambo's performance extended well into the twentieth century. Despite the vast demographic shifts of Blacks into major urban centers of the country, the racist underpinning which supported the development of slavery and segregation was rigidly maintained, and the image was still utilized as a means of continuing enforcement of Jim Crow practices. Yet, certain changes occurred later as a consequence of pressure from newly organized Black groups, such as the NAACP and the National Urban League, both of whom constantly protested the image of the mass media; and from the influence of powerful external events, namely the democratic ideology reflecting the country's position in both world wars.

FROM UNCLE TOM TO MR. T.: OTHER IMAGES IN POPULAR CULTURE

With the demise of the Sambo stereotype and the rise of Black nationalist movements in the 1960s, a different image of the Black male was rigidly fashioned in the media: the tough and resilient loner. In films particularly, and occasionally on television, Black detectives, private eyes, political radicals, and mavericks—their physical appearance of ruggedness and attractiveness comporting with Hollywood's ideal leading man—sallied forth across the screen combatting villains, Black and white, and winning the beautiful female, Black and white. The earliest television figure appeared in the "I Spy" series in 1962, starring Bill Cosby who played the second-fiddle partner to white actor Robert Culp. The duo struggled with spies and foreign intrigue around the globe and were noted for their clever and winsome ways. In the following decade, a spate of films depicted the tough ghetto figure, the most notable involving a "cool" and charming private detective called *Shaft*, a Black counterpart to James Bond, portrayed by Richard Roundtree. In "Mr. T.," the television character of the 1980s, a slight variation of this role was highlighted. Mr. T. was gruff yet good-natured, powerful yet gentle, and he collaborated with a team bent on combatting evildoers.

The major exceptions to this typecast character were the different roles performed by Sidney Poitier, whose film career from the 1950s to the 1970s paralleled that of accomplished white actors. From his first role in *Blackboard Jungle* (1955) to *Guess Who's Coming to Dinner* (1967), Poitier was the premier Black actor in films, and by the time the latter movie was released, he was one of the top box-office attractions in the country. There had been, of course, many other superb actors who had worked in the industry, but none were able to break through to achieve top billing. Poitier generally played an individual whose intellectual qualities were superior and whose morals were above reproach. For all his leverage, however, even Poitier was forced into constrained roles. He was usually an outsider or a loner who rarely became involved with the attractive woman. It was not until after many films in his career, in *Guess Who's Coming to Dinner*, that he was finally permitted to kiss a white woman, in this instance his fiancé, in an extremely brief scene observed only through the taxi driver's rearview mirror. Nonetheless, Poitier was one of many males whose roles were fairly complex and demanding and went far beyond the stereotyping which had so long plagued them over the years in the media. Additional discussion on this subject is given in chapter 3 and in chapter 9 of Daniel Leab's *From Sambo to Superspade*.

A POSITIVE VIEW OF THE BLACK AMERICAN MALE

It should be immediately noted that, during these same decades, the Black man was not always derogatorily portrayed in popular culture. Exceptions to the stereotype clearly existed, and although they were relatively few in number, they did indicate that on occasion Black men were accorded a semblance of normality, if not accomplishment. John Singleton Copley's famous painting, ''Watson and the Shark'' in 1778 depicted a man of perfect, normal proportions participating in the capture of a shark. (Chapter 1 elaborates on this positive view.) The angry character Bobo in Herman Melville's complex novella *Benito Cereno* (1858) was endowed with superior intelligence; *The Narrative of the Life of Frederick Douglass*, the extraordinary abolitionist and political activitist, appeared in print in 1845; Booker T. Washington's *Up from Slavery* (1900) was the first widely read work about a Black man in the Horatio Alger mode; the scientist George Washington Carver was heralded for his work with the peanut and sweet potato; the Black worker *John Henry*, that ''steel driving man,'' was extolled in folk song; the United States mint printed commemorative medals of such individuals as Frederick Douglass and Booker T. Washington at the turn of the century. At the same time, there appeared a work which would become a classic interpretation of Afro-American culture, W. E. B. DuBois' *The Souls of Black Folk* (1898); and the ''Ballad for Americans'' sung and narrated by Paul Robeson in the 1930s and 1940s was one of the most popular recordings of the period.

THE CHANGING IMAGE

Gradually, the exaggeration of Sambo's physical features was toned down so that by the 1930s the faces and bodies were no longer drawn in animalistic fashion. Gone also was the accent on exaggerated clothing; Blacks were portrayed in the accepted fashion of servant, valet, or service roles.

Other features, however, remained steadfastly intact. The electronic industry made extensive use of the stereotype in promoting their new technologies. Stereoscopic slides, silent and sound films, photographic stills, radio and television both synthesized and extended aspects of the images. Before the innovation of the moving picture, receptive audiences peered into gadgets which contained pictures of historical and geographical locations, exotic peoples, churches, wonders of the world—and humorous occurrences, including among them scenes of the comical Black male. Sambo moved from the stereoscope to the silent film. From its formative years, the industry depicted Black men—often white men disguised in blackface makeup (a practice seen in the minstrel)—as having a fondness for watermelon, fried chicken, dice, and razors and prone to crazy antics. In the halcyon days of the major studios, Sambo could be seen and heard in a variety of different movies. Minstrelmen Al Jolson and Eddie Cantor donned blackface and sang and danced before white audiences. And there were many other minstrel shows in the films. *Our Gang*, winsome little children with at least one Black member, staged as minstrel. So, too, did Judy Garland and Mickey Rooney, in their numerous musicals, adopt the minstrel style. Chorus lines and singing groups in many other musicals donned blackface. When Blacks were hired for parts, they were usually seen singing spirituals, dancing merrily on the old plantation, bubbling with gaiety in kitchens, smiling broadly as they red-capped bags at railroad stations, and snappily tap-dancing in musicals.

For pure mirth, however, the industry utilized the superstitious aspect of the stereotype. Here the Black servant and valet provided the action for white audiences. In hundreds of films, the Charlie Chan detective series being a major provider of the form, the Black chaffeur chattered at ghosts, fearfully skittered at spooks, and swiftly made his exit down the road where he passed horses and trains in his haste to escape from the "haunts." In certain films, his face turned white and his hair suddenly spiraled upward when he fearfully confronted danger. Furthermore, the Black male was depicted as the only person capable of entering into and carrying on a dialogue with the racing horse, usually the long shot in the formulaic racing story. The performer most associated with the film stereotype was Lincoln Monroe Perry, who assumed the name Stepin Fetchit. Mumbling, shuffling, slack-jawed, and befuddled about virtually every aspect of life, Perry parlayed the white image into stardom. Like many Black actors, he was forced into a mold, yet he honed the stereotype into an art form.

The electronic industry reinforced the image in the 1930s with three Black characters, two of whom were white and one Black. The "Amos 'n' Andy Show," begun in 1928, became one of radio's longest running serial programs. In keeping with the minstrel tradition, the two were white men who kept the dialect and antics but transferred them to an urban setting. The show presumably depicted life in Harlem during the Great Depression. The story line, played out over a series of fifteen-minute slots, allegedly drew from the life of the urban Black. Amos and Andy struggled for economic independence and harmonious female relationships for over thirty years by pursuing various schemes to satisfy both aims. By their quest for success and their rejection of work relief, though, Amos and Andy actually undercut some of the harsher aspects of the stereotype which were highlighted by thick dialect and comical scenes.

One of the most recognized voices on radio belonged to Eddie Anderson, dubbed "Rochester," who performed as Jack Benny's radio personal servant, valet, cook, and chaffeur. Intriguingly, Anderson spoke without any dialect and with a raspy voice that became his trademark. Despite his clearly subservient role, Anderson became the first Black male to publicly outsmart, outmaneuver, sass, and occasionally put down his "Boss." There was no question, however, that the stereotype was partially maintained on the show. In the late 1930s and 1940s, Rochester shot dice, dated several women simultaneously, ate watermelon, and visited bars. And his single name was in keeping with his inferior position. Yet his combative stance toward Benny and his intimate relationship, which permitted role reversals on the air, were suggestive of changes occurring in white sensibility, if not perceptions. In the post-World War II period, the Benny-Anderson duo, as well as the Amos and Andy radio personalities, were adopted for television, but they were the last of such shows.

To a considerable extent, Sambo virtually disappeared in the mass media in the decades following World War II. Several major events pulled the stereotype from center stage into the wings. The ideological thrust of the war combined with the civil rights movement and the rise of Black comedians to prominent media status essentially terminated its life. However, its form continued to breathe in many areas of the culture from the 1960s to the early 1980s. Sambo could be found in thousands of movie reruns on late night television and on Saturday and Sunday mornings; in a *Mutt and Jeff* comic series, which depicted grinning and avaricious cannibals in stove hats, straw skirts, and bones protruding from noses; on front lawns as jockeys; on postcards in drug and stationery stores; in the form of "Isaac," the bartender on the popular television series "Love Boat"; in advertisements in *Time, Newsweek, The New Yorker*, and other magazines, which pictured a smiling, single-named bartender "wanting to satisfy you in every way," or as jazz players in New Orleans; in the multicolored, turban-wrapped boy atop the *Sambo* pancake houses franchised across the country; and in the minstrel plays which were performed in small towns in all regions.

These were, however, passing images. For the most part, Sambo no longer frolicked on center stage in American culture. In 1955, the curtain rose on the act that would push the stereotype into history. In that year, Rosa Parks, a weary seamstress in Montgomery, Alabama, refused to relinquish her seat to a white man in a crowded bus. She was arrested in accordance with Jim Crow laws. Her action reflected the refusal of millions of other Blacks and led to the boycott which followed and to the rise of civil rights organizations. By the mid–1960s, after thousands of sit-ins, demonstrations, marches, beatings, and jailings, the country profoundly altered its view of the Black male and Black culture. Racist attitudes and practices would continue in American culture in variegated ways, but, in the aftermath of the movement, it could be said that Sambo had been laid to rest.

The change was reinforced by another development, namely, the rise of Black comedians in the mass media who not only did not play Sambo but mocked whites for their perception. When Dick Gregory, the first Black comic to achieve national awareness, wryly declared before a white audience in a Chicago nightclub in the 1960s, "Makes you wonder . . . when I left St. Louis I was making $500 a week for saying the same thing out loud that I used to say under my breath," the longest running stereotype was put to rest (Boskin, "Goodby" 30–31). Whatever the future of white-Black relationships in the remaining decade of the twentieth century, it was no longer possible for an image to influence whites and plague Blacks. The distance between fantasy and reality had finally been narrowed.

THE LITERATURE OF SAMBO AND THE BLACK MALE IMAGE

Studies of the Sambo image have been largely concentrated on its characteristics during the slave period. Stanley Elkins first posed the psychological problem of assessing the connection between the slave system and Black personality in *Slavery: A Problem in American Institutional and Intellectual Life* (1950). His conclusion, which wavered between the concept of "childishness" and "dependency" as the dominant response, brought the issue into sharp focus. Elkins' work impacted beyond the scholar's domain. William Styron's novel, *The Confessions of Nat Turner* (1966), awarded the Pulitzer Prize for Literature, drew heavily upon Elkins' thoughts. Many other social scientists, however, extracted different Black responses from the plantation culture. David B. Davis aptly noted in *The Problem of Slavery in Western Culture* (1966) that virtually all slave societies conceived of their slaves in servile terms, often equating them as children or animals.

In Eugene Genovese's salient works, particularly in *Roll, Jordan, Roll: The World the Slaves Made* (1972), religion became the organizing force for Blacks as they grappled with the problem of accommodation and resistance. More pointed was John Blassingame's *The Slave Community* (1979), which trenchantly argued that Sambo was a necessary survivalist tool within an entrapped circumstance, a clever albeit complicated form of behavior. One consequence of this action was to make it appear that Sambo was, in effect, a personality dimension of the Black male. Nevertheless, many southern whites and Blacks understood that a terribly serious game, one with defined roles, was being conducted for the maintenance of a system of complex relationships. George M. Frederickson's incisive study, *The Black Image in the White Mind* (1971), argued that white inventiveness in forestalling an egalitarian biracial society brought an insistence on both the Sambo and Savage images so that the elimination of one would automatically trigger the enactment of the other.

Analysis of the stereotype in the twentieth century has mainly been in conjunction with its projection in the movies. Thomas Cripps, *Slow Fade to Black: The Negro in American Films, 1900–1942* (1977); Donald Bogle, *Toms, Coons, Mulattoes, Mammies, and Bucks* (1973); and Daniel J. Leab, *From Sambo to Superspade* (1975) treat the image in the film industry in considerable depth.

An attempt to place the stereotype in the context of the popular culture is found in Joseph Boskin's *Sambo: The Rise & Demise of an American Jester* (1986).

For other important works pertaining to the image, see Winthrop Jordan's

White over Black (1968), Robert Toll's *Blacking Up: The Minstrel Show in Nineteenth Century America* (1974), and Kenneth Stampp, *The Peculiar Institution* (1956).

NOTES

1. Nat Turner was a slave and preacher in Southampton, Virginia, who, in 1831, led one of the most ferocious insurrections against slavery in American history. He and his followers killed sixty whites, including Turner's owner and family, in their futile attempt to escape from slavery. Just as other slaves joined Turner in their attacks, a powerful force of state and federal troops overwhelmed them. In retaliation, whites killed over 100 blacks, some of them who were free, and eventually executed Turner. For additional discussion, see *The Confessions of Nat Turner* (1831) and the controversial novel by William Styron, *The Confessions of Nat Turner* (New York: Random House, 1966), as well as John B. Duff and Peter M. Mitchell, eds., *The Nat Turner Rebellion: The Historical Event and the Modern Controversy* (New York: Harper & Row, 1971).

2. Gordon Allport, *The Nature of Prejudice* (New York: Doubleday & Co., 1954) 185; Allport's emphasis.

3. Harriet Martineau, *Society in America* (New York: Saunders and Otley, 1837), 381–82. Emphasis mine.

SELECTED REFERENCES

Books

Allport, Gordon. *The Nature of Prejudice.* New York: Doubleday and Co., 1954.

Berlin, Ira. *Slaves without Masters.* New York: Vintage Books, 1974.

Blassingame, John M. *The Slave Community.* 2nd ed. New York: Oxford University Press, 1979.

Bogle, Donald. *Toms, Coons, Mulattoes, Mammies and Bucks.* New York: Viking Press, 1973.

Boskin, Joseph. "*Goodby, Mr. Bones.*" *The New York Times Magazine* (May 1, 1966):30–31.

———. *Sambo: The Rise & Demise of an American Jester.* New York: Oxford University Press, 1986.

Cripps, Thomas F. *Slow Fade to Black: The Negro in American Films, 1900–1942.* New York: Oxford University Press, 1977.

Davis, David Brion. *The Problem of Slavery in Western Civilization.* Ithaca, N.Y.: Cornell University Press, 1966.

Douglas, Robert L. "Black Males and Television: New Images versus Old Stereotypes." *The Western Journal of Black Studies* 11 (Summer 1987): 69–73.

Douglass, Frederick. *The Narrative of the Life of Frederick Douglass.* Boston, Mass.: Published at the Anti-Slavery Office, 1845.

DuBois, W. E. B. *The Souls of Black Folk.* 1898. Chicago: A. C. McClurg, 1904.

Duff, John B., comp. *The Nat Turner Rebellion: The Historical Event and the Modern Controversy.* Eds. John B. Duff and Peter M. Mitchell. New York: Harper & Row, 1971.

Elkins, Stanley M. *Slavery: A Problem in American Institutional and Intellectual Life*. 2nd ed. Chicago: The University of Chicago Press, 1968.

Ellison, Ralph. *Invisible Man*. New York: Random House, 1947.

Farel, Joel. "Charles Waddell Chesnutt's Sambo: Myth and Reality." *Negro American Literature Forum* 9 (1975): 105–8.

Frederickson, George M. *The Black Image in the White Mind*. New York: Harper & Row, 1971.

Genovese, Eugene. *Roll, Jordan, Roll: The World the Slaves Made*. New York: Random House, 1972.

Harris, Joel Chandler. *Uncle Remus: His Songs and Sayings*. 1887. New York: D. Appleton & Co., 1920.

Jordan, Winthrop D. *White over Black*. Chapel Hill: University of North Carolina Press, 1968.

Leab, Daniel J. *From Sambo to Superspade*. Boston, Mass.: Houghton Mifflin Co., 1975.

Lippmann, Walter. *Public Opinion*. New York: Macmillan Co., 1922.

Melville, Herman. *Benito Cereno*. 1858. Barre, Mass.: Imprint Society, 1972.

Osofsky, Gilbert. *Puttin' On Ole Massa*. New York: Harper & Row, 1969.

Rose, Arnold. *The Negro in America*. New York: Saunders and Otley, 1944.

Stampp, Kenneth. *The Peculiar Institution: Slavery in the Ante-Bellum South*. New York: Alfred A. Knopf, 1949.

Styron, William. *The Confessions of Nat Turner*. New York: Random House, 1966.

"Tambo and Bones." In George C. D. Odell, *Annals of the New York Stage*. vol. 4. New York: Columbia University Press, 1927.

Toll, Robert C. *Blacking Up: The Minstrel Show in Nineteenth Century America*. New York: Oxford University Press, 1974.

Trevor-Roper, H. R. *The Crises of the Seventeenth Century*. New York: Harper & Row, 1956.

Turner, Nat. *The Confessions of Nat Turner, The Leader of the Late Insurrection in Southampton, Va*. 1831. New York: Thomas Hamilton, 1861.

Washington, Booker T. *Up From Slavery*. 1890. New York: A. L. Burt Co., 1901.

Wilkinson, Doris, and R. Taylor. *The Black Male in America: Perspectives on His Status in Contemporary Society*. Chicago, Ill.: Nelson-Hall, 1977.

Periodicals

EM *Ebony Man*. vol. 1–, 1986–. P.O. Box 549, Chicago, IL 60690.

MBM *Modern Black Man*. vol. 1–, 1984–. 475 Park Avenue South, New York, NY 10010.

The Toy Menagerie: Early Images of Blacks in Toys, Games, and Dolls

One of the most fascinating subjects, synthesizing a diversity of fields such as anthropology, art, history, and psychology, is the study of cultural artifacts. Such items are valuable for the information they provide about the beliefs, values, and customs of the societies in which they are created. Play objects are especially important cultural products, for they reflect given social contexts and offer restrospective accounts of traditions and behaviors. These filter through the imagination of the inventor of games, dolls, toys, or other items of amusement.

Basically, the shape and characterizations of play artifacts present evidence of the history and collective sentiments of a society. They express particular social and economic contexts and hence political realities. For example, in the United States one profound and revealing national incident involving dolls disclosed their influence on racial and economic relations. Attempts were made in the early 1900s to reduce the sale of "Negro" dolls designed to portray positive images as well as to discredit the National Negro Doll Company. Subsequently, a series of events occurred in Nashville, Tennessee, which graphically exposed racial attitudes toward constructive efforts to produce noncaricaturized children's toys depicting Blacks. One response to the discrediting scheme noted that

The most unkind cut that was ever given to a Negro enterprise was administered, or attempted to be administered, to the National Negro Doll Company of this city by a newspaper correspondent recently, who possibly was urged or persuaded by merchants, who feared the increasing popularity of the Negro dolls. . . . It was evident from the ovation given the advent of Negro dolls that practically every family which cared to instill race pride in their children would either have a Negro doll in their home or none at all. The merchants saw this, as the sale of white dolls among Negroes had fallen off to an alarming extent (*Afro-American Ledger*).

The belittling advertisements claimed that African American mothers would not purchase the dolls and that they were, in fact, opposed to the Negro doll movement. Yet, during a National Baptist Association convention at the time, the following resolution was endorsed:

Whereas, Our people for half a century, because of the uncomely and deformed features of Negro dolls, have spent thousands of dollars on white dolls at Christmas, etc., therefore be it Resolved, That we do here and now give our endorsement and hearty approval of the Negro Doll Factory, and not only urge the patronage of the people of our church, but of the race at large throughout the United States (*Afro-American Ledger*).

The popularity of these new racial pride dolls grew within the Black community. In fact, the National Negro Doll Company's products were often displayed at bazaars and fairs in many parts of the country. The role of Black women was especially important in the positive image movement. A number of women's groups supported the idea of Negro dolls. Churches in Nashville also distributed them. These activities represented significant transitions in collective self-definition as Blacks mobilized against racist imagery at the beginning of the twentieth century.

Cross-culturally, a matrix of social variables has been interrelated with games, toys, and dolls. The intimate connection of play objects with prevailing political sentiments was vividly demonstrated during the turbulent period of the 1960s "when longshoremen refused to unload Mao Tse-Tung dolls wrapped in leaflets containing quotations from Chairman Mao" ("Guys and Dolls" 109). Similarly, in 1974 the Cuban ministry publicly announced that dolls manufactured in that country were to be designed in the image of the people of the country. News accounts suggested that Cuban girls had played with the types which depicted Aryan images. Thus, the diffusion of national pride into the toy industry resulted in the emphasis on dolls with "Cuban type faces and clothing" ("New Image Planned for Cuban Dolls" 4B). During the same political era, the West German toy retailers association urged its members to avoid dealing in war toys. This initiative was supported by the German government with appeal coming from the justice minister who urged the industry to impose voluntary restrictions on toys which he felt encouraged violence (*Washington Afro-American* 14). Ten years later in the United States, counterfeit copies of Cabbage Patch dolls were seized by the U.S. Customs Service ("Cabbage Patch Fakes Seized from Maryland Firm" B1). In the following year, a controversy ensued after a public display of the Barbie doll to advertise tests of chylamdyia, a highly prevalent sexually transmitted disease. This action was defined as a violation of a valued symbolic artifact (Rovner B1, B4). Such examples of public and governmental responses to play artifacts reveal the intricate connection of toys, games, and dolls to deeply embedded societal values and beliefs.

THE SEARCH FOR PLAY OBJECTS AND THEIR
CULTURAL MEANINGS

In amusement and in play, toys and dolls continue to represent valuable cultural products which put forward a biographical sketch of a society—its customs, aesthetic values, and behavioral norms.[1] Historical accounts have demonstrated that dolls in particular have symbolized what little babies and girls who resemble them anatomically should look like and the category in which they should perceive themselves. Because of their sustained prominence over time as important cultural products in image creation, dolls are emphasized in this analysis. The time frame covers pre- and post-Reconstruction up to World War II. Several pertinent works which offer historical information on dolls as play objects are Kay Desmonde's and Angelo Hornak's *All Color Book of Dolls* (1974), Antonia Fraser's *A History of Toys* (1972), Ruth S. Freeman's *Encyclopedia of American Dolls* (1972), and Eleanor St. George's *The Dolls of Yesterday* (1948).

The various characterizations presented were obtained from department store catalogues located by using the resources of university libraries, *The National Union Catalog: Pre–1956 Imprints*, *Index to Periodical Articles By and About Blacks: 1974* (1977), and selected collectors' guides to American toys, games, and dolls. Documents from specific libraries were found in the 11th and 13th editions of *Symbols of American Libraries* (1976 and 1985). The toy and doll sections of the catalogs were examined thoroughly for those depicting Black Americans. Every distinct type was recorded, and its date of appearance was noted. Frequently, the precise origins were omitted. Each unique label was sought in encyclopedias, dictionaries, antique collectors guides, and works about children's early play objects. This was done to determine the meanings and the etymological derivations of the various labels used to describe and advertise Black portrayals in toys, games, and dolls. This method is consistent with the earlier content analysis of play artifacts (Wilkinson, "Play Objects as Tools of Propaganda: Characterizations of the African American Male" 1–16).

CARICATURES OF BLACK MALES

From the early 1880s through World War II, images of Blacks in toys were presented in caricature. In the 1880s and 1890s, the celebrated games for children as well as adults portrayed Black males most often. Typically, the artifacts constituted extensions of widely held beliefs about former slaves as musical and happy. Among the most popular and marketable amusements were musical play objects such as the "Mechanical Cake Walk"—a dancing couple advertised in an 1892 edition of *Marshall Field & Co. Catalogue* (Kelley 19–21). Yet it was the "Coon Jigger," a tap-dancing Black male, that achieved the status of "Toy King." Advertised as the "Alabama Coon Jigger" in the early part of the century, for many decades this mechanical play item was proclaimed as a realistic characterization of a Negro engaged in a Southern plantation dance (Goodstone 227).

13. "Alabama Coon Jigger," mechanical toy. Courtesy of the Edgar and Donna Orchard Collection.

In the 1912 *Sears, Roebuck & Co. Catalogue*, two smiling "Musical Negroes" were presented as "darkies playing accordian and flute." A similar toy was that of a "Musical Negro on Chair." It was also described as comical. Thus, along with many others depicting black males, these toys functioned to reinforce prevailing racial stereotypes at the level of play.

In addition to the musical items that attracted both children and adults, banks with indigenous American names such as "Uncle Tom" and "Jolly Nigger" were exceedingly popular. Conventionally, these were identified as amusing and comical. Those portraying Black males were the "Minstrel," "Stump Speaker," and "Cabin" banks. Throughout the nineteenth and twentieth centuries, the

14. "Ham and Sam," mechanical toy. Courtesy of the Edgar and Donna Orchard Collection.

names "Uncle Tom" and "Jolly Nigger"—two offensive labels—were applied to an array of amusement objects. Coinciding with these were the "Darkey Upset by Kicking Mule" (1914) and "Thrifty Tom Jigger." These items, illustrated in department store catalogues, are included in Joseph Schroeder's *The Wonderful World of Toys, Games and Dolls* (1971).

While the meaning of "nigger" is deeply entrenched as a highly derogatory term, not as much is known about the labels "tom" and "jigger," which have been associated with play objects depicting Black males in American amusements. The term "tom" in the English language system denotes the male of various animal species such as tomcat or tom turkey. As a proper noun, it is simply a boy's given name or a short form of Thomas. However, during slavery, the title "Uncle Tom" emerged as a dishonorable descriptor that evoked images of a Black man as abjectly servile and excessively deferential to whites. This contextual meaning originated from a key character in *Uncle Tom's Cabin* (1852), an antislavery novel by Harriet Beecher Stowe. Congruent with the historical translation of the image was "Uncle Tomism." This pertained to an agreed upon policy of racial interaction in which Americans of African ancestry exhibited willing submissiveness. Whites, on the other hand, displayed aggressive benevolence as well as patronizing attitudes toward submissive Blacks. Hence, dolls, toys, and games labeled "Uncle Tom," "Thrifty Tom Jigger," or "Jolly Nigger" functioned to crystallize existing American sensibilities toward happy and obsequious Black males.

The term "jigger" as a label for toys depicting Black males has had an interesting cultural transformation and chronology. Traditionally, the word "jig" has meant "a rapid, lively, springy, irregular dance for one or more persons, usually in triple meter; to move with a jerky or bobbing motion; jerk up and down or to and fro; to dance or play a jig" (*Random House Dictionary of the English Language* 767).

The jig in the sixteenth century was a popular dance in England. It became a part of concert music under the French name "gigue" in the seventeenth and eighteenth centuries. In this context, the "jig" or "gigue" comprises the concluding movement in a classical suite. Eventually, the dance diffused to America where it was incorporated as an important element in minstrel performances by whites in blackface. Among contemporary audiences, the jig is still known as a lively Irish dance.

Use of the words "jig" or "jigger" for American items of amusement has reflected the broader racial environment. For example, as a noun, the word "jigger" has been used disparingly and offensively whenever it has referred to a Black American. In fact, its social meaning and use have paralleled that of "nigger" (e.g., "Coon Jigger," "Jigging Dance"). Several definitions of the former have appeared: "One who or that which jigs; some contrivance, article or part that one cannot or will not name more precisely: *What is that little jigger on the pistol?*; also called jigger, flea, chigoe; chigger" (*Random House Dictionary* 767). A variant of this meaning is that for "jigaboo" (*jigger* + boo)—an insulting and disparaging term which has been used extensively by whites to designate a Negro.

At the beginning of the twentieth century, portrayals of Black males in toys assumed a variety of labels. Each shared the same physical attributes and characteristics. Among these were mechanical toys labeled "Musical Negroes," a "Musical Negro on Chair" (cited earlier), the "Dusky Dude," a "Tumbling Negro," and a game advertised as a "Jolly Coon Race." These play objects were marketed from the 1890s through World War I and up to the Depression years.

The following culturally based images, which survived for more than a century, expose the scope and social psychology of racist imagery in American history:

15. Rubber doll with melon. From the editor's collection. Photo by Vando Rogers.

1. "Darkey Upset by Kicking Mule," a dancing toy

2. "Dancing Coon"

3. Musical toys labeled "Ham and Sam"

4. "Jumping Jack"

5. "Whistling Coon," a novelty toy for children and adults

6. "Jolly Nigger" puzzle

7. "Alabama Coon Jigger"

8. A chain gang figure attired in a prison uniform (circa 1930s)
9. "Sambo"
10. "Chicken Snatcher"
11. "The Darkey's Coon Game"

Each of these labels mirrored broader underlying racial concepts and perceptions. With remarkable continuity over time, they came to symbolize images of Black males. The literature on the Black male in toys and other items of amusement includes Johana Gast Anderton, *The Collector's Encyclopedia of Cloth Dolls: From Rag Baby to Art Object* (1984); Tony Goodstone, ed., *1929 Johnson Smith & Co. Catalogue* (1970); Paula Parker, "Contemptible Collectibles" (1980); and Doris Wilkinson, "Play Objects as Tools of Propaganda" (1980).

Additional though similar characterizations of Black males were manufactured before and after the Depression. Yet, the visual patterns and the mode of expression that permeated adult and children's items of amusement remained virtually constant. For example, the 1928 Sears catalogue carried two stereotyped toys: "Chicken Snatcher" and "Charleston Trio." Their distinct descriptions, accompanied by pictures, appeared thus in the advertisements:

Charleston Trio. Some Steppers!
Very snappy action. When strong spring is wound up, Charleston Charlie dances with the small negro and the animal nods his approval (Sears 1928, 494).

Chicken Snatcher.
One of our most novel toys. When the strong spring motor is wound up, the scared looking negro shuffles along with a chicken dangling in his hand a dog hanging in the seat of his pants. Very funny action toy which will delight the kiddies (Sears 1928, 494).

The reverence attached to these toys is demonstrated by their assessed value in recent antique and collectors magazines. In some current issues one may find "Alabama Coon Jigger" (windup tin toy, patented 1912), "Amos and Andy Fresh Air Taxi" (windup tin toy, patented 1929), "Black Face Clown, "Black Magic" (advertising doll that accompanied "Buddy Lee," circa 1920), "Dapper Dan" (approximately 1920), "Thrifty Tom's Jigger Bank" (early 1920), "Jolly Nigger" play object, "Jazzbo Jim" (in various editions), "Rollo Chair" (a windup tin of a Negro man on boardwalk in Atlantic City pushing a three-wheeled chair), and "Hott and Tott" (1950s). Each toy, game, or doll reflected American racial thought and stereotypes at the time of its creation.

MASKING AS A BLACK MAN

Throughout the cultural histories of societies around the world, masking has had an integral connection with social, religious, and political events. Many of the basic values and beliefs of a nation are revealed through its masking rituals and rites of passage. In the entertainment sphere of the United States and Europe, masking has had important economic and cultural functions. For example, through the use of masks and wigs at the culmination of the nineteenth century in the United States, one could pretend to be a Black male. Minstrels popularized the Negro mask, which was used for entertainment principally by whites. In fact, for many years minstrel companies were made up of white men in blackface.

As early as 1799, the first documented American minstrel show was held in Boston. During the next fifty years, these popular musicals evolved as institutionalized modes of adult entertainment. Curiously, even Blacks who performed in the shows wore masks. In fact, talented performers such as Bert Williams had to wear blackface makeup to compete with comedians like Al Jolson and others. For the remainder of the nineteenth century minstrelsy held popular and nationwide appeal. (See chapters 2 and 4 for a more detailed discussion on Black minstrelsy in American culture.)

During the nation's severe economic crisis—the Depression—Negro masking served as a prominent recreational outlet, perhaps functioning as a means of escape from harsh social and economic realities. Throughout the cities and farm communities, minstrels and amateur theatricals in which one could mask as a Black flourished. Advertisements targeted at whites proclaimed that any young man with a "piece of charcoal and a wig [could] personate a negro perfectly" (Goodstone 283). Masking as a Black man thus became established in the milieu of adult play.

A number of traditional character masks appeared in the 1929 *Johnson Smith & Co. Catalogue*. Some of those with dark coloring—the tramp, the grotesque, and Negro masks—had striking facial features. Along with these and Negro wigs was the favorite "Uncle Tom" mask. The facial expressions and attributes were similar to those of "Uncle Mose" (a member of the "Aunt Jemima" family) and "Uncle Remus" (a plantation storyteller of animal tales). The "Uncle Tom" mask included imitation hair and eyebrows.

It is important to note here the use of the word "uncle" in the American race relations vocabulary. While the title has bestowed kinship status on the holder, other connotations have been apparent in the social history of racial interaction in America. Basically, the label has been applied to an elderly male. For many decades before the civil rights movement of the 1960s, Black domestic servants and laborers were designated as "uncle" (or "aunt" in the case of females) and were perceived as members of the households where they were employed [see Wilkinson, "Tactics of Protest as Media: The Case of the Black Revolution" (1970)]. Although the meanings in such instances could be construed as positive, the use of "uncle" represented an attempt to locate in social space Blacks who worked and lived in white households. The word has also been used in a derisive manner to refer to a pawnbroker. In addition, it has been applied to a behavioral response characterized by submission or the conceding of defeat. Coinciding with the "Uncle Tom" image, the use of "uncle" for Black males in America's early history embraced a complex synthesis of social and political meanings.

Joseph Boskin gives a fuller account of the "Uncle Tom" image in chapter 8 on Sambo and the male image.

Typically, masks depicting Black males were like the prototypic pre–1940 "Negro Make-Up Outfit." One catalogue, which graphically illustrates this, describes the costume as "the funniest and most laughable outfit ever sold." It consisted of "woven black cotton hood, realistic large eyes, thick red lips, and large teeth" (Goodstone 12). Similar to this was the "Nigger Make-Up" with a pronounced black color:

Nigger Make-Up without blacking. Complete with hat. Slipped on or off in a minute. No burnt cork or muss. The outfit comprises a black stockingnette mask, that can be slipped over the head in a moment, odd eyes, buck teeth, and imitation plantation straw hat. The entire make-up is instantaneous and most effective (Goodstone 12).

The description, accompanied by an illustration, contained its own message regarding the dominant perceptions of Americans of African descent. No other ethnic minority groups were portrayed in such bizarre and stereotypic ways.

THE LEGACY OF AUNT JEMIMA IN TOYS

The images embodied in games, toys, and dolls portraying American women of African ancestry coincided with those used to caricaturize Black males. Although limited in the types designed, most dolls were created to emit realistic portrayals. Many were advertised as character dolls with facial features and general appearance modeled after well-known persons in the society, especially in the entertainment industry. A discussion of these images is given in *The Encyclopedia of Collectibles* (1978) Wendy Lavitt's, *The Knopf Collectors' Guide to American Dolls* (1983), and in "The Doll Exhibit" (1987). One of the earliest and most renowned of this type was the classic Aunt Jemima figure. Appearing in the 1890s, this doll was typically fat with a round, smiling face and was customarily attired in a domestic outfit. Historical interpretations indicate that the figure, which appeared on kitchen items and foods, was perceived by whites as a replica of the "ideal Negro woman servant" (Pantovic 44–48). She was assigned an almost mystical status. Johana Gast Anderton noted in *More Twentieth Century Dolls from Bisque to Vinyl* (1979) that at least five generations of Black women were modeled after the original Jemima dolls. Permission to reproduce them was secured from the successors of Aunt Jemima Mills Company.

Although the basic image of this figure, depicted in dolls and in other items of amusement, was uncomplimentary to Black women, southern whites designated the symbol as positive and cherished it. Actually, the name Aunt Jemima is a feminine one; but the American caricature was that of an obese, darkly pigmented Black woman. While the products on which her face appeared were widely marketed, racially specific images were generated and reinforced. Despite the positive origins of the name "Jemima," found in Arabic and in Hebrew and tempered by the realism of race relations in the United States, the name was used derisively.[2]

Closely resembling the Aunt Jemima figure were the "Black Mamma Doll" (circa 1919), "Beloved Belindy," the "Old Nurse" with white doll (1875), "Mammy" (1880s), "Darkey Head," "Darky Nurse Rag Doll," and "Black Grandmother" (1800–1900). In *American Antique Toys: 1830–1900* (1980), Bernard Barenholtz and Inez McClintock describe the "Old Nurse" doll as a very comical mechanical toy. This doll conveyed the same demeaning images as those described in the catalogues of the 1890s. In a 1903 Montgomery Ward and Company *General Catalog*, the "Old Nurse" was advertised as well constructed and dressed in appropriate attire. She was considered an item of amusement for both children and adults.

Most Black dolls that were not European in appearance were anatomically similar to the "Old Nurse" and "Aunt Jemima" dolls. Traditionally wearing aprons, they were fat with thick red lips and broad, smiling expressions. The "Cake Walker" mechanical toys and the Mechanical Nurse, advertised in the early 1890s in Marshall Field catalogues, were in the same stylistic mode. Repeatedly, the images were rooted in stereotyped conceptions of women of African ancestry. Even a label such as "darky," which appeared frequently, denoted a desirable feature to whites. To Blacks, it suggested deliberate negative symbolism and was seen as fundamentally patronizing and contemptuous. After the Depression, similar "colored dolls" continued to be manufactured. They were always wearing bandanas and white aprons, usually holding a white baby doll.

During the early 1930s, the popular nineteenth-century Topsy and Eva babies were advertised in the Sears catalogues. Based on the character in Harriet Beecher Stowe's *Uncle Tom's Cabin* (1852), like Uncle Tom, Topsy had existed for many years. She was presented in the story as an ignorant but bright slave. In a 1930 Montgomery Ward and Company *General Catalogue*, she was described as a "mischievous pickaninny" beside a "dear little white baby." In Anderton's *The Collector's Encyclopedia of Cloth Dolls* (1984), a version of Topsy in the 1950s is identified. This doll is a replica of the earlier topsy-turvy version that could be changed from black to white by a simple flip of its long skirt. Although the original manufacturers are unknown, the dolls were prominent in the antebellum South. Racial stereotypes were illuminated in most of the early topsy-turvy dolls. Lavitt notes in *The Knopf Collectors' Guide to American Dolls* (1983) that the back side was often a caricature and dressed as a mammy. Later, the dolls were modified in physical appearance and marketed as "integration babies."

From the nineteenth through much of the twentieth centuries, baby dolls depicting Black females consistently symbolized negative images. They were often labeled "mischievous," "pickaninny" or "nigger." The forms of Black baby dolls included a "Negro doll in a melon," "darkey head" and "nigger baby." Pickaninny became a standard label for most Black baby dolls. As late as the post-World War II era, pickaninny was used to denote a Black child. While the term originated in Britain and was once endearing, it gained a different social meaning in the United States. *Roget's Thesaurus* (1972) identifies it with a number of negative synonyms: brat, elf, tomboy, flapper, whipper snapper, and urchin.

The term "nigger" is more intense in meaning and has been used extensively as a label for Black play objects. While the word has had a culturally distinct history in the United States, it evolved as an emotionally laden symbol for "any member of a dark-skinned race or [more] precisely a Negro" (Emery and Brewster 1140). It has historically represented a contemptuous and derogatory label; yet, the term was used to describe and market dolls that portrayed Black babies and males. *Roget's Thesaurus* (1972) lists the following synonyms: Blackness, swarthiness, cunning, and craftiness. (135–36). In American politics and diplomacy, "nigger" refers to "back-stairs" influence or Machiavellianism. As an adjective, the word has meant cunning as a fox, insidious, stealthy, sly, shrewd, and the like. Perhaps few words in the English language evoke such negative symbolism as the word "nigger." Using it to characterize toys created in the image of Blacks apparently produced no perceptual contradictions, for the label was maintained as one for play objects from the early 1800s to the 1950s. The psychological and cultural meanings of these dolls are presented in this author's work, "The Doll Exhibit: A Psycho-Cultural Analysis of Black Female Role Stereotypes" (1987).

Generally, the basic structural form of most Black female dolls, which were not babies, was the mammy character. In fact, Black mammy dolls emerged as the primary ones to remain on the market for decades. Like Aunt Jemima, mammy was defined as representing a realistic and acceptable image of a household servant. The term actually denoted a Black female serving as a nurse to white children. Often, as previously indicated, the mammy dolls were made cuddling white infants. Standard advertisements highlighted the physical features and emphasized broad smiles and large hands holding a white baby. Jan Foulke's *Fifth Blue Book: Dolls & Values* (1982) contains an illustration.

Although dolls representing Black females showed remarkable continuity in appearance, some diversity was reflected in the names. These names ranged from general ones, such as "Black woman" or "Black grandmother" to "Diana Jemima." The latter is illustrated in *Dolls & Values* (1982) as being in a collection in the mid–1920s. Significantly, most mammy dolls resembled the grotesque male golliwog figure which attained a highly marketable status after its genesis as a storybook character (Whitton 142). Eventually, the golliwog was found to induce fears in children.[3]

THE ADVENT OF NEW IMAGES

As racial sensitivities transformed the toy market in the 1950s and 1960s, most of the negatively labeled play objects of the nineteenth and mid-twentieth centuries receded to the background. One outcome from changed cultural imperatives was the debut of authentic Black dolls. Ultimately, pictures were taken of the heads of Black children and used for models for dolls. These included baby dolls as well as the "Flip Wilson–Geraldine" stuffed cloth doll. This plaything was reminiscent of an earlier "colored doll" advertisement in the 1931 Sears Roebuck catalogue, which contained the words "I'se in town, honey." There were, however, a few constructive role models with dolls representing athletes, writers, and movie stars. The eminent black writer Paul Laurence Dunbar was portrayed, for example. Similarly, the "Julia" doll was created in the likeness of Diahann Carroll who, in the 1960s, played in a television series by that name. Wendy Lavitt's *The Knopf Collectors' Guide* revealed that, prior to the 1940s, few artifacts represented the dignity and positive characteristics of American Blacks. Virtually all games, toys, and dolls depicting them were caricatures inspired by dominant racial themes.

Although changes have occurred in the cultural sphere of amusements, the past remains a part of American popular culture, particularly in the arena of adult films. To locate examples of toys and play objects discussed in this chapter, see chapter 10. Also see chapter 3 as well as the works listed in the bibliography in chapter 3. Despite the changing social environment in which children's play objects and adult items of amusement have been created and manufactured, the early images of Black Americans set the historical stage for enduring images of persons of African descent. Through play artifacts, deeply entrenched stereotyped conceptions were sustained. As cultural products, dolls, games, and toys thus served as mechanisms which established a context for reinforcement of racist belief and behaviors. While the past influences the present in innumerable ways, the nation's racial structure has changed dramatically and so have the racial sensibilities of its inhabitants. As these social tranformations have occurred, significant positive changes have taken place in the toy menagerie.

NOTES

1. This theme is discussed in Doris Wilkinson, "Racial Socialization through Children's Toys: A Sociohistorical Examination," *Journal of Black Studies* 5 (1974): 96–109 and in Ted J. Rakstis, "Debate in the Doll House," *Today's Health* 48 (December 1970): 28–31, 65–66.

2. Additional information on this topic may be found in Eric Partridge, *Name This Child: A Dictionary of Modern British and American Given or Christian Names* (London: Hamis, Hamilton, 1951): 158; *Webster's New World Dictionary of the American Language* 1 (New York: World Publishing Co., 1951): 373; and Nancie Swanberg, *Dolls through the Ages* (San Francisco, Calif.: Troubador Press, 1979): 25.

3. This is explained further in Antonia Fraser, *A History of Toys*: 190; and Doris Wilkinson, "Play Objects as Tools of Propaganda": 6–7. Images of Black women in dolls are discussed in "The Doll Exhibit: A Psycho-Cultural Analysis of Black Female Role Stereotypes": 19–29.

BIBLIOGRAPHY

"The Advent of Soul Toys." *Ebony* 24 (November 1968): 164–66; 168–70.

Afro-American Ledger, December 14, 1909.

Anderton, Johana Gast, *The Collector's Encyclopedia of Cloth Dolls: From Rag Baby to Art Object*. Lombard, Ill.: Wallace-Homestead Book Co., 1984.

————. *More Twentieth Century Dolls from Bisque to Vinyl*. Des Moines, Iowa: Wallace-Homestead Book Co., 1979.

Barenholz, Bernard, and Inez McClintock. *American Antique Toys: 1830–1900*. New York: Harry N. Abrams, Inc., Publishers, 1980.

Beck, Mindy. "Minority Images on T.V.: Up from Amos n' Andy." *Access* (October 6, 1975): 4–6.

Bergman, Peter M. *The Chronological History of the Negro in America*. New York: Harper & Row, 1969.

Boskin, Joseph. *Sambo: The Rise & Demise of an American Jester*. New York: Oxford University Press, 1986.

"Cabbage Patch Fakes Seized from Maryland Firm." *The Washington Post*, December 13, 1984: B1.

Coleman, Dorothy S., Elizabeth A. Coleman, and Evelyn J. Coleman. *The Collector's Encyclopedia of Dolls*. New York: Crown, 1968.

Desmonde, Kay, and Angelo Hornak. *All Color Book of Dolls*. London: Octopus Books, 1974.

"Dolls." *Collier's Encyclopedia*. vol 8. New York: P. F. Colliers, Inc., 1975, 318.

Emery, H. G., and K. G. Brewster. *The New Century Dictionary of the English Language*. vol. 2. New York: P. F. Collier & Son Corp., 1931.

The Encyclopedia of Collectibles. Alexandria, Va.: Time-Life Books, 1978.

Fife, Marilyn Diane. "Black Images in American TV: The First Two Decades." *Black Scholar* 5 (November 1974): 5–15.

Foulke, Jan. *Fifth Blue Book: Dolls & Values*. Cumberland, Md.: Hobby House Press, 1982.

Fraser, Antonia. *A History of Toys*. London: The Hamlyn Publishing Co., 1972.

Freeman, Ruth S. *Encyclopedia of American Dolls*. New York: Century House, 1972.

Gibbs, Patikii, and Tyson Gibbs. *Collector's Encyclopedia of Black Dolls*. Paducah, Ky.: Collector Books, [1986]. For a list of public and private collectors of Black dolls, see Acknowledgements, p. [3].

Goodstone, Tony. ed. *1929 Johnson Smith & Co. Catalogue*. New York: Chelsea House Publishers, 1970.

"Guys and Dolls." *Newsweek* 71 (June 24, 1968): 109–10.

Index to Periodical Articles By and About Blacks: 1974. Boston: G. K. Hall, 1977.

Kelley, Dale, ed. *1892–1893 Marshall Field Toy Catalog*. Des Moines, Iowa: Wallace-Homestead Book Co., 1969.

Klemensrud, Judy. "Award Winning Toys: Nonsexist, Nonracist, and Peaceful." *New York Times*, February 19, 1975: L–25.

Lavitt, Wendy. *The Knopf Collectors' Guide to American Dolls*. New York: Alfred A. Knopf, 1983.

McClintock, I., and M. McClintock. *Toys in America*. Washington, D.C.: Public Affairs Press, 1961.

Michener, Charles. "Black Movies." *Newsweek* 80 (October 23, 1972): 74–82.

Montgomery Ward & Co. General Catalogue. Chicago, Ill: Montgomery Ward & Co.,
    1903.

————. 1930.

National Union Catalog: Pre–1956 Imprints. London: Mansell Publishers, 1968–.

"New Image Planned for Cuban Dolls." *Minneapolis Star*, July 2, 1974: 4B.

Pantovic, Stan. "Black Antiques Reveal History of Stereotypes." *Sepia* 23 (July 23,
    1974): 44–48.

Parker, Paula. "Contemptible Collectibles." *Perspectives: The Civil Rights Quarterly*
    12 (Spring 1980): 19–23.

Partridge, Eric. *Name This Child: A Dictionary of Modern British and American Given
    or Christian Names.* London: Hamish, Hamilton, 1951.

Rakstis, Ted J. "Debate in the Doll House." *Today's Health* 48 (December 1970): 28–
    31, 65–66.

Random House Dictionary of the English Language. New York: Random House, 1967.

Roget, Peter Mark. *Roget's Thesaurus of Synonyms and Antonyms.* New York: Alahad
    Books, 1972.

Rovner, Sandy "Oh, Barbie! Does Ken Know?" *The Washington Post* (March 8, 1985):
    B1, B4.

St. George, Eleanor. *The Dolls of Yesterday.* New York: Bonanza Books, 1948.

Schroeder, Joseph, ed. *The Wonderful World of Toys, Games, and Dolls.* Northfield,
    Ill.: Digest Books, 1971.

Sears, Roebuck & Company General Catalogue. Chicago, Ill.: Sears, Roebuck & Co.,
    1912.

————. 1928.

————. 1931.

Stowe, Harriet Beecher. *Uncle Tom's Cabin.* London: J. Cassell Publishers, 1852.

Swanberg, Nancy. *Dolls through the Ages.* San Francisco, Calif.: Troubador Press, 1979.

Symbols of American Libraries. 11th ed. Washington, D.C.: Library of Congress, 1976.

————. 13th ed. Washington, D.C.: Library of Congress, 1985.

Washington Afro-American, March 13, 1979: 14.

Webster's New World Dictionary of the American Language. New York: World Publishing
    Co., 1951.

Whitton, Blair. *The Knopf Collectors' Guide to American Toys.* New York: Alfred A.
    Knopf, 1984.

Wilkinson, Doris. "The Doll Exhibit: A Psycho-Cultural Analysis of Black Female Role
    Stereotypes." *Journal of Popular Culture* 21 (Fall 1987): 19–29.

————. "Play Objects as Tools of Propaganda: Characterizations of the African American
    Male." *Journal of Black Psychology* 7 (August 1980): 1–16.

————. "Racial Socialization through Children's Toys: A Sociohistorical Examination."
    Journal of Black Studies 5 (1974): 96–109.

————. "The Stigmatization Process: The Politicization of the Black Male's Identity."
    In *The Black Male in America: Perspectives on His Status in Contemporary
    Society.* Eds. Doris Wilkinson and Ronald Taylor. Chicago, Ill.: Nelson-Hall,
    1977, 145–58.

————. "Tactics of Protest as Media: The Case of the Black Revolution." *Sociological
    Focus* 3 (Spring 1970): 13–21.

Wilkinson, Doris, and Ronald Taylor, eds. *The Black Male in America: Perspectives on
    His Status in Contemporary Society.* Chicago, Ill.: Nelson-Hall, 1977.

Black Americana Resources and Collections: Evidences of Black Imagery

Black images in American culture traditionally have been studied through paintings, sculpture, and other works of art; through historical documents, personal papers, treatises, and works of history; through fiction, poetry, and literary works; through the music and songs by Black Americans or those who wrote about them; and through an examination of other subject areas. Scholarship is lacking in the study of that category of Black Americana commonly known as artifacts or memorabilia. Considering the virtually limitless scope of Black memorabilia, for the collector this may be a monumental but rewarding task. Donna C. Kaonis elaborates on this point as she notes the range of materials that the collector of such works may own: antique advertising, artwork, books, clocks, dolls, ephemera, fine china, folk art, humidors, linens, sheet music, sports memorabilia, toys, or other items. Whether the items are produced commercially or by other means, Kaonis notes that they may be "outrageously stereotypical or exquisitely beautiful examples of Black culture" (Kaonis 33). Interestingly, however, within these evidences of Black culture are certain recurring motifs that are worthy of further examination and that will be identified subsequently in this chapter. Thus, the relationship between images of Black Americans as depicted in printed works and other areas of artistic creativity and those presented in various forms of memorabilia deserves systematic examination and interpretation to give more comprehensive values to the imagery. For researchers and the advanced collector of Black Americana, the two fields increasingly are assuming new meanings, and scholars may search for visual as well as printed examples of American culture. The surge of interest in Black collectibles, however, demonstrates a need to document the origins and meanings of the images that are found.

This reference work has been designed to bridge the gaps between the two fields and to stimulate further research and inquiry into the subject matter.

Discussion is given to the evidences of Black images in American culture, the manufacturers' reasons for creating the items, reasons for collecting, and the location or identification of resources. Except for the ubiquitous lawn jockey, Aunt Jemima, Uncle Ben, blackface comedians of earlier years, Amos 'n' Andy team, and a few other figures, the range of items and images is relatively foreign to the average American. While visual representations may be seen, as for example in the surging craft now labeled folk art where the watermelon-eaters and mammy figures abound, the full range of subject matter and objects is generally unknown. As this work builds bridges to understanding American culture and the images within it, it should also stimulate other research endeavors to bring the study of this subject matter into full flower.

EVIDENCES OF BLACK IMAGES IN AMERICAN CULTURE

The literature of Black images in American culture and the visual depictions of these images are being collected under the rubric of Black Americana, Black artifacts, Black collectibles, Black memorabilia, Negroabilia, niggerbilia (used by whites in some circles), and other names that are far less complimentary and descriptive than any given in this list. Some artists refer to the highly stereotypical works as inflammatory art. For the purposes of this chapter, the first four terms will be used interchangeably; however, the primary emphasis is on the images that the items portray.

The various chapters in this book document the negative, positive, mixed, and confused images of Blacks during the years of this country's existence. In each instance, however, some images are clearly discernable as threads that permeate subject matter and subsequently have been reinforced through visual representations in memorabilia. This research has shown that the image makers spared no opportunity to portray Blacks on various objects common in everyday life for those who chose to use them. While historically not all of the images have been degrading, and some are clearly works of art, many that have been in the general public's view or popularly promoted in books, films, yard art, and novelty items have been primarily negative or stereotypical. The finer works, such as Nippon or Staffordshire china, are so exquisite that some scholars and collectors disregard them as Black memorabilia items.

Many forms of Black memorabilia that flourished in popular culture from the mid–1800s to the late 1950s were produced in the industrial northern United States and sometimes were imported from Germany, England, Japan, and a few other countries. The highly agricultural South, complete with Blacks who served in a variety of roles, had neither the desire nor the commercial means to reproduce novelties of its slaves, free Blacks, or servants; they could observe them daily in the roles that the memorabilia supposedly showed them practicing. But for the industrial North, where fewer Blacks resided (and in some instances, in the earlier years, no Blacks were seen), the need to make their own "brutes" or "exotic primitives" seemed to be a compelling one. On this issue, noted collector

Ronald Carr commented that Blacks were used as subject matter because they attracted attention. He found that the Japanese considered Blacks unusual; Germans thought that Blacks were inferior; other countries that produced Black items were inspired by the far-reaching effects of slavery. Carr also found that some of the works were items of affection, such as the "caring mammy" and the "jolly minstrel." Moreover, trade cards used extensively between 1870 and 1880 were neither designed nor used to portray negative images. In later years, we drew negative conclusions to many of the items that had been produced. Many of the negative views of Black artifacts emerged from people in the lower economic strata. The motion picture industry compounded these views through the stereotypical and demeaning roles that Black actors and actresses played. Blacks, therefore, have been a contradiction (telephone conversation with Ronald Carr, September 9, 1986; see also Kader).

Other views on the historical depictions of Blacks in artifacts are documented in many references given throughout this volume. Like other cultural minorities, entities that are different are sometimes pronounced and attract attention. In any culture, there is a majority (or dominate) group, and minority (or subordinate) group. The desire to remain a majority is a natural one; therefore, other cultures that are different fail to fit into the majority mold. If ridiculed, as, for example through cultural artifacts, the minority culture is easier for the majority to accept. The pattern that follows is like that of voodoo worship—a way to release tension and frustration. Whites increasingly had difficulty accepting the idea that the U.S. slavery system had ended; thus, the idea of creating a pseudo-slave state seemed tenable and ludicrous. Historically, then, we see in the artifacts an array of slave likenesses, grotesques, subordinates, infantiles, and items that extol the virtues of Blacks as well. Carr's "Black contradiction" theory is therefore reinforced. This chapter makes no effort to delve further into the meanings and contradictions of Black Americana; rather, it gives examples of the material items in American culture that reinforce the images identified in the preceding chapters and refers the researcher to examples of the images in collections and in pertinent reference works in which they are illustrated, discussed, analyzed, and interpreted. The researcher needs only to examine the products of the artists cited in chapter 1 or to view the paintings and prints that Black Americana collectors seek today to capture the variety of images in paintings. The range is from Currier and Ives' "Darktown Series" to prints of watermelon-eating children, to the Harry Roseland series on children and Black women, to prints of Henry O. Tanner's famous *Banjo Lesson*. Further, Black memorabilia that strengthens Driskell's findings may be seen in Nardi's sculptures on the watermelon eaters as illustrated in the discussion of Carr's collection in the September/ October 1982 issue of *Collectors' Showcase* (Kader 8).

The two popular minstrel figures—Jim Crow, a buffoon characterized by poverty and limited mental capability, and Zip Coon, a citified dandy who wore exotic dress and was equipped with a zest for using malapropisms—are discussed in chapters 2 and 4 and are alluded to in other chapters as well. These stage comics embellish the covers of sheet music (particularly coon songs), adorn publicity materials for stage acts, and promote other negative and stereotypic views of Blacks in musical forms. Blacks as entertainers are easily available in the existing figurines, toys, and in almost any imaginable form. Both Zip Coon and Jim Crow, or the images they represent, serve as models for items depicting children or adult males, for it is common to find the Black figures dressed in the style of either character.

Uncle Toms, pickaninnies, mammies, coons, faithful servants, comics, savages, and contented slaves have been shown in both films and on television. The "tragic mulatto," damned for reasons that were not of her making, also emerges in the media, as does the stereotypical image of the highly sexual Black male and female. Some of the erotic collectibles found in the various collections identified illustrate these images.

Interestingly, Harriet Beecher Stowe's *Uncle Tom's Cabin* is mentioned in several of the chapters of this book, including chapter 5. Collectors discussed later in this chapter show less concern for developing extensive collections of the slave narrative, treatises, books, and other works that Clift-Pellow analyzes in chapter 5 and that preserve the full range and scope of the Black image in literature. But the collector has access to many literary works, some rare and choice first editions and some that are merely old and of dubious value.

Images of the pickaninny, mammy, Sambo, and the exotic primitive abound in early works for young people. The same was true of the terminology used, such as "shine," "coon," and "darkey." *Little Black Sambo*, published in various editions and also used to inspire the creation of games and toys, developed from a pleasant, fantasy picture book for children into one that defied every positive image that educators, librarians, and parents would want for Black children or for whites who were unfamiliar with Black culture. Other works, such as *Ten Little Niggers*, followed *Little Black Sambo* in the range of toys, pipe racks, and other items inspired by the book's images. These two works are popular items for the collector of black memorabilia. Collector Edgar Orchard of Missouri has obtained at least 28 versions of *Sambo*.

One of the strongest and most popular Black images in American culture is that of the female figure. The wide range of imagery has been promoted through advertisements, toys, household items, dolls, and every object imaginable. While the female character's image ranges from innocence to sexuality and from a lovable figure in the plantation "big house" to the defiant Sapphire, the mammy dolls, cookie jars, and salt and pepper shakers that portray some of these images are among the most widely collected items on the Black Americana market.

By contrast, Sambo and many other Black male figures were popular yet never fully enjoyed the strong, dominant role of mammy and the female. Collections of Black Americana document the Sambo or Sambo-like image among children and adults as well. In the mammy and Uncle Mose salt and pepper shakers, for example, the researcher observes frequently the male figure portraying a subordinate role to the female, depending, of course on the design of the item and

16. Glazed ceramic figure depicting the stereotype of the Black shoeshine boy. From the editor's collection. Photo by Vando Rogers.

on mammy's pose. But there are also sexually explicit items such as incense burners, novelties, and prints that demean children and adults; strength seems to be less important. Toys which further promote the comical, infantile male refer to him as "jigger," "coon," "Rastus," "dandy," or "Jazzbo Jim." In the case of some toys where two males are shown, they are referred to by catchy titles such as "Ham and Sam," "Hot and Tott," and "Spic and Span." (See illustrations in Kader 12.) Toy banks, some of which are rare and costly, are among the most stereotypical of all the items produced. Examples of the highly stereotypical ones that show male and female images are the "Jolly Nigger," its female counterpart "Dinah," and "The Stump Speaker." Bill Norman's *The*

17. Salt and pepper shakers, depicting the mulatto image. From the editor's collection. Photo by Vando Rogers.

Bank Book: The Encyclopedia of Mechanical Bank Collecting (1984) gives good illustrations of toy banks.

Male images as seen in such toys as the "Whistling Coon," "Jolly Nigger" puzzle, "Charleston Trio," and "Hey, Hey the Chicken Snatcher" show the recurring motifs discussed in various chapters. "Chicken Snatcher" reinforces the belief that Blacks were thieves, particularly when chickens were involved. One could also order by mail an appropriate costume to dress up and look like a Negro. The female image in toys includes the common Aunt Jemima but other dolls as well, such as "Beloved Belinda" and the "Black Mama Doll." Favorable images emerged in later years, as seen in the debut of the authentic Black doll. Toys, particularly dolls of all types, constitute a popular category among collectors. Of significance to this point is Len Hoyte's doll museum and collection of over 5,000 rare and antique dolls, many of which are Black. The reader should also see Ronald Carr's extensive list of box games that constituted a part of his collection before it was dispersed in 1986 (Carr, "Box Games" 5–6).

The vast number of cultural images and objects of material culture paralleled the ebb and tide of efforts to promote more wholesome race relations in this

18. "Lift Every Voice and Sing," reproduction of a work of art created by Augusta Savage for the New York World's Fair, 1939. From the editor's collection. Photo by Vando Rogers.

country. J. Stanley Lemons notes further the use of Blacks as comic figures in the period from the late nineteenth century forward. His article "Black Stereotypes as Reflected in Popular Culture: 1880–1920" notes that Blacks as entertainers and comics emerged twice in popular culture, and, at each time, race relations were poor (Lemons 104).

Collections and literature of Black Americana provide sources for study and new interpretations of events. For example, Thomas "Daddy" Rice has been credited for originating and popularizing the "Jim Crow" figure and act in minstrelsy. But an "Anonymous American" who wrote a small treatise on *The*

19. Woodcarvings showing the Black preacher and other stereotypes. Courtesy of James Cheek. Photo by Vando Rogers.

Origin of Jim Crow: Being an Authentic Account of the Life and Adventures of the Comic American Nigger, Jim Crow . . . (1937) gives another view. His claim is that a young man of South American Indian ancestry was sold into slavery, and while living on the plantation he was taught "Anglo-American niggerisms." One of his "nigger songs" was "Jump Jim Crow." The song and accompanying act were picked up by an old, deformed Black man from whom Rice learned the act and later made famous.

The researcher and collector of Black Americana must do more than examine the materials and form statements about their beauty, ugliness, distastefulness, or impropriety. They must question the portraits that the materials represent, analyze the reproductions of persons real or imagined, know the historical developments of the images or materials, and understand the social context in which they were created or flourished. Very often an idea originated in a positive vein and deteriorated into a negative one. For example, historically, the lawn jockey consistently aroused anger among Blacks and some whites, and perhaps curiosity among other cultural groups. Several legends that have caused mixed responses have circulated about the jockey's origin. Sometimes called "Jocko Graves," Earl Koger asserts in "The Legend of Jocko: The Negro Boy Who

Inspired George Washington'' that the lawn jockey was created to honor a young, courageous Black boy who performed a noble deed for General George Washington. It adorned the lawn of Washington's mansion (Koger n.p.).

William H. Siebert gives another explanation of the jockey, or ''iron manikin [sic].'' In *The Mysteries of Ohio's Underground Railroads* (1951), he states that one abolitionist operated an ''interrupted station'' on the underground railroad, ''a condition silently advertised to . . . conductors and their parties by the flag in the manikin's hand, or its absence.'' The appearance of the flag meant that the station was open for passengers (Siebert 145–46). Views on the black jockey legend are also given in ''The Hitching Post.''

Whether or not one accepts either legend, the black jockey figure also yields a positive image and should provide inspiration for students of Black history. Records show that Black jockeys played a key role in the shaping of American racing history. Of the fifteen riders in the inaugural Kentucky Derby, fourteen were Black. Oliver Lewis rode H. P. McGrath's Aristides to victory in the first ''Run for the Roses'' held in 1875; Isaac Murphy was the greatest jockey in history. In the early years of the racing event, Murphy led horses to win three Kentucky Derbys. ''Black Jockeys Shaped Early Churchill Kentucky Derby History'' in the *Churchill Downs News* illustrates the early Black jockey history.

Examination of images of Blacks in material culture shows that the Jim Crow, Zip Coon, and Sambo-type characters continue; that is, the use of bright colors, swallowtail coats, tattered clothing, or childlike figures are prevalent. This is true whether or not the item is in the form of a toy (the ''Jolly Nigger Bank''), a toothpick holder, or other collectible. Even when children are used in the artifact the same appearance is suggested. As noted earlier, a young child may be dressed in clothing that closely resembles or duplicates that worn by both minstrel figures.

In addition to minstrel characters, other stereotypes were popular. One prime example is the Black servant. In fact, use of Blacks as servants, such as mammies, butlers, and cooks, has been common. Images also include those of ministers, deacons, and musical comics or entertainers. Uncle Tom was common, as were Rastus and Sambo (mentioned earlier). While originally treated in illustrations as humans, by the 1880s Blacks became coarse, grotesque caricatures. They were ugly, animal-like, and obviously never neutral in the view which they aimed to represent. In many instances, too, grotesques were created more for comedy. This period may well be called the grotesque era, for the image was extended to whites and to other ethnic minorities. Examples of these images seen on trade cards, greeting cards, toys, and elsewhere, showed Blacks with oversized mouths, ears, hands, and feet. Again the ''Jolly Nigger Bank'' is a prime example, to which is added a sloping forehead clearly suggesting limited intelligence. Its counterpart ''Dinah'' extended the image to women.

The literature shows that such stereotypes or images in American culture remained near the turn of the century—so much so that some scholars suggest that ''honest'' whites had no idea that they were degrading to Blacks and to

20. Postcard portraying the stereotyped image in dress, and association with razors. From the editor's collection. Photo by Vando Rogers.

other groups. Many thought that they were simply funny. Even so, the images continued to spread, and the trade cards of that day did a very good job of promoting them. For example, one trade card advertising Fairy Soap shows a young white girl asking a stereotyped Black girl, "Why doesn't your mammy wash you with Fairy Soap?" thus rendering the two more alike in color. Similarly, a trade card for Coats and Clark thread shows a young Black boy sitting in the sun as the sun frowns upon him; the commentary reads, "We never fade." Aiden Fruit Vinegar trade cards show Blacks as chicken-stealing, watermelon-eating brutes. The Fourteenth Amendment and other Reconstruction amendments were not spared, as some of the cards of the 1880s found fun in them. One trade card for Magnolia Meat shows several Blacks eating a large ham while declaring, "What de use talkin' 'bout dem 'mendments?"

Use of caricatures or stereotypes of Blacks in cartoons has been widespread. Some show Blacks stealing or chasing chickens, shining shoes, or eating watermelon or show a wedding party whose characters are stereotyped.

Research for this chapter identified many collections that contain figural items with sexual connotations, thus reinforcing in visual form some of the stereotypes discussed in chapters 3, 5, 7, and 8. This discussion thus far shows that the creators of Black images in American culture have seized countless opportunities to produce and promote them. Black Americans have not been the only cultural minority group subjected to such forms of dehumanization; however, they have borne the brunt of them. Jewish, German, Mexican Americans, and American Indians frequently have also been targets of ridicule; of literary and cultural abuse, as seen in minstrel sketches (''The Coon and the Chink''); of signs (''No Dogs, Negroes, Mexicans''); and of other forms. Items known as Black collectibles and the images that they represent fail to achieve all that their creators expected. To render Blacks childlike, indolent, and grotesque through artifacts, books and other materials does not, in fact, cause Blacks to live up to these expectations. Since the items neither altered history nor actually caused Blacks to fit into one or two stereotypical molds, at best they only misguided the uninformed reader and viewer. If actually viewed, however, the materials in this chapter show that many of the negative images overpower the positive ones, thus giving some readers the impression that all of the items are stereotypical or negative. In reality, an image is negative or positive, depending on how one perceives it, and, as earlier noted, while an idea that is conceived as positive may degenerate into a negative one, the reverse may also happen. Fortunately, this is evident in the development and popularization of many Black collectibles.

ON COLLECTING BLACK MATERIALS

Why collect Black Americana? The literature on collectors shows an enormous range of interest and activities that extend from philatelists, numismatists, bibliophiles, and doll collectors. Their interests developed from an equally wide range of reasons—the gift of an item as a child, the presence of such items in the home, or simply a fascination or curiosity for the subject matter and representations of it. In gathering material for this chapter, collectors were asked to indicate their reasons for collection and to tell how their collecting practices began. Some, though not all, of the respondents supplied this information. For additional information on this question, the reader is referred to the end of the description of each private collection where the responses are located.

Evidences of positive Black images in the collections identified in this research are noteworthy. Interestingly, such collectors have very strong reasons for collecting Black Americana. An outstanding illustration is the Madame C. J. Walker collection in the hands of her granddaughter, A'Lelia Bundles. (The Indiana Historical Society also has an extensive collection of Walker memorabilia.) The Bundles collection consists of family items saved through the years and includes clothing, Black hair care and cosmetics items, advertising materials, correspondence, and other materials that document the life of this philanthropist, businesswoman, and entrepreneur. The materials have a very special meaning and help preserve and document the history of the Walker family. Naomi Wright of Maryland collects greeting cards, silver spoons, photographs, and an array of items that present a positive view. These items also document the wide range

21. Photograph showing Mrs. Paul Laurence Dunbar and scenes from Black life in America. Courtesy of Special Collections, Fisk University Library.

Mrs. Paul L. Dunbar

of materials that have been created in a positive vein. Elizabeth Norris of New York, a founder of the Council on Interracial Books for Children, extended her interest in removing negative and stereotypical images by collecting historical works and memorabilia that accomplished this end. Larry Lester of Kansas concentrates on Black baseball memorabilia (coins, stamps, and items from Black leagues) that present realistic and positive images of Blacks in American history. The collection is used for research, exhibits, and lectures, particularly to young people who are unfamiliar with Black history.

Some collectors are attracted to the negative and stereotypical images that others hold in disdain. For example, several respondents commented on their admiration of "those big red lips" of mammy figures, or the adorable Black, fat mammy cookie jar, or the cuteness of a pickaninny doll. Collector Pat Antonick of Ohio concentrates on highly stereotypical items that show Blacks with crocodiles, monkeys, cotton, and watermelon; however, her efforts grew out of curiosity rather than a desire to demonstrate prejudices. The same is true of Joseph A. Jacovino of Pennsylvania, whose collection is stereotypic in the use of Blacks to advertise products in specific areas from 1840 to 1900. For example, items in his collection show Blacks advertising agricultural equipment, shoe polish, clothing, foods, furniture, hardware, varnishes, thread, medicine, soaps, and starches.

There are collectors, most of whom are Black, whose primary interest is in gathering materials broad in subject matter and varied in the images that they represent, but who follow what this author identifies as the Schomburg syndrome—a desire to collect rigorously on Black themes and a mania for completeness of subject representations. Arthur Alfonso Schomburg (1874–1938), a Puerto Rican partly of Negro descent, noted bibliophile, and builder of the collections at Fisk University and at the Schomburg Center for Research in Black Culture in New York, set out early to disprove an elementary school teacher's claim that Blacks had no history. His personal collection had an international flavor, for Schomburg acquired Black materials on numerous subjects from all around the world. He employed bibliographic detective work so essential for one who has a mania for completeness. Schomburg explored publishers' catalogs and bibliographies in books, pamphlets, and obscure and well-known works with a view toward documenting history as a matter of record rather than a debatable issue. The pioneering and exhaustive efforts of Schomburg and other book collectors are discussed in Arna Bontemps, "Special Collections of Negroana."

LOCATING BLACK AMERICANA

This pioneer work has been limited to locating and identifying sources of Black Americana available in select collections throughout the United States. In this section of the chapter, data have been gathered through the following means: (1) the identification of collectors and dealers available from subscribers to Black Americana newsletters and recommendations from known collectors; (2) the distribution of questionnaires to collectors and dealers to determine their collecting interests and to obtain a description of the materials gathered; (3) consultation with scholars in the field, particularly those who at the time of the research had assembled collections; (4) consultation with dealers and examination of their materials; (5) visits to flea markets, antique shops, private collections, and collections in a select number of libraries and museums; and (6) a review of the published works that appear at the end of this chapter. The research explored the histories of the development of the collections, the geographic locations, the types of materials assembled, the existence of catalogs or indexes to the materials, and the special character of the collections.

As with other fields of study, research is never complete. Lacking in this case is the ability to assess more fully the range, scope, quality, and dispersion of materials. While the questionnaires and consultations revealed a wealth of information, the research also showed that numerous "closet" collectors exist. As far as can be determined, many are advanced collectors. Some live in California, Florida, Maryland, New York, and in the New England states. Their reasons for anonymity range from security of resources to an inability to negotiate with dealers when the potential value of a collection is known. Malinda Saunders estimated in an article on "Focusing on Black Art and Artifacts" that there are approximately 1,000 Black Americana collectors in the United States (Berry 12). This figure is at best a conservative estimate, for not only do "closet" collectors exist but countless numbers of other people have entered the arena. Don Kader believes that the number of avid collectors has decreased in the last few years from 10,000 to approximately 8,000 (from a conversation in Pasadena, California, on May 3, 1987). On the other hand, collector Larry Lester estimates that there are from 250 to 300 serious collectors of Black images (in a letter to Jessie Carney Smith dated February 9, 1987). The latter statements are tenable, for the size of many collections ranges from a few items to a large number; some collections are purposefully limited in scope and size. Until the extensive collections are pulled together in museums and libraries, closet collections are publicized, and more known collectors report the content of their resources, knowledge of the full range and scope of Black Americana available will remain fragmented.

Research shows further that there are among the circuit of known collectors several who also are advanced collectors. While the full list need not be given here, collectors who fit this category at the time of the research include Lillian Anthony (Georgia), Pat Bacon (Nevada), Marguerite Ross Barnett (Missouri), Diane Cauwels (Tennessee), Janette Faulkner (California), James Gregg (Maryland), Dick Horlick (California), Mildred Franklin (New York), Lenon Hoyte (New York), Paul Jeromack (Maryland), Gary Snell (California), and Edgar Orchard (Missouri). Their collections comprise extensive amounts of materials in many categories, or they are limited to an extensive number of items in a specific category, such as dolls, cookie jars, salt and pepper shakers, or postcards, or they are limited to specific themes, such as Blacks and watermelons. Such collections, vital sources for primary research on Black collectibles, provide new insights into Black and American history and culture. In the compilation of reference works recently published, both Dawn Reno, author of *Collecting Black Americana* (1986), and P. J. Gibbs, author of *Black Collectibles Sold in America* (1986), drew upon the resources in more than one collection. The specialized nature of some collections, coupled with the personal interests of the collector, result in the different character that the materials gathered will have. The researcher will benefit from the advanced collector's expertise, the resources that are available in a single source, and the rare finds that may be included in a modest collection of little note.

Current trends in the development of this field make interesting study. Several advanced collectors who are also scholars of Black Americana have dispersed their materials, thus making the resources available to a greater number of collectors. An early, advanced collector who initiated the trend is Ronald Rooks of Baltimore, Maryland, who in 1982 began to sell portions of his enormous collection of over 300 choice items through auction. Until that time, and as far as this research could determine, the nation had never had such a major sale of Black Americana. Since his first sale, many materials previously hidden subsequently resurfaced. The content of his collection, assembled over a thirty-year period, is described in the auction catalogues that accompanied his sales (Rooks 1983, 1984). Rooks sold his collection because he "thought it was time to sell, and to bring items into the limelight." He also shifted emphasis from collecting in the field to appraising antiques and collectibles and to working with dealers (conference with Ronald Rooks on February 20, 1987). Rooks is consulted frequently not only for advice on items for sale but also for his opinions for research and publication projects on this topic, such as John Denis Mercier's doctoral dissertation, "The Evolution of the Black Image in White Consciousness, 1876–1954: A Popular Culture Perspective (1984)."

Before dispersing his materials primarily through auctions in 1986, Ronald Carr of California held the largest collection known in the world. Partial descriptions of the Carr collection of numerous rareties manufactured in the United States and in other parts of the world have been published with illustrations in *Collector's Showcase* (Kader 8–17) and in various sections of *Black Collectibles*. His collection of over 5,000 items served as an index to the scope and variety of the resources produced. Seventy-five percent of the items were unique, but Carr acknowledges that whenever he visited other collections he always saw items that he had not previously known, thus attesting to the enormous size of the Black Americana pool of resources (telephone conference with Ronald Carr on September 9, 1986). Like Rooks, Carr is a scholar in this subject area, and he has generously offered his services as advisor, consultant, or appraiser at Black memorabilia shows and auctions and to researchers.

A third advanced collector who has subsequently dispersed his collection is Don Kader, also of California. The Kader collection of over 2,000 items was sold privately between 1985 and 1986. For a good pictorial view of the collection, the reader should purchase the videotape of the Kader collection (see bibliography at the end of this chapter). The videotape is also useful for educational purposes.

The toy collectors and other collectors as well welcomed an opportunity to enhance their resources through purchases from the sale of materials in Atlanta's Toy Museum. The first sale was held at auction on October 3–4, 1986, and others followed. While the collection was not exclusively Black, it contained a number of rare and unusual items that were in demand such as folk dolls, mechanical toys, and marionettes. Materials from the first sale are described and illustrated in the catalog for the Toy Museum of Atlanta listed in the bibliography for this chapter.

Other collectors, some advanced, some with interesting specialities, some whose collections are small, but eclectic in subject matter, continuously offer their materials to dealers for resale. The popularity of the subject matter, however, has stimulated considerable interest in building new collections or augmenting older ones to meet personal interests. Since collectors often exchange materials through swap meets or private contact, it is possible that items that fit a particular collector's interest may be easily acquired. This practice is also stimulated through advertisements in the *Antique Gazette*, *Antique Trader*, and other similar means.

TRENDS IN COLLECTING AND PROMOTING BLACK AMERICANA

In addition to the activities of American collectors in recent years noted above, a number of trends in the field of Black Americana have been established. These are important for the leads that they provide to the researcher of Black and American popular culture and history. On this issue, Marguerite Ross Barnett makes an interesting and important observation:

Although it is often painful to view these items [the artifacts], they are extremely significant to black scholars and the black community in general because they provide a crucial historical and cultural link from the past to the present. Because these materials depicting the pervasiveness and historical continuity of negative images of blacks have not been generally well known, there is a serious gap in our knowledge of the rise, subconscious internalization and stubborn persistence of racism against blacks. While there is a general, albeit vague, awareness that rationalizations of the subordinate position of blacks have been rooted in an ideology of black inferiority, what is less well known is that American popular culture has been an important vehicle for transmission of those ideological notions (Barnett 82).

Thus, the theses of scholars only a few years ago bear study from a variety of current perspectives. Barnett's views, along with those of collectors Mary Kimbrough, Janette Faulkner, Naomi Wright, and others have served as catalysts for the research that P. J. Gibbs has completed for *Black Collectibles Sold in America*, for John Denis Mercier's doctoral dissertation, for Sam Denison's classic work, *Scandalize My Name: Black Imagery in American Popular Music* (1982), and for new interpretations that are under way or that, hopefully, will be stimulated as result of the present reference volume and other works.

A brief accounting of activities in this field may suggest new areas for research:

1. There is a surging interest among Blacks in collecting Black Americana (including items with positive images as well as grotesques, segregation signs, lawn jockeys, mammy figures, pickaninny dolls, and other items that historically were insulting to Blacks). (Rooks noted in his conference with me on February 20, 1987 that the racial composition of buyers at his first sale was 15 percent Black and 85 percent white; his second sale, 40 percent Black and 60 percent white; and his final sale, 70 percent Black and 30 percent white. Ninety percent of the Blacks in attendance were from the District of Columbia, Maryland, New York, and Pennsylvania.) The primary interest is in identifying unknown parts of Black history and collecting visual representations of it.

2. There is a continuing and renewed interest in collecting among some white Americans; others have developed new interests along these lines.

3. Other cultural minority groups are collecting Black Americana as well as items pertinent to their own history. The attitude is one of sympathy toward others who have been enslaved, and inherent empathy in ties that bind groups (conference with Edgar Orchard on September 9, 1986).

4. The consequences of items 1 and 2 are a rigorous demand for almost any items that are remotely Black related; the costs for such items are becoming astronomical, and competition for purchases is keen.

5. Blacks have developed skills and expertise in identifying and appraising these materials and are beginning to enter businesses for themselves.

6. Items that were available on the market prior to the civil rights movement went underground during the movement but have resurfaced.

7. The major collections of Black Americana have been assembled privately and remain in private hands.

8. With few exceptions, the larger known collections are located outside the South.

9. The demand for Black Americana has stimulated several markets: acknowledged reproductions, unacknowledged fakes, and a surging interest in new folk items which show in new guises many of the stereotypical figures of earlier times.

10. Libraries and museums remain the primary source of the print media—books, periodicals, broadsides, art, and other historical documents that are useful to aid in interpreting Black history. These repositories note the need to collect and preserve historical documents in the form of artifacts as well.

What is important is the emotional acceptance that the Black community, especially, and the whole community, as well, are now making of another segment of American history and culture. They are now learning more about white America's shaping of the Black past and of images that whites had of Blacks. If current trends in collecting, preserving, promoting, and researching

Black American images continue, the diversity of ways in which Blacks contributed to or were viewed in American history and popular culture will be more widely known and understood.

THE SEARCH PROCESS

Findings in this exploration indicate that the collecting of Black Americana is still a virgin field. Many collectors are at the point where bibliophies in Black bibliography were twenty years or more ago. By comparison, bibliographer Monroe Nathan Work and scholar W. E. B. DuBois were concerned with bibliographical control of the vast amount of materials published in the early 1900s. Arthur A. Schomburg, Arthur Spingarn, and James P. Slaughter were to the book world what Ronald Rooks and Ronald Carr have been to the black memorabilia collector. The bibliophiles exhausted every known lead to works by and about Blacks on the many subjects and in a variety of languages. Professional guidance and advice are essential to the development of a good, balanced collection, whether that balance is within a specialized area or spans a broader range. Within this field, the problem of information access is wanting. Both the newer and retrospective price guides and lists are incomplete, and there is no volume comparable to Work's *A Bibliography of the Negro in Africa and America* (1928) which provides the indexing needed for these early stages of a developing field. The subject matter needs comprehensive guides and should be indexed, whether it is all encompassing or restricted to specific subject matter, such as Black salt and pepper shakers, Black cookie jars, Black majolica, or Black banks. Extensive narratives, historical documentation, illustrations, and locations should be included. Snell's forthcoming volume on Black salt and pepper shakers and Black banks typifies the type of research and publication needed in the field. In addition, the use of new technologies in accessing materials, sources, collectors, researchers, and similar data is ideally suited to the control of information on this theme.

Through the survey process for this chapter, 450 collectors were identified (including some dealers who also collect). Of that figure, 225 responded; most of these are included in the list of collectors below. Those who were eliminated had recently dispersed their collections, had only a few items, or were concentrating on subjects other than Black memorabilia. As noted earlier, the actual number of collectors is unknown, not only because of the "closet" collectors who wish to remain anonymous and whose anonymity is respected here, but because of the vast number of persons who do not appear on various lists, who are not registered with dealers, but who may, indeed, have unique items that remain unidentified. Dealers who have responded as collectors are included in the two categories. Thus, the importance of locating as many collections as possible is a critical issue.

While the advanced collector has already been discussed, hopefully that collector, as well as those who are just embarking on this venture, know the history of Black people and the periods that the materials address. Items are meaningless unless they can be related to actual time periods in American history and culture. When were they created? What was happening at that time? Thus, references given with each chapter will lead the collector to important sources for developing or enriching background that will make the art of collecting more rewarding and will provide new avenues for students and scholars of Black history.

The sections below have been grouped under the following primary and secondary headings: (1) Sources of Materials (list of galleries, museums, and historical societies (by state); libraries, research centers, and information centers (by state); private collectors (by state); dealers; and designers and manufacturers); (2) Collectors' Clubs; and (3) Exhibitions, Shows and Sales, and Special Programs. Attention is called to the introduction to the final section, "Bibliography," which guides the researcher and the collector to vital reference sources on Black Americana that conclude the chapter.

SOURCES OF MATERIALS

Selected List of Galleries, Museums, and Historical Societies

The African-American Museum Association, 1111 E Street, N. W., Suite B500 Washington, D.C. 20004 publishes a list of member museums and gives the names of the chief officer, curator, or other official. The list that follows includes some, but not all, Black museums. Those that are Black owned or operated or that concentrate on Black materials are indicated by an asterisk (*).

Alabama

*George Washington Carver Museum, Tuskegee University, Tuskegee, AL 36088.
*Southeastern Center for Afro-American Architecture, Tuskegee University, 308 Gregory Street, Tuskegee, AL 36088.

California

*Brockman Gallery, 4334 Degnan Building, Los Angeles, CA 90008.
*California Afro-American Museum, 700 State Drive, Los Angeles, CA 90037.
*Dunbar Hotel Cultural and Historical Museum, 6565 Sunset Boulevard, Suite 525, Los Angeles, CA 90028.
*East Bay Negro Historical Society, 5606 San Pablo Avenue, Oakland, CA 94608.
*Ebony Museum, 582 14th Street, Oakland, CA 94612.
*Museum of African American Art, 4005 Crenshaw Boulevard, 3rd Floor, Los Angeles, CA 90008.
*Museum of African American Art, 2617 Lincoln Boulevard, Suite 207, Santa Monica, CA 90405.
National Minority Military Museum Foundation, 549 Kerr Hall, University of California, Davis, CA 95616.
* San Francisco African-American Historical and Cultural Society, Fort Mason Center, Building C, San Francisco, CA 94123.

Colorado

*Black American West Museum and Heritage Center, 608 26th Street, Denver, CO 80205.

Connecticut

*Connecticut Afro-American Historical Society, Inc., 444 Orchard Street, New Haven, CT 06511.

Delaware

*Afro-American Historical Society of Delaware, 512 East Fourth Street, Wilmington, DE 19801.

District of Columbia

*African Studies and Research Program, Howard University, P.O. Box 231, Washington, DC 20059.
*Anacostia Neighborhood Museum, Smithsonian Institution, 1901 Fort Place, SE, Washington, DC 20020.
*Barnett-Aden Gallery, 2825 31st Place, NE, Washington, DC 20018. (by appointment only)
*Bethune Museum-Archives, Bethune Historical Development Project, National Council of Negro Women, 1318 Vermont Avenue, NW, Washington, DC 20005.
*Evans-Tibbs Collection, 1910 Vermont Avenue, NW, Washington, DC 20001.
*Frederick Douglass Home, 1411 W Street, SE, Washington, DC 20020.
*Frederick Douglass Memorial and Historical Association, 14th and W Streets, SW, Washington, DC 20020.
*Howard University Gallery of Art, Howard University, 2455 6th Street, NW, Washington, DC 20059.
*Moorland-Spingarn Research Center, Howard University, 2455 6th Street, NW, Washington, DC 20059.
*Museum of African Art, 316 A Street, NE, Washington, DC 20002.
*National Museum of African Art, Smithsonian Institution, Washington, DC 20560.
*Smith-Mason Gallery, 1207 Rhode Island Avenue, NW, Washington, DC 20005.
*Tomorrow's World Art Center, P.O. Box 56197, Washington, DC 20011.

Florida

*Bethune-Cookman College, Carl S. Swisher Library, 640 2nd Avenue, Daytona Beach, FL 32015.
*Black Archives Research Center and Museum, Florida A&M University, P.O. Box 809, Tallahassee, FL 32307.
*Gallery Antigua, Inc., 5138 Biscayne Boulevard, Miami, FL 33137.
*Joseph E. Zee Memorial Library and Museum, Jacksonville Public Library, 122 North Ocean Street, Jacksonville, FL 32202.

Georgia

*African American Family Historical Association, P.O. Box 115268, Atlanta, Georgia 30310.
*Art N Artifacts Gallery, 531 1st Avenue, Columbus, GA 31901.

*Atlanta University, Waddell Gallery, Chesnut Street, SW, Atlanta, GA 30314.

*Atlanta University Center, Inc., Robert W. Woodruff Library, Virginia Lacy Jones Exhibition Gallery, 111 James P. Brawley Drive, SW, Atlanta, GA 30314.

*Collections of Life and Heritage, 135 Auburn Avenue, NE, Atlanta, GA 30303.

*Herndon Home, 587 University Place, NW, Atlanta, GA 30314.

*King Library and Archives, Martin Luther King, Jr. Center for Nonviolent Social Change, 503 Auburn Avenue, NE, Atlanta, GA 30312.

*Laney Walker Museum, 938 Wrightsboro Road, Augusta, GA 30312.

*Morris Brown College, Ruth Hodges Gallery, Atlanta, GA 30314.

Illinois

*The DuSable Museum of African-American History, 740 East 56th Place, Chicago, Illinois 60637.
Concentrates on art, books (500), photographs, and sculpture (over 500 items) by Africans and Black Americans. Collection also includes some Black Americana such as advertising buttons (2,000) and other advertisement materials, dolls (100), greeting cards (550), banks (15), household items (100), posters (200), record albums (100), sheet music (100), and souvenir items (100). Collection acquired through gifts (over 300 in the Victor A. Travis Collection) and purchases.

*Southside Community Art Center, 3831 South Michigan Avenue, Chicago, IL 60653.

Indiana

Indiana Historical Society, William Henry Smith Memorial Library, 315 West Ohio Street, Indianapolis, IN 46202.
Houses papers and effects of businesswoman and philanthropist Madame C. J. Walker. Readers should contact the society for content and use of the collection. Other materials include the Black Indiana Archives. See also Eric Pumroy, *A Guide to Manuscript Collections in Indiana Historical Society and Indiana State Library*. Indianapolis, 1986.

*Madam Walker Urban Life Center, Inc., 617 Indiana Avenue, Indianapolis, IN 46202.

Kansas

*First National Black Historical of Kansas, 601 North Water, Wichita, KS 67203.

Louisiana

*Amistad Research Center, Tulane University, New Orleans, LA 70118.

Tulane University, Howard Tilton Library, Feret and Newcomb Place, New Orleans, LA 70118.

Maryland

*Banneker-Douglas Museum, 84 Franklin Street, Annapolis, MD 21401.

*Coppin State University, Library, Baltimore, MD 21216.

*Gallery Ligon, P.O. Box 1105, Columbia, MD 21044.

*Great Blacks in Wax Museum, 1601 East North Avenue, Baltimore, MD 21205.

*Lillie Carol Jackson Museum, Inc., Civil Rights Museum, 1320 Eutaw Place, Baltimore, MD 21217.

*Maryland Community on Afro-American History and Culture, 84 Franklin Street, Annapolis, MD 21401.

Maryland Museum of American Art, P.O. Box 1105, Columbia, MD 21044.

*Morgan State University, Gallery of Art, Hillen and Coldspring Lane, Baltimore, MD 21239.

*Orchard Street Cultural Museum, 24 South Abington Avenue, Baltimore, MD 21229.

Massachusetts

*African American Masters Artists in Residency Program (AAMARP), Northeastern University, 360 Huntington Avenue, Building 590, Michelson Hall, Boston, MA 02115.

*Afro-American Cultural Center, 30 Concord Terrace, Springfield, MA 01109.

*Harriet Tubman Gallery, United Southend Settlement, 566 Columbus Avenue, Boston, MA 02118.

*Museum National Center of Afro-American Artists, 300 Walnut Avenue, Boston, MA 02119.

*Museum of Afro-American History, Abiel Smith School, 46 Joy Street Corner of Smith Court, Boston, MA 02114.

*Parting Ways, Museum of Afro-American Ethnohistory, 130 Court Street, P.O. Box 1776, Plymouth, MA 02360.

Michigan

*Afro-American Museum of Detroit, 1553 West Grand Boulevard, Detroit, MI 48208.

*Graystone International Jazz Museum, 716 Lothrop, Detroit, MI 48202.

*Michigan Ethnic Heritage Studies Center, 71 East Perry Street, Detroit, MI 48202.

*Museum of African American History, 1553 West Grand Boulevard, Detroit, MI 48208.

*Your Heritage House, 110 East Perry Street, Detroit, MI 48202.

Minnesota

*African American Cultural Center, 2429 South 8th Street, Minneapolis, MN 55454.

Mississippi

*Booker/Thomas Museum of Southern Artifacts, Highway 12, Lexington, MS 39095. Includes family memorabilia and other items.

*Smith Robertson Black Cultural Center, P.O. Box 3259 YWCA, Jackson, MS 39207.

Missouri

*Black Archives of Mid-America, 2033 Vine Street, Kansas City, MO 64108.

*Vaughn Cultural Center, 1408 North Kings Highway, St. Louis, MO 63113.

Nebraska

*Great Plains Black Museum, 2213 Lake Street, Omaha, NE 68110.

New Jersey

*African Arts Museum, S. M. A. Fathers, 23 Bliss Avenue, Tenafly, NJ 07670.

*Afro American Historical & Cultural Society of Jersey City, Inc., 1841 Kennedy Boulevard, Jersey City, NJ 07305.

*Carter G. Woodson Foundation, P.O. Box 1025, Newark, NJ 07101.

*Merabash Museum, P.O. Box 752, Willingboro, NJ 08046.

*NAACP Historical and Cultural Project, 441 Bergen Avenue, Jersey City, NJ 07304.

New York

*African American Museum, 110 North Franklin Street, Hempstead, NY 11550.

*Afro-American Cultural Center, 2191 7th Avenue, New York, NY 10027.

*Afro-American Cultural Foundation, Westchester Community College, 75 Grasslands Road, Valhalla, NY 10595.

*Afro-American Historical Society of the Niagara Frontier, P.O. Box 1663, Buffalo, NY 14216.

American Gallery, 996 Madison Avenue, New York, NY 10021.
        Rare toys.

American Hurrah, Joel and Kate Hopp, 766 Madison Avenue, New York, NY 10021.
        Folk art and early rag dolls.

Antique Supermarket, 84 Wooster Street, New York, NY 10012.
        Advertisements and toys.

*Aunt Len's Doll and Toy Museum, 6 Hamilton Terrace, New York, NY 10031, (212) 926–4172
        Contains more than 5,000 rare and antique dolls, including many that are Black. Some of the Black dolls were made in Europe in the nineteenth century for the American market, and many of these typify the stereotypes of the day (exaggerated features). Current Black dolls, such as Huggy Bean (manufactured in 1985 by a Black doll company) are included.

*Black Fashion Museum, Harlem Institute of Fashion, 157 West 126th Street, New York, NY 10027.

*Black History Exhibition Center, 106 North Main Street, Hempstead, NY 11550.

*Community Folk Art Gallery, 2223 East Genessee Street, Syracuse, NY 13210.

*Genesis II Museum of International Black Culture, 509 Cathedral Parkway, New York, NY 10025.

Grinnell Gallery, 800 Riverside Drive, New York, NY 10032.

Hillman-Gimini Antiques, 6743 Madison Avenue, New York, NY 10037.
        Fine antiques, banks, dolls, folk art, and toys.

*Museum of African and African-American Art and Antiquities, 11 East Utica Street, Buffalo, NY 14209.

Museum of American Folk-Art, 444 Park Avenue South, Fourth Floor, New York, NY 10016.
        Paintings by unknown twentieth-century artists; self-portraits by Mose Tolliver; paintings on tin, including one of Jackie Robinson by Sam Doyle; and miscellaneous black memorabilia.

Museum of the City of New York, Steven Miller, Senior Curator, Fifth Avenue at 103rd Street, New York, NY 10029, (212) 534–1672.
        Large selection of stereotypic prints (approx. 129) in the Currier & Ives Collection "Darktown" Series (reproductions of some slides in this series available). Miscellaneous advertisements, dolls, playbills, sheet music, toys, trade cards, and other prints. Available for research by appointment.

*New Muse Community Museum of Brooklyn, 1530 Bedford Avenue, Brooklyn, NY 11216.

*Schomburg Center for Research in Black Culture, New York Public Library, 515 Lenox
    Avenue, New York, NY 10037.
    See also under libraries.
*Society for Preservation of Weeksville and Bedford, P.O. Box 120, St. John Station,
    Brooklyn, NY 11213.
*Store Front Museum/Paul Robeson Theatre, 162–02 Liberty Avenue, Jamaica, NY
    11433.
*Studio Museum in Harlem, 144 West 125th Street, New York, NY 10027.
*319 Gallery, 319 West 108th Street, New York, NY 10025.

North Carolina

*African American Cultural and Service Center, 401 North Myers Street, Charlotte, NC
    28202.
*Heritage Center, North Carolina A&T State University, Greensboro, NC 27411, (919)
    379–7874.
    Includes furniture by Thomas Day, quilts, African art, and other works.
*Martin Luther King Museum of Black Culture, 511 North Henry Street, Eden, NC
    27288.
*North Carolina Central University Museum of Art, 1805 Fayetteville Street, Durham,
    NC 27707.
*YMI Cultural Center, 39 South Market Street, P.O. Box 7301, Asheville, NC 28801.

Ohio

*Afro-American Cultural Center, Cleveland State University, 2121 Euclid Avenue, Cleve-
    land, OH 44115.
*Afro-American Cultural and Historical Society Museum, 1765 Crawford Road, P.O.
    Box 20039, Cleveland, OH 44120.
Black Art Plus, 51 Parsons Avenue, Columbus, OH 43215.
*Black Studies Division, Western Reserve Historical Society, 10825 East Boulevard,
    Cleveland, OH 44106.
*Dunbar House State Memorial, 219 Summit Street, Dayton, OH 45407.
*Karamu House, 2355 East 89th Street, Cleveland, OH 44106.
*National Afro-American Museum and Culture Center, Wilberforce University, Wilber-
    force, OH 45384.
Resident Art and Humanities Consortium, Black History Museum, 1515 Linn Street,
    Cincinnati, OH 45214.
*Watkins Academy Museum of Cultural Arts, 724 Mineola Avenue, Akron, OH 44320.

Oklahoma

*Ntu Art Association, 2100 NE 52nd Street, Oklahoma City, OK 73111.

Pennsylvania

*Afro-American Historical and Cultural Museum, 7th and Arch Streets, Philadelphia,
    PA 19106.
The Balch Institute, 18 South 7th Street, Philadelphia, PA 19106, (215) 925–8090.
    The institute comprises an ethnic museum and research library/archive which
    actively collects on all American ethnic groups. Major holdings in Black Amer-

icana contain advertisements (including trade cards), books, greeting cards, posters, metal face masks, and miscellaneous items.

*Crispus Attucks Community Center, 605 South Duke Street, York, PA 17403.

*Historical Commission, Mother Bethel AME Church, 419 Richard Allen Avenue, Philadelphia, PA 19147.

*Ile Ife Center, 2544 Germantown Avenue, Philadelphia, PA 19133.

Pearlman Antique Toy Museum, 270 South Second Street, Philadelphia, PA 19106.
    Collection includes Black mechanical and still banks, dolls, and other toys.

*Selma Burke Art Center, 6118 Penn Circle South, Pittsburgh, PA 15206.

Rhode Island

*Rhode Island Black Heritage Society, 1 Hilton Street, Providence, RI 02905.

South Carolina

*Avery Institute, P.O. Box 2262, Charleston, SC 29403.

*Avery Research Center for Afro-American History and Culture, College of Charleston, Charleston, SC 29424.

*Mann Simon's Cottage, 1403 Richland Street, Columbia, SC 29201.

*Old Slave Mart Museum, P.O. Box 459, Sullivan's Island, SC 29482.

*Pendleton Foundation for Black History & Culture, P.O. Box 122, Pendleton, SC 29670.

*Penn Center, Fogmore, P.O. Box 126, St. Helena Island, SC 29920.

*South Carolina State College, I. P. Stanback Museum/Planetarium, Orangeburg, SC 29117.

Tennessee

*Beck Cultural Exchange Center, 1927 Dandridge Avenue, Knoxville, TN 37915.

*Fisk University, Aaron Douglas Gallery, University Library, Nashville, TN 37208.
    Collection of African artifacts and thirty portraits by Winold Reiss of Black folktypes; the William H. Johnson Collection of Black folk paintings.

*Fisk University, Carl Van Vechten Gallery, Todd Boulevard and Jackson Street, Nashville, TN 37208, (615) 329-8543, -8544.
    Works by renowned Black artists such as Richmond Barthé, Romare Bearden, Aaron Douglas, David C. Driskell, Earl Hooks, folk artist Clementine Hunter, Alma Thomas; famous painting of the Fisk Jubilee Singers by Edmund Havel (artist in the court of Queen Victoria who commissioned the work); extensive collection of African art. Murals by Aaron Douglas are located in the administration building.

Museum of Tobacco Art and History, 800 Harrison Street, Nashville, TN 37203.

Texas

*African American Cultural Heritage Center, Nolan Estes Educational Plaza, 3434 S. R. L. Thorton Freeway, Dallas, TX 75224.

*Carver Museum, Public Library, 1165 Angelina Street, Austin, TX 78702.

*Museum of African-American Life and Culture, P.O. Box 41511, Dallas, TX 75241.

Sutton's Black Heritage Gallery, 5003 San Jacinto, Houston, TX 77004.

*Texas Southern University, 3201 Wheeler Street, Houston, TX 77004.

Virginia

*Harrison Heritage and Cultural Center, P.O. Box 194, Roanoke, VA 24002.
*University Museum, Hampton University, Hampton, VA 23668.

Libraries, Research Centers, and Information Centers

Libraries, research centers, or information centers that emphasize Black materials are indicated by an asterisk (*).

District of Columbia

Library of Congress, Prints and Photographic Division, Washington, D.C. 20540.
    Vast collection of lithographs, single pictures, stereographs, and portraits. The Brady Collection includes negatives of Civil War photographs recording the war, and the Francis Benjamin Johnston Collection contains information on actors, art and artists, caricatures, cartoons, and lynching.
*Moorland-Spingarn Research Center, Thomas Battle, Director, Howard University, 500 Howard Place, NW, Washington, DC 20059, (202) 636–7239.
    Chiefly books (over 97,000) and periodicals (over 10,000), record albums (approx. 1,100) and sheet music (over 4,000); also miscellaneous Black memorabilia such as advertisements, household items, minstrel sketches, playbills, posters, and prints. Small collection of pornographic material. Acquired through gifts, estate bequests, and purchases.

Illinois

*Johnson Publishing Company and Library, 820 South Michigan Avenue, Chicago, IL 60605.
    Contains current and retrospective files of *Ebony*, *Jet*; files of journals no longer published (*Ebony Jr.*, *Sepia*, *Black World*), photographs, books; and numerous other items.

Kansas

*Walkes Prince Hall Masonic Collection, Joseph A. Walkes, Jr., President, Phylaxis Society, P.O. Box 3151, Fort Leavenworth, KS 66027, (913) 651–4584.
    The Walkes Prince Hall Masonic Collection is the largest privately owned collection on Black (Prince Hall) Freemasonry in the world. It consists of books, pamphlets, magazines, newspapers, articles, private papers, microfilm, letters, and other items. There are proceedings, such as the minutes of African Lodge no. 459 charted by the Grand Lodge of England with Prince Hall as master in 1784, as well as the proceedings of the Prince Hall Grand Lodge of Missouri and Louisiana, both almost complete, comprising over 120 years each. It also consists of the letters (approximately 10,000) of Joseph A. Walkes.

Kentucky

Kentucky Derby Museum, 704 Central Avenue, Louisville, KY 40208.

New York

*AFRAM Alternative Information Marketing Service, Preston Wilcox, President, 68–72 East 131st Street, New York, NY 10037.
> A research and retrieval service; gathers information on Blacks from advertisements in newspapers, periodicals, and reprints.

*Schomburg Center for Research in Black Culture; Howard Dodson, Chief; Betty Gubert, Head, General Research and Reference; New York Public Library; 515 Lenox Avenue; New York, NY 10037; (212) 862–4000.
> Chiefly consists of books (87,000 volumes), manuscripts of works by Black authors, periodicals (2,000), playbills (28,000), posters (2,600), prints (1,000), and record albums (10,000). Photographic collection of 150,000 items. Collection also includes greeting cards and postcards (700), political and religious buttons (300), dolls, films (50), paintings (300), sheet music (300), soap powder boxes, toy books (5), stamps (200), medallions, mugs (porcelain, depicting frogs from a group by that name of which minstrel performer Bert Williams was a member), lantern slides (50), and numerous other items.

Niagara Falls Public Library, Local History Department, 1425 Main Street, Niagara Falls, NY 14305.
> Collecting interest in the music, letters, clippings, reviews, and other materials on composer R. Nathaniel Dett.

Pennsylvania

Balch Institute, David H. Sutton, Archivist, R. Joseph Anderson, Librarian, 18 South 7th Street, Philadelphia, PA 19106.
> See also entry under Museums above.

Free Library of Philadelphia, Music Department, Logan Square, Philadelphia, PA 19103.

Tennessee

*Fisk University Library, Jessie Carney Smith, University Librarian, 17th Avenue North and Jackson Street, Nashville, TN 37208.
> Collection consists chiefly of books and periodicals (over 40,000 on Black themes), minstrel sketches (200), oral history interviews (500), and sheet music (approximately 500). Other Black memorabilia include art (busts and figurines, 20), advertisements (30), films (3), dolls (including one slave-made doll, 10), lawn jockey (1), miscellaneous household items (30), segregation signs, mechanical banks (5), and numerous rare and special items. The Goodman-Chaney-Schwerner collection, a gift of Rose Agree, contains 1,000 books about Blacks for children. Most collectibles purchased or donated for lecture/exhibit series, "Images in Black Artifacts: Negative and Positive" funded in 1981 by the Tennessee Committee for the Humanities. Selected bibliography and brochure available.

Memphis State University, Brister Library, Memphis, TN 38104.
> The Radio History Collection contains over 500 tapes: over 1,000 hours of broadcast of news, entertainment, and historical shows.

Memphis/Shelby County Public Library and Information Center, 1850 Peabody Street,

Memphis, TN 38104.
Photographs by C. S. Pollard taken from about 1915 to 1940 portray Blacks in stereotypical terms.

Private Collections—Canada

Except for the single Canadian collector, private collections that have been identified below are located in the United States. Inquiries about these collectors should be addressed to the owner c/o the editor of this reference work. Addresses of collectors who are also dealers are listed under the section on dealers.

Misiewicz, Roger and Carol
Major portion of the collection consists of miscellaneous household objects (including 75 sets of salt and pepper shakers, ceramic containers, and figures), postcards and stereoptics (144), trade cards and smaller numbers of advertisement items, labels, and other materials. Concentrates on music-related items (blues and gospel, 1902–1943), and has 95 percent of all items ever commercially issued. Collection taped, consisting of 100 8-hour reel-to-reel tapes from their own 3,000 or more original 78s, 1,000 microgrooves, and over 100 tapes. Contains approximately 400 microgroove of post-World War II blues and gospel music, and extensive magazine and book collections related to this music. Black Americana collected in the United States and Canada; music assembled from worldwide sources.

Private Collections—United States

California

Bertelsen, L. John
Variety of materials with concentration on world-acknowledged assemblage of phonographs circa 1930–1953; extensive Amos 'n' Andy collection including life-sized cardboard figures used in advertising, books, toys, recordings, and statues; extensive record collection of various Black comedians circa 1900–1935 featuring the Two Black Crows, Hyde & Slyde, Licorice Drops, etc. Collection also includes books and periodicals, postcards, sheet music (700), trade cards, and other items. Nearly 99 percent of the materials were acquired in California over thirty-five years.

Boggan, Jacqueline
Miscellaneous items including Mohammed Ali decanter, candles, coins, comic books (Golden Legacy and Harlem Globetrotter), celebrity dolls, golliwogs, lead figures, lunch pails, celebrity stamps, and cache covers. Acquired in California, District of Columbia, Michigan, New Jersey, and Oregon.

Brinson, Lois Zinnerman
Concentration on books, cookie jars (including works by F & F Mold & Die Wőrks, Pearl China & Pottery Co., McCoy), dinner plates (including Coon Chicken Inn), dolls, door stops (one dated late 1800s), miscellaneous household items (including 26 sets of salt and pepper shakers), paintings (some used on the Bill Cosby television show), prints, and other rare and special items. Collection acquired from Ronald Carr and other collectors, antique shops, and flea markets.

Edge, Jan
Chiefly books (2,500) by or about Blacks in the United States, and Africa, especially on slavery and fiction; also greeting cards, dolls, miscellaneous household items, paintings and prints, record albums, and other items. Collection contains African artifacts and music. Acquired in California; African materials acquired directly from Africa.

Farkash, Heidi
Books, films (movies, negatives, and stills), household items, postcards, sheet music, souvenir items, and toys constitute the bulk of the collection. Additional miscellaneous items. Special or rare items include slave bill of sale, Civil War material, and chrome peanut crisper (with cannibals dancing around a fire). Acquired from swap meets, flea markets, and shows in California, Texas, Tennessee; through mail; and from travels in France and the Soviet Union.

Faulkner, Janette
Eclectic collector with a number of items in all categories. Special character of collection is that all items depict stereotypical image of Blacks produced in countries throughout the world. Most items were purchased or donated. Many items exhibited in 1982 at the Berkeley Art Center and reproduced in the catalogue, *Ethnic Notions: Black Images in the White Mind* (cited in bibliography for this chapter).

Hoke, Wandia Sylvia
Collection contains in excess of 500 items, chiefly greeting cards and postcards, household items (including approximately 100 sets of salt and pepper shakers), labels, periodicals, prints, and sheet music. Emphasis is on complete sets, such as the mammy cookie jar, spice set, and other items from F & F Die Works, which are in the collection. Acquired from flea markets and antique shops in Alabama, California, Illinois, Michigan, and New York.

Horlick, Dick
Focuses on picture postcards that feature Black images, the world's largest collection of cards (10,000) dating from 1896 to 1960s. Also concentrates on greeting cards, books, and periodicals, prints, record albums (500), sheet music (1,000), trade cards (2,000), and lobby cards from all-Black movies of the 1930s and 1940s. Special interest in pre–1963 Black vocal group music; collection contains thousands of ephemera relating to this subject. Acquired over thirty years. Videotape available.

Kader, Don
An advanced collector; subsequently disposed of most items. Remaining collection contains concentration of advertisement items, banks, cans, dolls, household items (including sets of salt and pepper shakers), labels, prints, sheet music, souvenir items, toys, trade cards, and approximately 300 additional items. Unique items include hand leather sewing box (ca. 1878), pocket watch with Blackwoman insert, slave bracelet (Nigeria, ca. 1790), hand-made miniature stage sets (from "Frankie & Johnnie"), and brass candlestick with slave in shackle (ca. 1850s). Acquired over twelve-year period from other collectors, shows, flea markets, malls, mail, and elsewhere. Videotape available.

Kimbrough, Jack
Collection consists of over 1,500 books, 150 periodical titles (including twenty years of *The Crisis*), paintings, African art, and 400 record albums. Book collection concentrates on the Black military (with works on William Nell, Ossian Flipper, and others); about 25 works on the Black cadet in 1877; slave narratives; works by nineteenth- and early twentieth-century Black writers William Wells Brown, Charles Waddell Chesnutt, Paul

Laurence Dunbar (almost all of his poems and fiction); many works by Harlem Renaissance writers and leaders of the era, including W. E. B. DuBois (many signed copies), Langston Hughes (near complete collection with several signed), and others. Materials acquired over many years and from a variety of sources. Catalogue of collection is in process.

Miller, Mary Atrice
The few artifacts in the collection include ashtrays, banks, advertising buttons, a clock (1910 peanut vendor), cookie jars, games, a lawn sprinkler, linens, mechanical toys, puppets, salt and pepper shakers, signs, soap powder boxes, syrup containers, tobacco (Nigger Hair) tins, and yarn holders. Limited specialty on watermelon and "coon" items. Collection also contains over 200 periodicals, record albums, African statues and busts; concentrates on items that give visual and positive rendition of the Black experience through books (over 1,000 on race relations, slavery, Blacks in films, Black politics, and other subjects); personality dolls of Blacks (George Washington Carver, Reggie Jackson, Willie Mays, Diana Ross, Harriet Tubman, and others); Black political posters (including works on Mayor Tom Bradley as well as the Black Panthers); and works on white Americans who were significant in the Black experience including John F. Kennedy, Abraham Lincoln, Franklin D. Roosevelt, and Eleanor Roosevelt. Collection began in 1979; items purchased through *Antique Trader* and shows and dealers in California. Plans are to open an exhibition hall or community museum.

Minnex, Michelé and Zelber
Collection with a folk art flair. Includes advertisements (approximately 90) and advertising buttons (15), ashtrays, greeting cards, banks, books (over 50), cans (20), dolls (over 100), films, games (10), cookie jars (40), miscellaneous household items (over 200), paintings, pipes, plates (20), postcards (over 60), posters, prints (over 20), record albums, salt and pepper shakers (25 sets), sheet music (30), soap powder boxes, souvenir items (over 50), sugar bowls, syrup containers, toys (10 mechanical and 15 others). Materials acquired from antique shops, private collections, and as gifts from friends. Considering opening Black folk art museum.

Oeland, Charles
Emphasis on postcards (50) and advertising cards (30); most are derogatory. Collection contains several ashtrays, dolls, produce labels (10), letter openers, salt and pepper shakers, and soap powder boxes. Materials collected during past two years; found at various local antique shops.

Patton, Harold L., III
Bibliophile, with collection of 6,000 volumes, over 2,000 by Black authors dated 1773–1986; over 1,500 first editions, many signed. Fiction by Black authors (1853–1986) is primary focus. Approximately 400 volumes of poetry dated 1773–1986 included. Other subject areas collected include art, folklore, dance, history, music, sports and athletics, television, and motion pictures. Purchased in United States and abroad.

Snell, Gary
Over 500 sets of salt and pepper shakers, matching sets (such as vinegar, oil, grease jars, and salt and pepper shakers), and banks. (See also Bibliography section.)

Tolbert, John A.
Basic collection consists of books and periodicals, paintings, playbills, prints, record albums, and miscellaneous items. Books, photographs, playbills, and records (78s) by Paul Robeson are signed. Art works of Blacks during the late 1930s and early 1940s by

Burr Singer included. Some military photographs of World War I and others from the period 1890s–1930s, and a 100-year-old blackamoor carving (6 ft.) with documentation. Acquired in California.

Connecticut

Bertrand, Valerie (also dealer)
Restricted to paper items and includes books (some autographed), documents signed by Booker T. Washington and Frederick Douglass, photographs (celebrity autographed), music (early sheet music with stereotypic caricatures), newsclippings from 1800s regarding Dred Scott case and slave trade in general, slave-related documents, and trade cards; few buttons, dolls, salt and pepper shakers and more.

Fourier, Richard
Bulk of collection is in advertising and includes candy boxes, Aunt Jemima pancake flour box, mammy recipe box, recipe box with Black chef, two Aunt Jemima masks, and other items. Also contains cookie jars and other household items. Began collection several years ago with purchase of set of salt and pepper shakers.

Gilmore, Barbara
Collection contains advertisements (6) and advertising buttons (2), ashtrays (3), greeting cards (6), playing cards, banks (2), dinner bells (3), books (25), candy boxes (2), dolls (30–40), games (6), cookie jars (9), miscellaneous household items (30–50), labels (3), letter openers, paintings (3), milk pitchers (3), postcards (50), prints (12), puppets, record albums, salt and pepper shakers (75–100 sets), soap powder boxes, songbooks, string holders (3), sugar bowls (3), syrup containers, tobacco tins (2), mechanical toys (3), miscellaneous toys (3), trade cards (30), and miscellaneous items (pincushions, noisemakers, 9 golliwogs). Special items include large selection of sheet music, graphic covers (many stereotypic), many positive illustrations of Blacks. One-of-a-kind items such as "The Alabama Pilgrims" by Alexander Watt (leather cover-gilt print of a true history of their wanderings; original hand-colored photographs on each page). Items collected in Connecticut, Indiana, Maine, Massachusetts, New Hampshire, New York, Pennsylvania, and Wisconsin.

McCumber, Robert (also dealer)
Approximately 50 mechanical banks, 50 still banks, and other items.

Maule, Margaret and Gerald
Modest collection of advertisements, ashtrays, dinner bells, dolls, cookie jars, miscellaneous household items, periodicals, salt and pepper shakers (14 pairs), souvenir items, sugar bowls, syrup containers, miscellaneous toys, and other items (Christmas decorations, Black firemen teapot, Black clown liquor set, and Black clown tea set). Acquired from tag sales, flea markets, and antique dealers and shops.

Rumohr, Elizabeth N.
Collection geared toward advertising and ephemera of a stereotypical nature; contains assortment of advertisements and produce labels, soap powder and miscellaneous boxes, signs, postcards, tin cans, tobacco tins, trade cards, and other items. Sheet music also collected. Purchased in Northeast. Computerized list in preparation.

Stevens, Barbara
Variety of materials including advertisements (buttons, general items, produce labels, and trade cards), books and periodicals, greeting cards and postcards (100), dolls, mis-

cellaneous household objects (including andirons, clocks, curtains, linens, sugar bowls, and 50 sets of salt and pepper shakers), souvenirs, toys (some mechanical), and other collectibles.

Thalberg, Jan
Diverse collection contains Coon Chicken Inn advertisements (25); greeting cards and postcards (95); banks (5 still and mechanical); books (including Howard Weeden and Edward Kemble items) and periodicals; dolls (100, including some paper); glass slides (10); games and puzzles (including Cream of Wheat); miscellaneous household items (500 including ceramic and metal clocks, Christmas ornaments, embroideries, hand-painted china and glass); jewelry (30); linens; salt and pepper shakers; sewing items (35); walking sticks (20); miscellaneous figural items, including Little Black Sambo (25); paintings (including original watercolors); prints (20, including Harry Roseland and Maud Humphrey); sheet music (30); souvenirs (50, including 30 sterling spoons); trade cards (50); and additional items. Prefers hand-made and unique items to those mass produced. Collected in New England and New York.

District of Columbia

Blalock/Lewis Collection, Albert Blalock and Stephen D. Lewis
A collection of over 300 works by and about Black subject matter. Concentrates on advertisements (40), as well as buttons (20), produce labels (26) and trade cards (10), Coon Chicken Inn items, greeting cards and postcards (75), books and periodicals (64), dolls (18), miscellaneous household item (26), ashtrays (10), cookie jars (6), figurines from mid- to late 1800s, linens, salt and pepper shakers (20 sets, including F & F Die Works and Luzianne), string holders, paintings (60), prints (100), record albums (50), sheet music, soap powder boxes, syrup containers, tobacco jars (10, several made in late 1800s), and other items. Collected from variety of sources and geographic areas.

Bundles, A'Lelia P.
Materials consist mainly of Black hair care and cosmetics items from the Madame C. J. Walker Manufacturing Company, with special emphasis on advertisements (50, including additional 50 advertising buttons), cans (10), books (50), periodicals (20), postcards (50), posters (15), and sheet music. Of equal importance are the materials relating to the Walker family. Numerous letters in the collection were written to businesswoman, philanthropist, and inventor Madam Walker; correspondents were Mary McLeod Bethune, Charlotte Hawkins Brown, Enrico Caruso, Mary White Ovington, William Pickens, Emmett Scott, and Mrs. Booker T. Washington. Family items include monogrammed silver; clothing of the Walker women; the wedding dress from the 1923 "Million Dollar Wedding" of A'Lelia Walker's adopted daughter, Mae; hair care implements; Walker products, containers, and furniture. Photographs in the collection show Madam Walker, her daughter A'Lelia (whom Langston Hughes called "the joy goddess of Harlem's 1920's and the Harlem Renaissance"), and their various friends and associates. The collector is the great-great granddaughter of Madam Walker, and she acquired most of the collection from the Walker family; other items were acquired through recent purchases. The collection will be expanded to include more hair care and cosmetics items, advertisements, and other materials, especially early Walker Company product containers manufactured prior to 1920. See also Indiana Historical Society (listed in this section under Galleries, Museums, and Historical Societies), which also contains a Walker Collection.

Ensminder, Mary Ann

Collection contains advertising items, banks, books, dolls, games, postcards, salt and pepper shakers, bottle stoppers, six-piece angel band, prints, and reprints. Items purchased all over the country; some in Germany.

Hames, Ronald S.
Advertising items, banks, candy boxes, dolls, cookie jars, playbills, postcards, puppets, salt and pepper shakers, sheet music, souvenir items, sugar bowls, syrup containers, toys, Carters Inky Racer, clay and terra cotta figurines, and other items. Began collecting in 1977 at the Ohio State Fair. Other items acquired in the District of Columbia, Maryland, and Virginia.

Hansberry, Gail
Chiefly a collection of late nineteenth- and early twentieth-century photographs of Black Americans and American Indians. Photographs include daguerrotype of Blacks in process of being enslaved; tintypes of individuals (children, adults, woman and child in process of being enslaved); tintype in leather case of woman and child; small leather photograph album of Cartes de Visite including image of Black Siamese twins; cabinet cards and Cartes de Visite ("Old Sam"; family portrait of mother, father, and daughter; outdoor scenes of slave children; portrait of woman in velvet frame); slave tag; and other slave documents. Materials purchased from photography dealers and private collectors in Washington, D.C. area, New York, and San Francisco.

Jacobs, Patricia D.
Variety of items collected, including advertising materials (34 general items, produce labels, and trade cards), greeting cards and postcards (80, including large variety of Valentine cards), banks (4), dolls (10), games (2), miscellaneous household items (27, including dinner bells, cookie jars, letter openers, 20 sets of salt and pepper shakers and string holders), prints (50, including some historic and signed by artist), sheet music (15), yard art (8), and miscellaneous linens and figurines (25). Several pornographic items. Collected from auction houses in various states.

Johnson, Julia B.
Primarily books (312) and periodicals (75), dolls (24), postcards (57), record albums (66), and sheet music (19). Also includes miscellaneous items, such as a lunch box from soccer player Pele, a vacuum bottle from the Harlem Globe Trotters, and first-day cancelled stamps of New York World's fair and Tuskegee Institute (Alabama), 1948. Acquired from flea markets and family.

Marzorini, A. L.
Collection primarily hand-made, one-of-a-kind folk art items without academic influence. Includes two unusual games ("Watermelon Frolic" and "Hit the Doger"), paintings (23) by Mose Tolliver, windup dancing woman (Baltimore, 1920s, on wood marked "coon dance"), nearly life-sized cut-out sign from traveling Western carnival show of Black banjo player (painted back and front), watercolors by Black artist from Reading, Pennsylvania. Also includes card holders (45 upright figures), dolls, lawn sprinklers (3), mechanical toys, puppets, signs, and other items. Collection gathered from Maryland, New York, New England states, Pennsylvania, and Virginia.

Saunders, Malinda (also dealer)
Doll collector; specializes in all types of dolls—old and new—especially ones with Black features. The twenty-five dolls in the collection were purchased from variety of sources. Until late 1986, the collector was the joint publisher of the newsletter, *Reflections of*

Sable Love: A Publication of the Black Memorabilia Collector (see Bibliography in this section).

Simmons, Charles E.

Collection contains advertisements (100) and buttons (10), cards (100 greeting and 60 playing), banks (2), books (200), cans (5 miscellaneous), dolls (5), household items (2 coffee jars, 1 cookie jar, 2 sugar bowls, 2 syrup containers, 21 sets salt and pepper shakers, 35 miscellaneous items), a letter opener, minstrel sketches (25), paintings (40), periodicals (300), pipes (2), playbills (10), postcards (70), posters (30), produce labels (10), prints (20), record albums (25), sheet music (60), signs (20), soap powder boxes (3), songbooks (5), tobacco tins (20), and toys (2). Ninety-nine percent of the advertisements, sheet music, postcards, and three-dimensional items emphasize distorted features and degraded character of Black men and women, portraying them as either docile or stupid. The unique character of the collection is the use of art (visual, poetry) and journalism to contrast the positive and negative portrayals of Blacks in similar periods and places, beginning with pre-colonial Africa and ending with the 1960s. Collection includes scholarly materials from *Journal of Negro History* and popular art and articles by Black journalists from the 1800s to the present; letters and articles of a former editor of the *Harlem Daily Worker* during World War II; and materials from personal research on Black journalists who have covered world affairs and civil rights. Journalism collection consists of reprints from *Mudhammad Speaks* and the *Chicago Defender* from the 1940s to 1960s; also extensive files on Robert Williams, William Worthy, and Adam Clayton Powell. Collection includes original Philadelphia newspaper dated 1792, which contains advertisements for runaway slaves; slave documents from Virginia and Maryland; segregation signs from Georgia; and Civil War documents and paintings of Black soldiers. Many items in the collection reproduced in extensive travelling exhibit entitled ''Black Americans and the Bicentennial of the U.S. Constitution: A Mass Media Perspective.'' Materials collected in California, District of Columbia, Georgia, Maryland, Michigan, North Carolina, and Pennsylvania. Catalogue of the exhibit available.

Wells, Clement

Needlepoint collection of Blacks who have been depicted on postage stamps (Louis Armstrong, Count Basie, Ralph Bunche, George Washington Carver, Ella Fitzgerald, W. C. Handy, Alexander Pushkin, Harriet Tubman, Booker T. Washington, Paul Laurence Dunbar, and others) and of contemporary figures Marian Anderson, Martin Luther King, Jr., Malcolm X, Dinah Washington, and others. All works completed by the collector.

Florida

Havris, Patrick J.

Collection consists of nine Staffordshire portrait figures from *Uncle Tom's Cabin* circa 1852; two are rare—Uncle Tom Tom and Aunt Chloe. Other items include rare commemorative pitchers from *Uncle Tom's Cabin* with scene on relief of a slave auction, handle in form of a praying slave scene of Eliza running away from Simon Legree; seven commemorative plates with painted scenes and verses from the book; prints of Nathaniel Currier and Uncle Tom and Little Eva; rare print by Thomas Strong Fust showing meeting of Uncle Tom and Little Eva; and five periodical versions of the work before it was published in book form. Collection contains volumes 8–12 of the thirteen periodicals issued, and a child's edition, c. 1910. Other Black memorabilia also collected. Purchased collection over five-year period from antique dealers and antique shows throughout the United States. Portion of the collection shown in *Antique Trader* (November 13, 1985).

Hensley, Larie
Formerly an advanced collector but now in process of disposing of most items. Collection includes numerous kitchen items and several ashtrays, greeting cards, cans, salt and pepper shakers, soap powder boxes, souvenir items, string holders, sugar bowls, syrup containers, tobacco tins, and yard art.

Georgia

Anthony, Lillian
Advanced collector. Materials include advertisements (50), ashtrays (10), greeting cards (10), playing cards (2), banks (12), dinner bells (7), books (1,525), advertising buttons (3), candy boxes (2), cans (15), dolls (24), games (5), cookie jars (4), lawn sprinklers (2), miscellaneous household items (150), labels (10), letter openers, minstrel sketches (25), paintings (over 50), periodicals (60), dinner plates (2), playbills (10), postcards (250), posters (15), prints (200), puppets (2), record albums (225), salt and pepper shakers (15 sets), sheet music (50), signs (4), soap powder boxes (5), souvenir items (50), string holders (4), sugar bowls (2), syrup containers (2), tobacco tins, toys (14 mechanical and still), trade cards (50), miscellaneous items (150). Unique items are spoons, decanters, cigar cutter, perfume containers, erotic items, diarama of cotton fields and indigo plantations. Collection has been used to research the reasons for creating the images and to explore their relationships to contemporary racist and sexist dehumanization of African and African-American people. Materials acquired from antique shops in Illinois, Indiana, Iowa, Ohio, Minnesota, and Nebraska, and from antique shows in the District of Columbia, Florida, Illinois, Indiana, and Nebraska.

Willingham, N. Louise
Advanced collector. Diversified collection of advertising items and buttons (40), greeting cards (50), books (400), dolls (12), miscellaneous household items (10), produce labels (3), minstrel sketches (6), paintings (30), periodicals (30), playbills (20), postcards (35), posters (20), prints (15), salt and pepper shakers, signs (12), souvenir items (20), yard art. Materials cover contemporary and historical Black images. There are pamphlets, brochures, invitations, programs, magazine and newspaper articles, and other materials on Black art and Black artists, including photographers and Black theater (about 1,000 pieces). Theater materials contain playbills for the last Broadway show performed by Josephine Baker, and some minstrel sheet music. Also a slave bill of sale (Wayne County, North Carolina, dated 1836), an issue of *The Liberator* dated 1865, and an assortment of about 150 pieces. There are political literature, note cards, and photographs (some hand colored). Button collection dates from 1960s and early 1970s; greeting cards are a collection of Black Christmas cards, including Kwaanza cards, and some images of famous Black women; 200 slides of historic Black sites mostly on the East coast and in the Southeast. Book collection contains about 45 children's books (many autographed), and adult books primarily on history and literature (some from the Harlem Renaissance period), several first editions and autographed copies. Doll collection includes likenesses of Maggie L. Walker, Phillis Wheatley, Bessie Smith, Sojourner Truth, a Jamaican slave woman (made by an 85-year-old woman), and Maasai (East African dolls). Numerous first-day issues of Black stamps and many African stamps are collected.

Illinois

McGrath, Mark and Patty
Collection limited to late nineteenth- and early twentieth-century cloth dolls (some clothed) and drawings by Bill Traylor. Items purchased from dealer and museum in Illinois.

Palensky, Roberta R.
Carefully assembled collection of advertisements (including figural Black man, "Banner Tobacco," buttons, and trade cards), mechanical banks (7, including "Dinah," "Jolly Nigger" (2), "Jolly Nigger with Top Hat," "Uncle Tom," "Bad Accident," and "Cabin"), still banks ("The Sharecropper," "Mammy" (3) and "Black Face Boy"), box ("Mason's Challenge Blacking"), dolls (8 folk type), games, miscellaneous household items (ashtray, baby feeding plate, Coon Chicken Inn items, mammy door stop and other bisque or iron figural items, nodder, tip tray), soap powder boxes (Sun-X Bleach, Fairbanks Gold Dust, Fun to Wash), slide (Civil War), postcards (large assortment), segregation signs, prints (reproductions of Bull Durham items), tin cans (including Nigger Hair tobacco, Severin Blend Coffee, Luzianne Coffee, Bowey's Hot Chocolate, and Uncle Remus Syrup), and other items. Collected for ten years from antique dealers in Illinois and New York.

Payne, Jeanene
Small collection used primarily for decoration. Concentrates on salt and pepper shakers (30 sets). Unique items include a mammy doll (4-inch handmade with faceless head made on top of black leather). Other items also collected. Interest began with purchase of cast-iron still banks—"Mammy," "Mammy with Spoon," and "Sharecropper." Acquired in various states.

Singley, Elijah
Collection includes ashtrays, advertising buttons, letter openers, postcards (300), prints (8), sheet music (35), souvenir items (15 spoons and forks), miscellaneous items (250 with heavy emphasis on medals, tokens, and other coin-like or numismatic items and on Green River Whiskey items). Materials acquired over the years from coin shows, hobby publications, antique shops, flea markets, and elsewhere.

Switzky, Harvey and Lynn
Eclectic collection includes advertisement items, produce labels and trade cards (56), greeting cards and postcards (16), books (cookbooks, children's and scholarly items, and periodicals), dolls (25), miscellaneous household items (13 ashtrays, 3 cookie jars, linens, planters, 28 sets of salt and pepper shakers, sugar and syrup containers, teapots, wall plaques), minstrel sketches, playbills, posters, prints, sheet music (209), songbooks (10), and miscellaneous items (28 figural items, noisemakers, golliwog items, and other materials). Included also is a pamphlet "Great Achievements of the Negro Race" with blank pages inside, and several erotic items. Most material purchased in Illinois and Iowa. Catalogue of collection pending.

Indiana

Colby, Joann Grandberry
Special items include a collection of original Paul Robeson 78-rpm records, over 100 postcards dating from 1906 depicting all aspect of Black life, and Harper's Weekly Print dated 1866 and titled "Uncle Tom and His Granddaughter." Other items include advertisements (30, as well as 25 buttons and 10 trade cards), miscellaneous household

items (55, including cookie jars, letter opener, collector's plates, 10 sets of salt and pepper shakers), prints (25), and yard art. Collection includes several items with sexual connotations.

Krethewey, Patricia
Special interest is in older Black items. Collection includes advertisements (100, as well as 15 produce labels), greeting cards and post cards (110), playing cards, books (27), miscellaneous household items (over 100, including cookie jars and 50 sets of salt and pepper shakers), prints (20), record albums (100), sheet music (50), and miscellaneous items. Collecting began in 1976, and materials were acquired in Illinois, Indiana, Michigan, and Texas.

Redwine, Barbara
Concentrates on string holders; collection also includes ashtrays (4), banks, books (5), dolls (7), cookie jars (3), lawn sprinkler (1), miscellaneous household items (12), postcards (6), posters (6), record albums (6), salt and pepper shakers (12 sets), sugar bowls (2), and syrup containers (1). Materials acquired from antique shows and flea markets.

Iowa

Voss, James
Small collection with several special items, such as book of "coon jokes," Amos 'n' Andy candy box; other items include advertisement items and buttons, miscellaneous cans, dolls, games, salt and pepper shakers, sheet music, tobacco tins, and mechanical toys. Most materials acquired in Iowa.

Kansas

Lester, Larry
Collection consists mainly of Black Americans on coins, stamps, currency; autographs; and all types of memorabilia on the old Negro baseball leagues. Coin collection contains set of Booker T. Washington and Washington/George Washington Carver coins in mint condition. Various gold and silver coins of Martin Luther King, Jr., Marcus Garvey, Frederick Douglass, and others from foreign countries; contains much U.S. coinage designed by Blacks. Currency collection consists of various dollar bills, with signatures of Blacks in the U.S. Treasury Department; includes foreign currency depicting Black Americans. Stamps include over 250 different items and cachet covers of Martin Luther King, Jr., issued from foreign countries; also over 100 different stamps of athletes, musicians, scientists, and abolitionists from around the world. (Conducts research on Black designers of U.S. postage stamps, and in 1986 produced special commemorative King stamp in honor of his first national holiday celebration.) There are about 275 autographs of famous Black Americans, including few atheletes or entertainers. The aim is to collect autographs of Blacks who made significant contributions to the Black cause, but who have had very little exposure and recognition. The few athletes' and entertainers' signatures are of those who have had a positive impact outside their respective fields, such as Olympian Tommie Smith, Harry Belafonte, and Paul Robeson. The oldest signature is that of Henry Highland Garnett. The collection also consists of the flip side of Black history: signatures of James Earl Ray, George Wallace, and members of the Ku Klux Klan. Negro baseball leagues are represented, reflecting the primary interest. There are ticket stubs, buttons, pennants, equipment, bats, uniforms, programs, pictures, and autographs. Many materials in this field pre-date Jackie Robinson's entrance into baseball.

Current research activities include the First Colored World Series, the First Colored All-Star (East-West) game, Josh Gibson, and a Negro baseball league calendar. Collection used for exhibitions, to encourage younger generations to be aware of their ethnic roots, and to promote Black history and restore it to its prominent place in American history. (Special stamp exhibitions are presented for schools, churches, and civic organizations.) Began collecting early in the 1960s.

Kentucky

Quisenberry, Rosetta Lucas
Primarily a collection of postcards (1,000 mostly negative and stereotypical), books (5 old and rare), dolls (10), and trade cards (approximately 150). Postcards collected throughout the southern states, New York, and Ohio. Collection is to be published in book form.

Rhodes, Lorena R.
Collection includes advertisements (55, with some buttons, labels, and trade cards), dolls (7), miscellaneous household items (ashtrays, cookie jars, linens, planters, 15 sets of salt and pepper shakers, 6 string holders, wall hangings), paintings, prints, sheet music, toys, and other items. Began collecting in 1971.

Simon, Elizabeth
Primary interest in Black folk and rag dolls (200 collected, including dolls made from nuts and cotton). Collection also contains advertisements (40 trade cards and 14 additional items), greeting cards (20) and postcards (1,200), books (25), games (10), miscellaneous household items (over 25, including baskets from Sea Islands of South Carolina), linens, minstrel sketches, prints, sheet music (15), soap powder boxes, souvenir items, toys, and other items.

Louisiana

Ohle, Jeanie (also dealer)
Collection limited to old quilts and folk dolls depicting Black subjects and made by Blacks.

Maryland

Brigance, Karen (also dealer)
Eclectic collector with items acquired in most categories. Collection heavily weighted in advertisements and in postcards. Materials collected over eighteen-year period and acquired throughout the United States.

Carson, Jeannette B. (also dealer; see Ethnic Treasures)
Collection consists primarily of dolls (50–60), majolica items, cast-iron figural items, and books.

Coleman, Rosalee L.
Chiefly a collection of record albums (1,247) from the 1950s through the 1970s covering rhythm and blues, and soul. Books (75) that relate to Blacks in entertainment, mostly in music, are also included. Materials acquired through purchase and gifts over a fifteen-year period.

Driskell, David C.
Collection consists of advertising boxes (20); labels (stereotypical); lithographs (over 100 from 19th century); photographs (early); postcards (Blacks picking cotton in Florida, and

with alligators), and other items. Special emphasis on paintings by Black artists (over 300 collected). Began collecting in 1973.

Fry, Gladys-Marie
Collection includes slave-made and other quilts by Blacks or depicting Black images, photographs, and print materials. The collector presents exhibitions and lectures and conducts research for publication on these items and on needlework by slaves.

Phillips, Glen and Ingrid
Special character of the collection is its excellent condition, the years covered (1850–1950), and its unique items, such as sterling souvenir spoons (110), some of which include enameled bowls with work scenes (Blacks picking cotton, cutting cane, leaning on a cotton bale). All spoon themes are stereotypical except of Frederick Douglass (silver plate); *Uncle Tom's Cabin* with Harriet Beecher Stowe, Topsy, and Eva; and a slave market in Tallahassee. Included in collection also are advertisements (20, as well as 35 buttons and 20 trade cards), greeting cards and postcards (130), banks, books (50) and periodicals (7), candy boxes, cans, dolls (10), miscellaneous household items (35, including ashtrays, dinner bells, syrup holders, sugar bowls, and string holders, 18 dinner plates, 16 sets of salt and pepper shakers), mechanical toys, paintings (5), pipes, posters, prints (15), puppets, sheet music, songbooks, and other items (35–50 bisque, porcelain, and majolica). Collection purchased throughout the United States and in some European countries from dealers, stores, antique shows, and other private collections.

True, William E.
Collection consists of ashtrays (approximately 15), greeting cards (20) and postcards (100–200), dinner bells (12), books (25), advertisement buttons, dolls (20), games (including 2 Little Black Sambo dart boards), miscellaneous household items (including 8 cookie jars, 80–100 sets of salt and pepper shakers, sugar bowls, 20 syrup containers), puppets, sheet music (10–20), soap powder boxes, souvenir items (20–30), tobacco tins (4), miscellaneous toys, and a metal lawn jockey. Special items include Topsy puppet from Uncle Tom's Cabin (new in box), Dancing Dan stick puppets (new), and bust of Roberto Clemente. Materials acquired from flea markets throughout the United States.

Winchester, Cora Lee
Small collection that focuses on bisque figurines of pickaninnies eating watermelon; special interest in watermelon figures (20). Collection also includes ashtrays, dolls (15), linens, salt and pepper shakers, and other items. Interest developed from pickaninny item in family collection. Items acquired in approximately 1981 from membership club in New Jersey.

Wright, Naomi
Advanced collector. The special character of the collection is on positive images; consists of greeting cards (50), banks (2), books (21), dolls (20), miscellaneous household items, paintings (7), pipes, prints (10), salt and pepper shakers, souvenir items (60 silver spoons), and miscellaneous items (60 figurines, 19 photographic items, 52 stereoptic cards and optical viewer, and assortment of 35 medals, coins, commemorative plates, jewelry, and plaques). Material acquired from antique shows throughout the United States and some foreign countries over a fifteen-year period.

Massachusetts

Boskin, Joseph
Small collection of advertisements, books (including 1 joke book), calendars, cookie tins,

comic strips (4 series), figural items, (4-ft cast-iron with lantern), linens, produce labels, paintings, postcards, prints, stereoptic slides, stamps, sheet music, soap powder boxes, and trade cards.

Conrad, Norman
Primarily interested in memorabilia and collectibles from the minstrel era, such as autographs, letters by minstrel performers, news clippings, postcards, posters, programs and tickets, radio and television programs, rare books and periodicals, recordings and miscellaneous items, and works on performers Bert Williams, Al Jolson, and Eddie Cantor. The collection includes these subject areas in books (100), films on video (2 of his mini-minstrels), minstrel sketches (50 booklets and publications), periodicals (25), record albums (several minstrel shows), sheet music (250), scrapbook of Karl Cartwright with articles on old-time minstrels (burnt cork, tamborines, bone, wigs, matchsafe from Christy minstrels), and an assortment of other Black memorabilia. Collection contains ingredients that go into the production of a minstrel show and are used by the collector to produce mini-minstrels. Materials acquired from antique dealers, private parties, flea markets, and gifts.

Minnesota

Matterson, Pat
More than 300 items in the collection. Included are advertisements (10) and advertising buttons (5), ashtrays (2, one from Coon Chicken Inn restaurant chain), greeting cards (3), banks (1 reproduction), dinner bells (4), books (10), cans (2), dolls (5), cookie jars (1), miscellaneous household items (31, including teapot, toaster cover, wall plaques, spoon rest), labels (15 cosmetics), periodicals, postcards (10), posters (2), puppets, record albums (100), salt and pepper shakers (30 sets), sheet music (12), signs (2, including reserved table sign from Coon Chicken Inn), soap powder boxes, songbooks (2), souvenir items (6), string holders (3), sugar bowls, syrup containers, tins (syrup and molasses), toys (6, including mechanical, tamborines, and noisemakers), trade cards, yard art, and miscellaneous items (50, including linens, hat hook, memo holders, drinking glasses). Also has an unusual lamp, believed to be handmade, depicting Black man with liquor bottle in hand. Materials purchased during travel in Canada and in California, Minnesota, Virginia, and Wisconsin.

Missouri

Consolo, Chris
Eclectic collection consists of advertisements (12, and 20 trade cards), cartoons, greeting cards (7) and postcards (70), playing cards, banks, books, dolls, films, games (including Sambo dart board), miscellaneous household items (50, as well as 1 coffee jar, 4 cookie jars, milk pitchers, 54 sets of salt and pepper shakers, 3 string holders, sugar bowls, and syrup containers), mechanical and other toys (10), minstrel sketches, puppets (6), sheet music (40), souvenir items (35), and numerous additional items. Among the special materials are a mammy biscuit jar (with cane handle), butler tie rack, clock (wooden), flue cover, pencil holder (native type), pencil sharpener, tip trays, and shot glasses. In addition, collection contains 45 rpm's sold under the counter after the civil rights movement, which include "Nigger Hatin' Me," "Who Likes a Nigger," "Looking for a Handout," "Kajun Ku Klux Klan," "NAACP Prayer," and "Cowboys and Niggers." Collection began with salt and pepper shaker and vastly expanded in scope. Materials

were acquired from flea markets, garage sales, shops, and other collectors and through the *Antique Trader*.

Holt, Mary Lou

Materials collected include advertisements, albums of greeting cards and postcards, books, cans, games, mechanical toys, and other items. Special items include Black Christmas items (rare, but held by members of the Christmas Club), "The Ghost Story" (a knockout relief in papier-mâché, framed), and an unusual tin advertising sign, "I'se in a Perdick-ermunt," which shows a Black man standing in a road with a live chicken under one arm and a watermelon in the other, contemplating a bottle of "free hootch" on the road.

Orchard, Edgar L. and Donna A.

Extensive collection that spans all subject areas. Estimated numbers of items are advertisements (25, as well as 20 buttons, 50 produce labels, and 100 trade cards), a cigar box, greeting cards (20) and postcards (150), playing cards, banks (30 mechanical), books (200), periodicals (15), cans (25), dolls (75), games (10), miscellaneous household items (100, as well as 50 ashtrays, 20 dinner bells, 10 cookie jars, 2 milk pitchers, 5 dinner plates, 100 sets of salt and pepper shakers, 15 string holders, 3 sugar bowls, 2 syrup containers), letter openers, posters (10), prints (25), puppets (7), record albums (10), sheet music (75), signs (10), soap powder boxes (10), songbooks (5), souvenir items (25), tobacco tins, toys (10 miscellaneous), yard art (10), and other items (150). Many other materials with sexual connotations. Collection acquired throughout the United States but mostly from Missouri. Materials catalogued and in 1987 displayed in the Vaughn Cultural Center, a division of the St. Louis Urban League. Catalogue available.

Riley, Calvin

Collection of 2,000 pieces includes books, figural items, folk art (hand-made by slaves), toys, and miscellaneous works. Most items are stereotypical. Began collecting in 1982 and acquired materials from antique dealers, estate sales and flea markets in Missouri, Ohio, and Wisconsin.

New Jersey

Bertoia, Jeanne and Bill

Collection includes ashtrays, banks (4), cans, paintings, toys (including "Two Coons" bell), doorstops (8), figural bottle openers (3), cast-iron miniatures (5), and other items. Began collecting doorstops in 1980 and mechanical banks and toys in 1984. Most Black memorabilia items have been sold. *See Doorstops Indentification and Value* listed in the Bibliography section.)

Brenner, Paul

Collecting practices concentrate on cancellations. Postcard collection numbers several thousand as do U.S. and foreign postage stamp cancellations. Black Expo, John Brown, Paul Cuffee's ship, Duke Ellington, Martin Luther King, Jr., the NAACP, National Urban League, Lincoln-Douglas debates, Prince Hall Masons, Rhode Island Black Regiment, Harriet Tubman, sickle-cell anemia, and the underground railroad are examples of the stamps collected. Materials acquired from various post offices. Initial cancellation catalogue for Black items in preparation.

Cuff, Jay W.

Included in the collection are advertisements (10), greeting cards (100) and postcards (100), banks (3), books (150), card holders, dolls (20), household items (20 miscellaneous, 4 dinner bells, 1 cookie jar, 3 sets salt and pepper shakers, string holders), letter openers

(2), pipes (3), posters (50), prints (25), puppets (10), record albums (50), sheet music (20), songbooks (10), souvenir items (over 100) and miscellaneous items (150, including bisque and majolica. Materials assembled from throughout the United States and from foreign countries.

Harris, Henry
Over 400 historical documents and important autographs constitute the collection. Includes Prester John Map by Ortelius (1571), and signatures and works by Toussaint L'Ouverture (1796), Henri Christoff (1802), Frederick Douglass, Henry Flipper (1901), Henry O. Tanner (1910), and William Hastie (1947). Materials acquired from dealers.

Mercier, Denis
Collection contains advertisements (75, as well as 3 buttons, 3 produce labels, 17 trade cards), greeting cards (15) and postcards (70), playing cards, books (15) and periodicals (20), candy boxes (2), cans (2), games (3), household items (2 ashtrays, 1 cookie jar, 4 sets salt and pepper shakers, 2 soap powder boxes, 1 syrup container, and 20 miscellaneous items), a letter opener, mechanical and other toys (4), minstrel sketches (5), pipes, playbills, posters, prints, record albums (100), sheet music (150), segregation signs, songbooks (5), souvenir items, and other materials. Several items with sexual connotations. Most items gathered as embodiments of American popular culture and used as part of data base for doctoral dissertation, "The Evolution of the Black Image in White Consciousness, 1876–1954: A Popular Culture Perspective" (University of Pennsylvania, 1984) and scheduled for publication by Greenwood Press under the title *Representations of Blacks in American Culture: An Analytical Sourcebook of Artifacts and Memorabilia.* Collection amassed from Midwest and Mid-Atlantic antique shops and dealers.

Wolverton, Howard
Materials cover all subject areas and classifications; especially weighted in sheet music. Most items acquired in New Jersey.

New York

Franklin, Mildred
Advanced collector. Materials include advertisements (15, and advertising buttons, 56), ashtrays (3), greeting cards (7), banks (2), books (150), candy box (1), dolls (5), films (3), miscellaneous household items (8), labels (29 produce), letter openers (4), minstrel sketches (3), paintings (8), periodicals (5), plates (2 dining), playbills (75), postcards (28), posters (14), prints (18), record albums (250), salt and pepper shakers, sheet music (10), signs (8), soap powder boxes (4), songbooks (3), souvenir items (14), syrup containers (2), tobacco tins (2), and trade cards (48). Unique item is a copy of "Le Pele-Mele," a French comic sheet dated January 25, 1903; cover depicts Black family. Special character of collection is its historical content. Incorporates Black contribution and presence in America and the world through autographs and the printed word. Range is from historic to contemporary Black achievers in all fields. Collection mainly ephemera, with over 300 autograph items, slave documents, photographs, and letters. Persons representing the Reconstruction are congressmen Robert Smalls, John Lynch, and John Mercer Langston. Other political personalities include Edward Brooke, Shirley Chisholm, Charles Diggs, Barbara Jordan, William Gray III, and Adam Clayton Powell. Rare or obscure works are a deed signed by Frederick Douglass (1885); a document signed by Blanche K. Bruce (1892); an Alabama marriage license (1886); a trade certificate signed by Marcus Garvey (1924); letters signed by Oscar De Priest (1932); playbills and programs from

The Green Pastures (1930), *Othello* (1944, signed by Paul Robeson), *Porgy and Bess* (1942 and 1985), *Cabin in the Sky* (1941, signed by Ethel Waters), and *Raisin in the Sun* (signed by entire cast); and documents of sale of slaves, autograph albums, photographs, and first-day covers. Also included are documents and photographs of African leaders and such well-known Black Americans as Alvin Ailey, Lena Horne, Leontyne Price, Bill "Bojangles" Robinson, Katherine Dunham, Pearl Primus, Joe Louis, Jackie Robinson, Jesse Owens, Althea Gibson, and Arthur Ashe, as well as writers James Baldwin, Gwendolyn Brooks, Charles Waddell Chesnutt, Countee Cullen, Langston Hughes, Margaret Walker, and others. Materials purchased at auctions and shows and through mail, catalogues, and trading across the United States.

Hart, Mark (also dealer)
Collector of fine and rare tobacco jars and few other items.

Jeromack, Paul
Collection concentrates on cookie jars circa 1920–1950s (45), salt and pepper shakers (50 sets), and ceramic items. Other materials consist of household items (25, including 1 dinner bell, 15 string holders, 8 sugar bowls, and 5 syrup containers). Collection acquired from flea markets.

Markowitz, Joel
Primarily collector of sheet music (1,200 pieces) on ragtime, blues, Black composers, Blacks on covers (stereotype drawings), Black performers (photos), early jazz, and other themes. Other items include advertisements (24), advertising buttons (24), minstrel sketches (12), record albums (100), single records (78s, 200), songbooks (30), trade cards (36), and piano rolls (1,000). Began collecting in 1977.

Norris, Elizabeth
Collection includes playing cards (3), books (over 100, including pamphlets and historical works from the 1880s to 1970), dolls (25), paintings (3), periodicals (over 20 issues), postcards (30–40), record albums (3), trade cards (over 12), miscellaneous items (including 75–80 civil rights buttons from the 1960s). Special collection of ephemera on Angela Davis. Special character of the collection is that all images are positive; the few exceptions are objects which are part of a different subject collection. The collector has been a librarian for interracial and intercultural organizations, one of the founders of the first Council on Interracial Books for Children, and editor of the annual bibliography, "Books for Brotherhood." All shared common goals: the eradication of derogatory racial stereotypes from popular culture and the encouragement of writers, artists, parents, and children to create and recognize realistic images of persons of all races.

Sailer, Edde
Collection consists of advertisement items, greeting cards, banks, dolls (12), household items (dinner bells, cookie jars, grocery note pad, milk pitcher, pot holders, 24 sets of salt and pepper shakers, string holder, sugar bowl, syrup container, wooden serving bowl), prints, souvenir items, and other materials. One item (mug) has sexual connotations. Materials have special meaning to the family and have inspired others to collect. Items purchased in New York and Pennsylvania.

Scharer, Jonathan
Interests are in potpourri, American-made mammy items, and foreign pieces. Included in the collection are advertisements (20, as well as 15 buttons and 6 produce labels), greeting cards (50) and postcards (50), books (10), cans (6), household items (10 ashtrays,

2 dinner bells, 2 coffee jars, 2 cookie jars, 6 sets of salt and pepper shakers), mechanical toys (2) and miscellaneous toys (10), prints, puppets, and signs (10). Items acquired from flea markets and dealers.

Steinke, Kathleen

Chiefly an art collection; includes watercolor sketch "Southern Dancer" signed H. Biggert (very early work); wood carved statues over two-feet tall of Uncle Tom and Eva and field workers; and primitive clay statue of Black bongo drummer (signed). Items acquired from antique shops and at auctions, in New Jersey and New York.

Watson, Yvonne (also dealer; see On the Dark Side under Dealers)

Varied collection of advertisements (12) and advertising buttons (20), ashtrays (4), greeting cards (12), banks (1), books (6), candy box (1), dolls (20), cookie jars (6), miscellaneous household items (100–150), linens (6), painting (1), playbills (4), postcards (12), posters (6), puppet (1), record albums (10), salt and pepper shakers (50 sets), sheet music, signs, soap powder boxes, souvenir items (6), sugar bowls (2), toys (7, mechanical and miscellaneous), trade cards (8), and Uncle Ben's Rice tins (4). Materials acquired in New York state.

Wickham, Vicki

Chiefly a collection of golliwog pins made by Roberson's Marmalade in London.

Williams, William T.

Small collection of books, dolls, household items (including 10 sets of salt and pepper shakers), sheet music, soap powder boxes, songbooks (10), and other materials. Special items include a doorstop and two walking sticks all from the nineteenth century. Materials acquired in Maine and Ohio.

North Carolina

Schulman, Norma N.

Primarily a collection of recordings (3,000 78 rpm's) and sheet music (350). Subject areas are pre-war jazz and blues, with emphasis on Black female artists. Few additional items include cans, coffee tins, produce labels, soap powder boxes, and miscellaneous household items.

Ohio

Antonick, Pat

Collection contains advertisements (over 50) and advertising buttons (5), ashtrays (2), bank (1), dolls (20, including some celluloid), cookie jar (1), letter openers (2), soap powder boxes, souvenir items (10–15), tobacco tins, toy (1 Amos 'n' Andy windup), trade cards (over 20), and miscellaneous items (pot holders, calendars, and outhouses). Included are souvenirs of the South depicting gullible and ignorant Southern Blacks; stereotypical items such as Blacks with crocodiles, monkeys, cotton, and watermelon. Collection started in 1972 out of curiosity rather than to demonstrate prejudices. Materials gathered from antique shows, auctions, and flea markets.

Burdine, E.

Concentrates on dolls (25) and salt and pepper shakers (16 sets). Collection also includes advertisement items (miscellaneous as well as produce labels), banks, books, card holders, household items (dinner bell, cookie jar, string holder, soap powder boxes, syrup containers), postcards, sheet music, toys, yard art, and other materials. One special item is a carved boat with ten Black men rowing. Materials purchased form antique shops and flea markets; some gifts.

Hart, Virginia L.
Collection comprises advertisements (chiefly Cream of Wheat), banks (5, including clear glass "Lucky Joe," "Sharecropper," "Mammy" metal and "Mammy" ceramic), box (Mason blacking), dolls (jointed, rubber, cloth, and others), household items (including ashtray, biscuit baker, bottle openers, 8 cookie jars (F & F, Pearl Co., McCoy), dinner bells, egg timers, flower pots, linens, match holders, 6 memo pads/grocery lists, pie bird, pin cushion, pot holders, salt and pepper sets, spice sets, string holders, tape measure (mammy), teapot, games, sheet music, and other materials. Primary interest is in usuable kitchen items. Most items were acquired in Ohio; some ordered form other parts of the country.

Knox, Theresa
Chiefly a collection of postcards (26) and salt and pepper shakers (14 sets). Several other items acquired, including unusual curved tray with woman's head (may be part of salt and pepper set, with one part missing). Materials collected from flea markets, garage and yard sales in Ohio and in other states; some gifts.

Price, Karl V.
Collection consists of advertisements (25, as well as produce labels), greeting cards (75) and postcards (55), books (45) and periodicals (10), dolls (10), games (10), household items (including 40 ashtrays, 3 dinner bells, 55 sets of salt and pepper shakers, 5 sugar bowls, 3 string holders, and 15 syrup containers), puppets (5), record albums (100), sheet music (40), songbooks (10), mechanical toys (13), miscellaneous toys (30), and other items. Seventy-five percent of the collection is in near mint condition. Items collected from yard sales and from other collectors.

Slater, Eva L.
Extensive collection consists of advertisements (numerous, including over 25 buttons, 12 produce labels, and 500 trade cards), autographs (35), banks (12), books (over 350) and periodicals (numerous), cans (5), dolls (25), figural bottles, household items (including cookie jars, dinner plates, 10 sets of salt and pepper shakers, 2 string holders), letter opener, minstrel sketches, paintings, pipes, playbills, posters (25), prints (100), record albums (numerous), sheet music (50), signs (15), soap powder boxes, songbooks (5), souvenir items (25), mechanical toys (12, and other toys, 5), and miscellaneous items including clocks, baseball items, fans, fraternal items, ink wells, paper clips, political buttons, slave bill of sale, statues, and tobacco humidors. Special items include a letter written by the King of England to Black soldiers of World War I, an extensive collection of works by poet Paul Laurence Dunbar, a large selection of children's books, a stamp collection, a sculpture of Louis "Satchmo" Armstrong, and some Ku Klux Klan items (including the Grand Wizard's complete costume—hat, sheet robe bag, medals, and secret code books). Paper goods collected cover a wide variety of subject areas and types. Collecting practices span a twenty-year period.

Wartinger, Kenneth R.
Collection consists of advertisements (produce labels, trade cards, and other items), greeting cards and postcards, banks, cans (10), dolls (10–15), games, household items (10 ashtrays, coffee tins, dinner bells, cookie jars, 10–15 sets of salt and pepper shakers, sugar bowls, syrup containers), letter opener, minstrel sketches, painting (watercolor),

sheet music, soap powder boxes, souvenir items, mechanical and other toys, and other items. Many works by F & F Tool & Die Co., including grocery list, "I'se Got to Buy," and varnish can depicting Black with slogan, "Our varnish won't turn white." Dolls of particular interest include two made by Pat Kolesar, showing exaggerated features, and one angel doll that won best show in Atlanta. Collection acquired in Ohio from flea markets, auction, and gifts.

Oklahoma

Gifford, Carol (also collector, dealer, and manufacturer; see Carol's Collectibles under Designers and Manufacturers)
Collection includes advertisements (miscellaneous as well as trade cards), greeting cards and postcards, books, cans, dolls, household items (3 ashtrays, 34 cookie jars, dinner bells, 1 dinner plate, 35 miscellaneous items, 23 sets of salt and pepper shakers, 1 sugar bowl, 3 string holders, 6 syrup containers), minstrel sketches, paintings, prints, sheet music, souvenir items, and yard art. Items obtained from local antique shops and flea markets. Cookie jars purchased through the *Antique Trader*.

Pennsylvania

D'Ambrosio, Joseph
Advanced collector. Materials number over 1,000 items including advertisements and advertising buttons, ashtrays (18), greeting cards (30), playing cards (1 deck), banks ("Jolly Nigger," "Plantation," and several composition), dinner bells, books (60, including works on Blacks and Africa, *Mother Gooseville*, several editions of *Little Black Sambo* and *Uncle Tom's Cabin*), cans (5), films, games (2), cookie jars (4) and candy jar (1), linens, letter openers, miscellaneous household items (brushes, match boxes), paintings (3), playbills (2), postcards, posters, prints (10), puppet (1 Stepin Fetchit), record albums (14, including "Little Black Sambo"), salt and pepper shakers (30 sets, including one complete with grease pot), sheet music (10), soap powder boxes, string holders (4), syrup containers (5), tobacco tins (4), mechanical toys (1 Kobe, 4 action Kobe), trade cards, yard art (including cast-iron jockeys, concrete fishing boys), and miscellaneous items (Black angels chalkware, door knockers, bottle openers, stoppers and caps, silent butler, match holder, Royal Daulton governor's cook, ceramic tobacco jar, incense burner, nodders, Martin Luther King, Jr., paperweight, clocks (including Redwing mammy electric), 8 chocolate cups, and other works. Collection began in 1977 from a fascination for different subjects and cultures. Most items acquired in Philadelphia.

Dennison, Sam
The collection of 500 pieces of sheet music and 100 minstrel songsters covers the imagery of Blacks in America from the early 1800s through the present; served as a major source for the collector's book *Scandalize My Name: Black Imagery in American Popular Music* (see Bibliography in this chapter). Collection began in 1966; items were purchased from library duplicates, flea markets, dealers, and other sources; some were gifts from persons interested in the research.

Jacovino, Joseph A.
Primary focus of the collection is on advertisement items. Included are general advertisements (55), advertising buttons (35), cans (55), produce labels (30), signs (25), and trade cards (50). The special character of the collection is the stereotypic use of Blacks to advertise products in specific areas during the period 1840–1900. These include ag-

ricultural equipment, blacking (shoe polish), clothing and shoes, foods, furniture, hardware (paints and varnishes), medicines (patent), sewing machines, soaps (detergents and starches), stove blacking (polish), and thread (spool). Erotic, or sexually explicit, items include a tobacco advertisement of a Black man from Millot's Cigars and a Malakov's Bitters advertisement of a Black woman (1846). Other parts of the collection include greeting cards (25), playing cards (10), books (20), games, household items (50), playbills (35), posters (20), soap powder boxes (30), souvenir items (60), tobacco tins (15), toys (2 mechanical and 18 others), and miscellaneous (50 die cuts). Most items, especially trade cards, were purchased during a twelve-year period from antique shows and flea markets, advertising shows in Maryland, New Jersey, and Pennsylvania, and from dealers located throughout the United States and Canada.

Johnson, Elaine
Included in the collection are advertisements (some buttons and labels), greeting cards and postcards, books (including a Sambo book with moving parts), candy boxes, cans, dolls, household items (ashtrays, dinner bells, coffee jars, cookie jars, milk pitchers, 15 sets of salt and pepper shakers, 1 string holder, 3 sugar bowls, 1 syrup container, and 24 miscellaneous items), posters, prints (including signed Sambo print), souvenir items, and yard art. Materials purchased from flea markets, yard sales, and a Black memorabilia show in Maryland.

O'Donnell, Rich
Collection includes advertisements (20) and advertising buttons (10), ashtrays (14), banks (5), dinner bells (12), books (8), cans (2), dolls (5), cookie jars (20), labels (4), letter openers (5), periodicals (2), plates (2 dinner), postcards (15), posters (4), prints, salt and pepper shakers (over 300), soap powder boxes, souvenir items (25), string holders (3), sugar bowls (8), syrup containers (2), miscellaneous items (5 spice sets, 7 oil and vinegar sets, 15 figurines, 16 outhouses, a pencil sharpener, and other works). Special or unique items include mammy in glass globe with snow, Black man and woman turnabouts, and Weller mammy items (of six known pieces made, the collector has three). Materials acquired from various dealers and collectors included in this list. Catalogue of collection in process.

Posner, Judy (also dealer)
Concentrates on cookie jars.

Tennessee

Cauwels, Diane
Advanced collector with extensive assemblage of materials. Included in the collection are advertisements (boxes, tins, 40 buttons, produce labels, and trade cards), banks (6 still), books (20), candy boxes, cans, dolls (toaster dolls only), games (6), household items (67 different cookie jars, large quantity of Coon Chicken Inn dinner plates), 220 different sets of salt and pepper shakers, 15 string holders, 4 sugar bowls, syrup containers, and several hundred miscellaneous items), letter openers (3), record albums (3), signs (Green River type), soap powder boxes, souvenir items, tobacco tins, and approximately 1,200 miscellaneous items. One of the special items in the collection is the complete set of 6 Weller pottery pieces made in the 1930s (only 144 complete sets were made for Quaker Oats/Aunt Jemima Company). The set consists of cookie jar, creamer, sugar bowl, syrup pitcher, tea kettle, and batter bowl. The items feature a mammy and small

black boy; all are hand painted and signed. Collection purchased from parties and flea markets all across the United States.

Cross, Joyce (also dealer, designer/manufacturer; see Memories under Designers and Manufacturers)
Collection primarily consists of dolls, linens, salt and pepper shakers, and needlepoint.

Keith, Stanley J.
The collection contains advertisements, banks, books (relating to the Reconstruction period) and periodicals, dolls, household items (ashtrays, cookie jars, 50 sets of salt and pepper shakers, syrup containers and other items), paintings, photographs (tintype), prints, sheet music, soap powder boxes, souvenir items, stereoptic viewer pictures, and miscellaneous materials. Items acquired from auctions, antique stores, flea markets, yard sales, and friends.

Smith, Jessie Carney
Eclectic collection of advertisements (boxes, buttons, calendars, signs, trade cards), greeting cards, playing cards (1 deck of famous Black Americans), banks (2 still and 5 mechanical), books (150) and periodicals (25), cans, dolls (15), films (2), games, household items (andirons, 15 ashtrays, 2 dinner bells, humidor, 3 dinner plates, including Coon Chicken Inn, figural bottle opener, 12 cookie jars, linens, 3 pitchers, 6 quilts, 50 sets of salt and pepper shakers, sugar and creamer, watermelon boy tip tray, and 50 miscellaneous items), lawn sprinkler, minstrel sketches (5), newspapers (Black, of mid–1900s), paintings, photographs (including tintypes), posters (including several of Blacks on postage stamps), phonograph records (including Bert Williams), puppets (3), prints (including golliwog), slides (200), sheet music (50), signs (including segregation), soap powder boxes, toys (including children in ring game and Sambo dart board), and miscellaneous items. Special pieces include replica of "Lift Every Voice and Sing" by Augusta Savage, Schenley Whiskey series of Black figures, majolica items, and golliwog nodder. Several erotic pieces. Materials acquired from antique shops in Georgia, Ohio, North Carolina, and Tennessee, from flea markets, mail order, and gifts. Began collecting in 1971.

Wilcox, Beverly Mitchell (also dealer)
Chiefly paper items such as postcards, photographs, and prints. Collection includes advertisements (buttons, produce labels, trade cards), greeting cards (15) and postcards (45), banks, books (20) and periodicals (9), dolls, household items (ashtrays, linens, salt and pepper shakers), films (Amos 'n Andy shorts), minstrel sketches, playbills, yard art, and miscellaneous pieces (Christmas package seals, church collection envelopes and perfect attendance pins, hand fans, Coon Chicken Inn matchbooks, and other items). Collection acquired from antique shops and flea markets in California, Georgia, Louisiana, Tennessee, Texas, and Washington.

Wilson, Rhonda Campbell
Collection includes advertisements (10), greeting cards (5), dinner bells (2), books (40, including autographed copies), advertising buttons (3), cans (10), dolls (10), games (3), miscellaneous household items (20), labels (10), periodicals (20), playbills (7), postcards (15), posters (20), prints (2), record albums (300), salt and pepper shakers (3 sets), sheet music (3), signs (3), soap powder boxes, songbooks, souvenir items (5), syrup containers, yard art, and miscellaneous items (Sambo puzzle, scrapbooks, late 1800 and early 1900 magazines and cartoons, and early items relating to Tuskegee Institute). Most items

purchased in Virginia; some in Maryland, Massachusetts, and Tennessee; others handed down in family.

Texas

Reed, Bernadette T.
The collection is oriented toward ceramics and kitchen items, and contains banks (still and mechanical), household items (ashtrays, cookie jars, cream and sugar sets, 16 sets of salt and pepper shakers, 1 set of honey jars, 6 spice sets, 5-piece kitchen set), postcards, prints, puppets, and miscellaneous items (golliwogs, thermometers, toothpick holders, and other items). Materials acquired in Texas and Washington.

Washington

Miller, Sandy
Advanced collector of dolls (195 acquired). Collection also contains advertisements (buttons, produce labels, trade cards, and 21 other items), greeting cards and postcards, banks, books (45) and periodicals (3), games, household items (10 ashtrays, 3 dinner bells, 10 cookie jars, 3 dinner plates, 70 sets of salt and pepper shakers, sugar bowls, 3 string holders, 4 syrup containers, and 30 miscellaneous items), 1 lawn sprinkler, 1 pipe, posters, puppets, sheet music, signs, soap powder boxes, souvenir items, toys (mechanical), yard art, and other items.

Virginia

Holoman, Verna
Materials consist of books (30), periodicals (10), and record albums (30). Items purchased from used bookstores, record shops, and library sales in Ohio. Acquisitions began while collector was graduate student and continued out of interest in history and books.

Wyoming

Wolford, Joyce
Collection is heavily weighted in advertisements (buttons, produce labels, 24 trade cards, and 103 miscellaneous items), and in household materials (10 ashtrays, 3 dinner bells, 23 cookie jars, dinner plates, 95 sets of salt and pepper shakers, 7 string holders, 4 sugar bowls, and 65 miscellaneous items). Included also are greeting cards (18), postcards (22), banks, books, candy boxes, cans, dolls (14), games (including Sambo dart board), letter opener, posters, prints, puppets, sheet music, signs, soap powder boxes, souvenir items, tobacco tins, toys (miscellaneous), yard art, and other items. Other special items collected include cast-metal Black workman (1932), plate (calendar, 1915), spoons (24 sterling silver, figural, Blacks on handles and etched or embossed in bowl), tape measure of cast-metal head (German), and vase (figural, Black bride, German). Several erotic or sexually explicit pieces. Collection purchased through various advertisements and collectors' lists in California, eastern, and midwestern states.

Dealers

This list of dealers is a sampling of many who are currently involved in buying, selling, and trading Black Americana. For additional information on sources of materials (flea markets, swap meets, trade days, and dealer auctions), consult *Great American Flea*

Market Directory, P.O. Box 455, Arnold, MO 63010. See also issues of *Collectors'*
Showcase, Dawn Reno's *Black Americana*, and introductory pages to specialized works
such as Gene Florence's *The Collector's Encyclopedia of Occupied Japan Collectibles*.
While this book has made no attempt to list appraisers, auctioneers, and consultants who
are experienced in handling Black collectibles, a number of such professionals are avail-
able. Examples are Ronald Rooks, appraiser, 880 Washington Boulevard, Baltimore,
MD 21230; Ronald Carr, appraiser c/o the editor; Richard Opfer, Harris Auction Galleries,
Inc., auctioneers, 873–875 North Howard Street, Baltimore, MD 21201; Barrett-Bertoia,
auctions and appraisals, 1217 Glenwood Drive, Vineland, NJ 08360; Hake's Americana
& Collectibles, P.O. Box 1444CS, York, PA 17405; P & T Antiquarians, 2813 West
End Avenue, Nashville, TN 37203; and Robert L. McCumber, 201 Carriage Drive,
Glastonbury, CT 06033.

Antiques and Collectibles, Helene Guarnaccia, 52 Coach Lane, Fairfield, CT 06430,
    (203) 374–6034.
Antonation, Linda; P.O. Box 1551; Bellevue, WA 98009.
    Black memorabilia catalogue. Illustrated. Items fully described. Range from com-
    mon to rare. Each issue includes kitchen items, paper, linens, bisques, and more.
Arnold, Verdia; 479 Westgate 9F; Pasadena CA 91103; (818) 792–6688.
The Back Porch, Chris Simmons, 429 Lakeview Terrace, Pemberton, NJ 08068, (609)
    894–4455.
    Send $1.00 and self-addressed stamped envelope for copy of Black memorabilia
    list.
Behind the Times, Fred and Shirley May, P.O. Box 8683, Chattanooga, TN 37411, (615)
    899–1058.
    Offers wide range of new, folk items.
Bertrand, Valerie; Black'abilia; 14 Vernon Street; Hamden, CT 06518.
Cerebro, P.O. Box 1221, Lancaster, PA 17603, (717) 656–7875.
    Lithographs of produce, cigar, and other labels.
Cookie Jar Antiques, C. Keith Lytle, 99 Greensboro Way, Antioch, CA 94509, (415)
    757–7731.
    Offers a variety of Black collectibles, including many common ones made in
    Japan. Specializes in cookie jars.
Discount Video Tapes, Inc., P.O. Box 7122, 3711 B West Clark Avenue, Burbank, CA
    91510, (818) 843–3366.
    Video scrapbooks as well as Black artist of the silver screen on video (VHS and
    beta).
Earlene's Orphanage, P.O. Box 7747, Silver Springs, MD 20907, (202) 829–7170.
    Offers Black collectible Cabbage Patch dolls.
Ella's Place, 9500 Croom Acres Drive, Upper Marlboro, MD 20870.
Ethnic Treasures, 1401 Asbury Court, Hyattsville, MD 20782.
    Also sponsors Black memorabilia shows and publishes newsletter.
Florence, Gene; P.O Box 22186; Lexington, KY 40522.
    Items from occupied Japan.
Franklin Antique Mall; Joan and Archie Glenn; Second Avenue, South, and South Margin;
    Franklin, TN 37064; (615) 790–8593.
    Black antiques and collectibles.

Gwen's Antiques, P.O. Box 151, Lafayette Hill, PA 19444.
   Extensive collection of paper items.
Haring, Donna; Rennigers Market; Adamstown, PA 19501
   Black-related items (ceramic, linens, cloth dolls).
Hart, Mark; P.O. Box 177; Old Bethpage, NY 11804.
   Specializes in, but not limited to, fine and rare items, such as tobacco jars, banks
   (mechanical and still), Nardi sculptures, and wall hangings.
Heritage Crafts; Page Jackson, Jennifer Jackson, Janice and Ronnie Meador; 503 Third
   Avenue West; Springfield, TN 37172; (615) 384–7701.
   Black folk items.
Just Like Mama Had, Barbara Friend and Mel Eisenberg, 2514 Kings Point Drive,
   Dunwoody, GA 30338.
   Black antiques and collectibles.
Ken-Neets Antiques, Route 1, Box R9C, Beaumont, TX 77706.
Kentucky Country, Mickie Carpenter Antiques, 4321 Smallhouse Road, Bowling Green,
   KY 42101, (502) 781–7435.
   Collects Black memorabilia, including quilts and furniture.
McCumber, Robert L.; 201 Carriage Drive; Glastonbury, CT 06033; (203) 633–4984.
   Appraisals; buys and sells toy mechanical and still banks and books on banks.
On the Dark Side, 309 South Franklin Street, Syracuse, NY 13202, (315) 428–0827.
P & T Antiquarians, P. J. and Tyson Gibbs, 2813 West End Avenue, Nashville, TN
   37203, (615) 320–1928.
   Fine, Black collectibles. Also offers appraisals of collections.
Pennywhistle Antiques, Ron Slaughter, P.O. Box 358, Amador City, CA 95601, (209)
   267–5966.
Pollack, Frank and Barbara; 1214 Green Bay Road; Highland Park, IL 60035; (312) 433–
   2213.
   Folk dolls and paintings.
Posner, Judy; R.D. #1, Box 273F; Effort, PA 18330; (717) 269–6583.
   Send $1.00 + 39¢ and self-addressed stamped envelope for illustrated list of
   Black memorabilia.
The Sheet Music Center, Box 367, Port Washington, NY 11050.
   Black sheet music and piano rolls.
Simply Country, Jeanie Ohle, 303 Timberlane Drive, Slidell, LA 70458, (504) 649–
   3168.
   Wide range of fine Black collectibles.
Smorgasbord Antique and Gift Mall, 4144B Lebanon Road, Hermitage, TN 37076, (615)
   883–5789.
Stebbins, Gwen; P.O. Box 388; Davidson, MI 48432.
Thalberg, Jan; 23 Mountain View Drive; Weston, CT 06883; (203) 227–8175.
Then, Now & When, 1401 Ashbury Court, Hyattsville, MD 20782, (301) 559–6363.
Totty, Gordon; 576 Massachusetts Avenue; Lunenburg, MA 01462.
   Specializes in scarce paper Americana, including books, periodicals, prints, sheet
   music, and nineteenth-century images on cabinet cards and stereoptic cards. Cat-
   alogue available for $1.00 subscription.
Wilcox, Beverly Mitchell; P & T Antiquarians; 2813 West End Avenue; Nashville, TN
   37203; (615) 320–1928.

All types of Black memorabilia, particularly trade cards, tin signs, and kitchen items.
Wonderful Things, 616 E Street, NW, Washington, DC 20004, (202) 393–8413.

Designers and Manufacturers

Carol's Collectibles; Carol Gifford, owner; 426 "E" Frank Street; Norman, OK 73071; (405) 366–8367.
    Designs and copyrights series of cookie jars and other items depicting early Black American heritage. Has the discontinued mold for "granny" jar which is being made in the series. The mammy watermelon jar produced in the 1930s by Pearl China Company is another in a series of approximately six jars being manufactured.
Country Accents; Thomas J. Miller, owner/designer; 522 Vincennes; New Albany, IN 47150.
    Designs and creates Black folk dolls.
Memories; Joyce Cross, owner; 111 Ashland Court; Franklin, TN 37064; (615) 790–8890.
    Designed and copyrighted dinner plates depicting Hattie McDaniel and Buckwheat (from the Our Gang Little Rascal's television series).

COLLECTORS' CLUBS

Although the interest of some of these organizations is not limited to Black items, they may be beneficial to Black memorabilia collectors. Excluded from the list is the Black Americana Memorabilia Collectors Association, a national group organized in 1984 but no longer in existence. For information on the association, see early issues of *The Black American Collector*.

Bay Area Collectors of Black Memorabilia, Jacqueline Boggan, 2804 Benvenuen, Berkeley, CA 94705.
Doorstop Collector's Club, 1217 Glenwood Drive, Vineland, NJ 08360.
The Ephemera Society, 124 Elm Street, Bennington, VT 05201.
Mechanical Bank Collectors of America, P.O. Box 128, Allegan, Michigan 49010.
National Association of Paper & Advertising Collectibles, P.O. Box 471, Columbia, PA 17512.
Occupied Japan Collectors Club, 18309 Faysmith Avenue, Torrance, CA 90504.
Salt and Pepper Shaker Club, Dottie and Bill Avery, 2832 Rapidan Trail, Maitland, FL 32751.
    Publishes newsletter.

EXHIBITIONS, SHOWS AND SALES, AND SPECIAL PROGRAMS

The activities below, in chronological order under various subheadings, are representative of the numerous exhibitions, special shows, sales, and programs presented on the theme of Black Americana. The recent groundswell of interest in or curiosity for Black memorabilia has prompted numerous local exhibits and lectures on this theme. For other information and dates, see current issues of *Black Ethnic Collectibles: Newsletter*

for the Black Memorabilia Collector, *The Black Americana Collector*, and *Collectors'*
Showcase listed in the bibliography in this section.

Auctions

Collectors' Auction, Black Americana Sale, Timonium, Maryland, March 7, 1981; October 17, 1981; September 1982; and October 5, 1985. Catalogues published.

Collector's Auction, Black Americana Sale, Baltimore, Maryland. The Ronald Rooks Collection, April 23, 1983; July 21, 1984. Catalogues published.

Collector's Auction, Black Americana Sale, Baltimore, Maryland. The Ronald Carr Collection, October 5, 1986. Catalogue published.

Lloyd Ralston Toys, Fairfield, Connecticut. The Frank Mitchell Collection of Still and Mechanical Banks, November 21, 1981; additional auction April 4–5, 1986.

Toy Museum of Atlanta, at auction, Philadelphia, Pennsylvania, October 3–4, 1986; second sale March 13–14, 1987. Many Black toys included. Catalogues published.

Conferences

See also lectures presented in connection with exhibitions listed below.

Atlanta University, School of Library Service, Atlanta, Georgia. "Conference on Materials by and about Negroes," October 1965. Proceedings published.

Howard University, Washington, D.C. "Black Bibliophiles and Collectors: A National Symposium," November 29–30, 1983. Section on "Black Memorabilia as Collectables and Material Culture" included lecture on "Image Collections," by collector/scholar Lillian Anthony; "The Johnson Foundation" (on materials on Blacks in the theater), by collector/scholar Helen Armstead Johnson; and "The Paul Robeson Archives," by scholar Paul Robeson, Jr. Publication of proceedings by Howard University Press pending.

Exhibitions

Dartmouth College, Hanover, New Hampshire. The Marguerite Ross-King (now Barnett) Collection, exhibition and lecture, March 1981.

Fisk University Library, Fisk University, Nashville, Tennessee. "Images in Black Artifacts: Negative and Positive," exhibit and lecture series at the university and throughout Tennessee, 1981–1983. Guide and bibliography published.

Berkeley Art Center, Live Oaks Park, California. "Ethnic Notions: Black Images in the White Mind" (the Janette Faulkner Collection), lecture and exhibit, September 12–November 4, 1982. Catalogue published.

Washington University, St. Louis, Missouri. "The Mae Smith Blount Collection of Black Stereotypic Memorabilia and Artifacts," exhibit and lecture, October, 1982.

South DeKalb Gallery, Mini Mall, South DeKalb, Georgia. "Famous Black Women in History" (dolls from the N. Louise Willingham Collection), exhibit, February 1983.

Martin Luther King, Jr., Memorial Library, Washington, D.C. "Reflection on the Past" (the Albert L. Blalock and Steven D. Lewis Collection), exhibit, May 1–June 30, 1986.

Wadsworth Atheneum, Hartford, Connecticut. "Afro-American: Images of Black American History from the Simpson Collection," July 4, 1986–January 18, 1987.

Vaughn Cultural Center, St. Louis, Missouri. "Recollections and Images," the Black memorabilia collection of Edgar and Donna Orchard, September 20–October 31, 1987.

Vanderbilt University, Bishop Johnson Black Cultural Center, Nashville, Tennessee. "How White Folks Saw Black Folks: An Introduction to Black Memorabilia," October 13, 1987.

Shows and Sales

Silver Spring, Maryland. "First Annual Black Americana Extravaganza Show and Sale," October 26–28, 1984, sponsored by M & J Productions.

Atlanta, Georgia. "Black Americana Show and Sale," November 8–10, 1985, sponsored by M & J Productions.

Richmond, Virginia. "Black Americana Show and Sale," February, 1986.

Pasadena Center Conference Building, Pasadena, California. "Second Annual Black Memorabilia Extravaganza Show and Sale of the West," sponsored by M & J Productions, May 17–18, 1986.

Silver Spring, Maryland, Armory Place. "Black Americana Show and Sale," sponsored by M & J Productions, October 3–5, 1986.

Howard University, Washington, D.C. "Black Memorabilia Show and Sale," sponsored by Ethnic Treasures, February 2–3, 1987.

Pasadena Center, Conference Building, Pasadena, California. "Third Annual Black Memorabilia Extravaganza Show and Sale of the West," sponsored by Ethnic Treasures, May 2–3, 1987. (At least two Black memorabilia shows and sales are now held annually: the West Coast show in Pasadena, California, in May, and the East Coast show in Silver Spring, Maryland, in October.)

Silver Spring, Maryland, Armory Place. "Fourth Annual Black Memorabilia Show and Sale," sponsored by Ethnic Treasures, October 2–4, 1987. Series of seminars on collecting Black memorabilia held on October 3, 1987.

BIBLIOGRAPHY

The literature on collecting Black Americana in a single, comprehensive source has been lacking; therefore, this section should provide an important tool in the access to information on this theme. To glean a reasonably good insight into the publications on this topic, the reader must search a number of sources. For example, information on toys may be found in catalogues of toy museums, such as *Perelman Antique Toy Museum* (1972). Similarly, information on salt and pepper shakers may be found in Helene Guarnaccia, *Salt and Pepper Shakers* (1985) and in Melba Davern, *Collector's Encyclopedia of Salt and Pepper Shakers* (1985); dolls in Patikki and Tyson Gibbs, *The Collector's Encyclopedia of Black Dolls* (1987); banks in Bill Norman, *The Bank Book: The Encyclopedia of Mechanical Bank Collecting* (1984), the "Cream of Wheat" man in Dave Stivers, *The Nabisco Brand Collection of Cream of Wheat Advertising Art* (1986); and under various topical issues examined in this book in references given at the end of each chapter. John Denis Mercier's doctoral dissertation, available through University Microfilms and the University of Pennsylvania and forthcoming in a revised version through Greenwood Press, is the most comprehensive resource available on Black Americana in popular culture. It includes excellent references to the origins of images or Black memorabilia; however, its purpose is not toward assessing the key literature on this general theme. For current information on collections, collectors, and related topics, two publications mentioned earlier are essential: *The Black American Collector* and *Black Ethnic Collectibles*. Subscription information for these newsletters is given in the alphabetical listing below. Two recent price guides, P. J. Gibbs' *Black Collectibles Sold in America* and Dawn E. Reno's *Collecting Black Americana*, help to balance the basic resources needed for the study of Black Americana. For current prices of Black collectibles, the reader should consult sections on Black Americana in various price guides to antiques. The list that follows includes a mixture of comprehensive and brief discussions; used together, however, they help to round out all but the obscure sources of information on collections and collectibles in Black Americana.

Ames, Alex. *Collecting Cast Iron*. Derbyshire, England: Moorland Publishing, 1980.
"Ann Says Slave Story a Myth." In Ann Landers Column. Nashville *Banner*, November 3, 1982.
  Discusses the legends of the Black lawn jockey figure.
Antique Shop Guide. P.O. Box 90, Knightson, IA 46148, 1986.
  Useful for locating antique shops.
Antique Week. Mid-Atlantic Edition. 15 Catoctin Circle, SE, Leesburg, VA 22075.
Antique Weekly (formerly *Tri-State Trader*). P.O. Box 90 AP, Knightstown, IA.
  See various issues for articles on Black Americana, items available, and locations of dealers and shows.
Axe, John. *Collectible Black Dolls*. Riverdale, Md.: Hobby House Press, 1978.
————. *Effanbee: A Collector's Encyclopedia*. Riverdale, Md.: Hobby House Press, 1983.
Bailey, Stanley. "Black Artifacts Collection Raises Interest and Price." *Washington Times*, March 10, 1987: 5–B.
Barenholz, Bernard, and Irene McClintock. *American Antique Toys 1830–1900*. New York: Harry B. Abrams, 1980.
Barnett, Marguerite Ross. "Nostalgia as Nightmare: Blacks and American Popular Culture." *The Crisis* 89 (February 1982): 42–45. Illustrations in color and black and white.
Berry, Heidi L. "Focusing on Black Art and Artifacts: A Growing Appreciation of Black Life, History and Culture." *Washington Home* (February 27, 1986): 9, 11–13.
  Illustrated. Contains information on several collections.
Bertoia, Jeanne. *Door Stops: Identification and Value*. Paducah, Ky.: Collector Books, c1985.
  Contains color illustrations of several Black door stops.
Black America on Stage. Text by Helen A. Johnson. New York: The Graduate Center of the City University of New York, October 1978.
  Catalog of the exhibit Black America on Stage from the collection of the Armstead-Johnson Foundation for Theatre Research, Helen A. Johnson, curator. Depicts the work of Blacks in the theatre in all phases and capacities.
The Black American Collector: The Magazine for the Collector of Black-Related Material.
  v. 1–, October 1981–. Publication irregular 1985–1986, but resumed in 1987.

Issued bimonthly by Ronald A. Rooks, 880 Washington Boulevard, Baltimore, MD 21230.

"Black Americana 1630–1984." *Antiques and Arts Weekly* (February 22, 1985).

"Black Collectors out of the Closet." In Lifestyles Weekender. Nashville *Banner*, November 20, 1986: B–1.

Black Ethnic Collectibles; Newsletter for the Black Memorabilia Collector. v. 1–, 1987–. Bimonthly. Ethnic Treasures, 1401 Asbury Court, Hyattsville, MD 20782. $13.00 yearly subscription.
    Contains articles on the collector; collections; sale and wanted items; advertisements; new subscribers and collecting interests; news regarding museums exhibits, auctions, consumer information, organization/clubs sponsorships, special events; featured articles on topical issues; regional news; opinions; reports on mystery items; and illustrations.

"Black Jockeys Shaped Early Churchill, Kentucky Derby History." *Churchill Downs News*, 1980 Black Expo Edition: 2–3. Illustrated.

The Black Memorabilia Collector's Monthly Newsletter. no. 1, 1982–85. Ed. Jacquie Greenwood.

"Black Memorabilia: Images in Racism." *The National Leader*, May 31, 1982: 23–24.

Bontemps, Arna. "Special Collections of Negroana." *Library Quarterly* 16 (July 1944): 187–206.

Carr, Ron. "Black Memorabilia Offers a Wide Range in Collecting." *The Black American Collector* (October 1981): 3–4.

———. "Some Goodies to Collect." *The Black American Collector* (October 1981): 12–14.

Carr, Ron, comp. *Collector's Auction: Black Americana Sale.* October 5, 1986. Catalogue. Baltimore, Md.: Harris Auction Galleries, 1986.
    Illustrated.

Carr, Ronnie. "Box Games." *Reflections of Sable Love* 1,6 (March 1986): 5–6.

Christie's East. "Christie's Collectibles." New York: Christie's East, 1975–1979.

Coleman, Dorothy S., Elizabeth A. Coleman, and Evelyn J. Coleman. *The Collector's Encyclopedia of Dolls.* New York: Crown Publishers, 1975.

"Colgate Drops 'Darkie' Toothpaste Logo." *Afro-American*, March 7, 1987: 15.
    Discusses controversy of the racially offensive package and tube of "Darkie" toothpaste marketed in the Far East and featuring blackface Al Jolson type.

"Collectibles: Black Memorabilia." *Black Enterprise* (February 1982): 101.

Collectors' Showcase. v. 1–, 1981–. Bimonthly. Accent Studios, 1018 Rosencrans, San Diego, CA 92106. Yearly subscription $20.
    Various issues contain illustrated articles on Black memorabilia and collecting practices for specific items such as dolls, toys, and others. Advertisements of shows, sales, and items from private collectors for sale are given. See also articles by Don Kader and Donna C. Kaonis.

Cornelius, Carlisle. "Antiques Tell Story of Blacks' History." In Washington Weekend, *The Washington Times*, October 1, 1987: M35.

Cranmer, Don. *Collectors Encyclopedia of Toys and Banks; with Price Guide.* Gas City, Ind.: L–W Book Sales, 1986.
    Arranged by broad category such as tin and heavy gauge, cast iron, and banks. Photographs and prices for Black toys and banks included in this arrangement. Gives list of other books on toys and banks published by L–W Book Sales.

Cull, George, and Alta Cull. *Cigar Advertising Price Guide: Signs, Tins, Labels, etc.* Evanston, Ill.: H. Fenrich, 1954.

Currier and Ives. *The Great Book of Currier & Ives' America.* Ed. Walton Rawls. New York: Abbeville Press, 1979.
  Includes illustrations from the "Darktown Series."

Curtis, Tony, comp. *Antiques and Their Values, Dolls and Toys.* Scotland: Lyle Publications, 1980.

Davern, Melba. *The Collector's Encyclopedia of Salt and Pepper Shakers: Figural and Novelty.* Paducah, Ky.: Collector Books, 1985. "Black Americana," 116–30. Includes prices.

Denison, Sam. *Scandalize My Name: Black Imagery in American Popular Music.* New York: Garland Publishing, 1982.

Driskell, David C. *Two Centuries of Black American Art.* New York: Alfred A. Knopf, 1956.

Eliot, Drew. "Black Collectibles." *Free Enterprise*, August 5, 1975: 31–39.
  Cover shows full-page color illustration of J. P. Alley's Hambone cigars. Article includes black and white illustrations.

Ethnic Notions: Black Images in the White Mind. An Exhibition of Afro-American Stereotype and Caricature from the Collection of Janette Faulkner. Berkeley, Calif.: Berkeley Art Center, September 12 to November 4, 1982.
  Text with black and white illustrations.

"Everybody's Happy." *Encore* (July 1973): 37–46.
  Illustrated article on Black memorabilia.

Ferris, William. *Afro-American Folk Art and Crafts.* Boston: G. K. Hall & Co., 1983.

Fisk University Library. Fisk University. "Images in Black Artifacts: Negative and Positive: A Selected Bibliography." Comp. Dorothy G. Lake. Nashville, Tenn.: Fisk University Library, 1981.
  Prepared as a part of a public exhibit/lecture series funded by the Tennessee Committee for the Humanities.

Flea Market Price Guide. Robert W. Miller. 5th ed. Lombard, Ill.: Wallace-Homestead Books, 1984.
  "Black Collectibles," 74–75. Illustrated.

Florence, Gene. *The Collector's Encyclopedia of Occupied Japan Collectibles.* Third Series. Paducah, Ky.: Collector Books, 1987.
  Alphabetical arrangement by subject categories, with prices included. Black items given within this arrangement. Also includes in back, price guides for Series I and II in the set.

Frederickson, George M. *The Black Image in the White Mind: The Debate on Afro-American Character and Destiny, 1817–1914.* New York: Harper and Row, 1971.

Freeman, Ruth S. *Encyclopedia of American Dolls.* New ed. Watkins Glenn, N.Y.: The Author, 1972.

Fritz, Richard. "On the Air: The Amos 'n' Andy Show." *Collectibles Illustrated* (May/June, 1983): 82–92.

Gaines-Carter, Patrice. "Black Memorabilia: Images of Racism." *The National Leader*, May 31, 1982: 23–24.

Gibbons, Louise J. *Buried Treasure in the Black Community.* New York: Vantage Press, 1978.

Gibbs, P. J. "Black Collectibles Catalog." Nashville, CGL, Box 158472, Nashville, TN. Monthly. Illustrated.

———. *Black Collectibles Sold in America*. Paducah, Ky.: Collector Books, 1986.
Contains text and over 500 full-color illustrations of Black collectibles. Photographs include advertising items, containers, dolls, entertainment, figural images, folk art, literary collectibles, novelties and souvenirs, pictorial images, toys, and other items. Current price guide and list of Black museums conclude the volume.

———. *Horsman Dolls, 1950–1970*. Paducah, Ky.: Collector Books, 1985.
Includes illustrations of Black dolls.

Gibbs, Patikki, and Tyson Gibbs. *The Collector's Encyclopedia of Black Dolls*. Paducah, Ky.: Collector Books, 1987.
Illustrated with description and prices. "Bibliography," 184–85; "Books with Black Dolls Listed," 185–90; "Price Guide Listing," 190; "Doll Companies Which Carried a Line of Black Dolls," 190.

Gite, Lloyd. "Memorabilia." *Essence* (October 1985): 99.
Gives notes on how to collect. Illustrated.

Goodstone, Tony, ed. *1929 Johnson Smith and Co. Catalogue: Suprising Novelties, Puzzles, Tricks, Joke Goods, Useful Articles, etc.* New York: Chelsea House Publishers, 1970.

Great American Flea Market Directory. P.O. Box 455, Arnold, MO 63010.
Lists flea markets, swap meets, trade days, and dealer auctions.

Guarnaccia, Helene. *Salt and Pepper Shakers*. Paducah, Ky.: Collector books, 1984.
Out of print.
Black and white illustrations of salt and pepper shakers depicting Black images, 40–45.

———. *Salt and Pepper Shakers*. Paducah, Ky.: Collector Books, 1985.
Color illustrations of salt and pepper shakers depicting Black images, 56–65. Other Black sets scattered throughout the subject arrangement, such as "Advertising and Promotion."

Hammond, Dorothy. *Confusing Collectibles: A Guide to the Identification of Reproductions*. Leon, Iowa: Mid-America Books Co., 1969.

Hampton, Chester M. "Jocko, Symbol of Pride." *Washington Post*, September 7, 1970, B1, B5.
Brief biographical information on Earl Koger, author of a leaflet on "Jocko," the Black lawn jockey figure. Also recounts the legend.

Harris, Jessica. "Collecting Black Memorabilia." *Essence* 8 (July 1977): 56–57, 130–31.
Illustrated article on Black collectors and collections.

Harris, Middleton, with Morris Levitt, et. al. *The Black Book*. New York: Random House, 1974.
Text with color and black and white illustrations of scenes from Black life, Black Americana materials, historical documents, and other information.

Hertz, Louis H. *The Toy Collector*. New York: Arco Publishing, 1980.

Hillier, Mary. *Dolls and Doll-Makers*. New York: G. P. Putnam's Sons, 1968.

"The Hitching Post." *The Black American Collector* 1,4 (May–June 1983): [5–7]
Legends of the hitching boy, stable boy, or jockey figure.

Holt, Patricia. "Shocking Study in Images." Review of *Ethnic Notions: Black Images in the White Mind.* From the collection of Janette Faulkner, Berkeley Art Center. *San Francisco Chronicle*, August 1, 1982: 3.

Hopkinson, William P. *Toys and Banks with Their Prices at Auction.* Concord, N.H.: Rumford Press, 1970.

Hudgeons, Thomas E., III., ed. *The Official 1983 Price Guide to Antiques by the House of Collectibles.* Orlando, Fla.: House of Collectibles, 1982.

Hyman, Tony. *Handbook of American Cigar Boxes.* Elmira, N.Y.: Arnot Art Museum, 1979.

Jeromack, Paul. "Black Plaster Wall Placques." *The Black Memorabilia Collector's Monthly Newsletter* (April 1983): 6–8.

———. "An Introduction to Black Cookie Jars." *The Black American Collector* 1,2 (December, January, February 1982): 3–4.

Kader, Don. "Collecting Black Memorabilia." *Collector's Showcase* 2,1 (September/ October 1982): 8–17.
    Cover illustration important for the collector. The article is illustrated in color and describes the collection of Ronald Carr before it was sold.

Kaduck, John M. *Advertising Trade Cards.* Des Moines, Iowa.: Wallace-Homestead Book Co., 1976.

Kaonis, Donna C. "Collecting Black Memorabilia." *Collectors' Showcase* 5,6 (July/ August 1986): 33–39.
    Illustrations in color. Many of the items shown are from the collection of Ronald Carr who, at the time of publication, had amassed the world's largest known collection of Black memorabilia.

"Keepers of the Story." *Ebony* (February 1981): 84–90.
    An illustrated article on Black museums as institutions that preserve and honor the Afro-American cultural heritage.

Ketchum, William C., Jr. *The Catalog of American Collectibles: A Fully Illustrated Guide to Styles and Prices.* New York: A Rutledge/Mayflower Book, 1979.

King, Constance Eileen. *Dolls and Dolls' Houses.* London: Hamlin, 1971.

Klamkin, Marian. *Picture Postcards.* New York: Dodd, Mead and Co., 1974.

Klug, Ray. *Encyclopedia of Antique Advertising.* Gas City, Ind.: L–W Promotions, 1978.

Koger, Earl, Sr. "The Legend of Jocko: The Negro Boy Who Inspired George Washington." n.p.: The Author, 1963.
    Leaflet giving the legend of the Black lawn jockey figure.

Kovel, Ralph, and Terry Kovel. *Kovel's Advertising Collectibles Price List.* New York: Crown Publishers, 1986.
    Covers the 1986–1987 market in advertising collectibles and includes names familiar to collectors, such as Green River Whiskey.

———. *Kovel's Antiques and Collectibles Price List.* 15th ed. New York: Crown Publishers, 1983–1984.

———. *Kovel's Antiques Price List.* 13th ed. New York: Crown Publishers, 1980–81.
    This volume and later editions are useful for the collector to show price changes. Some items shown in one edition are excluded from others.

———. *Kovel's Antiques Price List.* 14th ed. New York: Crown Publishers, 1981–1982.

———. *Kovel's Antique Price List.* 18th ed. New York: Crown Publishers, 1986.
    Contains alphabetical list of Black memorabilia. Illustrated.

———. *Kovel's Collectors Source Book.* New York: Crown Publishers, 1983.

Includes names and addresses of collectors' clubs, magazines, auction houses, mail order houses, and restoration services for over 100 different items. Essential.

———. *Kovel's Know Your Collectibles.* New York: Crown Publishers, 1981.

Lavitt, Wendy. *American Folk Dolls.* New York: Alfred A. Knopf, 1982.
Contains section on "Black Dolls," 74–83. Illustrations and text.

Lemons, J. Stanley. "Black Stereotypes as Reflected in Popular Culture: 1880–1920." *American Quarterly* 29 (Spring 1977): 102–16.

Lenburg, Jeff. *The Encyclopedia of Animated Cartoon Series.* Westport, Conn.: Arlington House Publishers, 1981.

Lesser, Robert. *A Celebration of Comic Art and Memorabilia.* New York: Hawthorne Books, 1975.

Levine, Lawrence W. *Black Culture and Black Consciousness: Afro-American Folk Thought from Slavery to Freedom.* New York: Oxford University Press, 1977.

Lipman, Jean. *American Folk Art: Mood, Metal and Stone.* New York: Dover Publications, 1972.

Livingstone, Jane, and John Beardsley. *Black Folk Art in America: 1930–1980.* Jackson, Miss.: Corcoran Gallery of Art/University of Mississippi Press Center for the Study of Southern Culture, 1980.

Maccay, James. *Childhood Antiques.* New York: Taplinger Publishing Co., 1976.

McClintock, Katherine M. *The Complete Book of Small Antiques Collecting.* New York: Bramhall House, 1953.

McCumber, Robert L. *Toy Bank Reproductions and Fakes.* Glastonbury, Conn.: The Author, 1970.
Discusses reproductions of mechanical and still banks, lists the reproductions, and provides tracings for detecting fakes. Many Black banks included.

Mackay, James. *An Encyclopedia of Small Antiques.* New York: Harper and Row, 1975.

McQuary, Jim, and Cathy McQuary. *Collector's Guide to Advertising Cards.* Gas City, Ind.: L–W Promotions, 1975.

Malveaux, Julianne. "Investing by Collecting." *Essence* 17 (December 1986): 113–14.

Margolin, Victor, Ira Brichta, and Vivian M. Brichta. *The Promise and the Product: 200 Years of American Advertising Posters.* New York: Macmillan Publishing Co., 1979.

Mebane, John. *Collecting Nostalgia: The First Guide to the Antiques of the 30's and 40's.* New Rochelle, N.Y.: Arlington House Publishers, 1977.

Mercier, John Denis. "The Evolution of the Black Image in White Consciousness, 1876–1954: A Popular Culture Perspective." Ph.D. diss., University of Pennsylvania, 1984.

———. *Representations of Blacks in American Culture: An Analytical Sourcebook of Artifacts and Memorabilia.* Westport, Conn.: Greenwood Press, in press.
A commercial edition of the author's doctoral dissertation. This is a scholarly work which delves into the origins of Black Americana. Both editions are illustrated.

Miller, Elizabeth W., and M. Fisher. *The Negro in America: A Bibliography.* 2d ed., rev. and enl. Cambridge, Mass.: Harvard University Press, 1970.

Miller, George, and Dorothy Miller. *Picture Postcards in the United States, 1893–1918.* New York: Clarkson N. Potter, 1976.

Miller, Robert W. *Wallace-Homestead Price Guide to Dolls.* Des Moines, Iowa: Wallace-Homestead Book Co., 1982.

Moore, Andy, and Susan Moore. *The Penny Bank Book; Collecting Still Banks through the Penny Door*. Exton, Pa.: Schiffer Publishing, 1984.
> Nearly 1,700 still banks, a number of which are Black.

Morrow, Lynn. *Black Collectibles: Descriptive Price Guide for Black Memoribilia* [sic], [Langley Park, Md.]: Karen Brigance, 1976.
> Illustrated.

——. *Black Collectibles: Descriptive Price Guide for Black Memoribilia* [sic]. [Langley Park, Md.]: Karen Brigance, 1983.
> Illustrated.

Murrell, William. *A History of American Graphic Humor*. New York: Whitman Museum of American Art, 1933. vol. I, 1747–1865; vol. II, 1865–1938.

"Museum for Rare Antique Dolls Has a Home in Harlem." Nashville *Tennessean*, January 23, 1987: D–10.
> Describes the collection of more than 5,000 rare and antique dolls in the Aunt Lev's Doll and Toy Museum in Harlem. Many of the dolls are Black.

Nicholson, Susan. "The Golliwog Collectibles." *Spinning Wheel* (January/February 1981): 12–16.

Norman, Bill. *The Bank Book: The Encyclopedia of Mechanical Bank Collecting*. San Diego, Calif.: Accent Studios, 1984.
> Illustrations of cast-iron, tin, wooden, musical, and vending banks; includes many Black items. Contains illustrations of trade cards and advertising flyers that further illustrate the banks. Bibliography, p. 158.

Null, Gary. *Black Hollywood: The Negro in Motion Pictures*. Secaucus, N.J.: The Citadel Press, 1975.

Official Sotheby Park Bernet Price Guide to Antiques and Decorative Arts. Ed. Charles Colt, Jr. New York: Simon and Schuster, 1980.

Opfer, Richard. *Collector's Auction: Black Americana Sale*, March 7, 1981. Catalogue. Timonium, Md.: Richard Opfer Auctioneering, 1981.
> Illustrated.

——. *Collector's Auction: Black Americana Sale*, October 17, 1981. Catalogue. Timonium, Md.: Richard Opfer Auctioneering, 1981.
> Illustrated.

——. *Collector's Auction: Black Americana Sale*. October 5, 1985. Catalogue. Timonium, Md.: Richard Opfer, 1986.
> Illustrated.

The Origin of Jim Crow: Being an Authentic Account of the Life and Adventures of the Comic American Nigger, Jim Crow. . . . by An American. London: James S. Hodson, 1937.

Parker, Paula. "Contemptible Collectibles." *Perspectives* (Spring 1980): 19–23.
> Describes the collection of Mary Kimbrough, advanced collector in Los Angeles, California.

Perelman, Leon J. *Perelman Antique Toy Museum*. Des Moines, Iowa: Wallace-Home-stead Book Co., 1972.

Peters, Harry T. *Currier and Ives: Printmakers to the American People*. Garden City, N.Y.: Doubleday, Doran and Co., 1941.

Porter, Dorothy. *The Negro in the United States: A Selected Bibliography*. Washington, D.C.: Library of Congress, 1970.

————. *A Working Bibliography of the Negro in the United States.* Ann Arbor, Mich.: xerox, University Microfilms, 1969.

Pratt, John Lowell. *Currier and Ives: Chronicles of America.* Maplewood, N.J.: Hammon Inc., 1968.

Presbrey, Frank. *The History and Development of Advertising.* New York: Greenwood Press, Publishers, 1968.

Reflections of Sable Love: A Publication for the Black Memorabilia Collector. 1985– 1986. Monthly. M & J Publications, 5406 9th Street, N.W., Washington, D.C. Ceased publication in 1986.

Contains classified advertisement section, articles on Black memorabilia and re-lated topics, lists of subscribers, and black and white illustrations.

Reif, Rita. "Black Stereotypes Featured in Dartmouth Exhibit." *New York Times*, March 3, 1981: A–11.

Brief article describing the Marguerite Barnett-King [sic] collection then on exhibit at Dartmouth College.

Reno, Dawn N. *Collecting Black Americana.* New York: Crown Publishers, 1986.

Includes text, black and white illustrations, price list, brief list of collectors, dealers, museums, and educational institutions that contributed to the book, and a bibliography.

Rogers, Carole G. *Penny Banks, A History and a Handbook.* New York: Subsistence Press, Dutton, 1977.

Rogers, William, ed. *The Official 1882 Price Guide to Old Books and Autographs.* Orlando, Fla.: House of Collectibles, 1982.

Rooks, Ronald, A., comp. *Collector's Auction: Black Americana Sale.* April 23, 1983. Catalogue. Baltimore, Md.: Harris Auction Galleries, 1983.

Illustrated.

————, comp., ed. *Collector's Auction: Black Americana Sale.* July 21, 1984. Catalogue. Baltimore, Md.: Harris Auction Galleries, 1984.

Illustrated.

Schatz, Walter. *Directory of Afro-American Resources.* New York: Bowker, 1970.

An index to primary and secondary resources on Black themes in libraries and in research and information centers.

Schroeder, Joseph J., Jr. *The Wonderful World of Toys, Games, and Dolls 1860–1930.* Northfield, Ill.: DBI Books, 1971.

Schwartz, Marvin D., and Betsy Wade. *The New York Times Book of Antiques.* New York: Quadrangle Books, 1972.

————. "Of Mammies and Golliwogs." *Northern California Express* 8, no. 51 (Sep-tember 26, 1986): 1–2.

Siebert, William H. *The Mysteries of Ohio's Underground Railroads.* Columbus, Ohio: Long's College Book Company, 1951.

Smith, Jessie Carney. *Black Academic Libraries and Research Collections: An Historical Survey.* Westport, Conn.: Greenwood Press, 1977.

Chapter 5, pp. 156–205, gives a historical analysis of Black collections and the anatomy of such collections in various Black academic institutions. Also discusses resources in the Schomburg Center for Research on Black Culture in New York. Reference works and types of materials that these collections should house are given.

Stivers, Dave. *The Nabisco Brand Collection of Cream of Wheat Advertising Art.* San

Diego, Calif: Collectors' Showcase, 1986.
> Contains color and black and white Cream of Wheat advertisements. Most feature "Rastus, the Cream of Wheat man." Includes biographical notes on artists who created the Cream of Wheat works.

Stix, Harriet. "Black Images in the White Mind." *Americana* 10, 1 (March/April 1982): 24–27.
> A review of the collection of Janette Faulkner in the Berkeley Art Museum, September 18 to November 4, 1982.

Time-Life Books, eds. *The Encyclopedia of Collectibles.* Alexandria, Va.: Time-Life Books, 1978.

Toy Museum of Atlanta. At Auction, October 3–4, 1986. *Catalogue, The First Sale.* Barrett Bertoia, auctions & appraisals. Richard Opfer, auctioneer. Atlanta: n.p., 1986.
> Includes black and white and color illustrations of Black toys.

Vesey, Tom. "Black Memorabilia Stirs Memories Good and Bad," *Washington Post,* October 5, 1987: D1, D7.

Vlach, John. *The Afro-American Tradition in Decorative Arts.* Cleveland, Ohio: Cleveland Museum of Art, 1978.

Wallace-Homestead Price Guide to Antiques. Ed. Robert W. Miller. Special Anniversary. 10th ed. Des Moines, Iowa: Wallace-Homestead Book Co., 1984.
> "Black Collectibles," 76.

Warman's Americana & Collectibles. Ed. Harry L. Rinker. Elkins Park, Pa.: Warman Publishing Co., 1986.
> "Black Memorabilia," 77–83.

Weltens, Arno. *Mechanical Tin Toys in Color.* Poole, England: Blanford Press, 1977.

Westfall, Ermagene. *Cookie Jars.* Paducah, Ky.: Collector Books, 1983.
> Contains color photographs and suggested prices of cookie jars. Arranged by manufacturer. Figural and other jars of Blacks are scattered throughout the book.

Weston, Helen. *Introducing the Song Sheet: A Collector's Guide to Song Sheets with Current Values.* Nashville, Tenn.: Thomas Nelson, 1976.

White, David Manning, ed. *Popular Culture: The Great Contemporary Issues.* New York: Arno Press, 1975.

White, David Manning, and John Pendleton, eds. *Popular Culture: Mirror of American Life.* Del Mar, Calif.: Publisher's Inc., 1977.

White, Gwen. *Antique Toys and Their Background.* New York: Arco Publishing Co., 1971.

Winchester, Alice, ed. *The Antiques Book.* New York: Bonanza Books, 1970.

Witkin, Lee D., and Barbara London. *The Photograph Collector's Guide.* Boston: Little, Brown, 1979.

Wood, Jane. *The Collector's Guide to Post Cards.* Gas City, Ind.: L–W Promotions, c1984.
> A reference guide useful for identifying types and prices of greeting cards. Contains section on Blacks (p. 49).

Work, Monroe N. *A Bibiography of the Negro in Africa and America.* 1928. New York: Octagon Books, 1965.

Yourse, Robyn-Denise. " 'Racially Offensive' Exhibit Points to Constitution's Inequities." *Washington Afro-American,* May 30, 1987: 1, 22.

Discusses the exhibit "Black Americans and the Bicentennial of the Constitution: A Mass Media Perspective," prepared by collector Charles E. Simmons.

Zeller, Leslie. *Book Collecting*. New York: Cornerstone Library, 1978.

Films

Ethnic Notions. 56-minute documentary. 1/2 VHS and 3/4 video. Producer/director Marlon Riggs. Narrated by Esther Rolle. 1987. Rental $85; sale $295. California Newsreel, 630 Natoma Street, San Francisco, CA 94103.
Explores more than 100 years of interaction between racial tensions and popular culture, illustrating how stereotypes such as the coon, mammy, uncle, pickaninny and sambo have helped to shape and mirror changing social-political attitudes toward race. It embraces images in a variety of sources ranging from feature films and animated cartoons, to musical recordings and pre–Civil War sheet music from the Harvard Theatre Collection. The film was inspired by the exhibition of Janette Faulkner's collection in California.

Kader, Don. *The Don Kader Collection*. Videotape. Color. 5–1/2 hours. Available from 1116 South Orange Grove Avenue, Los Angeles, CA 90012.

Index

Male images: in advertising, 259, 264, 269; African, 258; in collectibles, 264; in films, 245, 266, 270; in folk names, 259; literature on, 270–71; in plays, 239; in popular culture, 258, 267; Sambo, 257–70; Savage, 258–59, 270; in songs, 259; in toys, 278–82
Mamba's Daughters, 239
Mammy: in films, 244–50; in literature, 238–39; monument, 236. *See also* Stereotypes
"Mammy" (doll), 283
Mammy Pleasant, 241
Mammy Pleasant's Partner, 241
"Mannix" (TV show), 69
Mann Simon's Cottage, 313
Man's Duty, A (film), 244
Man Who Cried I Am, The, 157
Many Thousand Gone: The Ex-Slaves' Account of Their Bondage and Freedom, 148
Mapp, Edward, 53, 61, 243
Marie LeVeau's Daughter (painting), 18, 22
Markowitz, Joel, collection, 331
Mark Twain Journal, The, 149
Marrow of Tradition, The, 151, 239
Marshall, Arthur, 127
Marshall, Paule, 158, 236
Marshall, William, 64
Marshall Field & Co. Catalogue, 275, 283
Martin, Dellita, 143
Martin, Roberta, 129
Martineau, Harriet, 264
Martin Luther King Museum of Black Culture, 312
Mary Jane, 204
Maryland Commission on Afro-American History and Culture, 18, 23
Maryland Community on Afro-American History and Culture, 309
Maryland Gazette, 21 n.3
Maryland Historical Society, 4, 23
Maryland Museum of American Art, 309
Mary Poppins, 200, 204
Marzorini, A. L., collection, 321
Masher, The (film), 56

Masking: as Negro, 280–82; Uncle Mose, 281; Uncle Remus, 281; Uncle Tom, 281; and wigs, 281
Massachusetts, University of, 242
Master, Juba, 32
Mathews, Charles, 30
Mathis, Sharon Bell, 212
Matterson, Pat, collection, 328
Maule, Margaret and Gerald, collection, 319
Mayfield, Curtis, 44
Maynard, Richard, 52, 59
Mayr, Christian, 19, 23
M. C. Higgins, the Great, 213
Me and Bessie (musical), 43
Means, Florence Crannell, 202–4
"Mechanical Cake Walk" (toy), 275. *See also* "Cake Walker"
"Mechanical Nurse" (doll), 283
Me Day, 211
"Media Image of Black Women, The," 249
"Melba" (TV show), 250
Melies, George, 54
Melinda (film), 245
Melindy's Happy Summer, 203–4
Melindy's Metal, 203
Meltzer, Milton, 44
Melville, Herman, 141, 149, 267
Member of the Gang, 212
Member of the Wedding (film), 65–66
Memphis/Shelby County Public Library and Information Center, 315
Memphis State University, Brister Library, 315
Mencke, John G., 239
Merabash Museum, 310
Mercer, Johnny, 41
Mercier, Denis, 303–4; collection, 330
Meridan, 158
Meritt, Theresa, 249
Meriwether, Louise, 237
Merry Adventures of Robin Hood of Great Renown in Nottinghamshire, The, 195
"Metaphors of Mastery in the Slave Narratives," 148

About the Editor and Contributors

LOIS FIELDS ANDERSON has worked as reference librarian in public libraries in Ohio and Iowa, and as music cataloger at Fisk University. For the past fifteen years, she has been a library/media specialist in the Lexington, Massachusetts public schools. She has produced two video shows for local network in Lexington, and has organized a multicultural collection for the Harrington School. She is agent for T. J. Anderson's professional activities.

T. J. ANDERSON is one of the leading composers of his generation. He studied composition with George Ceiga, Scott Huston, Philip Bezanson, Richard Hervig and Darius Milhaud. Anderson is well known for his orchestration of Scott Joplin's *Treemonisha* which premiered in Atlanta in 1972. His opera, *Soldier Boy Soldier*, was commissioned by Indiana University, and his large cantata, *Spirituals*, based on a text by poet Robert Hayden and conducted by Robert Shaw, was performed for the dedication of the Martin Luther King, Jr. Center for Nonviolent Social Change in Atlanta. Anderson's interest in minstrels resulted in his participation in the 1984 celebration, *Thomas Jefferson's Orbiting Minstrels and Contraband*. He is Austin Fetcher Professor of Music at Tufts University.

JESSIE M. BIRTHA is a former children's librarian with over 20 years of service in the Free Library of Philadelphia. She has served as children's librarian in a variety of branches in the system, as children's specialist in the book selection unit of the Office of Work with Children, and as branch supervisor. She has been an adjunct staff member, Philadelphia Branch of Antioch Graduate School, where she taught children's literature, and consultant for McGraw-Hill Language Arts Program *American Language Today*. Birtha has lectured widely on minority children's books and reading, and has published a number of articles on this topic.

JOSEPH BOSKIN is Professor of History and Afro-American Studies and Director of the Urban Studies and Public Policy Program at Boston University. His research and writing have been directed toward analyzing the relationship between images and behavior, specifically, the role of pejorative stereotypes and humor in the formation and development of racist attitudes. His books include *Seasons of Rebellion: Protest and Radicalism in Recent America* (1971), co-author and editor; *Urban Racial Violence in 20th Century America* (1969), author and editor; *Into Slavery: Racial Decisions in the Virginia Colony* (1976); and *SAMBO: The Rise and Demise of an American Jester* (1986). He is currently working on a book entitled *Linkages in Culture: Social Conflict and Contemporary American Humor*.

ARLENE CLIFT-PELLOW is Professor of English and Director of the Division of Humanities and Fine Arts at Fisk University. Her postdoctoral research has been assisted by grants from the National Institute of Education, the National Endowment for the Humanities, and the Ford Foundation. Most recently, she was awarded a fellowship in the United Negro College Fund Distinguished Scholars Program. Active in the Modern Language Association as well as in other professional organizations, she is a former chairperson of the MLA's Division of Black American Literature and Culture. Among other publications, she co-authored the entry on folklore in *The Encyclopedia of Black America*.

DAVID C. DRISKELL is Professor of Art at the University of Maryland at College Park. The leading authority on Afro-American art, Driskell has published widely on Afro-American art and artists, and has written four books on Afro-American art: *Amistad II, Afro-American Art* (1975); *Two Centuries of Black American Art: 1750–1950* (1975); *Hidden Heritage: Afro-American Art, 1800–1950*, and *Contemporary Visual Expressions: The Art of Sam Gilliam, Martha Jackson-Jarvis, Keith Morrison and William T. Williams* (1987).

THOMAS RIIS is an Associate Professor of Music History at the University of Georgia. His research has concentrated on the issues surrounding Black American musical theater, and he has published articles in *The Black Perspective in Music*, *American Music*, and the *New Grove Dictionary of American Music*. In 1987 he served as the Senior Research Fellow at the Institute for Studies in American Music, Brooklyn College of the City University of New York. An active performer, Riis plays the cello and other early string instruments, conducts, and sings.

JANET SIMS-WOOD is Assistant Chief Librarian, Reference/Reader Service Department, Moorland-Spingarn Research Center, Howard University. Sims-

Wood is associate editor of *SAGE: A Scholarly Journal on Black Women* and founder and president of Afro Resources, Inc., a publishing company. Works on which she collaborated (under the name of Sims) include *The Black Family in the United States: A Selected Bibliography of Annotated Books, Articles and Dissertations on Black Families in America* (1978), and *Black Artists in the United States: An Annotated Bibliography of Books, Articles and Dissertations on Black Artists, 1779–1979 (1980)*. She also compiled *The Progress of Afro-American Women: A Selected Bibliography and Resource Guide* (1980) and *The Ku Klux Klan: A Bibliography* (1983) and has contributed numerous articles and reviews to Black studies journals.

JESSIE CARNEY SMITH is University Librarian and Professor at Fisk University. Smith in 1985 was named ACRL Academic or Research Librarian of the Year. At Fisk she has conducted numerous research, training and public lecture/exhibition programs funded by the U.S. Office of Education and the National Endowment for the Humanities. A scholar and lecturer on Black American collections and resources, Black American collectibles, ethnic resources, and ethnic genealogy, she has also published widely on these topics. Her writings have been published in journals such as *College and Research Libraries*, *ALA Yearbook*, *Black World*, and *Ethnic Treasures* (the journal for collectors of Black Americana). Smith has contributed chapters to *The Black Librarian in America*, *Library and Information Services for Special Groups*, and *Reference Services and Library Education*, and published an essay in *Dictionary of American Library Biography*. Her two published books are *Black Academic Libraries and Research Collections* (1977) and *Ethnic Genealogy: A Research Guide* (1983), both Greenwood Press publications.

NAGUEYALTI WARREN is Assistant Professor of English and chairperson of the Department of English at Fisk University. Warren is co-compiler of *Kumbe! The Writer Speaks: A Brief Annotated Bibliography of Books on Africa* for the 1985 Let's Talk About It in Tennessee Reading and Discussion Programs in American Libraries. Warren's poetry has been published in numerous journals including *Testimony: A Journal of Afro-American Poetry*, *Cotton Boll/Atlanta Review*, *American Poetry Anthology*, and is anthologized in *Mississippi Writers: A Record of Childhood and Youth*, vol. III.

DORIS Y. WILKINSON is Professor in the Department of Sociology at the University of Kentucky. She has made notable contributions to the profession and the field of sociology through her research and work with the American Sociological Association as an Executive Associate. Wilkinson's research and publications have pertained to the study of social stratification and the psychology of symbols. She is the co-editor of *The Black Male in America* (1977) and editor of *Black Male/White Female* (1975). A recognized authority on the Afro-American experience, she has pursued interests in clinical beliefs and the study of cultural artifacts and has published articles on these themes.